# Two Hundred Years

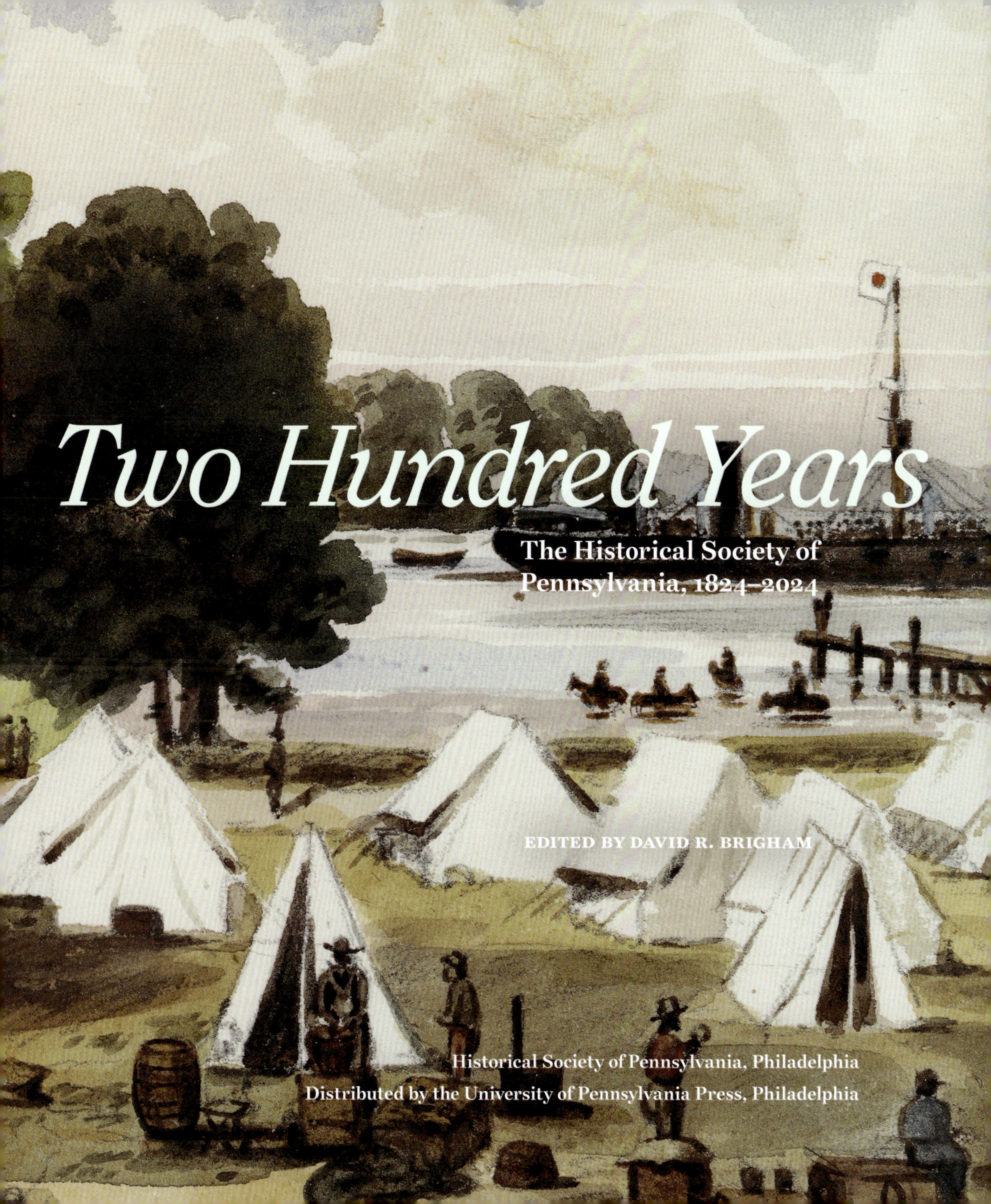

# *Two Hundred Years*

## The Historical Society of Pennsylvania, 1824–2024

EDITED BY DAVID R. BRIGHAM

Historical Society of Pennsylvania, Philadelphia
Distributed by the University of Pennsylvania Press, Philadelphia

LITHOGRAPHY
P. S. Duval,
Execute on Stone at the shortest notice all kinds of Drawings, Portraits, Landscapes, Historical Subjects, Animals &c.
Also all kinds of Writings: Maps, Charts, Plans, professional and visiting Cards, Circulars, Billheads
PHILADELPHIA
Delaware
Shipped in good
on board the
whereof
the port of
For similar afford great advantages in Circulars of Business by the facility which they can be Executed in Lithography & the despatch & cheapness of the work render it an object to Merchants and others
LITHOGRAPHIC ES
from the Exchan
ALOYS SENEFELDER
Inventor of Lithography. Munich A.D. 1796.
MERCHANTS' EXCHANGE.
PHILADELPHIA.
183
of this
tenor and date
or order
Dollars
To
London
Artist.
No. 7 Bank Alley
P. S. Duval
7
BANK ALLEY.
Philadelphi

# Editorial Committee

# Contents



## Entries

# Acknowledgments

This book has benefitted from a tremendous community effort. The concept for this project began with a strategic planning process that commenced shortly after I was appointed Librarian and CEO of the Historical Society of Pennsylvania (HSP) towards the end of 2020. It quickly became apparent as I was introducing HSP to potential partners, colleagues, and patrons that there was no single volume that encompassed the breadth and quality of the library's collections. With a desire to fill this void, I first approached fellow historians of American art and culture, Elizabeth Milroy and Martha Hutson-Saxton, both members of HSP's Board of Councilors, to help imagine and develop such a book. HSP's 200th anniversary in 2024 seemed like the perfect occasion to publish, but it meant that a manuscript and photography would have to be completed by mid-2022. In other words, all content would have to be assigned, researched, written, and edited in just a year and a half. This daunting task became achievable when we signed on five additional scholars to help us find the right balance of themes that could be researched at HSP through the collections in our possession and illuminated by exemplary items.

Thankfully, HSP's staff and board are rich with talent, and we enlisted five more experts to the Editorial Committee—Lee Arnold, now Librarian Emeritus; Alice L. George, Independent Historian; Christina Larocco, Editor of the *Pennsylvania Magazine of History and Biography* (PMHB) and Scholarly Programs Manager; Walter Licht, Walter L. Annenberg Emeritus Professor of History at the University of Pennsylvania; and Randall L. Miller, Professor Emeritus of History at Saint Joseph's University—to help select the content for the book. We met every two weeks and reviewed hundreds of possible topics for inclusion, including twenty-eight pages of nominations from HSP's staff and volunteers, some of them with decades of experience as scholars and facilitators of research by other readers at HSP. As we chose the items for the book, we also identified the ideal author for each essay. The Editorial Committee brought remarkable energy and insight to the Table of Contents, and without them, this volume would have taken much longer or simply never have been completed. With expertise in art, politics, industry, labor, women's history, and other topics spanning the seventeenth to the twentieth centuries, together the committee had an astonishing mental bibliography and list of contacts. Collectively, the eight members of the Editorial Team also wrote thirty-six of the one hundred essays. In short, they were indispensable to the scope and content of this book, both in shaping and writing its engaging and informative entries.

I am extremely grateful to the additional forty-nine authors who contributed their knowledge of HSP's collections and their historical significance to this book. They are professors, librarians, curators, journalists, and genealogists, each bringing a unique and valuable perspective to the project. The authors have been remarkably generous in sharing their original research and responding in a timely way to every deadline and request for edits or additional information. Some have been friends and colleagues for more than thirty years, while others I have met because of this project; I am thankful to have my circle of colleagues so richly expanded as a consequence.

HSP's staff has also been instrumental to this venture beyond those who participated on the Editorial Committee. Andrew Williams, Digital Services Archivist, took most of the photographs with HSP's high-resolution digital camera, giving the book crisp images that make the pages of text legible and lively. For oversized items, such as the Benjamin West portrait of William Hamilton and his niece Anna Hamilton Lyle, and reflective surfaces, such as the exquisite gold Freedom Box given to William's uncle Andrew, and the first photograph in the United States taken on a copper plate by Joseph Saxton, Williams engaged photographer

Jaime Alvarez, who expertly managed the unique challenges of such items. Williams wrote the captions for each entry, updated existing catalogue information, and worked closely with HSP Conservator Tara O'Brien to measure each document, book, photograph, map, manuscript, or artifact and to verify their medium and support. O'Brien also added to the book by conserving a handful of items to illustrate them at their best and preserve them for future generations. Additional thanks are due to Thomas Primeau, The Charles K. Williams, II, Senior Conservator of Works of Art on Paper at the Philadelphia Museum of Art, for lending his expert eye to confirm the materials used to create the rare, early portrait of Johannes Kelpius. Finally, I am grateful to each member of HSP's staff, especially Katy Bodenhorn Barnes, Justina Barrett, Tristan Bella, Selena Bemak, Katie Clark, Christopher Damiani, Anthony DiGiovanni, Jon-Chris Hatalski, Sarah Heim, Cary Hutto, Margaret Maxey, Ryan McCarthy, Aileen Murphy, Kris Myers, Sara Nash, Lexy Nilles, Mary Offenback, Erin Paulson, Sara Ruesch, Nova Sturchio, and Steve Smith for their help with every aspect of this project, from verifying facts to locating selections within HSP's collection of more than twenty-one million items.

A book of this scale is possible only with substantial resources. Therefore, I am deeply grateful to the Richard C. von Hess Foundation and its trustees, Thomas Hills Cook, Managing Trustee, and Anne Gentner and Warren A. Reintzel, trustees, for approving funding for the entire project. This inspiring gift enabled us to achieve our full ambitions for this publication. We hope it meets their expectations and our shared goals of making HSP more widely known to students, educators, scholars, librarians, genealogists, and everyone with a passion or curiosity for history.

The team at Marquand Books has made this book gorgeous. Adrian Lucia and Ed Marquand have produced many memorable publications for museums, libraries, and other cultural institutions. I was delighted by their immediate interest in helping HSP achieve its vision for a book that could appeal to scholars and general audiences alike and be simultaneously beautiful and substantive. Ryan Polich did an excellent job creating the overall design language and laying out the individual spreads, as well as attending to such details as recommending materials for the cloth cover and the head/tail bands. Melissa Duffes did a masterful job editing essays by so many experts to create a cohesive whole; many authors expressed appreciation for her light but impactful touch. Kestrel Rundle has overseen the project and kept it on time and carefully coordinated.

At the University of Pennsylvania Press, I owe great thanks to Robert Lockhart, Senior Editor, who enthusiastically embraced the concept for this book and supported adding it to Penn's distinguished list of titles. I appreciate the work of the staff at the University of Pennsylvania Press in promoting this book to its likely audiences.

I am grateful to my family—Holly, Noble, and Flora—for listening to countless tales of new discoveries, authors who agreed to contribute to the book, and the incremental steps achieved towards completion. They even provided ideas that benefitted the final outcome, including suggestions of topics by Holly and Noble and an expanded finding aid for the Bartram Family Papers at HSP by Flora.

Finally, I would like to thank HSP's Board Chair Eric Noll and the entire Board of Councilors for embracing this project as the cornerstone for our 200th-anniversary celebration in 2024. Around it, we will build lectures and panel discussions, document displays, and community events for a wide variety of audiences, raising awareness and continuing to build on HSP's two-century tradition of inclusion.

David R. Brigham

LA'FAYETTE

# Introduction

David R. Brigham

The Hall of Independence *has been fitted up in the most splendid manner. The Room is 40 feet square, the walls and ceiling painted with stone colour, the windows hung with scarlet and blue drapery studded with stars. In the east side stands a statue of the immortal Washington, in a recess which was formerly occupied by the Chair of the first Congress. Behind the statue there is an azure star drapery suspended from spears and wreaths. To the right and left of the statue hung the Portraits of William Penn, Franklin and Robert Morris and Francis Hopkinson. The intermediate spaces are filled with the Portraits of Greene, Wayne, Montgomery, Hamilton, Gates, Rochambeau, Charles Carrol, of Carrolton, and Gov. M'Kean.*

*Over the door of entrance is placed the celebrated Portrait of Washington by R[embrandt]. Peale, relieved on each side by crimson and azure drapery suspended from spears and laurel wreaths. On the right and left of the entrance are placed the Portraits of Jefferson, Hancock, Adams, Madison, Monroe, and the venerable Charles Thompson.—On the north and south windows are draped to the floor with crimson and azure, the carpet of similar colours, and the furniture of mahogany tastefully and appropriately disposed.*[1]

This display of Revolutionary soldiers and statesmen (and the colonial proprietor) in Independence Hall set the stage for the ceremonial reception in Philadelphia for the Marquis de Lafayette (1757–1834), whose tour of the United States of America in 1824 and 1825 was the apex of the fiftieth-anniversary celebration of the War of Independence. He was feted in American cities and small towns as the last surviving major general of the Revolution. Lafayette's visit to Philadelphia in September–October 1824 featured a large procession with military honors through the Grand Civic Arch, which had been designed by the architect William Strickland, and decorated with sculptures by William Rush and paintings by Thomas Sully, along with a team of scenery painters from the New Theatre **(no. 46)**. Lafayette was further celebrated at a fashionable gala ball at the Chestnut Street Theatre **(no. 45)**.[2] Souvenirs such as portrait engravings, cockades, badges, handkerchiefs, ceramics, and other commemorative items fed the hunger for mementos of this historic occasion. During his stay in New York, Lafayette was inducted as an honorary member into the New-York Historical Society, a moment that could not be replicated in Philadelphia since there was no parallel institution in Pennsylvania.[3]

Also during this season of historical tributes, a small dinner was held to remember the 142nd anniversary of William Penn's arrival in the colony that would bear his name, with the hope that the event would become an

**Fig. 1** Max Rosenthal (1833–1918), *Peter Stephen Du Ponceau*, ca. 1875; lithograph on wove paper, 12 ¹¹⁄₁₆ × 10 inches (32.3 × 25.5 cm); Historical Society of Pennsylvania Portrait Collection [V88]

**Fig. 2** Albert Newsam (1809–1864), after Henry Inman (1801–1846), *William Rawle Sr.*, ca. 1832; lithograph on wove paper, 12 ½ × 9 ½ inches (31.7 × 24.2 cm); Historical Society of Pennsylvania Portrait Collection [V88]

annual occasion.[4] Eighteen people gathered in a Letitia Street house believed to have been constructed for the proprietor of the colony, now an inn operated by John Doyle, with Peter S. Du Ponceau (1760–1844) presiding over the event **(fig. 1)**. Du Ponceau was then president of the American Philosophical Society and in 1837 would become the Historical Society of Pennsylvania's (HSP) second president. Citing the regularity with which their peers in Massachusetts memorialized the Pilgrims' landing at Plymouth, Du Ponceau hoped that Pennsylvania would place equal weight on Penn's arrival and the principles which inspired him to establish the colony. Du Ponceau's speech was published in the newspapers and a pamphlet, and the occasion planted a seed that would result in the founding of HSP on December 2, 1824, with the selection of William Rawle Sr. **(fig. 2)** as its first president. Recognition of Penn and Lafayette were but two circumstances that led to the formation of a society in Philadelphia dedicated to preserving the past. By late 1824, just three of fifty-six signers of the Declaration of Independence and six of fifty-five delegates to the Constitutional Convention survived, and Charles Thomson (1729–1824), who served as secretary to Congress, had died that summer. These dwindling ranks added urgency for establishing a repository of American history in Philadelphia, where the Declaration and Constitution were both written.

HSP immediately identified itself as an institution formed "to collect and preserve the evidences of its own history from the earliest date" in order to "honour the character and advance the prosperity of their commonwealth" **(fig. 3)**.[5] The founders defined ten categories of inquiry around which they would organize the collections, and they formed standing committees to pursue these subjects:

1. On the national origin, early difficulties and domestic habits of the first settlers.

2. On the biography of the founder of Pennsylvania, his family and the early settlers.
3. Biographical notices of persons distinguished among us in ancient and modern times.
4. On the Aborigines of Pennsylvania, their numbers, names of their tribes, intercourse with Europeans, their language, habits, character, and wars.
5. On the principles to which the rapid population of Pennsylvania may be ascribed.
6. On the revenues, expenses, and general polity of the provincial government.
7. On the Juridical history of Pennsylvania.
8. On the literary history of Pennsylvania.
9. On the medical history of Pennsylvania.
10. On the progress and present state of agriculture, manufactures and commerce in Pennsylvania.[6]

These themes revealed HSP's original motivations—from keeping the Commonwealth's history from slipping into oblivion to telling stories of achievement in a variety of fields and noting trends in population growth and the development of a diverse economy as models of future success. Both antiquarian interests and an Enlightenment quest for useful knowledge drove its founding. In his inaugural address, president Rawle pronounced that in contrast to the American Philosophical Society, which granted access to its historical collections only to members, "all who feel a strong interest in its general views ought to be admissible [to HSP], and every inhabitant of our State ought to feel that interest."[7] The scope of the collections was defined broadly, and its audience was to be inclusive.

News accounts in 1824 identified key topics in the daily lives of Pennsylvanians as HSP came into existence. Regular notices of civic, economic, cultural, and benevolent organizations demonstrated the concerns of the community, ranging from the activities of the Pennsylvania Institution for the Deaf and Dumb, including the laying of the cornerstone of its building, to the efforts of the Magdalen Society to redeem women from prostitution **(no. 39)**, the founding of the Provident Society for the employment of the poor, and the Franklin Institute to educate working men.[8] The latter organization signaled the emergence of Pennsylvania as a site of technological innovation and industrial might, an identity that would grow over the next fifty years with the establishment of the anthracite coal, steel, and locomotive industries as well as the construction of canals, railroads, and other internal improvements.

HSP's founders recognized the signs of America's industrial promise and encouraged reflection on the past as inspiration for the future. Also in 1824 a new system of locks along the Schuylkill would open the river to navigable travel for 110 miles, thereby promoting commerce and industry within Pennsylvania's interior.[9] In July the first half of the Schuylkill Navigation Canal was dedicated, connecting Philadelphia to Reading. The first two toasts delivered at the opening ceremony clearly state the importance of the new canal to industrialization:

> The Internal Improvements of Pennsylvania—
> May the completion of the Navigation of the Schuylkill, lead to a speedy connection of the Western with our Eastern Waters.
> Coal Mines of Pennsylvania

The news account of the opening festivities asserts, "Pennsylvania may well boast of her vast magazines of mineral wealth" and specifically mentions the Lehigh and Lackawanna mines.[10] HSP founders also promoted industrialization and recent investments in expanding infrastructure and the coal industry in reports such as Thomas C. James's account (1826) of the anthracite coal industry and Erskine Hazard's 1827 "history of the origin and progress of the Lehigh Coal and Navigation Company's works at Mauch Chunk."[11] With these and other publications, HSP employed history to advance the next chapter in the Commonwealth's economic fortunes.

As HSP commemorates its 200th anniversary, this volume celebrates the growth of its extraordinary collections of more than twenty-one million manuscripts, books, photographs, maps, broadsides, prints, and drawings. Just as our founders wrestled knowledge into ten broad categories, HSP now embraces a new system of five themes to organize collecting, programming, staffing, and other activities:

- Pennsylvania: Crucible of the Nation

Land deeds between the Lenni Lenape people and William Penn, the first handwritten drafts of the Articles of Confederation and the United States Constitution, and clippings of George Washington's hair that were saved by his barber are among the treasures that document the deeply entwined histories of Pennsylvania and the United States of America.

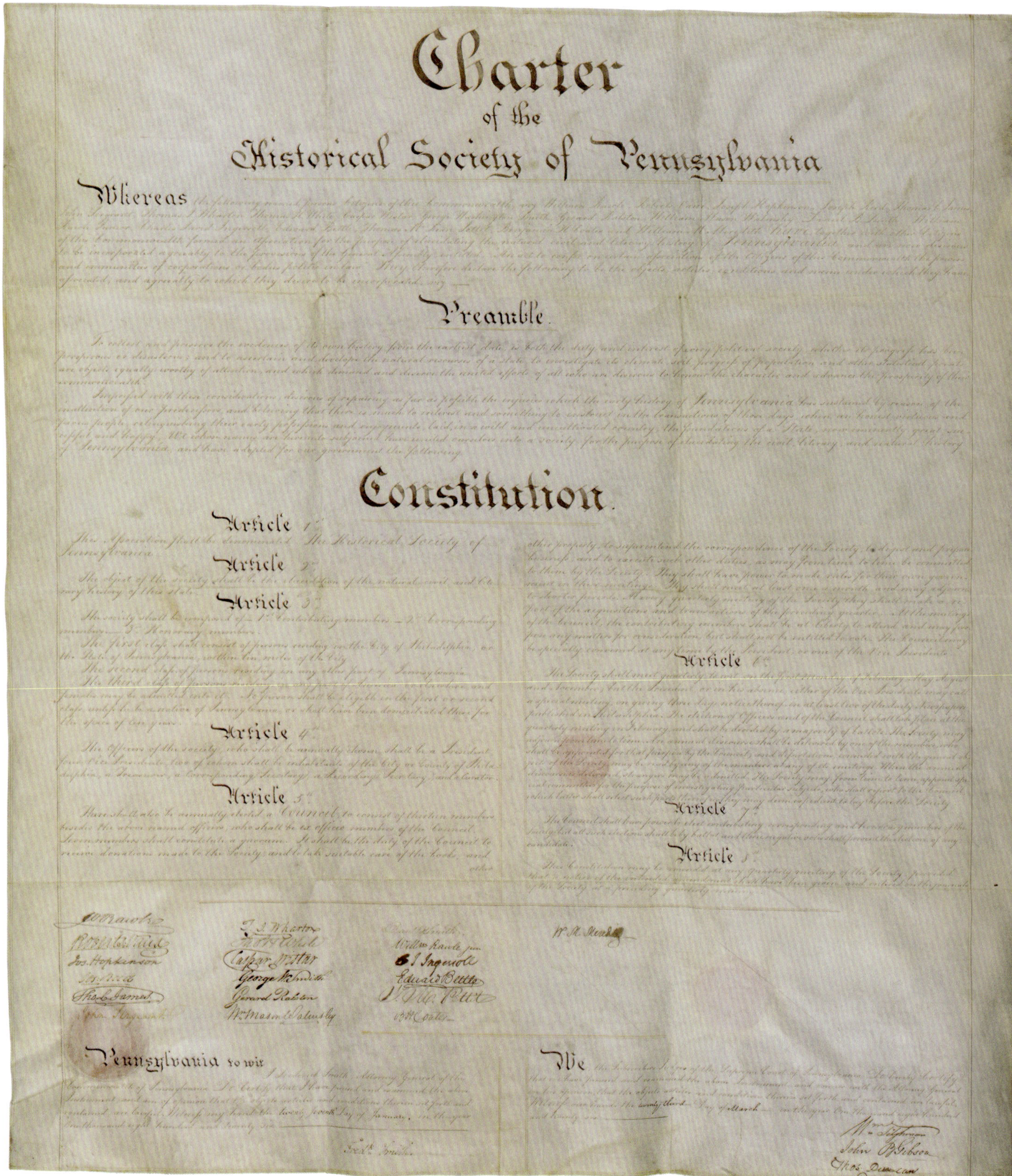
Charter
of the
Historical Society of Pennsylvania

Whereas

Preamble

Constitution

Article 1st

Article 2d

Article 3d

Article 4th

Article 5th

Article 6th

Article 7th

Article 8th

Pennsylvania to wit

We

**Fig. 3** *Charter of the Historical Society of Pennsylvania*, June 2, 1826; manuscript; ink on parchment, 29 ¾ × 25 ¾ inches (75.5 × 65.5 cm); Historical Society of Pennsylvania Institutional Archives [3136]

- What's Your Story? Chronicling Families and Communities

Whether descended from a founding father and mother, an enslaved couple, or recent immigrants, genealogists of all backgrounds can make "aha" discoveries about their family histories by delving into HSP's unique archives. Likewise, maps, photographs, and graphic arts enable residents to explore their homes, neighborhoods, and communities.

- America's Promise and Its Many Voices

The United States is a melting pot where people of all races, ethnicities, genders, and religions can achieve success. However, many have experienced a substantial gap between this ideal and reality. As they strive to overcome legal, economic, and other barriers, the voices and actions of women, people of color, immigrants from around the globe, and LGBTQ people are richly reflected in HSP's collections.

- Americans and Innovation: Science, Technology, and Enterprise

The spirit of enterprise is embedded at HSP in the first map of Philadelphia that was used by William Penn to sell plots of land, the natural history and nursery work of Mark Catesby (1683–1749) and the Bartram family, and the rapid development of industry exemplified by Baldwin Locomotive Works. Wanamaker's Department Store reinvented retail, creating abundant displays of new fashions amid dining venues and organ concerts, making shopping an experience for the growing middle class rather than merely the fulfillment of basic needs. Philadelphia is also a city of many firsts, including the first American photograph **(no. 51)**, taken in 1839 by inventor Joseph Saxton (1799–1873) from his vantage point in the United States Mint, just a few blocks from HSP, where it is now preserved.

- The Soul of America: Visual, Performing, and Literary Arts

In the eighteenth century, Peale's Museum was established as a popular entertainment space aimed at providing ordinary people access to science and art, and in the nineteenth century, the Academy of Music was created to rival the grandeur of European opera houses while opening such venues to wider audiences. In the twentieth century, the WPA art projects and community arts organizations, such as those led by H. August Wilson, more fully realized the democratization of arts and culture.

The one hundred short entries that follow feature highlights from HSP's collections. Rather than provide a comprehensive view of the collection, these essays by emerging and leading scholars will hopefully entice readers to seek answers to their questions about the past in HSP's Reading Room. Together, they form an impression of the range of perspectives, topics, materials, and times that can be investigated at HSP.

## Pennsylvania: Crucible of the Nation

In its first years, HSP devoted more energy to preserving the history of William Penn (1644–1718) and the founding of the Pennsylvania colony than to any other topic. The first item to enter the collection was a "Silver medal of William Penn accompanied by a description," donated by Joseph Sansom.[12] Also in its first year, HSP reached out to Deborah Norris Logan (1761–1839) about the "manuscript correspondence of Wm Penn and James Logan, which she has collected and arranged, in order for its publication by this Society" **(no. 47)**.[13] In November, HSP vice president Roberts Vaux read a paper "on the locality of the first treaty held [by Penn] with the Indians in Pennsylvania."[14] HSP continued to actively collect Penn's papers when it approached the estate of William Hamilton (1745–1813), an effort that resulted in the donation by Joshua Fisher of "one hundred original letters of Thomas Penn and a copy of William Penn's Instructions to his Commissioners . . . from documents in the possession of the representatives of the late William Hamilton."[15] Penn family correspondence and related items continued to trickle in throughout the nineteenth century. These early efforts bore mature fruit a half-century later with the acquisition of over 20,000 documents from William Penn and his family, a collection that had been sold in England for its scrap value.[16] A century later, five volumes of richly edited and annotated Penn papers were published, featuring HSP's collection as well as holdings in other repositories in the United Kingdom and United States. These important volumes make HSP's collections and the unique stories of the Quaker experience more widely accessible to scholars and students of colonial history.[17]

Penn's closest allies became wealthy families in positions of official power that extended throughout the eighteenth century, including the Logan, Norris, Fisher, Chew, Shippen, and Pemberton clans, whose vast, multigenerational papers are preserved at HSP in collections that

**Fig. 4** Unknown, original map by Peter Mårtensson Lindeström (1632–1691), *Nova Suecia: Eller the Swenska Revier in India Occidentali*, ca. 1875; hand-drawn facsimile; black and red ink on paper, 9 × 28 ¾ inches (22.7 × 73.0 cm); foldout leaf in 19th century transcription of Peter Lindeström's journal [Am .0925]

span from the seventeenth to the twentieth centuries. They reflect all aspects of colonial life, including the growth and function of the colonial government, the development of the transatlantic economy, slavery, border disputes with other colonies, and relationships with Indigenous peoples, as well as family, religion, and culture. James Logan (1674–1751), for example, served as Penn's secretary, managing the proprietor's affairs in the colony after his return to England, and his son William (1718–1776) became a successful merchant and landowner. On behalf of William Penn's sons, Logan expanded the Penn family's land holdings through the now notorious Walking Purchase of 1737. That transaction is documented through a map that survives in the Logan Papers **(no. 9)**.

The early Swedish and German communities in Pennsylvania are also represented in HSP's collections. Swedish immigrants first arrived in the Delaware Valley in 1638, a generation before Penn. HSP's early records of the New Sweden settlement include the journal of Peter Lindeström, a military engineer in the Swedish colony from 1654 to 1655, which contains notes about geography, social and economic development, and a map of the Delaware River **(fig. 4)**. Andreas Sandel's (1671–1743) diary spanning 1701–43 covers his time as minister to the Swedish Lutheran congregation at Gloria Dei, the eighteenth-century church that still stands. The papers of the nineteenth-century collector Joseph J. Mickley (1799–1878) include documents relating to New Sweden, including Lindeström's eyewitness account of the Dutch overtaking the Swedish settlement in 1655.

Francis Daniel Pastorius (1651–1719), the founder of Germantown, ventured to London in 1683, purchased 15,000 acres in Pennsylvania from Penn to enable German settlement in the New World, and emigrated there himself to lead the effort.[18] His papers at HSP demonstrate his enterprise as well as his religious beliefs as a Lutheran pietist, later Quaker, and an intellectual whose interests ranged from gardening to alchemy and literature. A decade later, Johannes Kelpius (1667–1708) led a community of forty members of the celibate Chapter of Perfection on their millennial quest to the Wissahickon Creek in the wilderness of Pennsylvania. Kelpius composed volumes of poems and hymns in preparation for the second coming of Christ. Hymns and elaborate calligraphy of other pietist utopian communities are preserved in the Abraham Cassel Collection, including exquisite manuscript volumes from the

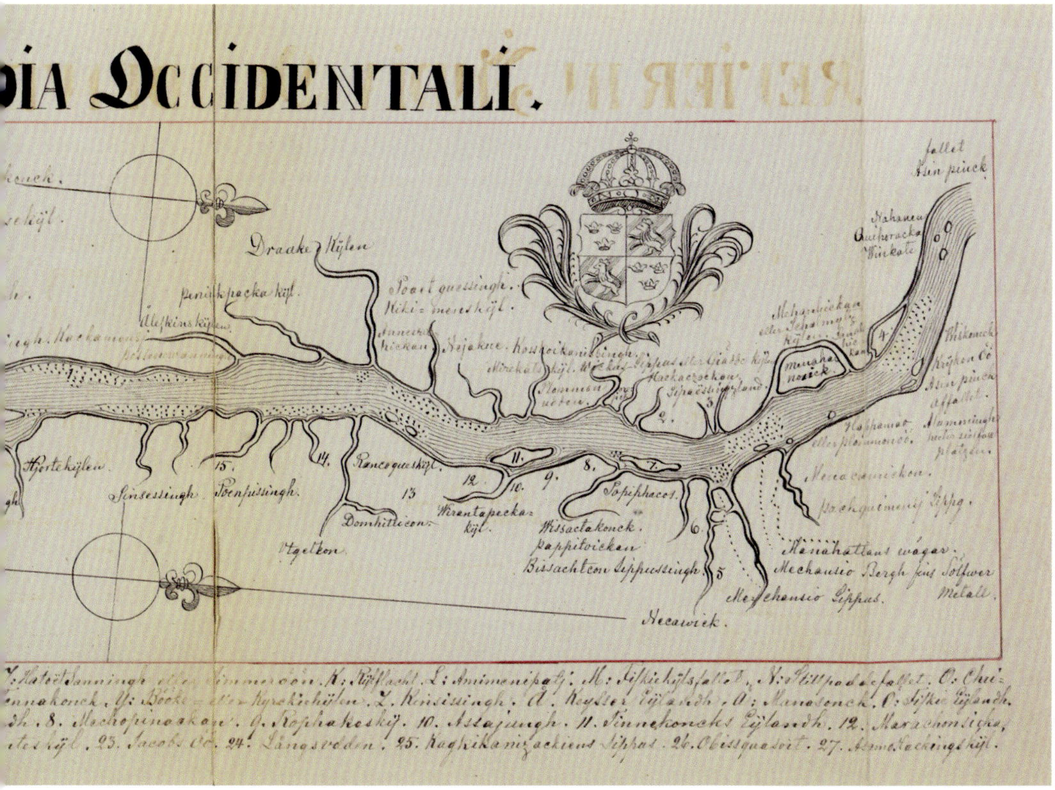


Ephrata Cloister, Snow Hill, and Schwenkfelder communities. The Pastorius and Kelpius Papers and Cassel Collection at HSP document the German dimension of ethnic diversity that developed early in Pennsylvania, as well as the religious, economic, literary, musical, artistic, and intellectual traditions that emerged in a transatlantic context.[19]

HSP's holdings of Revolutionary War materials are also astonishingly vast and varied. In collaboration with the American Philosophical Society and the Library Company of Philadelphia, HSP has digitized and shared over 37,500 pages of documents from the founding generation on The Revolutionary City website (https://therevolutionarycity.org/). Broadsides, pamphlets, and newspapers from the 1760s demonstrate the growing displeasure with British Parliament's efforts to tax the North American colonies to recoup the debt from the French and Indian War **(no. 12)**. Colonial resistance reached a fever pitch in 1765 with the passage of the Non-Importation Agreement signed by prominent Philadelphia merchants with surnames like Wharton, Biddle, Cadwalader, and Morris as well as by small shopkeepers **(no. 16)**.

HSP's collections hold many stories of the founding of the United States. These include the only surviving printer's proof of the Declaration of Independence **(no. 21)**, John Dickinson's draft of the Articles of Confederation **(no. 22)**, Charles Thomson's secret diaries of the Continental Congress **(no. 20)**, and the first two handwritten drafts of the United States Constitution **(no. 29)**. Letters to and from the canonical figures of the Revolution—George Washington, John Adams, Thomas Jefferson, Benjamin Franklin, Alexander Hamilton, and Robert Morris—are complemented by manuscript maps of Valley Forge by French officers and engineers **(no. 24)**, broadsides and pamphlets, as well as diaries written by ordinary soldiers such as John Hawkins **(no. 25)** and women such as Sarah Logan Fisher (1751–1796) **(no. 23)** and Elizabeth Drinker (1735–1807) **(no. 18)** who commented on events ranging from the British occupation to the Yellow Fever epidemics. One breathtaking exchange between General Washington and his confidante John Cadwalader details real-time planning and an account of Washington's surprise attack on the British forces at Trenton on December 26, 1776. Washington first writes to ask Cadwalader to join in the assault or at least to create a diversion. Then, when Cadwalader missed the action because of the Delaware River's icy waters, Washington sent an account of the conflict and a tally of the numbers by rank of the 919 men he captured that day **(fig. 5)**.

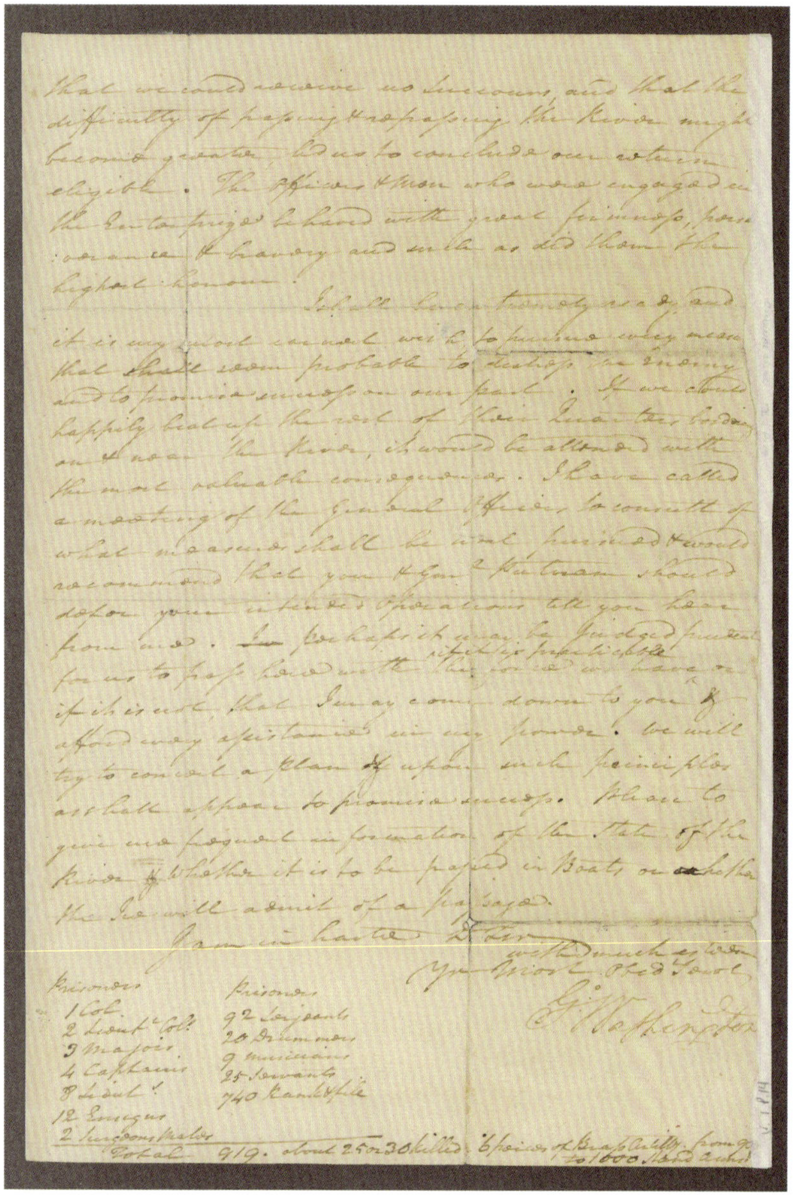

**Fig. 5** *George Washington Letter to John Cadwalader*, verso, December 27, 1776; manuscript; ink on laid paper, 12 ¾ × 8 ½ inches (32.3 × 21.5 cm); Cadwalader Family Papers [1454], Gift of the Cadwalader Family

## What's Your Story? Chronicling Families and Communities

To understand who we are and where we came from, especially in a nation of immigrants, many Americans have become avid genealogists. Thanks to resources such as FamilyTree.com, FindaGrave.com, and Ancestry.com, as well as public records of births, deaths, and marriages, decennial censuses, newspapers, and even DNA tests, family history has become one of the most popular hobbies in the United States. Among the various types of researchers at HSP, approximately half enter the Reading Room to populate their family tree and tell the stories of immigration, struggle, community building, and achievement that have shaped their own lives. Whether looking for data or trying to provide context for personal histories, HSP is an extraordinary resource for genealogical historians.

While the formation of legacy societies in the late nineteenth and early twentieth centuries connected individuals of like backgrounds, they could also exclude people. To offset this, the Genealogical Society of Pennsylvania (GSP) was founded at HSP in 1892 to broaden access to lineage information by making its resources democratically available. GSP's members committed to "preserve the genealogies of all persons who have lived in these parts, so far as we can get at them, no matter whether they were rich or poor, distinguished or humble."[20] While GSP maintains its independence today, in 2008–2009 it transferred thousands of volumes to HSP, thereby providing a rich store of information.

Family papers are one place to begin, especially when one's ancestry can be traced to a recognizable surname, such as Biddle, Cadwalader, Chew, Logan, Mifflin, Montgomery, Morris, Peters, Powel, Price, Richards, Shippen, or Wharton. But embedded in the papers of prominent families are also the stories of the people who worked for them—builders, gardeners, farmers, furniture makers, employees, servants, and slaves. These records include correspondence, diaries, commonplace books, ledgers, and other business papers, each with its own set of opportunities and challenges.

A broader spectrum of family histories can be accessed through census data, church records, gravestone inscriptions, deeds, wills, tax records, and passenger lists, which are available at HSP through manuscripts, microfilms, and published reference volumes. The papers of the R. R. Bringhurst (1877–1924) and Oliver H. Bair (1920–1980) funeral companies add to the knowledge of deaths across a century. Published local, county, and state histories provide narratives built on oral traditions that are otherwise hard to obtain. Family bibles similarly register information not available elsewhere, especially before the mandatory registration of vital statistics in public records **(no. 5)**. The archives of the Orphan Society of Philadelphia **(no. 42)** and the Children's Aid Society also help to recover family histories that would be lost without the meticulously detailed records of a particular child's origins.

In addition to family histories, HSP's collections contain vast resources related to the changing character of communities, with special strength in documenting the

**Fig. 6** Edmund Woolley (ca. 1695–1771), *Plan of the Pennsylvania State House*, 1732; ink on parchment, 12 ½ × 28 ¼ inches (31.7 × 71.7 cm); Historical Society of Pennsylvania Large Graphics Collection [V65], Gift of Robert R. Logan

built environment of Philadelphia through prints, drawings, maps, photographs, city directories, newspapers, and insurance company surveys. In 1682, William Penn commissioned his surveyor Thomas Holme (1624–1695) to draw a conceptual map that outlined the anticipated development of Pennsylvania's capital between the Delaware River and the Schuylkill. HSP also holds the copper plate on which the city plan was engraved; multiple impressions pulled from this plate **(no. 2)** affirm the map's promotional value to Penn as a real estate developer eager to attract investors and prospective settlers. Subsequent maps of Philadelphia, including Peter Charles Varlé's (ca. 1770–1835) 1802 plan, capture the extent of the bustling mercantile city more than a century later **(no. 32)**. William Birch's (1755–1834) nearly contemporary published collection of hand-colored engravings of Philadelphia informs the scholar and curious reader about the civic, political, religious, commercial, charitable, and cultural buildings that defined the character of the second largest city in North America at the end of the eighteenth century **(no. 37)**.[21]

Benjamin Franklin famously introduced property insurance in the United States as a safety net for people living in densely populated, fire-prone cities. The property surveys of the Franklin Fire Insurance Company document over one hundred thousand buildings with specific floor plans of humble and grand homes alike in Philadelphia and the surrounding region. These remarkable records show us how dwellings were organized, with interior spaces defined in relation to one another and labeled with their primary functions **(no. 57)**. They help to tell family as well as social histories.

Architecture in the eighteenth century was designed mainly by craftsmen-builders or gentleman-amateurs, whose well-rounded education and European travels gave them the skill and inspiration to design public buildings and grand private dwellings. For example, Andrew Hamilton (ca. 1676–1741), born and educated in Scotland, was a prominent attorney and a member of the committee formed to design the new State House that would later be known as Independence Hall **(fig. 6)**. The north elevation and plan is the earliest surviving architectural drawing for a building in Philadelphia. Drawn by builder Edmund Woolley (ca. 1695–1771), it demonstrates his knowledge of the Palladian style that had gained popularity in seventeenth-century Britain. HSP also possesses an extraordinary collection of approximately eighty eighteenth-century drawings for buildings commissioned by the Norris family. These drawings appear to have been completed by Samuel Rhoads (1711–1784), a builder and mayor of Philadelphia whose name appears in the Norris Family Ledger over decades, and by merchant and amateur architect John Dorsey (1759–1821) **(fig. 7)**. These include plans and elevations for town houses, country houses, and stables, designs for a town square with plot plans, details for windows and a porch, and practical instructions with dimensions for the carpenters to build a house.[22] This rare collection gives a

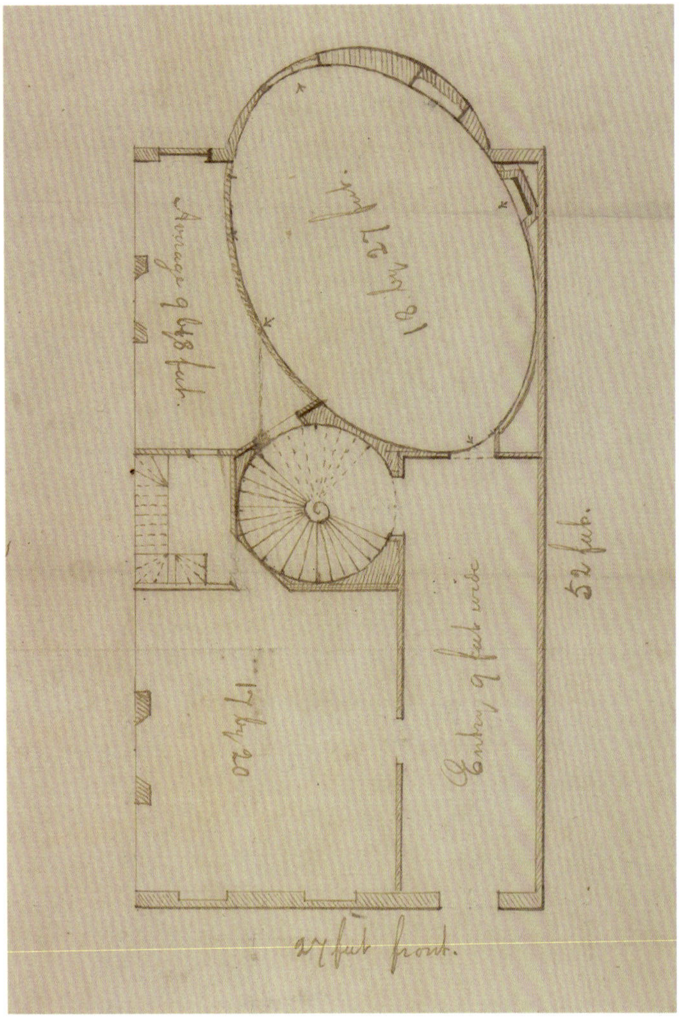

**Fig. 7** Attributed to John Dorsey (1759–1821), *Plan for townhouse with elliptical parlor*, ca. 1790; ink on laid paper, 11 15/16 × 8 inches (30.4 × 20.3 cm); Norris Family Papers [0454], Gift of the Norris family

unique glimpse into the design and construction of buildings in eighteenth-century and early nineteenth-century Philadelphia.

Visualizing the business district of Center City Philadelphia in the late nineteenth century is possible through the vivid depiction of entire blocks in DeWitt Clinton Baxter's (1829–1881) panoramas **(no. 76)**. Philadelphia's active business in lithography augments these views with specific full-color portraits of buildings ranging from drug stores to stone carvers' shops, breweries, sugar refineries, and places of worship **(no. 73)**. Individual depictions of modest and grand buildings, domestic, commercial, and civic, are also preserved in drawings and watercolors by W. L. Breton (ca. 1773–1855), David J. Kennedy (1816–1898) **(nos. 46 and 72)**, and other artists.[23] Lithographs by John T. Bowen and Co. vividly depict the businesses, places of worship, civic organizations, and other structures of nineteenth-century Philadelphia.[24] The expanse, urbanization, and industrialization of Philadelphia are evident in the aerial panorama view of the city made in 1908 amidst its 225th-anniversary celebration **(no. 79)**.

HSP preserves abundant stores of architectural plans, elevations, and renderings by leading architects of the eighteenth and nineteenth centuries. These include large holdings by Frank Furness (1839–1912) **(no. 73)**, Horace Trumbauer (1868–1938) **(no. 82)**, and small but significant groups of drawings by John Dorsey, Benjamin Henry Latrobe (1764–1820) **(no. 36)**, Robert Mills (1781–1855), William Strickland (1788–1854), Thomas U. Walter (1804–1887), Samuel Kneass (1806–1858) **(no. 43)**, John Notman (1810–1865), William Struthers (1812–1876), Stephen Decatur Button (1813–1897), Napoleon LeBrun (1821–1901) and Gustavus Runge (1822–1900) **(no. 60)**, Henry Augustus Sims (1832–1875), Addison Hutton (1834–1916), who designed HSP's current Georgian revival building, and George W. Hewitt (1841–1916), among others.

## America's Promise and Its Many Voices

HSP's collections go beyond the lives of famous individuals. For many decades, historians emphasized the accomplishments of leaders in politics, business, religion, education, the judiciary, military, science, and the arts at the expense of marginalized groups. In the 1960s, social historians began to rectify this glaring gap in the historical record by turning their attention to the stories of the working class, women, immigrants, people of color, and other groups often left out of the narratives of American exceptionalism and progress. The range and depth of HSP's collections provide unique opportunities to reexamine the diversity of voices that reveal our past.

Women's history is illuminated at HSP by letters, diaries, commonplace books, and other documents. Eighteenth- and early nineteenth-century diaries and letters written by Elizabeth Sandwith Drinker (1735–1807) **(no. 18)**, Sarah Logan Fisher **(no. 23)**, Sarah Wister (1761–1804), and Deborah Norris Logan (1761–1839) **(no. 47)** provide direct observation of women's lives concerning family, education, crises like the British occupation of Philadelphia in 1777–78 and the Yellow Fever epidemics of the 1790s, public events, and cultural life. Early public documents at HSP, such as tax assessments and censuses, expand our understanding of colonial and early national women as wives and mothers, as well as business owners, educators, artists, and activists.

Similarly, Emilie Davis's (1839–1889) diary from 1863–65 provides a view of everyday life in Philadelphia during another momentous time in American history, the Civil War, this time from the perspective of a free Black seamstress and domestic servant. Tucked among her daily notes about the comings and goings of friends and family and her regular attendance at school and church, on April 15, 1865, Davis wrote: "very sad news was received this morning of the murder of the President the city is in deep mourning we had a meeting of the [Ladies' Union] association."[25]

Evidence of women's activism spanning a century leading up to the passage of the Nineteenth Amendment, granting women the right to vote, has recently been digitized and published online in collaboration with other regional special collections libraries on a website called *In Her Own Right*, where the stories they tell are accessible to all. In addition to women's suffrage, HSP's collections demonstrate women's support for the abolition of slavery **(no. 50)**, protection of animals, women's athletics, nursing on the frontline of World War I, and fair treatment in the workplace. In the twentieth century, Thelma McDaniel collected posters, fliers, bumper stickers, and other ephemera related to her activism for Civil Rights: these are now catalogued and readily available for study **(no. 100)**.

**Fig. 8** Maria Louise Kirk (1860–1938), *Pinocchio and Candlewick*, 1919; ink and watercolor on board, 12 3/8 × 9 1/16 inches (31.5 × 23.0 cm); J. B. Lippincott Company Records [3104], Gift of Lippincott Williams and Wilkins, 2002

Women's creativity is reflected in the papers of visual artists Emily Sartain (1841–1927) and Violet Oakley (1874–1927) **(no. 80)**, as well as the composer, musician, and inventor, Mary Elizabeth Hallock Greenewalt (1871–1950) **(no. 87)**. Sartain and Oakley were born into families of prominent artists, giving them access to training, art supplies, and a circle of patrons to help them succeed. Maria Louise Kirk (1860–1938) was a children's book illustrator whose original watercolor illustrations for *Pinocchio* and *Heidi* are preserved in the J. B. Lippincott Company records at HSP **(fig. 8)**. The Lantern and Lens Guild and the Plastic Club Collections record women's efforts to organize themselves into mutually supportive groups of painters, illustrators, and photographers starting in the late nineteenth century.

Evidence of African American experiences is well sourced at HSP, including the histories of slavery and the formation of a Free Black community striving for freedom, seeking education, and promoting religious worship, economic opportunity, and creative expression. HSP's collections trace the determined emergence of community through the formation of independent businesses, civic associations, churches, and other organizations.[26] One of the central narratives of Black American history in HSP's collection is William Still's (1821–1902) diary **(no. 63)**, recognized as "the most detailed record now extant of how the Underground Railroad operated." The Still Papers also include his correspondence with Frederick Douglass, Sojourner Truth, and Booker T. Washington, as well as several copies of his published memoir.[27]

The multigenerational papers of such prominent families as the Norrises, Logans, and Chews, and the South Carolina senator Pierce Butler (1744–1822), who resided in Philadelphia after retiring from politics, record the history of slavery from the point of view of the enslavers, often with businesslike precision inventorying the monetary value of enslaved people according to their age, gender, and skills **(no. 61)**. By contrast, the Pennsylvania Abolition Society (PAS) united prominent Quakers with Free Black leaders, both men and women **(no. 50)**, in a common cause to end slavery. Although Quakers enslaved Africans and their descendants starting in 1684, by the second quarter

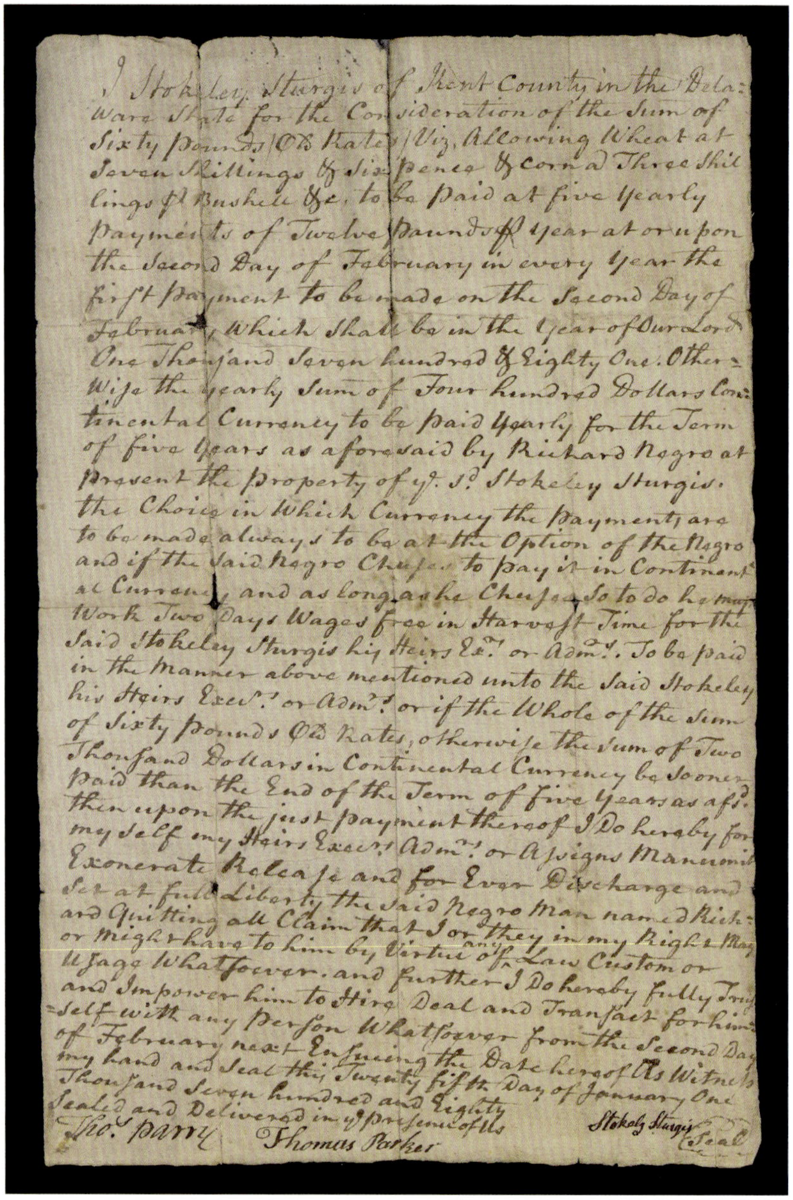

I Stokeley Sturgis of Kent County in the Delaware State for the Consideration of the Sum of Sixty Pounds Old Rates Viz. Allowing Wheat at Seven Shillings & Six pence & Corn at Three Shillings pr Bushel &c. to be Paid at five Yearly payments of Twelve Pounds pr year at or upon the Second Day of February in every year the first payment to be made on the Second Day of February which shall be in the Year of Our Lord One Thousand Seven hundred & Eighty One. Otherwise the yearly Sum of Four hundred Dollars Continental Currency to be paid Yearly for the Term of five Years as aforesaid by Richard Negro at present the property of ye sd Stokeley Sturgis. the Choice in which Currency the payments are to be made always to be at the Option of the Negro and if the said Negro Chuses to pay it in Continental Currency and as long as he Chuses so to do he may Work Two Days Wages free in Harvest Time for the said Stokeley Sturgis his Heirs Ex. or Adm. To be paid in the manner above mentioned unto the said Stokeley his Heirs Exec. or Adm. or if the Whole of the Sum of Sixty Pounds Old Rates, otherwise the Sum of Two Thousand Dollars in Continental Currency be Sooner paid than the End of the Term of five years as afd then upon the just payment thereof I Do hereby for my self my Heirs Exec. Adm. or Assigns Manumit Exonerate Release and for Ever Discharge and Set at full Liberty the said Negro man named Richard and Quitting all Claim that I or they in my Right may or might have to him by Virtue of Law Custom or Usage Whatsoever. and further I Do hereby fully Trust and Impower him to Hire Deal and Transact for himself with any Person Whatsoever from the Second Day of February next Ensuing the Date hereof As Witness my hand and Seal this Twenty fifth Day of January One Thousand Seven hundred and Eighty
Sealed and Delivered in ye presence of us
Thos. Parry Thomas Parker Stokely Sturgis (Seal)

**Fig. 9** *Richard Allen's Manumission Papers*, 1780; manuscript; ink on laid paper, 12 15⁄16 × 8 1⁄8 inches (32.8 × 20.7 cm); Pennsylvania Abolition Society (PAS) Papers [0490], Gift of the Pennsylvania Abolition Society, 1992, 2001, 2015

of the eighteenth century, significant numbers of Pennsylvanians had manumitted their slaves. In 1775 abolitionists formed the Society for the Relief of Free Negroes Unlawfully Held in Bondage, but the Revolution soon halted their efforts, and they did not resume until after the conclusion of the conflict. Prominent attorneys, including William Lewis (1752–1819) and HSP's first president, William Rawle, drafted the Gradual Abolition Act in 1780—the first American law of its kind—that ended the slave trade in Pennsylvania and widened a path to freedom for enslaved people. In addition to correspondence and business records, the PAS Papers have descriptions of individual manumissions. These remarkable documents include one for "Richard Negro," known today as Richard Allen (1760–1831), one of the founders of the African Methodist Episcopal Church in Philadelphia **(fig. 9)**.

The American Negro Historical Society (ANHS) was founded in 1897 by members of Philadelphia's Black community, including Robert Adger, W. M. Dorsey, and Jacob C. White Jr., to document and celebrate their peers' social, intellectual, religious, and civic lives. Other key figures represented in this collection include Frederick Douglass, James and William Still, and Octavius Catto, the educator and civil rights activist who was murdered at the age of twenty-five. In addition, the records document the work of the Banneker Institute to establish a learned society for African Americans **(no. 64)**, the Pythian Baseball Club, and Lebanon Cemetery **(no. 58)**. Correspondence and portraits, including a rare watercolor of the successful African American businessman James Forten **(no. 44)**, lend a biographical and personal character to these stories that enriches our understanding of the institutions they founded at the heart of their communities. While the ANHS Collection spans 1715 to 1962, the majority of the papers date from the second half of the nineteenth century. A united record of vigorous self-determination, HSP's collection also demonstrates violent racism and resistance against Black prosperity and full citizenship, as illustrated in the graphic depiction of the destruction of Pennsylvania Hall days after it was dedicated to promote abolition **(fig. 10)**.

The lives of Indigenous people can also be chronicled through HSP's collections, from the earliest contact with English settlers in the 1680s, through the effort to establish treaties, to the struggle to define Indian policy in terms of coexistence, separate sovereign nations, removal, or extermination. Founded to foster assimilation, the Indian Rights Association sought a better alternative to warfare or corralling native peoples onto reservations, though their efforts have since come into question. These included the formation of Indian Boarding Schools, lessons in western standards of dress and hygiene, as well as training in useful occupations. This work also eradicated the cultural specificity of hundreds of Indigenous nations and tribes. This complex history is documented in a collection of more than one thousand boxes of archival records that date from the founding in 1882 to the late twentieth century, encompassing the continental United States and Alaska.

In 2002, HSP absorbed the vast and important collections of the Balch Institute for Ethnic Studies, creating a national resource for the exploration of the immigrant experience in America as well as genealogical research. Founded in 1971, the Balch actively collected private and institutional papers that relate to Native Americans as well as immigrants from various parts of Asia, Africa, Europe, Australia, and Central and South America. For example, the extensive papers of Leonard Covello (1887–1982) tell of an Italian immigrant who became a leading educator in New York City, founder of Benjamin Franklin High School in East Harlem, and advocate for community-centered schools **(fig. 11)**. He helped Italian immigrant children and later African American and Puerto Rican students to balance the demand for assimilation with the need to preserve their ethnic identity through language, religion, cultural production, and association.[28]

The Fujita, Kobayashi, and Iwata Family Papers record the struggles of Japanese immigrants whose lives were disrupted during World War II when they were placed in internment camps in California, Arizona, New Mexico, and Utah. During her detention, teenaged Sumiko Kobayashi (born 1923) made a series of drawings that depict the stark environment—a former racetrack, repurposed as a prison—where she and her family were forced to live **(no. 91)**. The drawings are a beautiful, haunting testament to her perseverance in adversity. Despite their internment, the Iwata correspondence declares their loyalty as Americans and their commitment to live in the United States as productive citizens whenever the change in geopolitical circumstances would permit.

In addition to these personal stories, the Balch collections document organizations established within ethnic communities to assist immigrants in their adopted country while ensuring the preservation of their ethnic identities. The extensive records of the Russian Brotherhood Organization, Danish Brotherhood in America, Netherlands Society of Philadelphia, Alliance Française de Philadelphie, French Benevolent Society of Philadelphia, National Carl Schurz Association, Pan-Macedonian Association, Ancient Order of Hibernians in America, American Institute for Italian Culture, and other civic, cultural, and benevolent associations comprise a trove of information about the ways ethnic organizations in America supported their communities. The Balch is also rich in ethnic newspapers **(no. 93)**, published in native languages and in English, that helped immigrants stay connected with their homeland. Personal and institutional manuscripts are complemented

**Fig. 10** John T. Bowen (ca. 1801–1856), *Destruction of Pennsylvania Hall*, 1838; lithograph on wove paper, 10 13⁄16 × 14 3⁄16 inches (27.5 × 36.1 cm); Historical Society of Pennsylvania Medium Graphics Collection [V65], Presented by Mrs. John E. Brown, 1918

**Fig. 11** *Leonard Covello with Club Borinquen at Benjamin Franklin High School*, ca. 1940; gelatin silver print, 3 3⁄4 × 4 7⁄8 inches (9.5 × 12.3 cm); Leonard Covello Photographs [PG107], The Balch Institute

by over 60,000 books and periodicals, microfilm of ethnic collections in other archives, photographs, posters, broadsides, and ephemera.

LGBTQ communities are also reflected throughout HSP's collections, most notably in the papers of Dr. John Fryer (1937–2003) **(no. 98)**. At the American Psychiatric Association's (APA) national meeting in 1972, while disguised by a mask and an altered voice, Fryer delivered a speech in which he made history by challenging the APA to remove homosexuality from the *Diagnostic and Statistical Manual of Mental Disorders* (DSM). A year later, the APA acted on Fryer's powerful plea, setting the way for professional acceptance and legal changes that would eventually include protections for same-sex marriage. The 217 boxes of Fryer's Papers at HSP have inspired an acclaimed original play by the award-winning playwright Ain Gordon, and a documentary called *Cured*, a title that ironically references the millions of people who were suddenly "cured" by the removal of homosexuality from the DSM.

## Americans and Innovation: Science, Technology, and Enterprise

Even before Alexander Hamilton (1755/1757–1804) promoted the formation of the First Bank of the United States, Philadelphia was the national banking center. The Bank of North America was chartered by the Continental Congress in 1781 under the authority of the Articles of Confederation and ratified by the states. Conceived by Robert Morris (1734–1806) to establish a national currency and to finance the ongoing needs of the American Revolution, the Bank of North America is extensively documented at HSP in 672 volumes of ledgers, journals, and other official records as well as through correspondence written by Morris and by the bank's first two presidents, Thomas Willing (1731–1821) and John Nixon (1733–1808). Correspondence between Hamilton and his assistant secretary of the Treasury, Tench Coxe (1755–1824), adds to the record of the Bank of the United States, whose 1791 charter resulted in the shift of federal funds away from the Bank of North America and its subsequent reinvention as a private bank. The Biddle Family Papers at HSP document the Second Bank of the United States, chartered in 1816 and dismantled by Andrew Jackson in the 1830s.[29]

Financing the Civil War also depended upon banking in Philadelphia. Lincoln's secretary of the treasury Salmon P. Chase (1808–1873), built the National Bank and found an able partner in Philadelphia financier Jay Cooke (1821–1905) to sell bonds that funded the effort to maintain the Union. Chase later served as chief justice of the Supreme Court of the United States, and his personal and business records at HSP help to tell that story. Cooke backed Chase for the presidential nomination in 1868, but the Republican nod went to Ulysses S. Grant (1822–1885). Cooke's postwar career focused on financing the Northern Pacific Railway, though that venture and Cooke's fortune were gravely injured by the Panic of 1873. Cooke's papers and a substantial collection of Chase's are preserved and accessible at HSP.

Technological innovation is reflected in multiple disciplines throughout HSP. From the 861 books written, printed, or collected by Benjamin Franklin **(no. 17)** to the synesthetic light organ created by Mary Elizabeth Hallock Greenewalt (1871–1950) **(no. 87)**, the quest for improving the world through invention is embedded in the collections. The steam engine is typically credited to the British inventor Thomas Newcomen (1664–1729), with improvements by Scotsman James Watt (1736–1819). In the United States, John Fitch (1743–1798) and James Rumsey (1743–1792) independently built steamboats in the late 1780s and received patents simultaneously in 1791. Their contest for intellectual property rights ended up in the Pennsylvania Supreme Court and is partially captured in the papers of Justice George Bryan (1731–1791) at HSP. Steam technology was also used to solve public health crises, such as the steam-powered pump at Centre Square that Benjamin Henry Latrobe designed to distribute clean water and reduce the threat of yellow fever epidemics **(no. 36)**.

The roots of industrial development in Pennsylvania and in other colonies lay in the establishment of the earliest iron furnaces and forges in the first quarter of the eighteenth century. Successful iron production depended on water for power and transportation, level and well-maintained roads, wood to fuel the furnaces, and, of course, iron ore. These factors determined the most productive sites. Many early iron producers worked in partnership with one other person, though by the middle of the eighteenth century, wealthy merchants such as James Logan connected their activities in land speculation and trade to iron manufacturing. The small partnerships sold locally, while the Logan family and other groups exported iron to England. The Pennsylvania iron industry is documented at HSP in the papers of Colebrook Furnace, Cornwall Furnace, Durham Iron Company (in which Logan invested), Hopewell Forge, Mary Ann Furnace, New Pine Forge, Pequea Works, and Speedwell Forge, as well as in the Logan and Penn Family Papers. By the mid-nineteenth century, these smaller concerns were being eclipsed by industrialized production at anthracite-fueled ironworks and rolling mills that were more highly capitalized and organized into sophisticated companies.[30]

The Industrial Revolution in the United States also developed from small manufacturing enterprises located in rural areas throughout the state, such as the many cotton and paper mills that operated in Chester County during the nineteenth century. These mills were located in prosperous villages of a few thousand people each and, while quieter and cleaner than such mammoth factories as the Baldwin Locomotive complex in Philadelphia, were also part of a global economy. Buying cotton from the South, employing immigrant laborers from England and Ireland, and supplying fabric to Europe, these companies played an important role in the emergence of the United States as an industrial economy and power. HSP preserves the business and personal papers of such cotton and paper manufacturing families as the Gilpins, Martins, and Willcoxes, and their records provide a multidimensional account encompassing technology, economics, industrialization, education, social life, religion, and politics.

The Coxe Mining Company was crucial in developing the anthracite coal industry, which drove the need for internal improvements by literally fueling industrial production **(no. 74)**. An enterprise made possible by Tench Coxe's visionary acquisition of 80,000 acres of coal-rich land between 1790 and 1824, the mining of anthracite transformed northeastern Pennsylvania. As Alexander Hamilton's assistant secretary of the Treasury, Coxe collaborated on a draft of Hamilton's signature policy statement, "The Report on Manufactures" (1791), now held by HSP. Coxe foresaw the potential of anthracite, and his grandsons profited from it between the 1860s and the sale of the company in 1905 to the Lehigh Valley Railroad. Hundreds of boxes and volumes of Coxe-family and -company correspondence, legal documents, land deeds and surveys, and photographs inform the story of the coal industry from the perspectives of both the mine owner and the miner. At a particularly heated moment in 1885, the Molly Maguires—alternately understood as a secret labor union protesting unfair practices or a terrorist organization that notoriously used violence to pursue its agenda—sent illustrated death threats to company executives **(fig. 12)**, to which the company responded by hiring Pinkerton investigators.[31] An anonymous informant warned the Coxes that twenty-two Irish, English, Scotch, Welsh, and Dutch employees were planning to sabotage equipment in retribution for the unbearably hard treatment they received from a Mr. Koodley, "your inside boss," who had fired many miners and replaced them with "Hungarian cheap labor." This episode reflects the ongoing tensions between an immigrant workforce and the industrialists who depended upon their labor to extract the rich stores of Pennsylvania coal.

Internal improvements, starting with canals and later followed by railroads, sped the movement of raw materials, people, and manufactured goods and increased economic opportunities exponentially. As early as 1761, the Pennsylvania Assembly created a public commission to improve navigation on the Schuylkill River. This project was expanded in 1791 when the Commonwealth appropriated funds to begin the construction of canals. HSP's collections of papers from the Delaware and Schuylkill, Union, Delaware and Raritan, and Susquehanna and Tidewater Canal companies **(fig. 13)** help to trace the legal, technological, and economic histories of these canals.

An emblematic account of the Industrial Revolution in Philadelphia is the rise of the Baldwin Locomotive Works **(no. 49)**, which originated in 1828 when Franklin Peale (1795–1870), then managing the Peale Museum, asked jeweler Matthias Baldwin (1795–1866) to craft a model steam engine. By the late nineteenth century, Baldwin was the world's largest manufacturer of locomotives. At its peak in the early twentieth century, it employed 18,500 people at an industrial campus that spanned seven city blocks. A leader in innovative design, production, and management, the Works supplied engines to North America, Asia, and Europe. Numerous scholars of labor and transportation history have mined the vast Baldwin Locomotive Works records, deposited at HSP by the company in the mid-twentieth century, to tell the story both from the perspective of the industrialists who built the company as well as their employees. This example illustrates one of the strengths of the collections at HSP: they provide the evidence necessary to weave multiple narratives from different points of view.[32]

## The Soul of America: Visual, Performing, and Literary Arts

The breadth of HSP's manuscript holdings in the arts is defined by two great autograph collections assembled by jeweler Ferdinand J. Dreer (1812–1902) and lawyer and politician Simon Gratz (1837–1925). Both men were voracious collectors: Dreer amassed more than 40,000 documents, and Gratz exceeded 175,000. Letters, drawings, and documents by artists include painters, sculptors, printmakers, poets, dramatists, novelists, musicians, composers, singers,

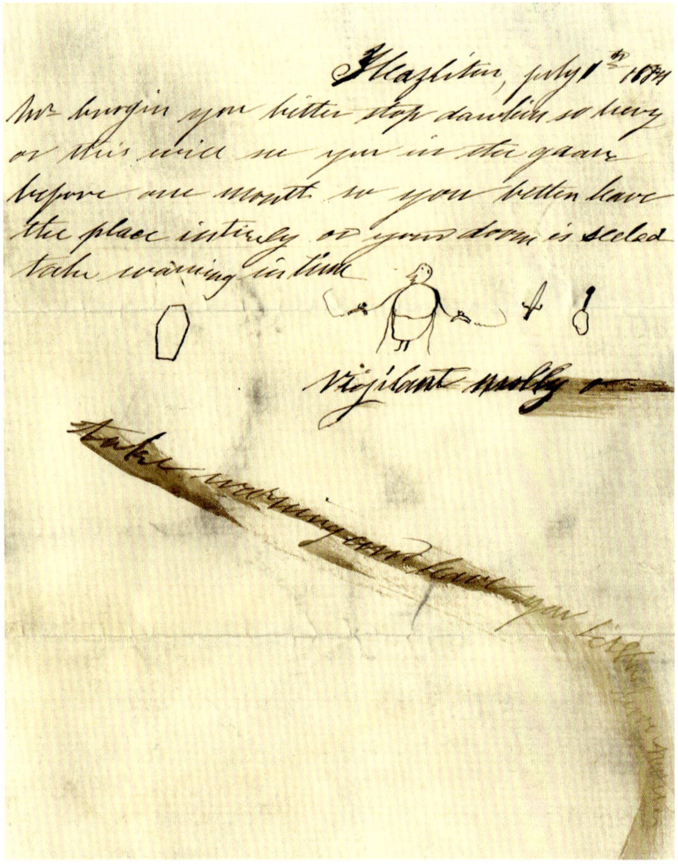

Hazleton, July 1st 1884
Mr. burgin you better stop dawdling so long
or this will see you in the grave
before one month so you better leave
the place intirely or your doom is sealed
take warning in time
Vigilant molly
take warning and leave

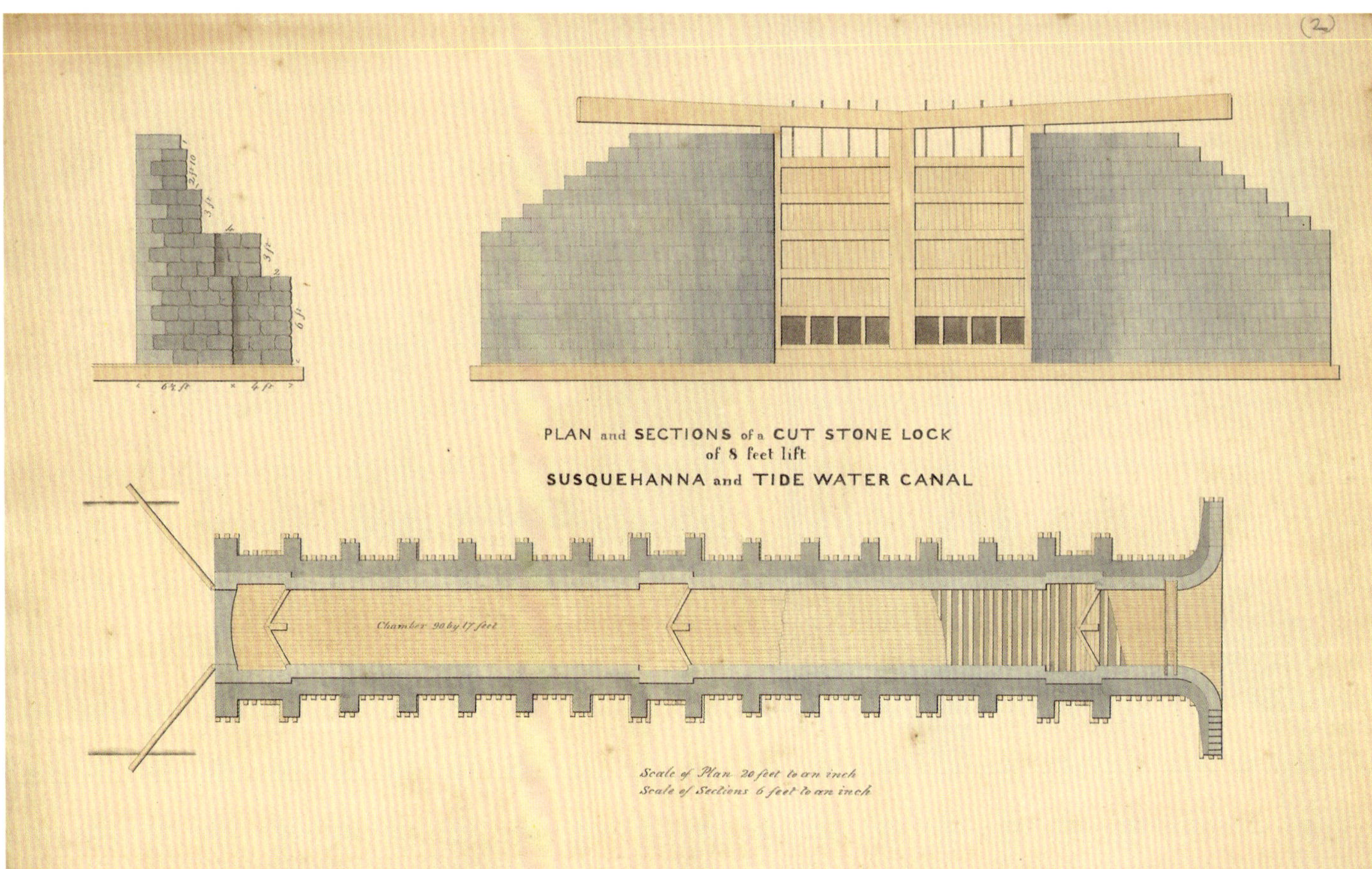


**Fig. 12** Molly Maguires, *"Coffin notice" to Mr. Burgin of the Coxe Mining Company*, July 1, 1884; manuscript; ink on paper, 8 × 5 ⅞ inches (20.5 × 15.0 cm); Coxe Family Mining Papers [3005], Gift of the Trustees for the Heirs and Devisees of Tench Coxe, 1967

**Fig. 13** Susquehanna & Tidewater Canal Co., *Plan and Sections of a Cut Stone Lock of 8 feet lift, Susquehanna and Tide Water Canal*, ca. 1835; ink and watercolor on wove paper, 10 × 15 7⁄16 inches (25.4 × 39.2 cm); p. 2 of *Construction of Locks For the Susquehanna and Tidewater Canal (plans) By Susquehanna & Tidewater Canal Co.*; Historical Society of Pennsylvania Bound Graphics Collection [V66], Gift of Miss Sarah H. Wilson, 1931

dancers, and actors from Europe and the United States. Several subjects included in this volume—Phillis Wheatley (1753–1784) **(no. 19)**, Benjamin West, William Birch, and Thomas Sully—are represented in these collections. The Dreer Collection also includes items from the hand of Michelangelo[33] **(fig. 14)**, and both collections contain manuscripts by Galileo, Queen Elizabeth I, and Sir Isaac Newton. Many of the documents are substantive, speaking directly to what makes each individual important. Dreer and Gratz also collected engraved portraits of the authors of these documents.

The arts in colonial and early national Philadelphia reflect the transatlantic nature of the bustling port city. The intertwined life stories of early American artists—Benjamin West, Charles Willson Peale and his sons, Peale's former slave Moses Williams (1777–ca. 1825), William and Thomas Birch, Thomas Sully, and John Neagle—cannot be told without reference to HSP's collections of manuscripts and original artwork. Born in nearby Springfield, twenty-two-year-old Benjamin West (1738–1820) traveled to Italy and settled permanently in London. He taught three generations of American painters, some of whom lived with him and worked with him on his large-scale canvases. In 1768, West was a founder and later president of the Royal Academy of Arts in London, a school and exhibiting society that served as a model for the short-lived Columbianum art academy (1794–95) and later the Pennsylvania Academy of the Fine Arts (PAFA, founded 1805). Prominent Philadelphians sat for portraits by West during their travels to England, including William Hamilton (1745–1813) and his niece Anna Hamilton Lyle (1769–1798) **(no. 28)**. King George III appointed West surveyor of the King's pictures and court history painter, and the artist counted colonial proprietor Thomas Penn among his patrons.[34]

Charles Willson Peale (1741–1827), one of West's first students, studied with him from 1767 to 1770. Back in Philadelphia, Peale maintained a lively studio practice, actively participated as a soldier and legislator in the American Revolution, painted the first seven presidents of the United States from life, and helped found the Columbianum and PAFA, as well as a private museum of art and science **(no. 30)**. In 1805, Peale, his son Rembrandt, and the sculptor William Rush joined forces with sixty-eight civic-minded Philadelphians to establish PAFA, and West advised the founders, including HSP's first president William Rawle, on the advisability of focusing on classical principles in concert with contemporary trends in art. Peale aligned himself with the Democratic-Republicans yet was among the last slave owners in Philadelphia. In addition to training his children to paint, he also taught an enslaved person in his household named Moses Williams to cut silhouette portraits **(no. 31)** at the Peale Museum, where Williams continued to work for several decades as a free Black concessionaire.[35]

Among the artists in Peale's orbit were British-born William (1755–1834) and Thomas Birch (1779–1851), who emigrated from London to Philadelphia in 1794, just in time to play a role in the ambitious but tumultuous efforts to form the Columbianum as an art academy that would train artists and exhibit their work. When this institution expired after just one exhibition, William Birch turned his attention to creating an ambitious collection of engraved, hand-colored views of the principal sites in what was then the capital of the new United States **(no. 37)**. Birch's book provided a comprehensive tour of the burgeoning city by encompassing images of Philadelphia's chief government, economic, cultural, religious, and charitable institutions. William's son Thomas, just eighteen when the project began, prepared preliminary drawings and watercolors of many of the scenes and translated one of them—the port in Kensington and the Treaty Elm under which William Penn was said to have signed his famous treaty with the Lenni Lenape—into a large oil painting **(no. 38)**. The younger Birch later pursued a career as a landscape and marine painter, themes that would dominate American painting throughout the nineteenth century.[36]

The next generation of leaders of the visual arts in Philadelphia included Thomas Sully (1783–1872), who was also closely associated with the theater community. Born in England, Sully crossed the Atlantic as a child with his family; both of his parents were actors. Sully would travel back to England in 1809 and return to Philadelphia to paint in a sophisticated style influenced by Sir Thomas Lawrence (1769–1830), West's successor as the president of the Royal Academy **(no. 46)**. Sully's pupils included John Neagle (1796–1865), who would marry Sully's stepdaughter Mary **(no. 48)**. Sully served on the board of PAFA (1816–31), and Neagle became its director. Sully also remained active in theater circles, patronizing both the Chestnut and Walnut Street Theatres, and his most successful portraits include the British actors George Frederick Cooke and Fanny Kemble.[37]

Late nineteenth-century and early twentieth-century visual arts are represented by the collections of the Sartain family, the sculptor William R. O'Donovan (1844–1920), and muralist Violet Oakley (1874–1927). Like the Peales and the Sully-Neagle family, John (1808–1897), William

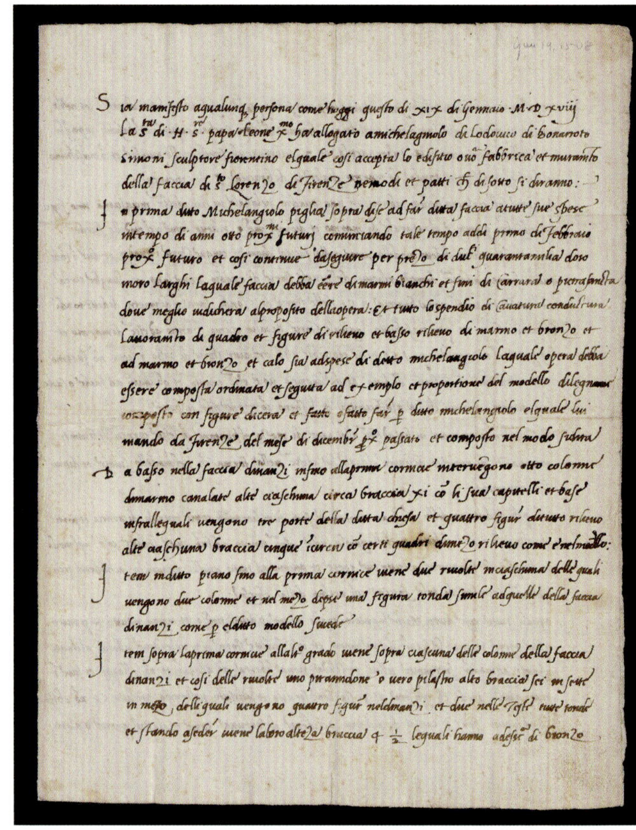

**Fig. 14** *Michelangelo Buonarroti Contract with Pope Leo X*, January 19, 1508; manuscript; ink on laid paper, 11 ½ × 8 ½ inches (29.3 × 21.7 cm); Simon Gratz Autograph Collection [0250A], Gift of Simon Gratz

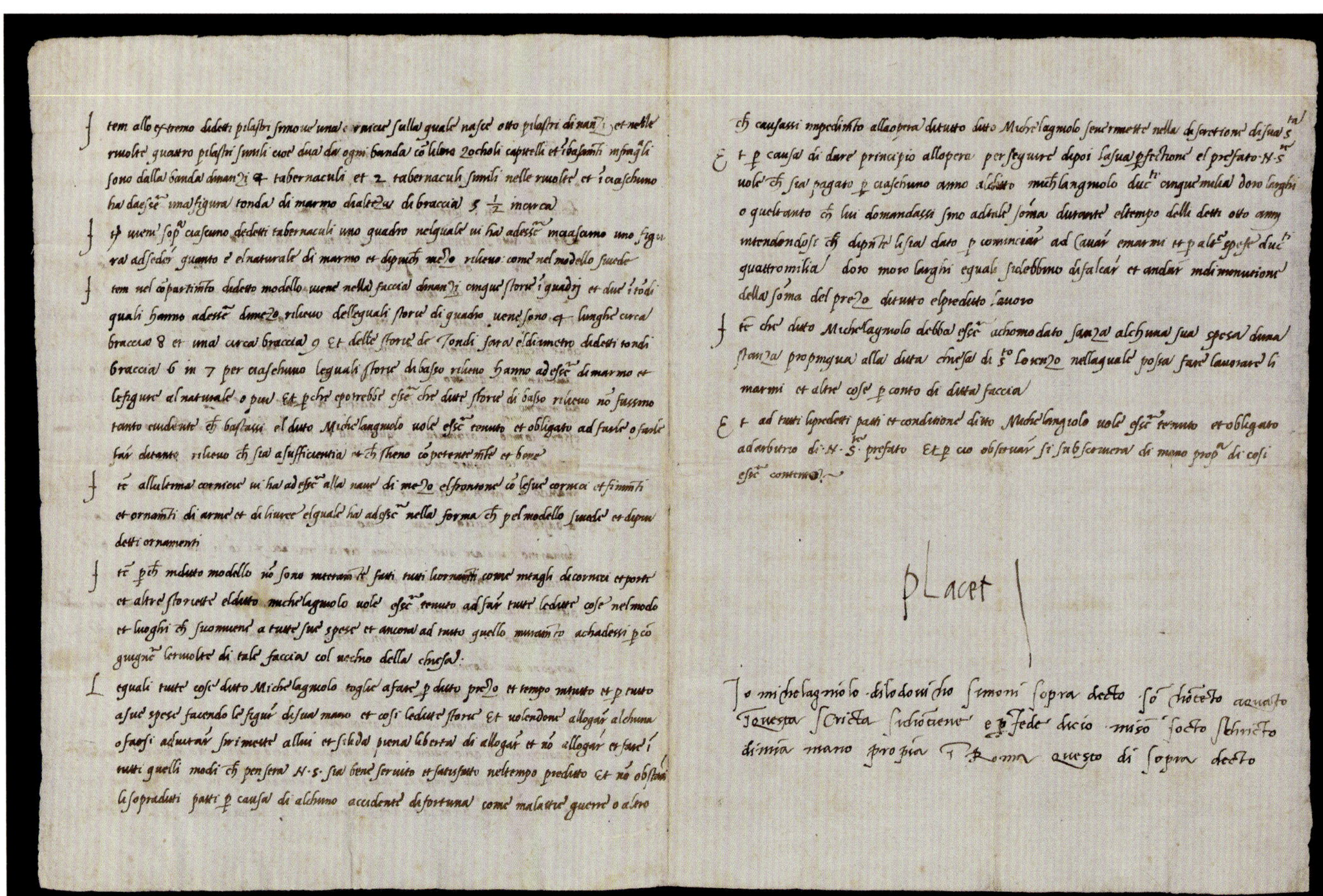

(1843–1924), and Emily Sartain played leading roles in the Philadelphia arts community. In addition to his career as a printmaker and editor, John was a member of the board of directors of PAFA and assisted in developing the program for the new PAFA building on Broad Street designed by Frank Furness and his partner George Hewitt. John also served on the boards of the Pennsylvania Museum of Industrial Art (now the Philadelphia Museum of Art) and the Philadelphia School of Design for Women (now Moore College of Art). Emily was also a champion of women artists at Moore and through her own professional example as a painter. O'Donovan fought in the Civil War on the side of the Confederacy and despite a lack of formal training, became a successful sculptor in New York who earned prominent commissions, including a collaboration with Thomas Eakins (1844–1916) for a monument to Washington at Trenton. A small but interesting collection of O'Donovan's correspondence, mainly from the early 1870s, documents his aspirations and struggles to gain a foothold in the art world. Oakley, like the Sartains, was part of a multigenerational family of artists and was awarded important commissions as a muralist and a teaching position in mural arts at PAFA **(no. 80)**. The stories of these and other artists are told in HSP's rich holdings.

In 1935 in response to the Great Depression, the Roosevelt administration started the Works Progress Administration (WPA), best known for building roads, bridges, airports, housing, and other public works. The program expanded to support creative workers, such as artists, playwrights, and writers. In Philadelphia, the Fine Print Workshop was established in 1937, and after the program ended in 1941, about five hundred prints were transferred to HSP. These include works by several dozen printmakers, including five African American artists: Samuel Brown, Claude Clark, Bryant Pringle, Raymond Steth, and Dox Thrash (1893–1965) **(no. 89)**. The WPA art projects were the first to provide equal opportunities and funding to Black and White artists. Artists were paid a wage to come to the studio each day and produce artwork. Thrash not only created lithographs and etchings, he also invented the carborundum printmaking technique during his time working for the WPA, a process that was refined in collaboration with fellow artists Michael Gallagher and Hubert Mesibov.

Important practitioners and institutions associated with the performing arts are also represented in HSP's collections. For example, the history of the Academy of Music, one of Philadelphia's architectural treasures and the home of opera, symphony, and ballet performances, is well documented at HSP. A prospectus published in 1852 outlines a plan to raise $300,000 to erect a 5,000-seat opera house that would rival European venues. The founders envisioned a fireproof building, comfortable in all weather that would offer inexpensive programs to a broad audience rather than only the wealthy elite. A handwritten note enlisted the support of a prospective donor and warned of potential failure if a gift were not forthcoming: "You are politely requested to subscribe for 300 shares—unless you do so—the project will certainly fail—Respect[full]y Yours &c—Joseph R. Ingersoll Pres't." At $100 per share, the solicitation was for $30,000. Architectural drawings by the team of Gustav Runge and Napoleon LeBrun show both the beauty of the building and the mechanical systems that would provide the promised comforts **(no. 60)**. The Academy of Music Collection at HSP includes playbills, programs, libretti, advertisements, and benefit gala invitations, from its opening in 1857 to 1972, starting with a series of classic operas by Italian and German composers performed by touring companies. Playbills name the opera and performers as well as the scenery painters. Elaborate productions are promised, supported by ample machinery, and many are annotated with brief critiques of the performances.

Performing arts activities in Philadelphia in the twentieth century are represented in the papers of the Theatre of the Living Arts (TLA) (1931–71) and actor, dancer, and educator H. German Wilson (1923–2014). Following early iterations as a concert hall and movie theater, the TLA became known as a repertory theatre, producing dozens of plays between 1959 and 1971 under the direction of Anne and Logan Ramsey and Andre Gregory, and later became a cinema. The TLA Papers include business records as well as documentation of the creative life of the theater, including scripts, headshots, correspondence, and contact sheets of photographs taken of plays as they were rehearsed and performed. Wilson created opportunities in North Philadelphia to make creative careers accessible in the Black community. He taught at the Community College of Philadelphia, directed the Model Cities Cultural Arts Program, led community outreach for the Philadelphia Museum of Art, founded the Venture Theatre, and established performance at The Village of Arts and Humanities **(fig. 15)**.

HSP's music collections include manuscript and printed sacred, patriotic, and popular music from the eighteenth to the twentieth centuries. The highlight of HSP's sacred music holdings is the Abraham Cassel Collection [1610], which encompasses eighteenth- and nineteenth-century

**Fig. 15** *H. German Wilson and Company*, 1974; gelatin silver print, 10 × 8 inches (25.3 × 20.3 cm); Archives of Mr. H. German Wilson [4140], Gift of Heidi Warren, 2017

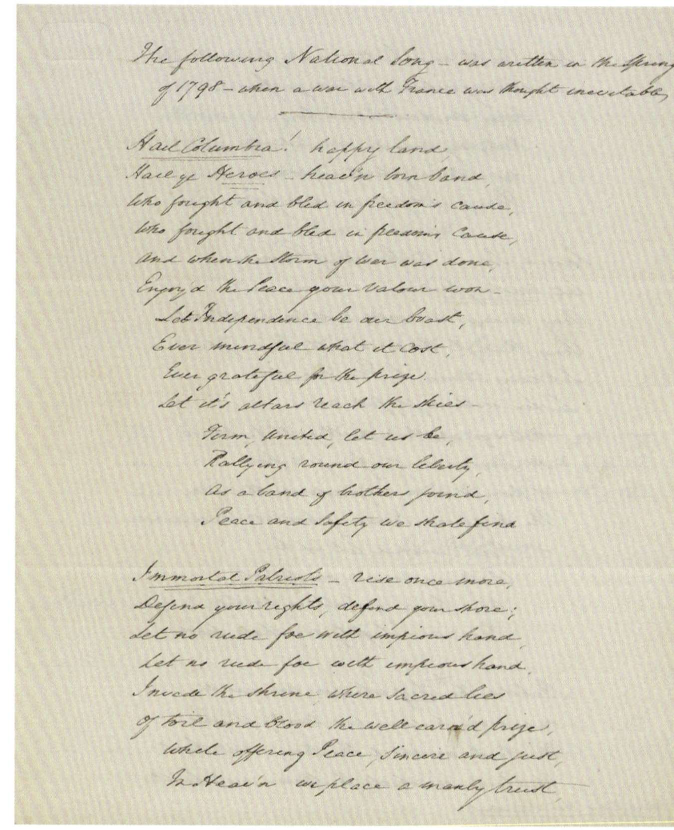

The following National Song — was written in the Spring of 1798 — when a war with France was thought inevitable,

Hail Columbia! happy land
Hail ye Heroes — heav'n born band,
Who fought and bled in freedom's cause,
Who fought and bled in freedom's cause,
And when the storm of war was done,
Enjoy'd the Peace your valour won —
Let Independence be our boast,
Ever mindful what it cost,
Ever grateful for the prize,
Let it's altars reach the skies —
Firm, united, let us be,
Rallying round our liberty,
As a band of brothers joined,
Peace and safety we shall find

Immortal Patriots — rise once more,
Defend your rights, defend your shore;
Let no rude foe with impious hand
Let no rude foe with impious hand
Invade the shrine where sacred lies
Of toil and blood the well earn'd prize,
While offering Peace, sincere and just,
In Heav'n we place a manly trust

**Fig. 16** Joseph Hopkinson (1770–1842), lyrics to *Hail, Columbia!*, May 2, 1838; manuscript; ink on wove paper, 9 7/8 × 7 7/8 inches (25.0 × 20.0 cm); Simon Gratz Autograph Collection [0250A], Gift of Simon Gratz

German manuscripts. The German mystic Johannes Kelpius is represented by a transcript of the hymns he wrote during his leadership of a religious community rooted in the Book of Revelation in Germantown, located in the Wissahickon Valley, just northwest of Philadelphia **(no. 4)**. The collection also includes a beautifully illustrated, handwritten eighteenth-century Choral Book and Chronicon from Ephrata Cloister **(no. 11)** and a manuscript music book from Snow Hill Cloister, both celibate communities devoted to awaiting the Second Coming of Christ.

Patriotic music at HSP includes "Hail, Columbia!," composed by Philip Phile (ca. 1734–1793) in 1789 with lyrics added by Joseph Hopkinson (1770–1842) in 1798 when the United States was in the midst of the quasi-war with France. Informally accepted at that time as the national anthem and often played at state occasions throughout the nineteenth century, it was favored by the Federalists but seen by the Democratic-Republicans as too steeped in pomp. Today it is still played as a ceremonial march for the vice president of the United States. Hopkinson sent the song to the retired first president of the United States, and Washington's reply is in the Hopkinson Papers at HSP. Washington wrote, "To expect that all men should think alike upon political, more than on Religious, or other subjects, would be to look for a change in the order of nature; but at so dangerous a crisis as the present, when every thing dear to Independence is at stake, the well disposed part of them might, one would think, act more alike;—opposition therefore to the Major will, and to that self respect which is due to the National character cannot but seem strange!—" HSP has several early printed versions of the song **(fig. 16)**, as well as manuscript versions that Hopkinson sent out in the late 1830s and early 1840s to explain the political context of his effort to unite the country through music. In the volume illustrated here, this Federalist anthem is bound with a printed copy of "Jefferson's March" **(fig. 17)**.[38] HSP also has a manuscript score by Hopkinson's contemporary Francis Scott Key (1779–1843) of "The Star-Spangled Banner," written during the War of 1812 but not recognized as the official national anthem until 1931. HSP's manuscript was a souvenir penned by Key around 1842 and mailed to General George May Keim (1805–1861) **(no. 54)**.

HSP's popular music collections include published sheet music and music scores composed by African American musicians ranging from Francis Johnson (1792–1844) to W. C. Handy (1873–1958). Johnson led a brass band that played at the Lafayette Ball in 1824, the records of which are held by HSP. The collection includes sheet music for cotillions and marches, as well as a lithographic portrait of Johnson by Robert Douglass Jr. (1809–1887), an African American artist in Philadelphia **(figs. 18 and 19)**. The Balch Collection includes manuscript and published music by Handy, known as the "Father of the Blues," and other musicians in his circle: William "King" Phillips, William Nash, James Price Johnson, Eddie Green, James Berni Barbour, William Benton Overstreet, Alec Lovejoy, and J. Lawrence Cook. Handy's beloved classics "Loveless Love" and "Careless Love" **(figs. 20 and 21)** were recorded by Louis Armstrong, Shirley Bassey, Ray Charles, Fats Domino, and other leading vocalists of the twentieth century.

Pennsylvania's colonial literature, both its writers and publishers, was among the earliest material studied and collected by the founders of HSP.[39] Soon after arriving in Pennsylvania in 1685, William Bradford (1663–1752) set up the first printing press in the middle colonies. HSP owns the only known surviving copy of his first book, an almanac printed in 1685 **(fig. 22)**. Although Bradford later moved to New York, his son Andrew founded the first newspaper in Pennsylvania, *The American Mercury*. Benjamin Franklin established his press in 1723 and, in the following decades, rapidly advanced publishing activities in the city by printing a wide range of imprints from broadsides to newspapers and books. More than a quarter of Franklin's personal library is also in HSP's collection, and these books are housed today at the Library Company of Philadelphia.

Perhaps HSP's greatest contribution to the study of literary history can be found in the papers of the Philadelphia-based international publishing house, J. B. Lippincott & Co. **(no. 81)**. Business records and correspondence document the firm's activities as a publisher, importer, and retailer. Joshua B. Lippincott (1813–1886) founded the firm in 1836, carrying on the bookselling business established by his bankrupt former employer, David Clark. Lippincott expanded the business to include reference and medical books, as well as literary works. Among the reference books were *Chamber's* Encyclopedia and

**Fig. 17** Richard H. Hobson (ca. 1780–ca. 1835), title page of *Hours of Harmony: A Selection of Admired Pieces of Music, composed and arranged for Piano Forte,* and *Hail Columbia! The Presidents March*, ca. 1820; published by Fleetwood's Lith. Co.; lithograph on wove paper, 12 ½ × 9 ⅞ inches (31.7 × 25.0 cm); Historical Society of Pennsylvania Music Collection [0948], Gift of Mrs. Knight, 1947

**Fig. 18** Alfred M. Hoffy (ca. 1790–ca. 1860), after daguerreotype by Robert M. J. Douglass Jr. (1809–1887), *Francis Johnson*, 1846; published by Wagner & McGuigan; lithograph on wove paper, $15\frac{15}{16}$ × $12\frac{3}{16}$ inches (40.5 × 31.0 cm); Ferdinand J. Dreer Autograph Collection [0175], Gift of Ferdinand J. Dreer, 1890

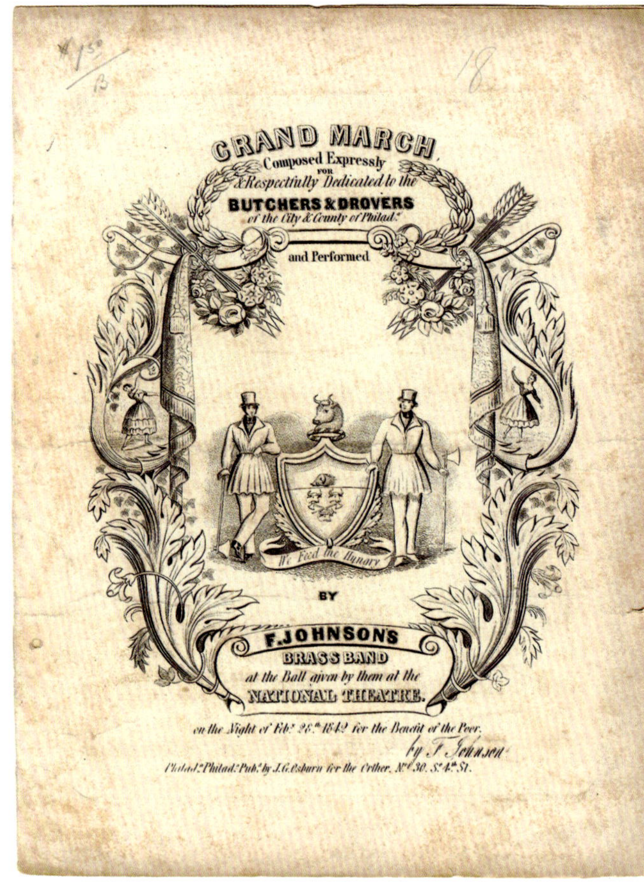


**Fig. 19** *Butchers and Drovers Grand March, composed expressly for & respectfully dedicated to the Butchers and Drovers of the city and county of Philad[elphia] by F. Johnson's Brass Band at the Ball given by them at the National Theatre*, 1842; published by J. G. Osburn; engraving on wove paper, $13\frac{3}{8}$ × $9\frac{7}{8}$ inches (34.0 × 25.0 cm); Historical Society of Pennsylvania Music Collection [0948]

Horace Howard Furness's compendium of Shakespeare's plays and commentary on them. In 1868, the firm began publishing *Lippincott's Monthly Magazine*, which printed the works of Arthur Conan Doyle, Oscar Wilde, and Rudyard Kipling, among others. In the twentieth century, Lippincott published important novels, including Zora Neale Hurston's *Their Eyes Were Watching God* (1937) and Harper Lee's *To Kill a Mockingbird* (1960). Today, the medical publishing business continues under the international brand of Wolters Kluwer.

## Conclusion

It is a humbling task to summarize the importance of HSP's vast and varied collections. Two hundred years after it was founded to "collect and preserve the evidences of [Pennsylvania's] own history from the earliest date," HSP continues to feed the curious inquiries of students, scholars, family historians, and artists alike. Every year, several thousand readers explore the archives, which range in size from a single sheet or volume to several mammoth collections that fill one thousand boxes or more. Because of the sheer enormity of the holdings, not all collections are fully catalogued or indexed yet. Archival resources available online—including HSP's digitized collections that relate to such themes as the nation's founding to abolitionism, women's activism, labor history, and world's fairs—are growing but still offer only a small sample of HSP's holdings. A determined and inquisitive researcher may be the first person in a generation or even a century to handle an important and irreplaceable document.

Reflecting the perspectives of both the powerful and the dispossessed, HSP's collections embody the hopes and

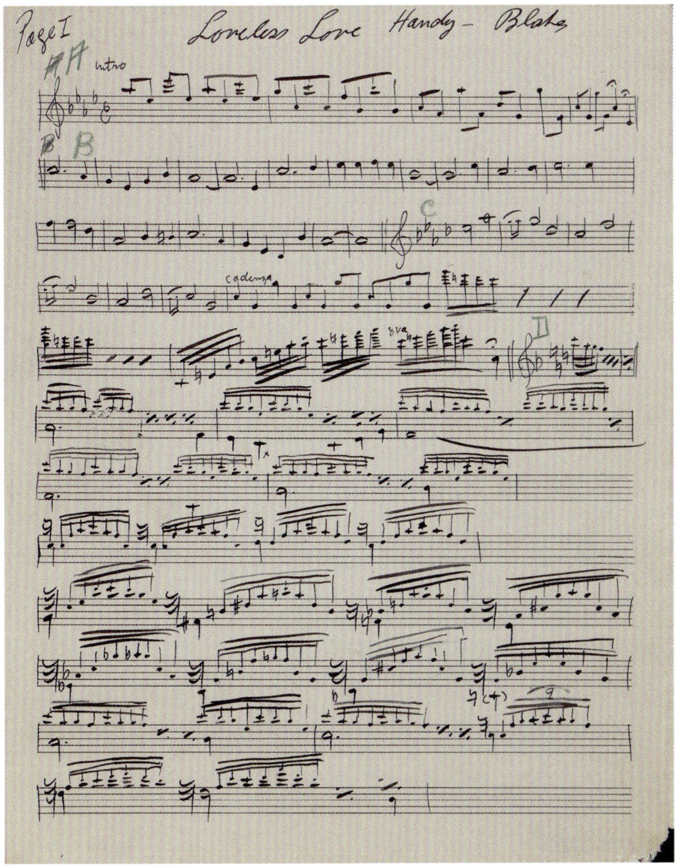


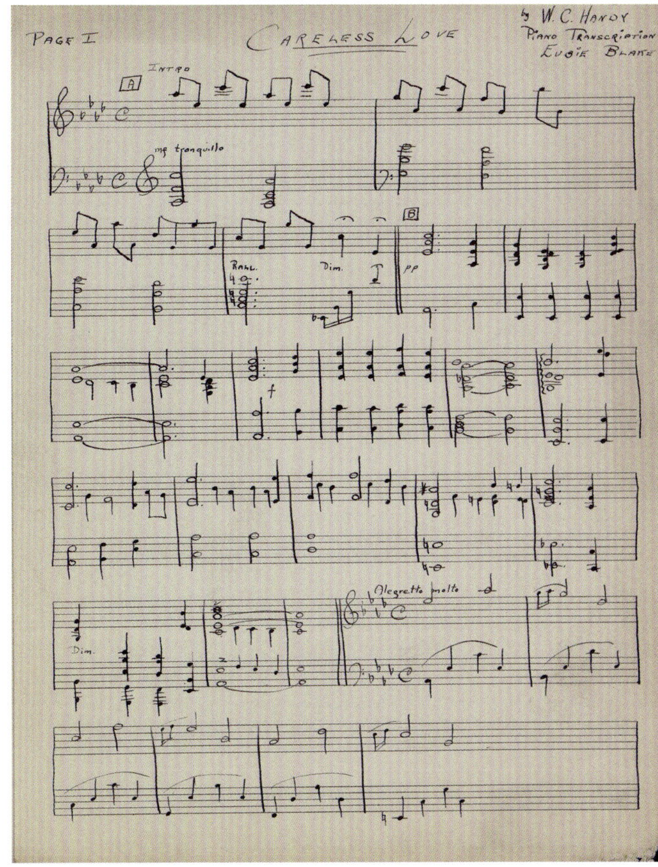


**Fig. 20** W. C. Handy (1873–1958), instrumental part of *Loveless Love*, 1921; manuscript; ink on paper, 12 ⅜ × 9 7⁄16 inches (31.4 × 24.0 cm); Handy Brothers Music Company Blues Composition Collection [MSS026], The Balch Institute

**Fig. 21** W. C. Handy (1873–1958), piano score of *Careless Love*, 1921; manuscript; ink on paper, 12 ⅜ × 9 7⁄16 inches (31.4 × 24.0 cm); Handy Brothers Music Company Blues Composition Collection [MSS026], The Balch Institute

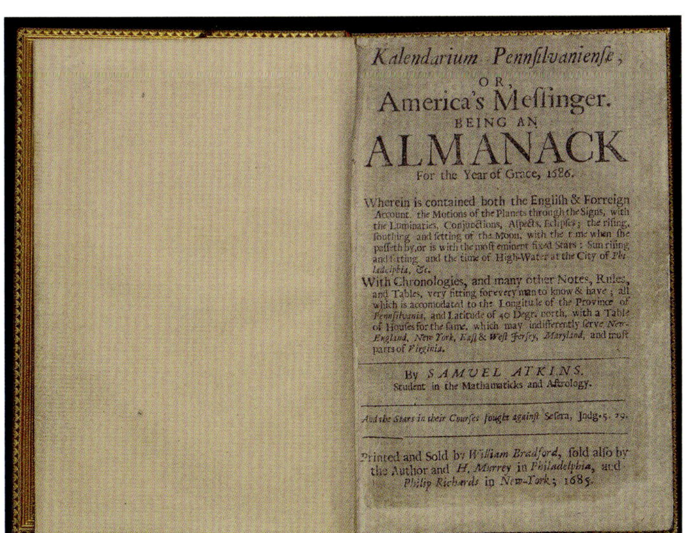

*Kalendarium Pennſilvanienſe*,
OR,
America's Meſſinger.
BEING AN
ALMANACK
For the Year of Grace, 1686.

Wherein is contained both the Engliſh & Forreign Account, the Motions of the Planets through the Signs, with the Luminaries, Conjunctions, Aſpects, Eclipſes; the riſing, ſouthing and ſetting of the Moon, with the time when ſhe paſſeth by, or is with the moſt eminent fixed Stars: Sun riſing and ſetting, and the time of High-Water at the City of *Philadelphia*, &c.

With Chronologies, and many other Notes, Rules, and Tables, very fitting for every man to know & have; all which is accomodated to the Longitude of the Province of *Pennſilvania*, and Latitude of 40 Degr. north, with a Table of Houſes for the ſame, which may indifferently ſerve *New-England*, *New York*, *Eaſt* & *Weſt Jerſey*, *Maryland*, and moſt parts of *Virginia*.

By *SAMUEL ATKINS*,
Student in the Mathamaticks and Aſtrology.

*And the Stars in their Courſes fought againſt* Seſera, Judg. 5. 20.

Printed and Sold by *William Bradford*, ſold alſo by the Author and *H. Murrey* in *Philadelphia*, and *Philip Richards* in *New-York*; 1685.

**Fig. 22** Samuel Atkins, title page of *Kalendarium Pennsilvaniense, or, America's Messinger. Being an Almanack For the Year of Grace, 1686*, 1685; published by William Bradford (1663–1752); laid paper bound in 19th-century full brown leather with gilt border and decorations, 6 × 4 inches (15.3 × 10.2 cm)

ideals of the American Republic as well as the crushing realities of wars, economic collapses, epidemics, political turmoil, inequality, and ferocious competition. HSP offers constantly evolving human stories that can satisfy every kind of curiosity and the changing needs of those living and writing histories. Thanks to many generous donors, HSP continues to grow. In recent years new acquisitions have arrived at a pace of about eighty to one hundred new collections per year. Sometimes these fill a gap in a colonial story and other times bring a narrative up to date or introduce an entirely new aspect of American history.

The date range of the items featured in this book, from 1682 to 1976, only hints at the breadth and depth of the collections. However, it also reflects the need to limit our scope. We deliberately left out the European and other global dimensions, though HSP's collections span every inhabited continent and reach back to a fourteenth-century letter written by King Charles VI of France (1368–1422). Not every work selected is a masterpiece, but many of the items stand in for a trove of related sources, either preserved by a donor or cobbled together by HSP's librarians and archivists over the decades. In these cases, we suggest the opportunities for research by describing their scope and quantifying the number of photographs, broadsides, political cartoons, or other like materials. Our hope is that this volume is a worthy celebration of HSP's first two centuries of collecting, and that it will inspire more students, scholars, collectors, genealogists, and patrons to explore and support these collections in fresh and exciting ways.

**Notes**

1. *Poulson's American Daily Advertiser*, September 30, 1824, 2.

2. *Poulson's American Daily Advertiser*, September 30, 1824, 2, and October 7, 1824, p. 3.

3. *Poulson's American Daily Advertiser*, August 21, 1824, 3.

4. *Poulson's American Daily Advertiser*, November 4, 1824.

5. Constitution of the Historical Society of Pennsylvania, recorded in the Minutes of the Historical Society of Pennsylvania, November 7, 1825, 23.

6. Minutes of the Historical Society of Pennsylvania, May 2, 1825, 6–7, henceforth Minutes.

7. "An Inaugural Discourse, Delivered on the 5th of November, 1825, Before the Historical Society of Pennsylvania, By William Rawle, Esq., President of the Society," in *Memoirs of the Historical Society of Pennsylvania,* vol. 1 (Philadelphia: McCarty and Davis, 1826; repr., Philadelphia: J. B. Lippincott & Co., 1864), 39, henceforth *Memoirs.*

8. Pennsylvania Institution for the Deaf and Dumb: *Poulson's American Daily Advertiser*, January 21 and June 19, 1824; Magdalen Society: *Poulson's American Daily Advertiser*, February 24, 1824; Provident Society: *Poulson's American Daily Advertiser*, January 28, 1824; and Franklin Institute: *Poulson's American Daily Advertiser*, February 9 and 19, April 7, July 13, and October 19, 1824.

9. *Poulson's American Daily Advertiser*, December 8, 1824, 2.

10. *Poulson's American Daily Advertiser*, July 10, 1824, 2.

11. Thomas C. James, "A Brief Account of Anthracite Coal on the Lehigh," in *Memoirs*, vol. 1, 321–31; and Erskine Hazard, "History of the Introduction of Anthracite Coal into Philadelphia," in *Memoirs of the Historical Society of Pennsylvania*, vol. 2, part 2 (Philadelphia: E. Littell, 1828), 155–64.

12. Minutes, May 13, 1825, 11; this medal is now in the Philadelphia History Museum Collection at Drexel University, part of which was donated by HSP in 2009.

13. Minutes, August 1, 1825, 12; and *Memoirs*, vol. 2, 223–38.

14. Minutes, September 19, 1825, 14.

15. Minutes, May 7, 1827, 43. The documents are listed in Joshua F. Fisher, "A List of the Instructions, Letters, &c. from Thomas and Richard Penn, Proprietors and Governors of Pennsylvania, to James Hamilton, Esq.," in *Memoirs*, vol. 2, 223–38.

16. Sally F. Griffith, *Serving History in a Changing World: The Historical Society of Pennsylvania in the Twentieth Century* (Philadelphia: Historical Society of Pennsylvania, 2001), 32.

17. Mary Maples Dunn et al., *The Papers of William Penn*, 5 vols. (Philadelphia: University of Pennsylvania Press, 1981–2016).

18. Marion Dexter Leonard, *The Life of Francis Daniel Pastorius: The Founder of Germantown* (Philadelphia: William J. Campbell, 1908), 110.

19. Patrick M. Erben, *A Harmony of Spirits: Translation and the Language of Community in Early Pennsylvania* (Chapel Hill: University of North Carolina Press, 2012); and Jan Stieverman and Oliver Scheiding, *A Peculiar Mixture: German-Language Cultures and Identities in Eighteenth-Century North America* (University Park: Pennsylvania State University Press, 2013).

20. Griffith, *Serving History in a Changing World*, 41.

21. Elizabeth Milroy, *The Grid & the River: Philadelphia's Green Places, 1682–1876* (University Park: Pennsylvania State University Press, 2016).

22. Jeffrey Cohen in James F. O'Gorman et al., *Drawing Toward Building: Philadelphia Architectural Graphics, 1732–1986* (Philadelphia: University of Pennsylvania Press, 1986), 33–38, 41–42.

23. George B. Tatum, *Penn's Great Town: 250 Years of Philadelphia Architecture Illustrated in Prints and Drawings* (Philadelphia: University of Pennsylvania Press, 1961).

24. Nicholas B. Wainwright, *Philadelphia in the Romantic Age of Lithography* (Philadelphia: Historical Society of Pennsylvania, 1958).

25. Elaine Forman Crane, ed., *The Diary of Elizabeth Drinker* (Boston: Northeastern University Press, 1991); Karin Wulf, *Not All Wives: Women of Colonial Philadelphia* (Ithaca, NY: Cornell University Press, 2000); and Emilie Frances Davis, *Emilie Davis's Civil War: The Diaries of a Free Black Woman in Philadelphia, 1863–1865*, ed. Judith Giesberg (University Park: Pennsylvania State University Press, 2014). Emilie Davis's diaries have also been digitized and transcribed and are available at https://davisdiaries.villanova.edu.

26. Gary B. Nash, *Forging Freedom: The Formation of Philadelphia's Black Community, 1720–1840* (Cambridge, MA: Harvard University Press, 1988); and Richard S. Newman, *The Transformation of American Abolitionism: Fighting Slavery in the Early Republic* (Chapel Hill: University of North Carolina Press, 2002).

27. Eric Foner, *Gateway to Freedom: The Hidden History of the Underground Railroad* (New York: W. W. Norton & Co., 2015), 152; and Library Company of Philadelphia and Historical Society of Pennsylvania, *Afro-Americana, 1553–1906*, 2nd exp. ed. (New Castle, DE: Oak Knoll Press, 2008).

28. Leonard Covello, *The Heart is the Teacher* (New York: McGraw-Hill, 1958); and Michael C. Johanek and John L. Puckett, *Leonard Covello and the Making of Benjamin Franklin High School: Education as if Citizenship Mattered* (Philadelphia: Temple University Press, 2007).

29. F. Cyril James, "The Bank of North America and the Financial History of Philadelphia," and A. J. McClurkin, "Summary of the Bank of North America Records," *Pennsylvania Magazine of History and Biography*, January 1940, vol. 64, 56–96; and Cordelia Biddle, *Biddle, Jackson, and a Nation in Turmoil: The Infamous War* (Boiling Springs, PA: Oxford Southern Press, 2021).

30. Paul F. Paskoff, *Industrial Evolution: Organization, Structure, and Growth of the Pennsylvania Iron Industry, 1750–1860*, Studies in Industry and Society, ed., Glenn Porter (Baltimore: Johns Hopkins University Press, 1983).

31. Kevin Kenny, *Making Sense of the Molly Maguires* (New York: Oxford University Press, 1998), 3–12.

32. Walter Licht, *Working for the Railroad: The Organization of Work in the Nineteenth Century* (Princeton, NJ: Princeton University Press, 1983); and John K. Brown, *The Baldwin Locomotive Works, 1881–1915: A Study in American Industrial Practice*, Studies in Industry and Society, ed., Philip B. Scranton (Baltimore: Johns Hopkins University Press, 1995).

33. HSP appreciates the authentication of Michelangelo's signature by Robert Tallaksen, who is an expert on this subject.

34. Helmut Von Erffa and Allen Staley, *The Paintings of Benjamin West* (New Haven, CT: Yale University Press, 1986). HSP has a unique, extra-illustrated version of John Galt's *The Life, Studies, and Works of Benjamin West, Esq.*, the first biography of West as well as correspondence, account books, drawings, prints, and books illustrated by West

35. David R. Brigham, *Public Culture in the Early Republic: Peale's Museum and Its Audience* (Washington, DC: Smithsonian Institution Press, 1995). HSP's collections include two important manuscript volumes relating to Peale's Museum: one containing the signatures of subscribers to annual admission tickets and the accessions book that records the museum's acquisitions from 1802 to 1844. Also at HSP are numerous silhouette portraits cut at Peale's Museum, very likely by the manumitted slave Moses Williams, and donated to HSP by various descendants of the sitters.

36. In addition to William Birch's *Views* and Thomas Birch's oil painting of Penn's Treaty Tree in front of the busy port in Kensington, HSP has a typescript of Birch's autobiography and numerous prints and drawings.

37. William Keyse Rudolph and Carol Eaton Soltis, *Thomas Sully: Painted Performance* (Milwaukee: Milwaukee Art Museum, 2013). HSP has Thomas Sully's manuscript register of each of the paintings he completed from 1801 to 1871 as well as the notebooks kept by his son-in-law, John Neagle.

38. Burton Alva Konkle, *Joseph Hopkinson, 1770–1842: Jurist, Scholar, Inspirer of the Arts* (Philadelphia: University of Pennsylvania Press, 1931), 69–84; George Washington to Joseph Hopkinson, May 27, 1798, Hopkinson Papers, vol. 2, Letters 1736–1800, 106 ½.

39. Thomas I. Wharton, "Notes on the Literature of Pennsylvania, read September 21, 1825," in *Memoirs*, vol. 1, 107–62; and Joshua Francis Fisher, "Some Account of the Early Poets and Poetry of Pennsylvania," read at a meeting of the Council, July 15, 1828, in *Memoirs*, vol. 2, 53–103.

| | | | | | | |
|---|---|---|---|---|---|---|
| 1 Schrauf | : | Lapisen | 24 spiels | 2 faden | Org | 200 Yds |
| 1 | " | Figur | 117 " | 1 " | " | 200 " |
| 1 | " | Ground | 160 " | 1 " | " | 200 " |

warps made about 159 Yards

* 8 rows weighed 3 lb 2 5/8 oz Org — 66 hours = per warp 6 33/ oz Organsin

10 " " 4 " 11 1/4 " " — 77 " = " " 7 52/ " "

Broché. 3 Yds White Sewing Cotton 2/100. 5 quills 4 3/100 oz Cotton. made 4 Yds 11 inch
equal 144 Yds Belt uses 14 38/ oz Cotton

June 8/66.* Aug Richter. 106 1/2 dez 21 lb 10 1/2 oz = 1 dz 3 26/ oz 48/100 oz Organsine

430 1/4 hours weaving 96.54
30 " fix 7.49 — 104.03 = 1 dz 98 cts

## Calculation of 212 Ps or 106 dozn

| | | | |
|---|---|---|---|
| 3 3/4 lb Organsine | | @ hn.nx | wwi.rn |
| 8 " Sewg Cotton # 2/100 | | o.nx | hi.nx |
| 10 3/4 " Glazed " | 2/40 | h.nx | hi.ir |
| Blocks Labels &c | | h | s.hs |
| Warping | r | wn.sn | wmh.ww |
| Weaving | rn | wns.nx | |
| Quills | s | wi.ti | |
| Dressing | wh | h.hm | |
| Sundries | i | o.om | |
| ss% wns.nx | | tn.sn | |
| hh% hn.am | | wn.hh | iwt.at |
| | | | onw.nm |

per piece w.ma

charged to Store at w.mn

May 1/66 24 dz 4 lb 11 1/2 oz = per dozn 3 15/ oz — = 104 dz 90 1/

117 3/4 hours weaving 23.55 = per dzn 98 cts
30 " fix 7.49 a 104 dz = 70

warps 8 rows 3 lb 2 5/8 oz will make about 104 dz 1/2 dz

# 1. **William Penn** (1644–1718)

## *Deed from Lenape Sachems to William Penn*

July 15, 1682
Manuscript; ink on parchment
11 13/16 × 20 1/2 inches (30.0 × 52.0 cm)

Collection no.: [0978]
Gift of Thomas Kimber, Jr., 1867

Lenape and Quaker oral traditions alike recall the first treaty with William Penn taking place under the Treaty Elm at Shackamaxon shortly after the proprietor's arrival in October 1682. No documentary evidence of that meeting exists, although we do know that Penn met with Lenape sachems on several occasions during his two-year sojourn in the colony. On at least a dozen occasions, Penn or his agents convinced an array of local sachems to sign documents conveying legal title to their kin's ancestral lands to him. In most cases, Lenape people no longer lived on these tracts, which scattered Swedish, Dutch, and English settlers had been occupying for several decades based on deeds, informal agreements, or other arrangements with local Natives. Penn's insistence on purchasing, or more often repurchasing, Lenape lands was partly motivated by his Quaker principles and his practical understanding that English-Native relations needed a peaceful reset in the wake of the brutal violence that had wracked New England and the Chesapeake respectively, the events known as King Philip's War and Bacon's Rebellion a few years earlier. But mostly Penn needed Indigenous signatures to prove in English courts that he—rather than other European claimants, particularly Maryland's Calvert family—had clear title to the land and thus could assure the settlers to whom he planned to sell or rent that their own titles would be valid. Somewhere in this mix of peaceful diplomacy and hardheaded real estate transactions, the legend of Penn's Great Treaty was born. Yet this document—the first surviving record of Penn's purchase of Lenape land title—dates from several months before Penn himself arrived in his colony; it was the work of his cousin and deputy governor, William Markham (1635–1704).

The contents are fairly mundane, couched in English legalese. A dozen sachems sold Penn approximately one hundred square miles of land south of the falls of the Delaware River (opposite today's Trenton, New Jersey); a few weeks later, several others gave their assent, as documented on the back of the parchment. The lands described were already claimed by Europeans, including a tract occupied by a man named John Wood and boundaries delineated by several trees strategically marked with the letter *P*. In exchange for what was thus really a quitclaim rather than an outright sale, the sachems received 300 guilders in Dutch money, 350 fathoms of wampum beads (strung together end to end, they would stretch about four-tenths of a mile), and a long list of cloth, clothing, tools, weapons, and other trade goods. Most of these items came in multiples of ten and so were ideally suited for redistribution to individual members of the sachems' kin and townsfolk. All of this compensation was apparently worth about £300 sterling, although Penn's agents may have paid nearly twice that much for the inventory. Penn was planning to charge immigrants £100 for every 5,000 acres of land. A hundred square miles, which contains 64,000 acres, ideally would yield him £1,280. The profit would be handsome, but by later American standards for such one-sided deals, the markup was not that outrageous. DANIEL K. RICHTER

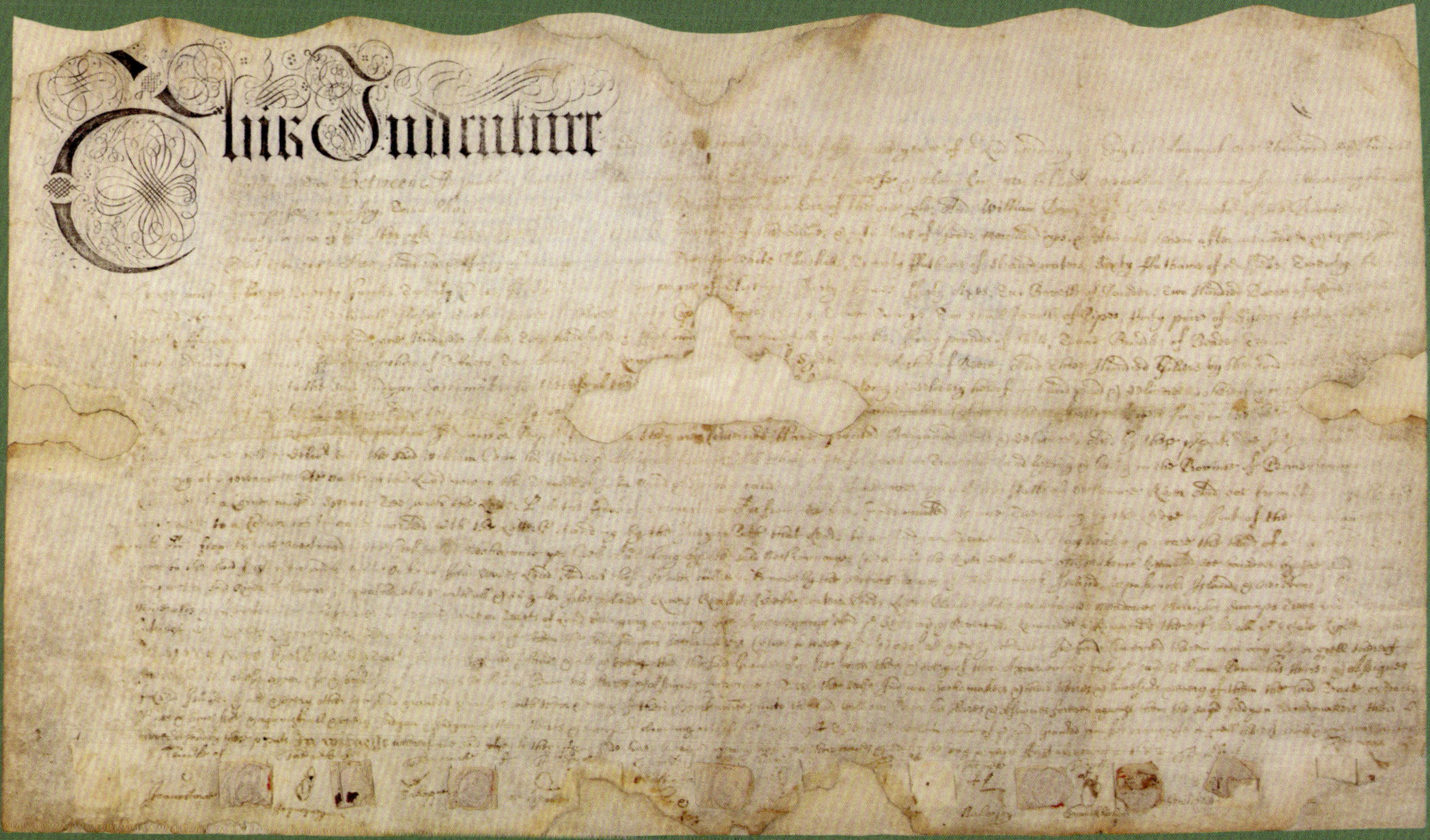
This Indenture

## 2. **William Penn** (1644–1718) and **Thomas Holme** (1624–1695)

# *A Portraiture of the City of Philadelphia in the Province of Pennsylvania in America*

1683
Engraving on laid paper
11 3/4 × 17 3/4 inches (29.7 × 44.9 cm)
Foldout leaf in *A letter from William Penn proprietary and governour of Pennsylvania in America to the Committee of the Free Society of Traders of that province, residing in London.*
Inscribed above map: *A Portraiture of the City / of / Philadelphia / in the Province of / PENNSYLVANIA / in / America / by Thomas Holme Surveyor General. / Sold by Andrew Sowle in Shoreditch / London*

Historical Society of Pennsylvania Map Collection

The settlement of Pennsylvania was a real estate venture as well as a "holy experiment" in religious tolerance. A year after he arrived in the colony, William Penn published this innovative plan for Pennsylvania's commercial center, devised by his chief surveyor Thomas Holme, in a promotional pamphlet containing a report on the colony's physical characteristics and agricultural potential initially prepared for London-based investors called the Free Society of Traders. The Historical Society of Pennsylvania owns eight impressions of the map, as well as the copper plate from which it was printed.

"Portraiture" in the title can mean either an imagined likeness or the delineation of an existing entity. The plan gave concrete form to a still abstract vision, and in an accompanying report, Holme labeled the *Portraiture* a "draught" that might "hereafter when time permits be augmented." But in his commentary, Penn, the eager developer, described the city as if already formed: "Philadelphia . . . is at last laid out to the great content of those here," assuring readers that building was well underway, awaiting the arrival of more settlers.

The *Portraiture* describes a compact one-mile by two-mile site covering roughly twelve hundred acres between the Delaware and Schuylkill Rivers. Holme included only a rough approximation of topography, leaving out most of the streams that flowed through the area to suggest that streets could be laid out quickly and easily extended. The gridlike layout was derived from ancient military- and commercial-settlement designs where ease and efficiency of movement were important. Penn and Holme adapted this format by arranging the streets in modular quadrants defined by the intersection of Broad Street, running north-south, and High Street (renamed Market), running east-west. These arteries and two "front" streets along the Delaware and Schuylkill Rivers were one hundred feet wide, an unusual size at this time. The remaining streets would be fifty feet wide, also unusually generous. At the central intersection of Broad and High Streets was a ten-acre square where "houses for public affairs" could be erected. Four other eight-acre squares sat within the surrounding quadrants. Holme drew trees in each of these zones to indicate that they would be landscaped as public parks. He also sketched in 550 house lots, the largest in the most desirable locations facing High Street and along the two riverfront streets. Smaller lots filled several blocks back from each river to each of the public squares. The rest of the plan was left blank because the proprietary land office had not yet surveyed these areas.

Landscaped squares and the tidy street layout echoed progressive urban planning projects in Europe and Great Britain, notably plans for rebuilding London after the

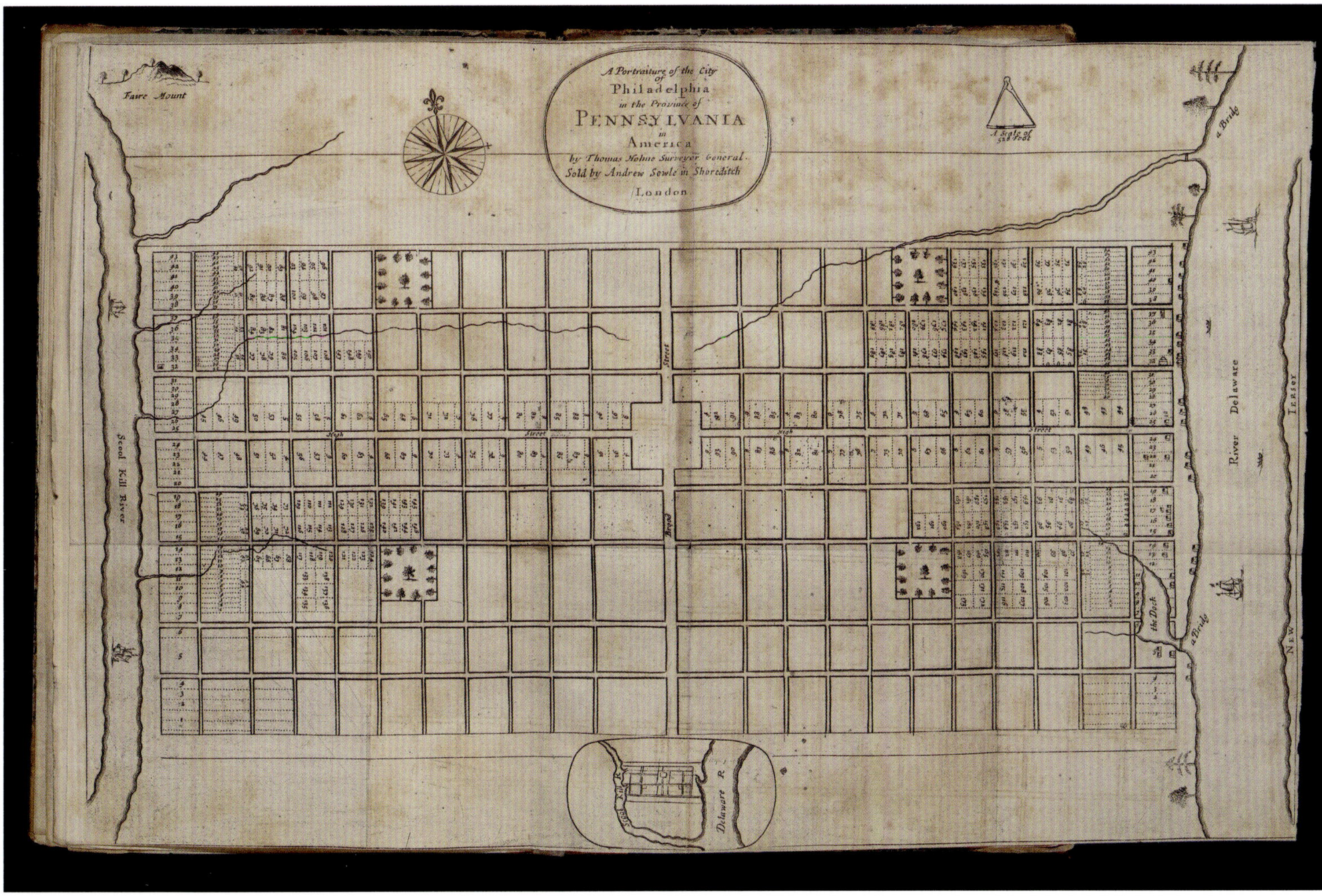


devastating fire of 1666. Fire prevention was uppermost in Penn's mind, and, in addition to wide streets, he urged that brick construction be encouraged whenever possible. However, similarities between the *Portraiture* and rebuilding plans for London should not be overemphasized. Fifteen years separated these proposals and Penn's acquisition of Pennsylvania, and though building reforms were instituted, London's basic shape changed very little because financial constraints prevented large-scale expropriations and resettlement. Nonetheless, London was Penn's touchstone, and he envisioned Philadelphia both as a tribute and an improvement—a "re-presentation" of his native city.

ELIZABETH MILROY

Further related information in the Historical Society of Pennsylvania archives can be found in the Logan Family Papers and the Penn Family Papers.

# 3. **Francis Daniel Pastorius** (1651–1719)

## *Alvearialia*

---

ca. 1700
Manuscript; ink and leaf prints on laid paper bound in parchment
6 ⅛ × 4 ¼ inches (15.5 × 10.8 cm)

Francis Daniel Pastorius Papers [0475]
Purchase, Library Fund

A few years after arriving in Philadelphia on August 20, 1683, and founding Germantown later that year, Francis Daniel Pastorius began a series of notebooks collecting much of the knowledge of his time. Yet he was busy enough without the task of gathering, selecting, and storing thousands of excerpts, original poems, and commentaries; Pastorius had left Germany as the agent of the "Frankfurt Land Company," European investors who had purchased land from William Penn to create a religious community in America. Trained as a law scholar, Pastorius managed the affairs of the Frankfurt Pietists in Pennsylvania for years. He became the civic and intellectual center of the fledgling immigrant community, joining the local and provincial meetings of the Quakers. He authored, with three other Germantown residents, the first public protest against slavery in North America. He married fellow German immigrant Ennecke Klostermanns, and the couple had two children—Johann Samuel and Heinrich. At schools in Philadelphia and Germantown, Pastorius taught a multilingual group of students, for whom he wrote school books. Aside from conducting a range of public affairs, Pastorius built a diverse garden and experimented with beekeeping, which inspired the naming of his most extensive manuscript commonplace book, entitled the "Bee-Hive" (a metaphor for the process of collecting and storing valuable knowledge and the ideas he pursued therein).

Yet, Pastorius's hope for a life free from the moral corruption and worldly vanity he had rejected in Europe left him sorely disappointed. In Pennsylvania, his early friendship with William Penn ended with the Quaker leader's departure for England. The Pennsylvania Quakers soon became mired in a religious schism known as the Keithian Controversy, which turned former "Friends" into bitter enemies and triggered a vicious pamphlet war in which even the peace-loving Pastorius became involved. With the community split, his association with the Frankfurt Pietists was a continuing burden. The group eventually appointed other agents, followed by a fraud scandal that left many Germantown residents, including Pastorius, without secure titles to their lands and even resulted in the loss of the hard-won Germantown charter.

Against this background of migrating, building, and unraveling, Pastorius assiduously sought other opportunities to stitch the fragments of his life together. Featured here, the title page of his "Alvearialia" manuscript encapsulates this attempt at creating order and cohesion ("Alvearialia," meaning things relating to beehives, thus establishing a connection between the excerpts collected in it and the larger "Bee-Hive" manuscript). Pastorius had been storing notes from his voracious reading (borrowing books from prominent Quakers) on scattered pages but now started anew—by literally stitching and binding together fragments in a process he described thus: "Looking over of late my Rejectanea or Waste papers, among a great heap of others, I met also with these here partly Inclosed, & Stich'd together which making (as you see) a pretty Little Book, deserve (me thinks,) a Frontispiece or Title page." He adorned this cover with intricate leaf prints that also brought the natural world into cohesion with the notes he had gathered. Though never quite whole again, Pastorius's new world was brought into harmony between the covers, bindings, and seams of his many manuscript books.

PATRICK M. ERBEN

Further related information in the Historical Society of Pennsylvania archives can be found in the Francis Daniel Pastorius Papers, George W. Norris Papers, Society Collection, Etting Papers, and Logan Papers.

# 4. **Christopher Witt** (1675–1765)

## *Johannes Kelpius*

ca. 1705
Watercolor on laid paper on canvas
9 × 6 ½ inches (23.0 × 16.5 cm)

Inscribed upper left: *Joha*[nnes] *Kelpius*

Historical Society of Pennsylvania Treasures Collection
Owned by John Leibert of Germantown, who later gave it to Abraham H. Cassel. Purchased from Cassel by the Historical Society of Pennsylvania in 1882.

What do a religious leader and his followers do when the Second Coming for which they prepared does not occur? Does their quest fall apart, dashing their trust in God and each other? For Johannes Kelpius, the enigmatic leader of the "Hermits of the Wissahickon," which established a celibate experiment outside Philadelphia in 1694, that seems to have happened when the world did not end that year. Popular accounts often assume that their failed end-time expectations led to conflict and dissolution after Kelpius's death in 1708. As with most historical narratives, however, the story is more complicated: the portrait that Christopher Witt (an English member of the group) painted in 1705 shows Kelpius in a posture of withdrawal from the world. When Christ returned, he would look for souls quietly waiting for him. Witt thus portrayed a vision of Kelpius close to his own transfiguration—from a person occupied with worldly things to a mystical seeker preparing for union with the divine.

Before coming to Pennsylvania, Kelpius had been a wanderer. Born in a German-speaking enclave in Transylvania in 1667, Kelpius studied theology in Tübingen, Leipzig, and Altdorf, where he earned a master of theology. He embraced Pietism, a reform movement within German Protestantism, which critiqued church doctrine and sought a personal relationship with the redeemer. Radical Pietists explored mysticism through the ideas of lay-theologian Jakob Böhme (1575–1624), the Jewish Cabbala, hermeticism (a pseudoscience associated with alchemy), and possibly the occult. During the 1680s, Kelpius met disgraced pastor Johann Jacob Zimmermann (1644–1693), who interpreted Halley's comet as a sign of the apocalypse, which he hoped to escape in America. After arranging for the passage of his "Chapter of Perfection" in Rotterdam, Zimmermann died, and Kelpius was voted the new leader before leaving for Pennsylvania.

The mystics' life on Wissahickon Creek is a matter of speculation, and their legendary tabernacle and observatory left no trace. Yet the archival record provides a fuller picture. The "Chapter" soon became embroiled in the Quakers' "Keithian schism" and a land fraud scheme in nearby Germantown. Some members left to marry, live in town, and even return to Germany. Kelpius and followers like Witt turned to mystical contemplation, prayer, and hymnody. Witt's portrait of Kelpius—in a study containing only a chair, table, book, and clock—visualizes his resigned waiting for a union with Christ. Kelpius's hymn books, such as the bilingual "Lamenting Voice of the Hidden Love," likened this pursuit to the cooing of the turtledove for its lost partner. Kelpius also wrote a widely read prayer manual and corresponded with like-minded individuals such as

Esther Palmer from Long Island, describing a process of mystical perfection known as the "three wilderness states." The hermit in Witt's portrait, hand raised mysteriously to his temple, played a key role in the transmission of Christian mysticism. Until his death in 1765 (at age ninety), Witt worked as a physician, trader in medicine, and famed botanist. Together, Kelpius and his portraitist left an indelible mark on early American religion and culture.

PATRICK M. ERBEN

---

Further related information in the Historical Society of Pennsylvania archives can be found in the Abraham H. Cassel Collection [1610], the Ferdinand J. Dreer Autograph Collection [0175], which includes Johannes Kelpius's journal and letters and the Francis Daniel Pastorius Papers [0475].

# 5. *Wharton Family Bible*

1727–1925
Laid paper bound in reverse calf with brass furnishings
18 13/16 × 11 13/16 inches (47.8 × 30.0 cm)

Collection: Wharton Family Bible [D0248]

Family bibles can be valuable sources in genealogical research, particularly for Protestant ancestors of western European heritage. Unfortunately, there are typically few resources for eighteenth- and nineteenth-century families that will provide exact dates of birth or death or even mention the existence of family members such as first spouses or children who died young or unmarried.

Bibles of this era—sometimes among the only books a family would ever own—were usually printed with specially designated pages either in the front or between Testaments intended to include handwritten family data. This record keeping could stretch across generations, with the book handed down to one of the children who then added their own family details to it, and so on.

One of the reasons these heirlooms are so precious is their rarity. For bibles to enter the collections of a historical or genealogical society usually requires them to have survived and ultimately been donated to an organization like the Historical Society of Pennsylvania. There is no centralized repository of family bibles and no single database that can be queried to determine if one exists for a specific family. They are still frequent finds for lucky hunters at antique shops or resale sites like eBay.

Still, efforts to gather, preserve, and share the contents of these priceless heirlooms have boomed in the Internet age. HSP alone holds thousands, a collection that includes both original bibles themselves and copies of genealogical material extracted or scanned from others still in private hands. Much of this collection was initially compiled by the Genealogical Society of Pennsylvania.

The Wharton bible at HSP is a beautiful example, and for a genealogist, the pleasure of gingerly pulling it from its archival box is something like Christmas morning. Especially with so many historical records now conveniently online, direct interaction with a piece of history in this way is increasingly special. This heavy bound volume contains genealogical material handwritten in both the front and middle sections, with one of the family's earliest ancestors referenced, Joseph Wharton, a notable Philadelphia merchant born in the city in 1707 to immigrant parents from Westmorland, England, and Monmouthshire, Wales. For such an early record to connect a family so definitively to their European origins is unusual. The bible was kept in the family for centuries, the latest entry documenting a descendant born in 1925.

Other family bibles in HSP's collection contain memorabilia such as church programs, yellowed newspaper clippings, photographs, and even—in at least one case—a lock of hair tucked into the pages. These are fascinating and tender insights into the world of people to whom they belonged—their values, their loves, their memories. While a bible's primary value to researchers may be extending a family line, it also serves as a tangible reminder of the humanity behind why such research is done in the first place.

KATY BODENHORN BARNES

## 6. **Mark Catesby** (1683–1749)

### *Smilax lævis Lauri folio non Serrato, baccis nigris. Pica cristata cærulea. The crested Jay.*

1731
Hand-colored etching on laid paper
13 3/4 × 10 inches (35.0 × 25.4 cm) (plate); 20 7/8 × 14 1/2 inches (53.0 × 37.0 cm) (volume)

pl. 15 of *The natural history of Carolina, Florida, and the Bahama Islands: Containing two hundred and twenty figures of birds, beasts, fishes, serpents, insects, and plants,* volume I
Inscribed upper right: *Smilax lævis Lauri folio non Serrato, baccis nigris*; lower right: *Pica cristata cærulea / The crested Jay.*

### *Rana maxima, Helleborena*

1731
Hand-colored etching on laid paper
13 3/4 × 10 inches (35.0 × 25.4 cm) (plate); 20 7/8 × 14 1/2 inches (53.0 × 37.0 cm) (volume)

pl. 72 of *The natural history of Carolina, Florida, and the Bahama Islands: Containing two hundred and twenty figures of birds, beasts, fishes, serpents, insects, and plants*, volume II
Inscribed lower left: *Rana maxima*; lower center: *Helleborena*; lower right: *MC* [monogram]

Between 1729 and 1747, the English naturalist Mark Catesby issued *The Natural History of Carolina, Florida and the Bahama Islands*, the first major illustrated publication on the flora and fauna of the British colonies of North America, which also augmented earlier works on the natural productions of the Caribbean. Catesby's publication, usually bound as two volumes, contains 220 plates, largely etched by his own hand and generally hand-colored under his supervision. These prints were based principally on drawings that Catesby had executed on sojourns to Virginia, Bermuda, and Jamaica, from 1712 to 1719, and to South Carolina and the Bahama Islands, from 1722 to 1726.

Catesby's *Natural History* was a work of empire, promoted by the Royal Society, and supported by members of the Royal Family, aristocrats, gentry, merchants, naturalists, gardeners, and horticulturalists with stakes in Britain's colonial possessions. Additionally, his publication advanced the interests of a colonial plantocracy based on slave labor, who sought to exploit America's natural resources as they appropriated Indigenous people's lands.

Catesby intended his *Natural History* to illustrate species previously unknown to Europeans, focusing on trees and shrubs for their practical value, often with animals that frequented them. While concentrating on birds, he illustrated fishes, crustacea, reptiles, amphibia, mammals, and insects as well. His work not only contributed to systematic knowledge of the world's species but also to a new environmental understanding of the relationships among flora and fauna from the same habitats. Catesby also observed the interactions of species introduced to the Americas by peoples from other regions of the globe. With tragic irony, he was cognizant of his dependence on Native Americans and enslaved peoples of African descent for his understanding of much that he observed, and, in some ways, his *Natural History* challenges the imperatives of empire that drove his work.

Of Catesby's many transatlantic colleagues, the Philadelphia botanist and collector John Bartram shared his deep knowledge of North America's natural productions and his interest in environmental associations observed in the field. Catesby was introduced to Bartram through the London merchant Peter Collinson (1694–1768) who shared Bartram's letters, live plants, seeds, and specimens with Catesby from the early 1730s. Bartram first mentioned Catesby by name in 1738, after he had received drawings from "friend Catesby" and had examined eight parts of the *Natural History* owned by the Pennsylvania proprietor Thomas Penn. Bartram and Catesby apparently continued communication through Collinson for two years longer, and Catesby sent Bartram at least the majority of volume I of his publication.

Only four letters from Catesby to Bartram and three from Bartram to Catesby are known to survive, and they are preserved primarily in the Bartram Papers at the Historical Society of Pennsylvania. However, in Bartram's wider correspondence, references to Catesby frequently appear. Catesby's *Natural History* both shaped Bartram's scope of North American natural history and widened Catesby's knowledge of America's natural productions. Catesby illustrated no fewer than nine specimens from Bartram at the end of his second volume, and he depicted as many as nineteen Bartram-sourced plants and animals in the plates of his Appendix.

JOEL T. FRY AND AMY MEYERS

## 7. **Charles Le Roux** (1688–1748)

### *Andrew Hamilton's Freedom Box*

1735
Gold
2 ¾ × 3 ½ × ¾ inches (7.0 × 9.0 × 2.0 cm)

Engraved on top of box, around edge, in Latin: *Demersae Leges—Timefacta Libertas—Haec Tandem Emergunt;* top of box: *Sigill Civitat Nov Eborac.*; interior of lid: *Non Nummis—Virtute Paratur.*; edge of box: *Ita Cuique Eveniat Ut De Republica Meruit.*

Historical Society of Pennsylvania Treasures Collection
Gift of Lena Cadwalader Evans, 1939

## **Paul Richard** (1667–1756) and the New York City Common Council

### *Certificate of Appreciation*

September 29, 1735
Manuscript; ink on parchment
21 ¼ × 24 ⅜ inches (54.0 × 62.0 cm)

Historical Society of Pennsylvania Treasures Collection
Gift of Lena Cadwalader Evans, 1939

"Though the Laws are sunk and liberty trembles at the deed, yet shall they rise again. Not by money, but by virtue gained. Thus let each receive what he has deserved of the republic." So reads the Latin inscription on this small gold box, presented to Andrew Hamilton in 1735. Hamilton, a Scottish-born lawyer, speaker of the Pennsylvanian Assembly, and vice-admiralty court judge, received the box from New York's Common Council on the occasion of his successfully defending the printer John Peter Zenger against charges of libel brought by the colony's governor, William Cosby. In his newspaper Zenger had lampooned Cosby as an aging lion unable to come to terms with his diminishing power. Cosby retaliated by trying Zenger under laws that sought to suppress criticism of authority figures in Britain and its overseas colonies.

This box is representative of the deep appreciation for Hamilton's skillful defense of Zenger by members of the Common Council who served as New York's city government. It is an elegant object that would have been costly to commission from its maker, silversmith Charles Le Roux. The council took the trouble to send it down to Philadelphia after Hamilton had returned to his adopted hometown. It is not known how Hamilton used it, though it would have made a very fine snuff box. But why would such a lavish gift be sent to a lawyer for winning a trial?

The significance of Hamilton's victory lies in the issue of the freedom of press, something now enshrined in the US Constitution's First Amendment. When Zenger made fun of the thin-skinned Cosby, he was pushing the envelope on the limits of free speech as they existed at the time.

City of New York ss. Paul Richard Esquire Mayor the Recorder Aldermen and Assistants of the City of New York convened in Common Council To all to whom these Presents shall come Send Greeting Whereas Honour is the just reward of Virtue and Publick Benefits demand a Publick Acknowledgment We therefore under a gratefull Sense of the remarkable Service done to the Inhabitants of this City and Colony by Andrew Hamilton Esquire of Pensilvania Barrister at Law by his learned and generous Defence of the Rights of Mankind and the Liberty of the Press in the Case of John Peter Zenger lately tryed on an Information exhibited in the Supream Court of this Colony do by these Presents bear to the said Andrew Hamilton Esquire the publick Thanks of the Freemen of this Corporation for that signal Service which he chearfully undertook under great Indisposition of Body and generously performed refusing any Fee or Reward And in Testimony of our great Esteem for his Person and Sense of his Merit do hereby present him with the Freedom of this Corporation These are therefore to Certify and Declare that the said Andrew Hamilton Esquire is hereby admitted Received and allowed a Freeman and Citizen of the said City to have hold Enjoy and Partake of all the Benefits Liberties Priviledges Freedoms and Immunities whatsoever granted or belonging to a Freeman of the same City In Testimony whereof the Common Council of the said City in Common Council assembled have Caused the Seal of the said City to be hereunto Affixed this Twenty Ninth day of September Anno Domini One Thousand Seven hundred and Thirty five

The idea that any opinion might be freely expressed was not widely accepted in 1735 when the trial took place, especially when it involved someone of lower social status criticizing an elite or royal person. Prepublication censorship had only ended in 1695, when the English act of parliament banning "heretical, seditious, schismatical, or offensive books" had lapsed. Although political writers in England were beginning to include some veiled criticism of politicians in their publications, this was still a dangerous business as the laws to prosecute libel were still very much in force. With his victory, therefore, Hamilton championed free speech as legal.

The engraving on the box itself seems only to address the main issue of the Zenger trial obliquely. This is because the conflict was also a contest between the factions vying for political power in colonial New York. Each accused the other of corrupt and illiberal behavior. Hamilton's triumph was also a win for those who had accused the royal governor of venality while portraying themselves as the protectors of justice, liberty, and virtue. In other words, this box represents an episode in New York politics which is quite easily connected to today's political conflicts and concerns.

EMMA HART

# 8. Benjamin Franklin's Indian Treaties

## *A Treaty of Friendship held with the Chiefs of the Six Nations, at Philadelphia, in September and October, 1736*

1737
Published by Benjamin Franklin (1706–1790)
Laid paper bound in half red morocco and marbled paper boards
13 3/8 × 8 1/4 inches (34.0 × 21.0 cm)

## *Minutes of Conferences, held with the Indians, at Easton, in the months of July and November, 1756*

1757
Published by Benjamin Franklin (1706–1790) and David Hall (1714–1772)
Laid paper bound in quarter brown grain-cloth and marbled paper boards
16 1/2 × 10 1/4 inches (42.0 × 26.0 cm)

Donated by the Subscribers to the Penn Papers, 1877

The Indian treaties printed by Benjamin Franklin and David Hall between 1736 and 1763 document the large, multiday diplomatic meetings between Native and colonial officials that shaped Pennsylvania politics for four decades. They also shed light on a period in which multiple communities competed and negotiated for land, sovereignty, and economic and cultural survival, with neither group entirely dominating the other. As alliances and frontiers between Pennsylvanians and the Native communities to the west, north, and south became increasingly unstable, and white-Native encounters grew increasingly violent, leaders on all sides struggled to respond.

Sometimes referred to as "Franklin's" Indian treaties, these texts were not authored by Franklin. Instead, they were final, public versions of conference proceedings, or minutes, drawn up by colonial secretaries and interpreters and printed in Philadelphia by Franklin and his partner Hall, both of whom were responsible for producing official Pennsylvania documents. The Historical Society of Pennsylvania holds nine of the thirteen treaties that were printed. Creating conference proceedings like these was rare, and no comparable series was produced in other colonies. Also notable is their folio format, layout, and typography. They are carefully designed to follow each conference day, listing the principal attendees, summarizing diplomatic speeches, and recording presentations of wampum and trade goods.

A twentieth-century publication project by HSP helped situate these works within a canon of colonial records. In 1938, Julian P. Boyd, HSP librarian, supervised the publication of an elegantly produced, limited edition of the treaties. These facsimiles were accompanied by a census and bibliographical essay; editions of manuscript journals by Conrad Weiser, Benjamin Chew, and James Pemberton held at HSP; and accompanying articles by Boyd and Carl Van Doren. In addition, Boyd documented surviving copies of the treaties and manuscript sources of the conference negotiations. During his research for the volume, Boyd also uncovered the Lewis Evans map of the 1737 Walking Purchase **(no. 9)**.

For Van Doren, these treaties were "diplomatic dramas" featuring powerful Native characters whose "actual words" could be read. More recently, historians have cautioned not to accept these printed texts as verbatim records of diplomatic interactions, which were mediated by many interpreters and for which, in some cases, multiple sets of notes survive. These printed works obfuscate as well as clarify aspects of colonial-Native politics. They hide as much as they reveal.

Although these are not Native-authored documents, they do show how colonial leaders carefully followed Native diplomatic practices and protocols. In them Native leaders also vigorously defend their lands and peoples, exposing colonial leaders' duplicity or refusal to intervene in settler conflicts. For example, one reader of the HSP copy of the 1756 Easton treaty minutes carefully bracketed and underlined numerous passages, focusing on speeches

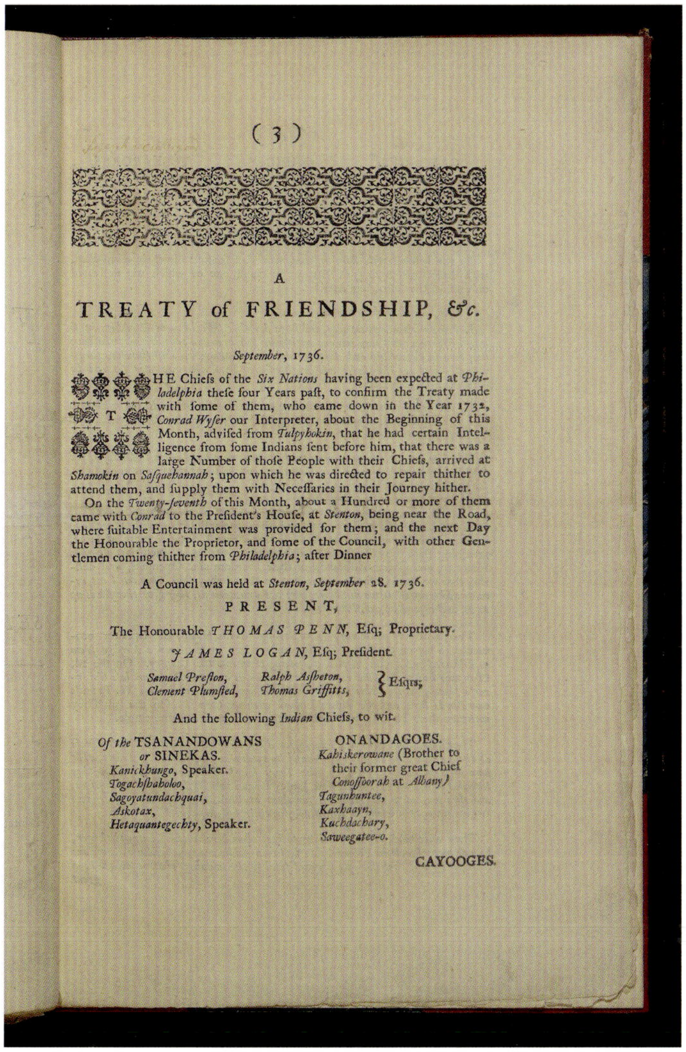

( 3 )

A

TREATY of FRIENDSHIP, &c.

*September*, 1736.

THE Chiefs of the *Six Nations* having been expected at *Philadelphia* theſe four Years paſt, to confirm the Treaty made with ſome of them, who came down in the Year 1732, *Conrad Wyſer* our Interpreter, about the Beginning of this Month, adviſed from *Tulpyhokin*, that he had certain Intelligence from ſome Indians ſent before him, that there was a large Number of thoſe People with their Chiefs, arrived at *Shamokin* on *Saſquehannah*; upon which he was directed to repair thither to attend them, and ſupply them with Neceſſaries in their Journey hither.

On the *Twenty-ſeventh* of this Month, about a Hundred or more of them came with *Conrad* to the Preſident's Houſe, at *Stenton*, being near the Road, where ſuitable Entertainment was provided for them; and the next Day the Honourable the Proprietor, and ſome of the Council, with other Gentlemen coming thither from *Philadelphia*; after Dinner

A Council was held at *Stenton*, *September* 28. 1736.

PRESENT,

The Honourable *THOMAS PENN*, Eſq; Proprietary.

*JAMES LOGAN*, Eſq; Preſident.

*Samuel Preſton*, *Ralph Aſheton*,
*Clement Plumſted*, *Thomas Griffitts*, } Eſqrs;

And the following *Indian* Chiefs, to wit.

*Of the* TSANANDOWANS *or* SINEKAS.
*Kanickhungo*, Speaker.
*Togachſhaholoo*,
*Sagoyatundachquai*,
*Askotax*,
*Hetaquantegechty*, Speaker.

ONANDAGOES.
*Kahiskerowane* (Brother to their former great Chief *Conoſſoorah* at *Albany*)
*Tagunhuntee*,
*Kaxhaayn*,
*Kuchdachary*,
*Saweegatee-o*.

CAYOOGES.

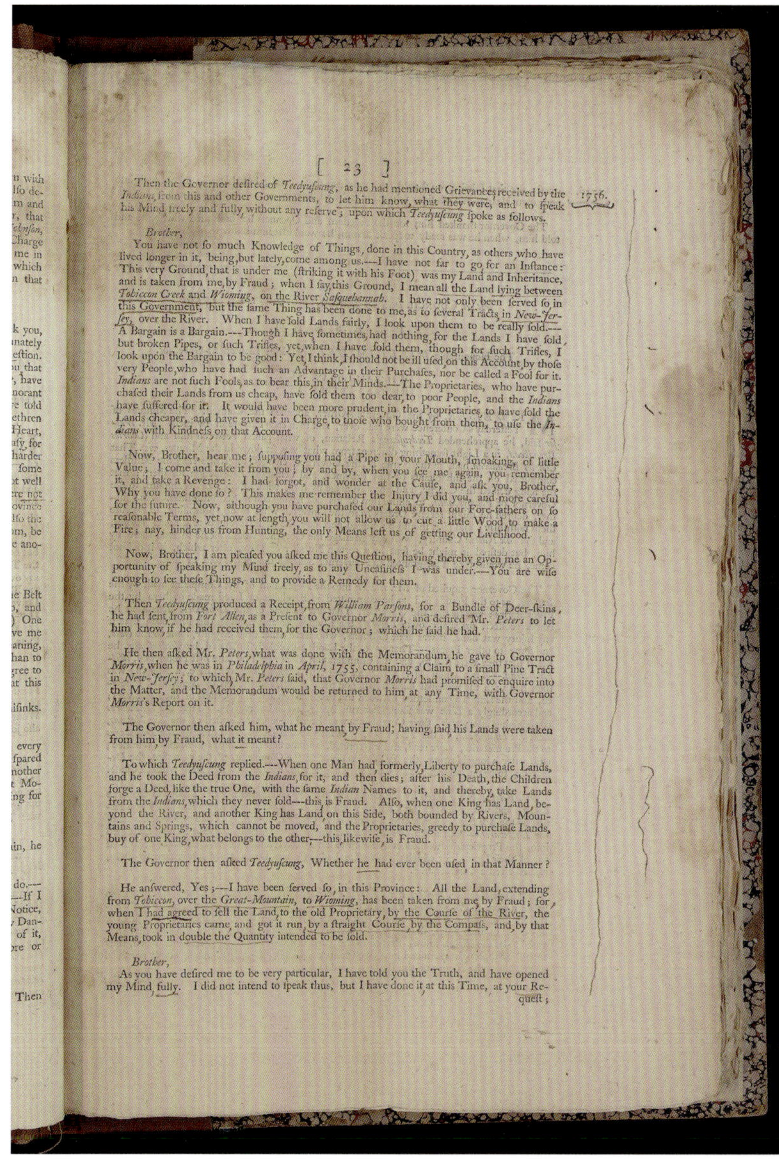

[ 23 ]

Then the Governor deſired of *Teedyuſcung*, as he had mentioned Grievances received by the *Indians*, from this and other Governments, to let him know, what they were, and to ſpeak his Mind freely and fully, without any reſerve; upon which *Teedyuſcung* ſpoke as follows. 1756.

*Brother*,

You have not ſo much Knowledge of Things, done in this Country, as others, who have lived longer in it, being, but lately, come among us.---I have not far to go for an Inſtance: This very Ground, that is under me (ſtriking it with his Foot) was my Land and Inheritance, and is taken from me, by Fraud; when I ſay, this Ground, I mean all the Land lying between *Tohiccon Creek* and *Wioming*, on the River *Saſquehannah*. I have not only been ſerved ſo in this Government, but the ſame Thing has been done to me, as to ſeveral Tracts, in *New-Jerſey*, over the River. When I have ſold Lands fairly, I look upon them to be really ſold.---A Bargain is a Bargain.---Though I have, ſometimes, had nothing, for the Lands I have ſold, but broken Pipes, or ſuch Trifles, yet, when I have ſold them, though for ſuch Trifles, I look upon the Bargain to be good: Yet, I think, I ſhould not be ill uſed, on this Account, by thoſe very People, who have had ſuch an Advantage in their Purchaſes, nor be called a Fool for it. *Indians* are not ſuch Fools, as to bear this, in their Minds.---The Proprietaries, who have purchaſed their Lands from us cheap, have ſold them too dear, to poor People, and the *Indians* have ſuffered for it. It would have been more prudent, in the Proprietaries, to have ſold the Lands cheaper, and have given it in Charge, to thoſe who bought from them, to uſe the *Indians* with Kindneſs, on that Account.

Now, Brother, hear me; ſuppoſing you had a Pipe in your Mouth, ſmoaking, of little Value; I come and take it from you; by and by, when you ſee me again, you remember it, and take a Revenge: I had forgot, and wonder at the Cauſe, and aſk you, Brother, Why you have done ſo? This makes me remember the Injury I did you, and more careful for the future. Now, although you have purchaſed our Lands from our Fore-fathers on ſo reaſonable Terms, yet, now at length, you will not allow us to cut a little Wood, to make a Fire; nay, hinder us from Hunting, the only Means left us, of getting our Livelihood.

Now, Brother, I am pleaſed you aſked me this Queſtion, having, thereby, given me an Opportunity of ſpeaking my Mind freely, as to any Uneaſineſs I was under.---You are wiſe enough to ſee theſe Things, and to provide a Remedy for them.

Then *Teedyuſcung* produced a Receipt, from *William Parſons*, for a Bundle of Deer-ſkins, he had ſent, from *Fort Allen*, as a Preſent to Governor *Morris*, and deſired Mr. *Peters* to let him know, if he had received them, for the Governor; which he ſaid he had.

He then aſked Mr. *Peters*, what was done with the Memorandum, he gave to Governor *Morris*, when he was in *Philadelphia* in *April*, 1755, containing a Claim, to a ſmall Pine Tract in *New-Jerſey*; to which, Mr. *Peters* ſaid, that Governor *Morris* had promiſed to enquire into the Matter, and the Memorandum would be returned to him, at any Time, with Governor *Morris*'s Report on it.

The Governor then aſked him, what he meant, by Fraud; having ſaid, his Lands were taken from him, by Fraud, what it meant?

To which *Teedyuſcung* replied.---When one Man had, formerly, Liberty to purchaſe Lands, and he took the Deed from the *Indians*, for it, and then dies; after his Death, the Children forge a Deed, like the true One, with the ſame *Indian* Names to it, and thereby, take Lands from the *Indians*, which they never ſold---this, is Fraud. Alſo, when one King has Land, beyond the River, and another King has Land, on this Side, both bounded by Rivers, Mountains and Springs, which cannot be moved, and the Proprietaries, greedy to purchaſe Lands, buy of one King, what belongs to the other;---this, likewiſe, is Fraud.

The Governor then aſked *Teedyuſcung*, Whether he had ever been uſed, in that Manner?

He anſwered, Yes;---I have been ſerved ſo, in this Province: All the Land, extending from *Tohiccon*, over the *Great-Mountain*, to *Wioming*, has been taken from me, by Fraud; for, when I had agreed to ſell the Land, to the old Proprietary, by the Courſe of the River, the young Proprietaries came, and got it run, by a ſtraight Courſe, by the Compaſs, and, by that Means, took in double the Quantity intended to be ſold.

*Brother*,

As you have deſired me to be very particular, I have told you the Truth, and have opened my Mind, fully. I did not intend to ſpeak thus, but I have done it, at this Time, at your Requeſt;

of the Lenape leader Teedyuscung (1700–1763). Teedyuscung accused the Pennsylvanians of stealing Lenape lands, exclaiming, "All the Land extending from *Tohiccon,* over the Great Mountain to *Wioming*, has been taken from me by Fraud" (23). His words testify, bitterly, to the end of an era of relatively cooperative relations between Pennsylvania and its Native neighbors.

JOHN H. POLLACK

Further related information in the Historical Society of Pennsylvania archives can be found in the Penn Manuscripts, Indian Affairs, the Penn Family Papers, the James Logan Papers, and the Conrad Weiser Papers.

A Map of that Part of
Bucks County
released by the Indians to the Proprietaries
of Pensilvania in September
Part of Bucks County
The Upper
Kittatinny
PART of WEST
NEW JERSEY.
A Scale of English Miles
PART OF
PHILADELPHIA COUNTY.

# 9. *Map of that Part of Bucks County Released by the Indians to the Proprietaries of Pensilvania on September 1737*

1737
Ink and watercolor on laid paper
16 5/8 × 14 inches (42.2 × 35.5 cm)

Logan Family Papers [0379]
Gift of Members of the Logan Family

Among the Historical Society of Pennsylvania's massive collection of the papers of the Logan Family is this earliest known work by cartographer Lewis Evans, who would later craft some of the finest maps of eighteenth-century North America. Evans's signature is so faded that many scholars, and HSP's own cataloguers, have misattributed it to surveyors John Chapman or Benjamin Eastburn, one or both of whom drew no-longer surviving sketches from which Evans probably worked. James Logan apparently commissioned Evans to make this elegant hand-drawn version to commemorate the infamous "Walking Purchase" of 1737. Logan—an intellectual who accumulated the second-largest private library in British America—was the Penn family's secretary and right-hand man. In the 1730s, William Penn's cash-strapped sons found themselves trapped by their father's strict policy of only granting land to settlers that he had previously purchased from Indigenous owners. The Penns had little such land left to sell until the Walking Purchase added some 1,200 square miles to their domain, including what would become the cities of Allentown, Bethlehem, and Easton.

The audacity of the caper continues to astound: a probably forged "ancient deed" that conveyed the amount of land a person could walk in a day and a half, with convenient blank spaces for such details as where, exactly, they should go; a trail that Pennsylvanians blazed two years in advance; a misleadingly sketched map that convinced relentlessly pressured Lenape sachems to consent to give up what they thought was a relatively small patch of ground; the Olympics-worthy speed at which walkers covered the planned distance in precisely eighteen clock-measured hours; a final trick of triangulation that laid out from the end of the speed walk a line that did not return directly eastward to the Delaware River but instead set off at a right angle to grab vast tracts that did not even belong to the Lenapes.

To a modern eye, Evans's map seems to celebrate this skulduggery. It proclaims proudly that the land had already been "part of Bucks County" long before it had been "released by the Indians to Proprietaries of Pensilvania." A double line that resembles a highway more than a path traces the walkers' route, accompanied by text recounting their eighteen-hour odyssey. Another string of words charts "A right Line . . . to a Poplar tree by the River Delaware marked with the Letter P," for Penn. The resulting triangle encloses two ranks of mountains flanking, in case we have forgotten, "The Upper Part of Bucks County."

More interesting are three figures that frame this triangle with another. Toward the upper right, a feline growls triumphantly over the walkers' accomplishment. Superimposed on a stylized body that one versed in the heraldry of the English crown would recognize as a "lion passant" is the very American face of a cougar or mountain lion, evoking, perhaps, a hybrid transatlantic British imperial victory. Meanwhile, at the map's lower left, a wolf (or maybe just a particularly vicious dog) leaps toward the Purchase in the heraldic attitude known as "salient." This lively canine contrasts dramatically with the dejected dog who trudges faithfully behind a walking human figure just below the map's title. This is not one of the Penn's speed walkers but instead a Lenape man wearing the kind of matchcoat often included among the trade goods used to pay for land. With a hint of sadness on his quickly rendered face, he strides resolutely westward to parts unknown—presaging the later trope of the last, vanishing Indian.

DANIEL K. RICHTER

# 10. *Articles of the Fellowship Fire Company*

1811
Manuscript; ink on wove paper
12 7/16 × 7 3/4 inches (31.6 × 19.8 cm)

From the *Fellowship Fire Company List of Members, 1811–1813*

Historical Society of Pennsylvania Fire Companies of Philadelphia Collection [0205]

There is a saying that in every organization, there are those who "carry water," the people who take on thankless tasks and without whom nothing would get done. Among the treasures of the Historical Society of Pennsylvania is a large, leather-bound volume, a testament to the literal water carriers of colonial Philadelphia—volunteer firefighters.

Voluntary fire companies were invented in Philadelphia, the brainchild of Benjamin Franklin in 1736. They were necessary because the municipal government never organized public firefighting, as was the norm elsewhere in the British Atlantic. Before the Revolution, Philadelphians formed at least twenty voluntary fire companies, with names like Union, Friendship, Amicable, and Hand-in-Hand. HSP has most of the extant records of these fire companies, but few with more completeness than the second fire company to be formed, the Fellowship Fire Company in 1738.

The thirty original members "reposing special Confidence in each others Friendship" promised to equip themselves with leather buckets and sturdy bags (with which to carry goods out of a burning house) and to use them exclusively to help one another "in case of Fire." Over time, they extended their services to anyone in the community who needed their help and acquired more equipment, including ladders, a hand-pumped "fire engine" in 1749, and fire hooks in 1766 to help remove burning debris.

Their efforts were difficult and dangerous. The Fellowship Fire Company fought a fire from 7:00 a.m. until 2:00 p.m., but noted proudly that compared with other volunteer companies, their "Engine play'd to Admiration far Exceeding all others there." The notorious brawls among fire-competing companies came only in the nineteenth century. These firefighters put the task first, and loyally (many of them for decades) came to monthly meetings, maintained their equipment, paid their fines, and protected their city from one of the deadliest menaces of the era.

JESSICA CHOPPIN RONEY

# ARTICLES OF THE Fellowship FIRE COMPANY

We, whose names are hereunto subscribed, reposing especial confidence in each other's friendship, do, for the better preservation of our Houses, Goods, and Effects from Fire, mutually agree to be governed by the following Articles:

1

The number of Members composing this Company shall not exceed thirty five.

2

Each of the Members shall provide, at his own expence, two Leathern Buckets, and one Bag of good Oznabrigs or wider Linen, containing four Yards at least, with a String fastened near the Mouth, which said Buckets and Bag shall be marked with our Names respectively and Company, and shall be applied to no other use than that of preserving thᵉ Houses, Goods, and Effects, of ourselves, and of our fellow-Citizens, in case of Fire.

# 11. Ephrata Cloister

## *Chronicon*

1745
Ink on laid paper bound in cloth
5 7/8 × 7 1/4 inches (15.0 × 18.5 cm)

Inscribed in German Fraktur: *Die Rose / oder: / Der angenehmen Blume / zu Saron geistliche Ehe-verlőbnűs / mit ihrem himmlischen Bråutigam, wel- / chem sie sich als ihrem Kőnig, Haupt, / Mann, Herrn, und Bråutigam, auf's ewig / hin verlobt.*

Abraham H. Cassel Collection [1610]

Perhaps the title of "The Rose," the chronicle of the Ephrata Sisterhood, was more than a metaphor expressing the soul's longing for Christ, the heavenly bridegroom; such tropes were typical for the radical Pietists who settled in early Pennsylvania to seek religious tolerance. Written in the ornate calligraphy reminiscent of medieval manuscripts (used in hymnals, chronicles, and other manuscripts at Ephrata), the title page reads: "Die Rose, Oder: Der angenehmen Blume zu Saron geistliche Ehe-verlöbnüs mit ihrem himmlischen Bräutigam, welchem sie sich als ihrem König, Haupt, Mann, Herrn, und Bräutigam, auf's ewig hin verlobt" (The Rose, Or: the pleasant flower of Sharon's spiritual betrothal to her heavenly bridegroom, to whom she promises herself forever as her king, head, husband, lord, and bridegroom). Under the leadership of Maria Eicher, the sisters lived at Ephrata—a communitarian experiment consisting of German Seventh Day Baptists—in a condition entirely unusual for their contemporaries: they never married or had children, lived apart from their families, and took monastic names. In a time of compulsory marriage, childbearing, and submission to patriarchal figures, they found a radical alternative: sexual celibacy, material simplicity, and a spiritual betrothal to Christ. When scores of unwed and married women—such as the Eicher sisters and the wife of prominent German printer Christoph Saur—joined the "Cloister," they scandalized the agricultural heartland of eastern Pennsylvania.

Granted, Ephrata was not devoid of patriarchal authority. Its founder and leader, Conrad Beissel (1691–1768), reportedly governed with a near-tyrannical style. Yet Beissel's personality matched the subversive, gender-bending mystical philosophy he brought to Pennsylvania when he emigrated from Germany in 1720. Beissel had imbibed the belief of German mystic Jakob Böhme that the virgin Sophia, identified as the female aspect of God, had once been united with Adam in a spiritual union. Böhme interpreted the fall of man as a separation from this female principle of divine wisdom, which moved Adam from an original state of androgyny toward a destructive male self-will. To reunite humanity with divine wisdom, a shedding of material desires was necessary.

At Ephrata, Beissel devised a system of self-mortification, including monastic life and dress, denial of food, drink, sleep, and sex, as well as continuous labor, to refine the human spirit into a prelapsarian perfection. Brothers and sisters worked in the "writing school," creating elaborate manuscript illustrations and hymnals. In the "singing school," Beissel taught his musical system and prescribed strict measures for purifying the human voice (such as a vegetarian diet). Ephrata brothers ran the printing

press, which produced the largest single volume printed in colonial America—the Mennonite *Martyrs' Mirror*. As a result, Ephrata brothers and sisters created a treasure trove of early American manuscripts, which present tremendous opportunities for scholarship in musicology, religious history and theology, utopian studies, German-language immigration, and women's studies. Over two centuries after the last celibate "nun" died at the "Cloister" in 1813, the Ephrata sisters still await a full scholarly assessment—especially of their radical experiment in eschewing contemporary gender roles. PATRICK M. ERBEN

---

Further related information in the Historical Society of Pennsylvania archives can be found in the Conrad Weiser Papers [0700], the Ferdinand J. Dreer Autograph Collection [0175], which includes Johannes Kelpius's journal and letters, the Francis Daniel Pastorius Papers [0475], and the Johannes Kelpius Collection of German Hymns [Am .088].

## 12. *An Act for Granting the Sum of Sixty Thousand Pounds to the King's Use; and for Striking Fifty-five Thousand Pounds thereof in Bills of Credit; and to Provide a Fund for Sinking the Same*

1755
Broadside; letterpress on laid paper
16 1/4 × 10 inches (41.3 × 25.5 cm)

Archives like the Historical Society of Pennsylvania are full of documents that look insignificant and dull. For example, one may wonder of the need to admire densely printed sheets of paper that advertise a 1755 tax act of the Pennsylvania Assembly. While this "broadside" (a flyer, in modern terminology) is no Declaration of Independence, many historians would argue that it is very important to the story of America's eventual separation from Britain. Indeed, scholars rely on HSP's collection of more than two thousand broadsides to tell them about many vital aspects of America's colonial past.

This act, passed by the Assembly in November of 1755, mandated raising roughly $4 million in present-day money. This vast sum was to be collected through a property tax, with poorer Pennsylvanians paying a flat rate while richer residents would pay 2.5 percent of each pound sterling of wealth. As the document explains, Pennsylvanians passed the act "desirous of demonstrating our Duty to our Sovereign, and willing to give a further Testimony of our Loyalty, and the most sincere Affection of his loving Subjects within this Province." However, this was not just a random expression of allegiance to King George II. Rather, the money was needed to wage war against the French and their Indigenous allies. This war would become known as the French and Indian War in North America and the Seven Years' War elsewhere. Perhaps the first world war, fighting raged on four continents, including in western Pennsylvania, where thousands of European colonists and Native Americans died or were taken prisoner. Finally, Britain emerged victorious, and the French were permanently ejected from North America after almost two hundred years of colonization.

Because Pennsylvania was a pacifist Quaker colony, this bill was more controversial than it might seem. Quakers opposed military action and, therefore, the raising of money to pay for it. These funds were destined to pay soldiers and buy them food, uniforms, and weapons. The Assembly's political factions had argued for months before the act became law precisely because Quakers' commitments to peace prevented them from endorsing it. Meanwhile, on the colony's western fringes, settlers and Indians were dying by the hundreds as the French and Native peoples launched successive attacks. Feeling aggrieved and abandoned by their leaders, European colonists cried out for action. Eventually, with this bill, help was on its way—but not before many lives had been lost.

The inaction of the colony's leadership created long-term distrust between poorer, rural settlers and the urban elites in Philadelphia. More critical, however, was the discord that the war fostered between the British and colonial Americans. As the tax act suggests, colonists were deeply loyal to the British. They committed large quantities of time and money to the war against the French. As a result, British policy after the war was won in 1763 seemed like a bitter betrayal of this loyalty. Arguing that the Americans had not contributed enough to the victory, the British looked to increase their tax take from the colonies with the Stamp Act of 1765. And that, of course, was the beginning of the Revolution.

EMMA HART

# *An* ACT *for Granting the Sum of Sixty thouſand Pounds to the* King's Uſe; *and for Striking Fifty-five thouſand Pounds thereof in Bills of Credit; and to provide a Fund for Sinking the ſame.*

WHereas the King's Service at this Time requires extraordinary Supplies from this Province, and the Treaſury (by the ſeveral Sums of Money already given by former Aſſemblies for purchaſing Proviſions for the King's Forces, erecting and maintaining Poſts, Payment of Expreſſes, Clearing of Roads, Maintaining of *Indians*, and other heavy Charges for the King's Uſe) is exhauſted; We, the Repreſentatives of the Freemen of the Province of *Penſylvania*, being deſirous of demonſtrating our Duty to our Sovereign, and willing to give a further Teſtimony of our Loyalty, and the moſt ſincere Affection of his loving Subjects within this Province, do pray, That it may be **Enacted; And be it Enacted**, by the Honourable *Robert Hunter Morris*, Eſquire, Lieutenant-Governor, under the Honourable *Thomas Penn* and *Richard Penn*, Eſquires, true and abſolute Proprietaries of the Province of *Penſylvania*, and Counties of *Newcaſtle*, *Kent*, and *Suſſex upon Delaware*, by and with the Advice and Conſent of the Repreſentatives of the Freemen of the ſaid Province in General Aſſembly met, and by the Authority of the ſame, That Fifty-five thouſand Pounds, in Bills of Credit, to be ſtruck by virtue of this Act, ſhall be **given to the King's Uſe**.

**And**, to the end the Fifty-five thouſand Pounds in Bills of Credit, ſo as aforeſaid given, may be duly ſunk and deſtroyed, **Be it further Enacted**, by the Authority aforeſaid, That there ſhall be levied upon all the Eſtates, real and perſonal, within this Province, of all and every Perſon and Perſons (the Eſtates of the Honourable *Thomas Penn* and *Richard Penn*, Eſquires, Proprietaries of the Province of *Penſylvania*, only excepted, in Conſideration of their free Gift herein after-mentioned) the Sum of Six Pence for every Pound, clear Value of the ſaid Eſtates yearly, for the Space of Four Years, to be paid by the Owners or Poſſeſſors thereof: And that every ſingle Freeman, whether reſiding with his Parents or elſewhere, who, at the time of the Aſſeſſment, ſhall be of the Age of Twenty-one Years, and hath been out of his Apprenticeſhip, or Servitude, for the Space of Six Months, and is not worth in Goods or Chattels Thirty Pounds, ſhall pay the Sum of Ten Shillings; except ſuch as now are, or hereafter ſhall be, engaged in his Majeſty's Service: All which ſaid ſeveral Sums, ſo to be raiſed as aforeſaid, ſhall be aſſeſſed and levied as in and by an Act, paſſed in the Eleventh Year of the late King *George* the Firſt, intituled, *An Act for Raiſing of County Rates and Levies*, is directed to be aſſeſſed and levied: And that every Article, Clauſe, and Thing therein contained, concerning the aſſeſſing and levying Taxes, ſhall be uſed, exerciſed, and put in Practice, for aſſeſſing and levying the Tax hereby impoſed, as if the ſame Articles, Clauſes, and Things, were inſerted in this Act; except in ſuch Caſes as are herein aſcertained, provided for, or altered.

**And be it further Enacted**, by the Authority aforeſaid, That the Commiſſioners of the reſpective Counties, or any Two of them, ſhall, as ſoon as may be after the Expiration of Six Months next following the Publication of this Act, iſſue forth their Precepts, directed to the Conſtables of every Townſhip, requiring them to bring to the reſpective Aſſeſſors, within Three Weeks next after the Date of ſuch Precepts, fair and true Certificates in Writing, upon their Oaths or Affirmations, of the Names and Surnames of all and every the Perſons dwelling or reſiding within the Limits of thoſe Townſhips or Places, as in and by the herein before mentioned Act for raiſing of County Rates and Levies, and as by this preſent Act is particularly ſet forth, and directed to be aſſeſſed: But, before the Commiſſioners and Aſſeſſors ſhall take upon them the reſpective Service and Duty by this Act required of them, they ſhall take an Oath, or Affirmation, to the Effect following; that is to ſay,

"Thou ſhalt well and truly cauſe the Rates and Sums of Money, by virtue of this Act impoſed, to be duly and "equally aſſeſſed and laid, according to the beſt of thy Skill and Knowledge; and herein thou ſhalt ſpare no Perſon "for Favour or Affection; nor grieve any for Hatred or Ill-will."

Which Qualification ſhall be adminiſtred as in and by the ſaid Act for raiſing County Rates and Levies is enjoined and required.

**And be it further Enacted**, by the Authority aforeſaid, That if the ſaid Commiſſioners, or Aſſeſſors, ſhall refuſe or neglect to perform and diſcharge the Duties required of them by this or the before-mentioned Act, each and every of the ſaid Commiſſioners, or Aſſeſſors, ſo refuſing, ſhall forfeit and pay to the Provincial Treaſurer the Sum of Twenty Pounds.

**Provided always**, That all Fines and Forfeitures ariſing by virtue of this Act, ſhall be levied as in the aforeſaid Act for raiſing of County Rates and Levies is directed; and ſhall be paid and added to the publick Provincial Stock.

**Provided alſo**, That the Conſtables ſhall have and receive, for their Care and Trouble in executing and returning the Receipts by this Act directed and enjoined, One Peny *per* Pound, and no more; and that the Aſſeſſors, for their Time and Labour in their Aſſeſſments, ſhall be allowed Three Pence *per* Pound upon the whole Sum contained in the Rates of their reſpective Counties, after the Aſſeſſment is rectified and adjuſted by the Commiſſioners, and no more; and that the County Treaſurers ſhall be allowed, for their Care and Trouble, One *per Centum* for all Monies by them received and paid, and no more; and that the Collectors ſhall retain in their Hands, for all Sums of Money by them reſpectively collected, Six Pence *per* Pound, and no more; any thing in this Act, or in the aforeſaid Act for raiſing of County Rates and Levies, to the contrary notwithſtanding.

**And be it further Enacted**, by the Authority aforeſaid, That if the ſaid Collector or Collectors ſhall refuſe or neglect to take upon him or themſelves the Truſt and Duty required of him or them by this Act, he or they ſo refuſing ſhall forfeit and pay to the County Treaſurer the Sum of Ten Pounds each; and the Aſſeſſors ſhall appoint ſome other fit Perſon or Perſons in the place or ſtead of the Collector or Collectors ſo refuſing or neglecting, as aforeſaid.

**And be it further Enacted**, by the Authority aforeſaid, That all the Sum or Sums of Money levied by the Collectors of the reſpective Diſtricts throughout this Province, by virtue of this Act, ſhall be paid by the ſaid Collectors to the County Treaſurers, and by the County Treaſurers, reſpectively, into the Hands of the Provincial Treaſurer.

But

## 13. **Gerard Van der Grucht** (1696–1776), after **George Heap** (ca. 1715–1752)

### *An East Prospect of the City of Philadelphia; taken by George Heap from the Jersey shore, under the Direction of Nicholas Scull Surveyor General of the Province of Pennsylvania*

1756
Published by Nicholas Scull (1687–1761) and Thomas Jeffrys (ca. 1719–1771)
Engraving on shellacked laid paper mounted on linen
20 ½ × 37 ½ inches (52.0 × 95.2 cm)

Historical Society of Pennsylvania Large Graphics Collection [V65]

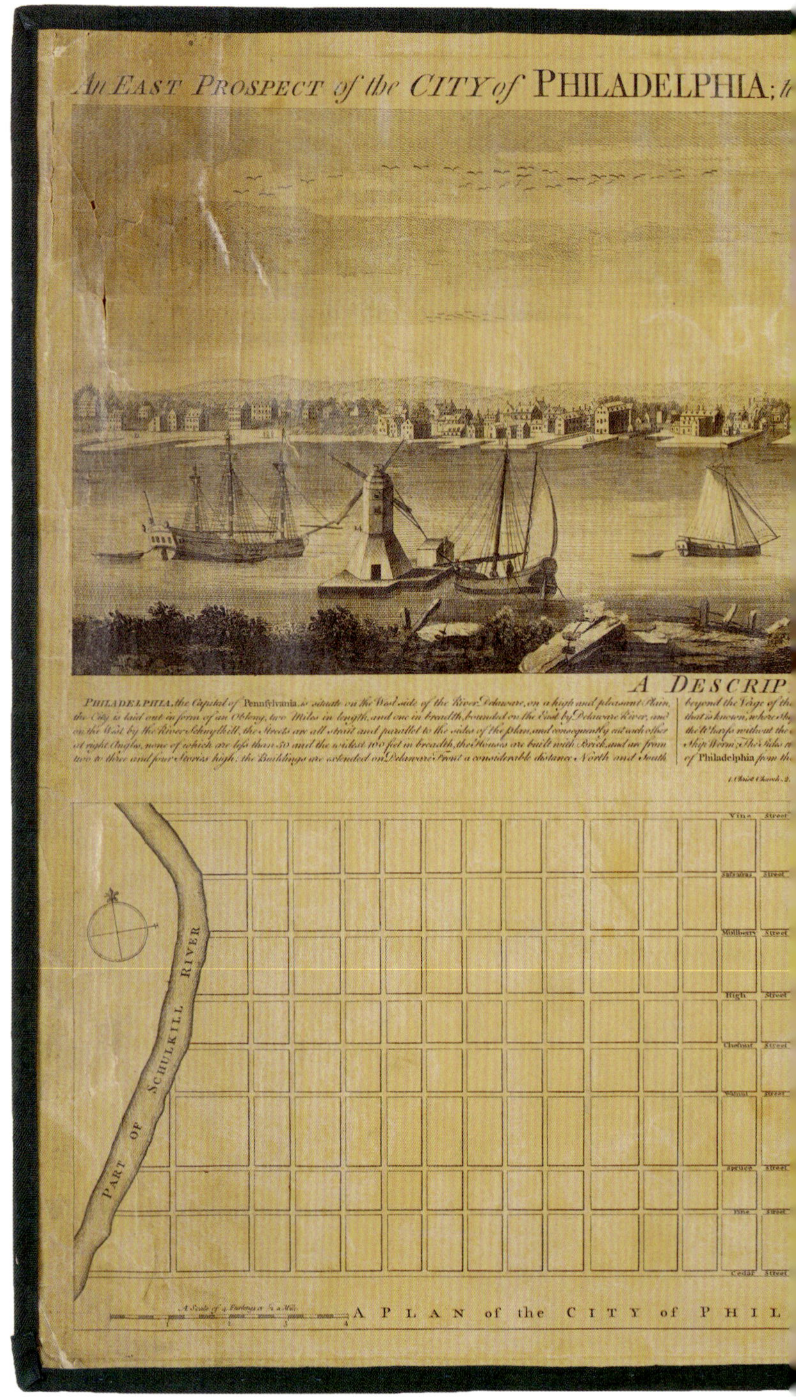


This is a reduced version of a promotional print commissioned by Pennsylvania proprietor Thomas Penn. By the 1750s more than 12,000 people lived in Philadelphia, making it the second-largest city in Britain's North American colonies after Boston. Eager to promote his bustling colonial capital, Penn learned that local artist George Heap had made a series of views of the port and hired Heap to translate them into an engraving, production costs for which would be paid by subscription. City "prospects" were a popular form of landscape art in the colonies. The earliest surviving "prospect" of Philadelphia is an oil painting by Peter Cooper made in about 1718, and engraved prospects of the ports of New York and Boston had been published in London as early as 1720 after on-site sketches by William Burgis.

Heap made his drawings from an elevated location on the New Jersey side of the Delaware River, centering the panorama on Christ Church, then the tallest building in the city. His first priority was to accurately render the appearance and location of major landmarks such as the State House (still under construction), the Court House, and various houses of worship. Penn's land agent in Philadelphia, William Peters, thought Heap's view was boring because there were so few church spires along the horizon—perhaps not surprising in a city founded by Quakers. As one historian noted, the unrelenting line of houses and warehouses along the many wharves with warships, merchant ships, and smaller vessels tacking along the river in the foreground celebrated Philadelphia's prosperity "but missed its bustle." Detailed statistics presented in the lengthy caption further attest to the city's robust economy.

Because there were few fine-art engravers in the colonies, Heap embarked for London with his drawings but died during the voyage. His widow then sold them to Nicholas Scull, who, as Pennsylvania's surveyor general, had already supervised the publication of several maps of

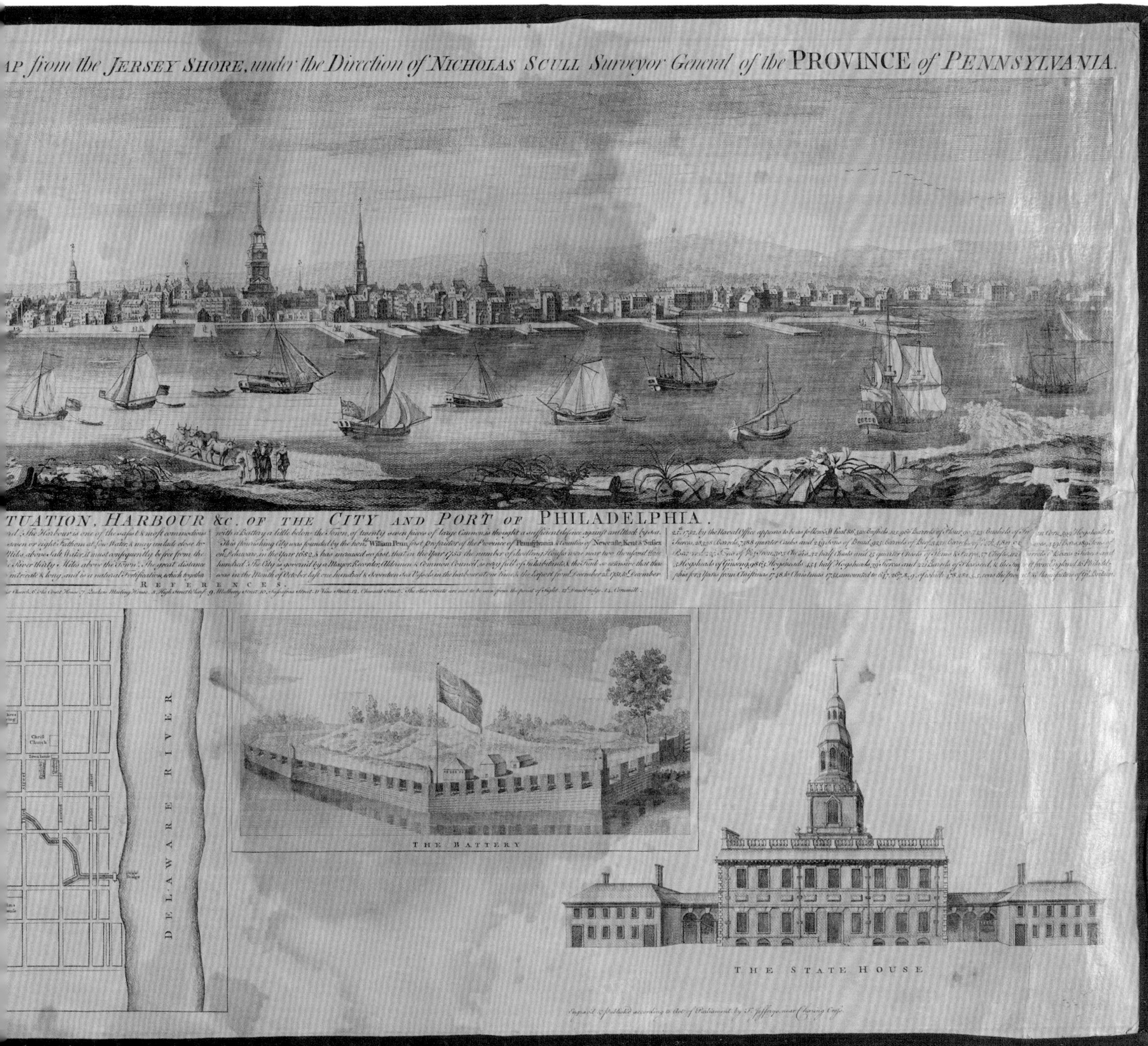


Philadelphia and Pennsylvania. Scull hired John Winter to clean up Heap's sketches and forwarded them to London, where Gerard Van der Grucht engraved them on four separate plates, which, when printed, combined to form a seven-foot-wide image, published in 1752. Seven hundred and fifty impressions were printed and sold quickly.

But Thomas Penn evidently objected to the massive print and directed Van der Grucht to draw a smaller version which was engraved by Thomas Jeffrys (or Jefferys), cartographer to the Prince of Wales, and published in 1756. Yet even though Van der Grucht and Jeffrys added new elements such as the city plan, a detailed view of the Battery, and the recently completed State House, buyers were unimpressed—perhaps because no ships were shown berthed at any of the many wharves. Philadelphians also criticized the inaccuracy of the city plan. From an edition of three hundred copies, only twenty were sold in the first year. Nevertheless, Jeffreys retained the plate and reused it for his 1768 *General Topography of North America and the West Indies*.

ELIZABETH MILROY

# 14. **James Claypoole Jr.** (1743–1822)

## *A Perspective View of Pennsylvania Hospital with the Buildings as Intended to be Erected*

1762
Hand-colored engraving on laid paper
12 3/8 × 15 3/4 inches (31.4 × 40.0 cm)

Inscribed below image: *A Perspective view of the Pennsylvania Hospital, with the Buildings as intended / to be erect*; lower left: *Jas. Claypoole Jun^r. delin^t et sculp^t*; lower center, in seal of hospital: *TAKE CARE OF HIM / & I WILL REPAY / THEE*

Historical Society of Pennsylvania Large Graphics Collection [V65]

On Pine Street between Eighth and Ninth Streets in Philadelphia, the stately Colonial-cum-Federal façade of Pennsylvania Hospital's original buildings (1755–1804) looks out over a dignified lawn and gardens. The serene tableau belies the bustle behind the walls, where a major urban hospital continues to test, diagnose, and treat 20,000 inpatients and 213,000 outpatients every year.

Pennsylvania Hospital often figures in Philadelphia's proud list of medical firsts: America's first hospital, first medical school (University of Pennsylvania School of Medicine, 1765), and first medical association (College of Physicians of Philadelphia, 1787), among others. But it might just as well be grouped with two other eighteenth-century Philadelphia institutions: the Alms House (founded in 1732) and the Walnut Street Gaol [jail] (founded in 1773). When the hospital was created in 1751, the goal of getting disorderly people off the streets was as important as providing medical care.

Dr. Thomas Bond originally conceived the idea of the hospital, and after he enlisted his friend Benjamin Franklin as a co-sponsor, the proposal gained momentum. Franklin's 1754 account of the hospital's creation similarly recalled that the "Inhabitants of the Province, who unhappily became disordered in their Senses, wandered about to the terrour of their Neighbours, there being no place (except the House of Correction or Almshouse) in which they might be confined, and subjected to proper treatment for their Recovery." Pennsylvania Hospital consistently fulfilled this therapeutically carceral function from the time it received its first patient in 1752, treating both mental and physical illnesses and injuries. Indeed, in its early years the mentally ill regularly constituted the majority of patients, and through the work of physicians such as Benjamin Rush (beginning in 1783) and Thomas Story Kirkbride (starting in 1841), the hospital became a pioneering institution in the humane treatment of mental illness.

Women were treated alongside men on a separate floor of the building, and Blacks were treated alongside whites. French political writer J. P. Brissot de Warville visited Pennsylvania Hospital in 1788 and marveled at both the quality and *equality* of accommodations there: "Blacks are here mingled with the whites and lodged in the same apts. This to me seemed a balm to my soul.... I saw a negro woman spinning with activity by the side of her bed. She seemed to expect a word of consolation from the director; she obtained it, and it seemed to be heaven to her to hear it."

Concern for the well-being of the poor and marginalized stemmed from a deep-seated paternalism. Patients who could not afford to pay for their care were treated free of charge, but only if they could present a letter from a respected member of the community attesting to their

good character. Such were the progressive impulses of Enlightenment-era reformers. Carceral motives and demeaning paternalism nevertheless resulted in an institution that made medical care (including the basics of nursing: clean bedding and clothing, food and drink, and rest) available to far more people residing in a far larger region than had previously been the case.

Today, the peaceful gardens and the inspiring façade of the original Pine building invite reflection as much on the elusive ideal of providing care to all regardless of economic circumstances as on the state-of-the-art medicine practiced behind the walls.

James Claypoole Jr.'s hand-colored engraving from 1762 captures the hospital as its original architect, Samuel Rhoads, intended for it to look rather than as it actually materialized. The east wing (at right in this image) was built first and completed in 1755. Construction on the west and central sections did not begin until forty years later when Rhoads's design was given a Federal-style update.

DAVID BARNES

John Tilton's Land
286a Land & Marsh granted to James Steel
Tobacco House
Whitehall 632a Land Marsh & Swamp
Negroe
Quarter
new Tobacco House
Barn
Swamp
N2d W 430 Perches
Charles Hillyard's Land
A Draught of the Lands bought by Samuel Chew Esqr. Decd. of Andrew Hamilton of Philada. Gent.
Situate in Duck-Creek Hundred & County of Kent upon Delaware containing nine hundred & eighteen Acres
within the Lines & Bounds above described Resurvey'd the 31st. of October & 1st. of November 1745
℘ Geo Stevenson Surr. of Kent
& Newcastle Counties on Delaware

# 15. *Plan of Whitehall Plantation*

October 31–November 1, 1745
Ink on laid paper
11 13⁄16 × 14 3⁄8 inches (30.0 × 36.5 cm)

Chew Family Papers [2050]
Gift of the Chew Family

Whitehall Plantation was established in the 1680s in Kent County, Delaware, and purchased by the Chew family in the 1760s. Multiple generations of Chew family members left records detailing the semidiversified farming operation for over a century. The collection of business records is broad and notable both for the insights it gives into market-oriented agriculture and how much the enterprise relied on enslaved persons for its profits. There is extensive documentation of how the white family deployed enslaved labor and treated those laborers from the 1760s to the beginning of the nineteenth century. The plat itself clearly identifies the "Negroe Quarter" next to one of the tobacco houses as part of the 918-acre property.

Benjamin Chew employed overseers and was a hands-off yet demanding manager of his enslaved people and their output. His agent and business manager handled the negotiations and arrangements when he rented out his enslaved laborers to others. His overseers handled the plantation, but Chew dictated goals and tasks. His letters reveal his oversight of matters such as his slaves' shoe sizes and the quality of shoes and clothing he wished to secure for them. These letters also reveal a continuing power struggle between Chew and his overseers. His overseers wished him to become more personally involved in the physical discipline of slaves, while Chew largely disavowed such unpleasant personal commitments. He also tended to provide far less clothing and food for his enslaved workers than even his overseers thought appropriate. They had trouble maintaining the command of the enslaved people that they expected they should have, as many letters in the collection make clear. The correspondence also reveals the reality of the intermixing of free Black people and enslaved people in the mid-Atlantic. Anyone who wished to argue that enslavement conveniently disappeared in the early republic North would find these records a real barrier to that view. The Chew family's multigenerational prosperity and status depended on the profits extracted from generations of enslaved laborers.

The much larger Chew Family Papers are a gem—a sizable and varied collection chronicling the extended family over seven generations. The documents bring alive the complexities of late eighteenth-century elite business practices. Most of the papers reflect the combination of lawyering, land speculation, and market-oriented farming typical of so many fortunes of the American Revolutionary era. In the nineteenth century, the family diversified into industrial investments as well. The collection is also valuable for family and social history, and men's and women's voices are represented for both the eighteenth and nineteenth centuries.

Benjamin Chew's letters reveal a political moderate during the American Revolution who hated his time as a political prisoner. He had a warm yet tense relationship with his namesake son, who also served as his business agent. Uncles and nephews, aunts, sisters, and nieces all cheerfully corresponded, gossiped, and fought with each other. Family squabbles and business affairs were often the same for this family, culminating in a mid-nineteenth-century estate dispute that consumed many packets of paper, much time, and good feelings among kin. Several members of the family also struggled with alcoholism and mental health. Benjamin's grandson William White Chew endlessly obsessed over drafts of suicide notes—a detail in the papers that gives rare insight into mental-health expectations and how people tried to cope with intrusive thoughts.

REBECCA BRANNON

# 16. *Resolution of Non-Importation Made by the Citizens of Philadelphia*

October 25, 1765
Manuscript; ink on laid paper
11 11⁄16 × 7 11⁄16 inches (29.7 × 19.5 cm)

Resolution of Non-Importation Made by the Citizens of Philadelphia [Am .340]
Gift of William Bradford, 1854

Among the treasures of the Historical Society of Pennsylvania rank the many rich materials that help us understand the coming of the American Revolution. How did Americans move from loyal subjects of Britain to angry protesters, then to rebels, separatists, and ultimately nation-builders on their own behalf?

One document that sheds light on those earliest steps into protest and later open revolt is a list of resolves agreed to by the "merchants and traders of Philadelphia." The document itself might not seem so remarkable, just one of numerous petitions and protests from the period, except that it is followed by six full pages of signatures, each with three columns per page crammed with names. These signatures represent the breadth and diversity of Philadelphia's mercantile community, including the wealthiest men in the community and their humbler neighbors; merchants, men who worked with their hands, lawyers, and even clergymen; Quakers, Protestants, Jews, and Catholics; future Patriots alongside future Loyalists; and six remarkable women who signed on their own behalves. This document, then, was no run-of-the-mill complaint but touched the entire community so deeply that a wide and diverse range of people found common cause to act as one.

The signatories objected to the "late unconstitutional" Stamp Act and connected their protest with action. "Until the Stamp Act is Repeal'd," the men and women who put pen to paper vowed to stop importing British goods, the first known economic boycott in western history. These inhabitants of a port city were putting their own livelihoods on the line with this promise, and that they did so speaks to how overwhelmingly their community rejected British taxation and advocated their own ideas of constitutionalism and American rights. Humble though the document itself may be, it is also potent with purpose and patriotism.

JESSICA CHOPPIN RONEY

Lydia & Eliz Hyde
Joseph Jacobs
Wm Symonds
J. West
Jas. Pinnock jun
Will^m Taggart
Wm Falconer
William Craig
Owen Biddle
Benj^a Hooton
David Wason
Saml Carruthers
Jacob Shoemaker jun
Bartram & Dundas
Robt Bass
Peyton & Adcock
Nath Twiddy
Rich & Peter Footman
A. Hopps
Caleb Hewes
Saml Fisher
Joseph Baker
Coxe & Furman
Robt Wall
Geo. Robotham
Andw Bankson
Hugh & Geo Roberts
Jere^h Warder
Rob. Tuckniss
John Steinmetz
Hugh Forbes
B. F. for Randle Mitchell
Joseph Claypoole
Richd Swan
Wm & Turner
John Ingles
John Pringle
[illegible]
Saml Bunting
Tho Clifford
I. Wallace
Ezra Lash
James Hartley
I. Shoemaker
Wm Allison
Hyman Levy jun
Jas. Wharton
John Bell
Magee & Sanderson
Henry Keppele jun
John Hughes
Reuben Haines
Owen Jones
Edwd Paschall
Benjamin Davies
Hudson Emlen
Richd Waln
John Knowles
William Vanderspiegel
Peter Thomson
Wm Pollard
Tho Lawrence
Judah Foulke
John Cox
Theo Gardner
Jn Bond
James Eddy
Philip Kearny jr
Richd Wells
Jonas Evans
Anthony Stocker
[illegible]
Hugh McCulloch

# 17. **Josiah Tucker** (1712–1799), marginalia by **Benjamin Franklin** (1706–1790)

## *A Letter from a Merchant in London to his Nephew in North America, Relative to the Present Posture of Affairs in the Colonies*

---

1766
Published by John Walter (d. 1803)
Laid paper bound in 19th-century half maroon morocco and marbled paper boards
9 × 5 11⁄16 inches (22.8 × 14.4 cm)

Purchased from Nicolas Gouin Dufief, 1801–1803, by Colonel William Duane; sold by him in 1822 to the Athenaeum of Philadelphia; sold in turn by it, December 22, 1885, to the Historical Society of Pennsylvania.

The Historical Society of Pennsylvania has one of the largest collections of books owned by Benjamin Franklin, 861 out of a total of about 3,000. Among the many things learned from them is that he hardly ever wrote in the margins of his books—with one important exception. In the aftermath of the Stamp Act, from 1765 to 1770, Franklin intensively annotated a dozen anti-American British pamphlets, of which four are at HSP. The one pictured here is among the most interesting because of his spectacular marginalia and the glimpse it gives into his thinking during this period of crisis.

All the pamphlets Franklin annotated argued that Parliament had the authority to tax the colonies, whereas many colonists believed that internal taxes (as opposed to external taxes, such as import duties) could only be levied by their own assemblies. In his marginal notes, Franklin advanced a deeper constitutional argument: England and the colonies were separate states with coequal legislatures, held together by their loyalty to the king. In claiming jurisdiction in the colonies, Parliament usurped an authority it did not rightfully possess.

When the author of this pamphlet, the argumentative Dean of Gloucester Josiah Tucker, asserted that it would be illegal for the king to exempt the colonies from Parliamentary taxes, Franklin scoffed, "What Stuff!" When Tucker claimed that all the colonial charters reserved to Parliament the right to tax them, or if not, they "must be supposed virtually to imply" it, Franklin gleefully called "A Fib, Mr. Dean." In fact, all but one were chartered by the Crown and contained no such concession to Parliament. Franklin wrote dramatically, as if he were debating Tucker in person.

When Franklin first tried out these arguments in marginalia in 1765, he was in London on a mission to placate a hostile Parliament, and he did not dare to share them with anyone. In 1770, when he annotated the Tucker pamphlet, he confided his thoughts in a letter to the Boston clergyman Samuel Cooper, saying he was preparing a manuscript on the subject for publication, but for the moment it was more prudent to be quiet.

He never published that manuscript, but through letters to his friends Franklin's ideas made their way into public discourse. In 1773, for example, when Massachusetts Governor Hutchinson rashly declared that denying the supreme authority of Parliament was tantamount to rebellion, Samuel Adams replied that Parliament could not claim that authority because it had not been granted in the colony's charter. It was widely believed on all sides that Adams was applying what he learned from Franklin. These revolutionary ideas helped tip the colonies toward independence, and in Franklin's marginalia, they can be seen taking shape. JAMES N. GREEN

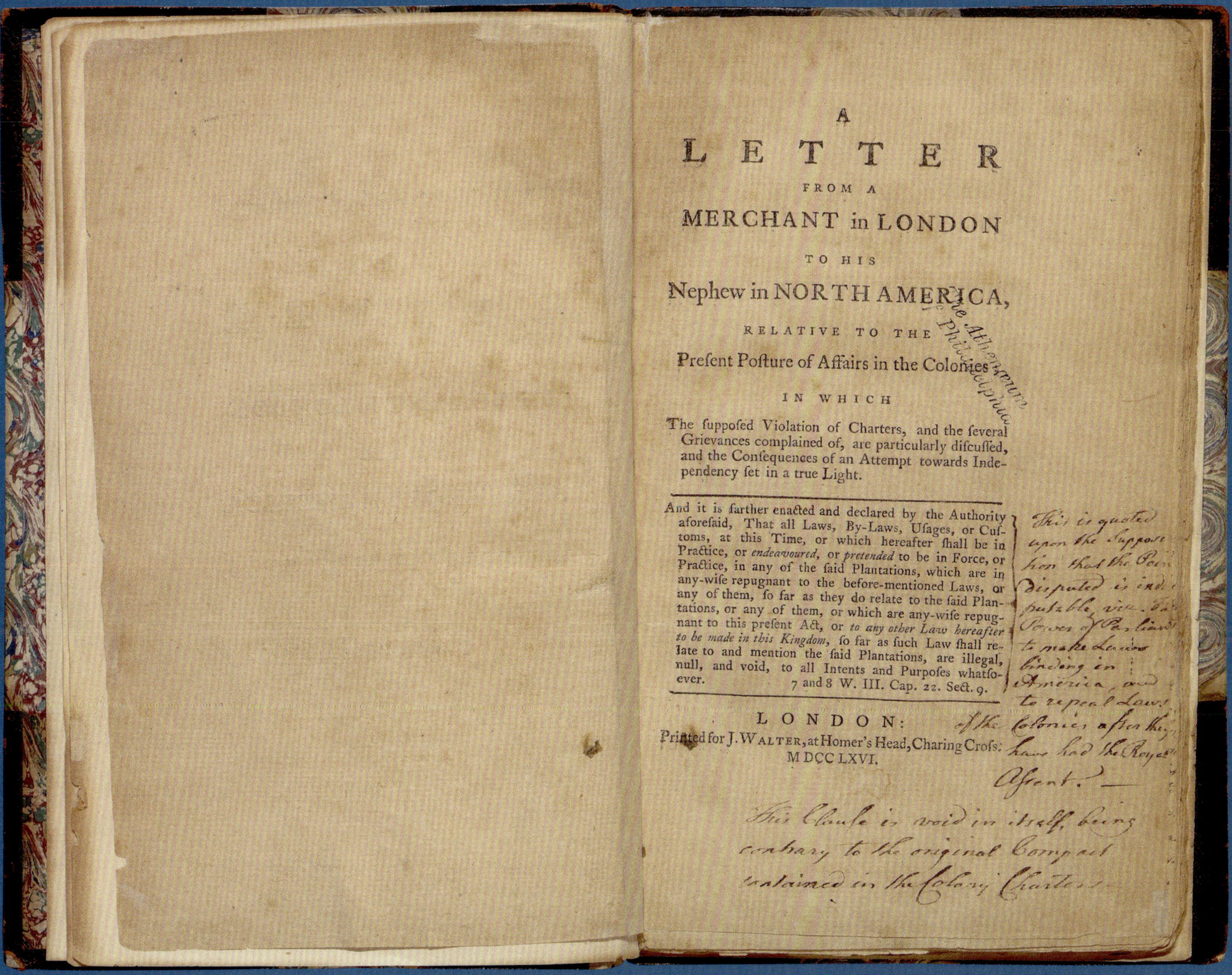

A
LETTER
FROM A
MERCHANT in LONDON
TO HIS
Nephew in NORTH AMERICA,
RELATIVE TO THE
Present Posture of Affairs in the Colonies;
IN WHICH
The supposed Violation of Charters, and the several Grievances complained of, are particularly discussed, and the Consequences of an Attempt towards Independency set in a true Light.



And it is farther enacted and declared by the Authority aforesaid, That all Laws, By-Laws, Usages, or Customs, at this Time, or which hereafter shall be in Practice, or *endeavoured*, or *pretended* to be in Force, or Practice, in any of the said Plantations, which are in any-wise repugnant to the before-mentioned Laws, or any of them, so far as they do relate to the said Plantations, or any of them, or which are any-wise repugnant to this present Act, or *to any other Law hereafter to be made in this Kingdom*, so far as such Law shall relate to and mention the said Plantations, are illegal, null, and void, to all Intents and Purposes whatsoever.
7 and 8 W. III. Cap. 22. Sect. 9.

This is quoted upon the Supposition that the Point disputed is indisputable, viz. the Power of Parliament to make Laws binding in America, and to repeal Laws of the Colonies after they have had the Royal Assent. —

LONDON:
Printed for J. WALTER, at Homer's Head, Charing Cross.
MDCCLXVI.

This Clause is void in itself, being contrary to the original Compact contained in the Colony Charters.

any Length, according to the Diſtance
Extent of his Dominions. Good Heave
what a ſudden Alteration is this! An Ar
rican pleading for the Extenſion of the P
rogative of the Crown? Yes, if it co
make for his Cauſe;—and for extending
too beyond all the Bounds of Law, of R
ſon, and of Common Senſe!

But though I have for Argument's ſa
and merely to confute you in your own W
here ſuppoſed, that the Crown had been
ill adviſed, as to grant Charters to the Co
nies ſo unconſtitutional and illegal, as th
undoubtedly muſt have been; — yet
Fact itſelf is far otherwiſe *; for no ſu
Charters were ever granted. Nay, many
your Colony Charters aſſert quite the co
trary, by containing expreſs Reſervations

* Our former Princes claimed a Right, and freque
exerciſed the Power of levying Taxes, without the Con
of Parliament. But upon ſettling the Colonies, this ſupp
Right, which coſt Charles I. his Crown, and his
was not inſiſted on in any of the Charters, and was expre
given up in that which was granted to Lord Baltimore
Maryland. Now this Clauſe, which is nothing more
the Renunciation of *obſolete* Prerogative, is quoted in
News Papers, as if it was a Renunciation of the Right
Parliament to raiſe Taxes.× Whereas the King in
Charter ſtipulated only *for himſelf, his Heirs, and Succeſ*
not to raiſe Taxes by virtue of the Prerogative Royal: w
certainly he might do; and which was very proper t
done for the Encouragement and Security of a new Colo
But he could not ſtipulate for the Parliament; and ind
he did not attempt to do it.

P

What Stuff! Why may not an American plead for the just Prerogatives of the Crown? It is not a just Prerogative of the Crown to give the Subjects Leave to settle in a foreign Country, if they think it necessary to ask such Leave? Was the Parliament at all considered or consulted in making these first Settlements? or did any Lawyer then think it necessary

× It was not a renunciation of a Right of Parliament; There was no need of such a Renunciation, for Parliament had not then pretended to such a Right.

But since the Royal Faith was pledg'd by the King for himself & his Successors, how can any succeeding King, without violating that Faith, ever give his Assent to an Act of Parliament for such Taxation?

× A Fib, Mr Dean; In one Charter only, & that a late one, is the Parliament mentioned: And the right reserved is only that of laying Duties on Commodities imported from the Colony or exported to it. —



'arliamentary Rights, particularly that great
ne of levying Taxes.× And those Charters
which do not make such Provisoes in ex-
ress Terms, must be supposed virtually to
nply them; because the Law and Consti-
ition will not allow, that the King can do
nore either at home or abroad, by the Pre-
ogative Royal, than the Law and Constitu-
on authorize him to do.×

Suppositions & Implications will not weigh in these important Cases. —

× No Law or Constitution forbad the King's doing what he did in granting these Charters.

However, if you are still doubtful, and if
ou would wish to have a Confirmation of
his Argument by some plain Fact, some
riking Proof, and visible Example;—I will
ive you one; and such an one too, as shall
onvince you, if any thing can, of the Folly
nd Absurdity of your Positions: the City of
ondon, for instance,—a Body Politic as
espectable, without Offence, as the greatest
f your Colonies with regard to *Property*,
nd superior to many of them with respect to
*Numbers*;— this great City, I say, the Me-
ropolis of the whole British Empire, hath
ong enjoyed, before the Colonies were ever
hought of, the threefold Power of Juris-
liction,—Legislation,—and Taxation in cer-
ain Cases: but no Man in his Senses ever
et supposed, that the City of London either
was, or could be exempted by these Char-
ers from Parliamentary Jurisdiction, or Par-
iamentary Taxes; and if any Citizen should

This Instance would be something, if London was not within the Realm, whereas the Colonies are without; and therefore 'tis nothing to the purpose, convinces no American of any thing but the pert positiveness & Ignorance of the Author. —

March y^e 24 : 1760 - - -

Went to Meeting this Morning: divers Testimonyes deliverd, — R Rawle, Catty Howell, ~~and~~ Sally Smith, from Burlinton, and H Callender drank tea at A Warners — Hannah Hicks, Mary Rhoades, and Anna Pole came after, and spent some little time with us. — — — — — —

25th:

Went to meeting this Morning, John Storer, with several other Frd^s. appeard in testimony, Mary Kirby concluded the meeting in Prayer, went after dinner to Smiths to buy cruels, from thence went to Uncles, and to Betsy Moodes, had a long confab in the counsel Chamber, stay'd tea there, call'd again at Uncles and at Sam^l. Sansoms, at F Rawles, and at Jos^a. Howells, then came home, was told that Polly was at Neigh^r. Callenders, went to her, and stay'd supper there, Bobby Smith came home with us. — — — ————

26

Spent this afternoon at W^m. Fishers, with R. Callender, Anna Warner Sen^r. — y^e Evening we spent at Jos^a. Howells, Jos^h. Radolph came home with us

March y^e 27 : 1760 -

Went to Meeting this Morning, call'd after at Isaac Howells, Hannah Hicks dinn'd at A Warners, she and George Bound, drank Tea with us — — — — — — — —

28th:

Went to Monthly Meeting this Morning, 4 Couples past, Viz^t. Ben^n. Swett and Sus^h. Siddon, Ruban Hanes, and M Wister, Jos^h. Drinker & H Hart, the other couple unknown by me, call'd after I left meeting at John Searsons, to see Molly, who has been unwell, — Betsy & Hannah Moode, came to our house after dinner stay'd but a little time Hannah Hicks call'd in the Evening, Polly and self, took a walk after she was gone, to Tho^s. Says — and to Uncles, Charles came home with us.

29

Went out after Dinner, with sister, call'd at Isaac Howells, at Uncle Jerviss, and at Wades Shop, drank Tea at B Moodes with Nurse Mary: spent part of the Evening there, with Nancy Mitchel &c: Hannah Hicks, Polly Rhoades, and Polly Pemberton, call'd while we were out.

# 18. Elizabeth Sandwith Drinker (ca. 1735–1807)

## *Diaries*

1758–1807
Manuscript; ink on laid paper
6 7/16 × 4 inches (16.3 × 10.4 cm)

Elizabeth Sandwith Drinker Diaries [1760]
Gift of Mr. Henry S. Drinker, 1955–1957

The Historical Society of Pennsylvania is full of manuscripts that reveal what it was like to walk the streets of colonial Philadelphia. The diaries and letters of the early residents are an endless treasure trove of details documenting everyday life in the eighteenth-century city. The overwhelming majority of surviving material was written by wealthy white men who had access to education, ink, and abundant paper, none of which came cheaply. Almost nothing written by the city's enslaved Black population, who were often illiterate, survives. Rare also are the voices of white women.

This rarity makes Elizabeth Sandwith Drinker's diary an invaluable guide to city life from a woman's perspective. Its value lies not only in its detail but also in Drinker's remarkable consistency and longevity; she regularly wrote for over forty-nine years. Her most frequent entries come from her youth, an era before she married Henry Drinker and birthed numerous children. These notes, made two years after she started the diary and in her twenty-fifth year, present the routines of Philadelphia life for a young, wealthy Quaker woman in her courting years. Fans of Jane Austen's novels and Netflix's *Bridgerton* will find recognizable activities of single womanhood in this extract of entries from a week in late March of 1760. Elizabeth visited with friends, "drank tea at . . . warners," "went out after dinner, with sister, call'd at Isaac Howells . . . and at Wade's shop." As a well-off woman with a houseful of servants to cater to her needs, she could live a life of leisure.

Nevertheless, there is one prominent feature of Elizabeth's routines that is uniquely Philadelphian: her participation in weekly and monthly Quaker Meetings. As members of the city's Quaker elite, Elizabeth, her sister, and her social circle were part of an important religious group whose presence was connected to the colony's origins as a place of toleration that strongly shaped the tenor of urban life. Visitors from other colonies observed how Quakers' plain dress and objection to lavish entertainments—like balls and concerts—made social life in Philadelphia more sedate than even Puritan Boston and much less raucous than New York and Charleston.

Drinker's thousands of diary entries also show how the course of a woman's life worked with the era's revolutionary events to create an ever-changing experience of Philadelphia. In her childbearing years, Elizabeth went to live in the countryside, while during the Revolutionary War and occupation by the British, she took refuge in her town home as her Quaker pacifist husband suffered imprisonment by the Patriots. There she remained until her death, with Philadelphia growing around her from a modest colonial town to an industrializing city. The Drinker residence on Front Street was long ago demolished; a freeway now stands in its place. Through Elizabeth's diaries, however, one can get some sense of what it was like to live in early Philadelphia, both a typical and an atypical eighteenth-century town.

EMMA HART

## 19. **Phillis Wheatley** (1753–1784)

### *Poems on Various Subjects, Religious and Moral*

1773
Published by Archibald Bell
Engraving (frontispiece); laid paper bound in full brown calf with gilt border (volume)
7 × 4 13⁄16 inches (17.7 × 12.2 cm)

### *Phillis Wheatley Letter to Samuel Hopkins*

February 9, 1774
Manuscript; ink on laid paper
9 5⁄16 × 7 ½ inches (23.7 × 19.0 cm)

Simon Gratz Autograph Collection [0250B]
Gift of Simon Gratz

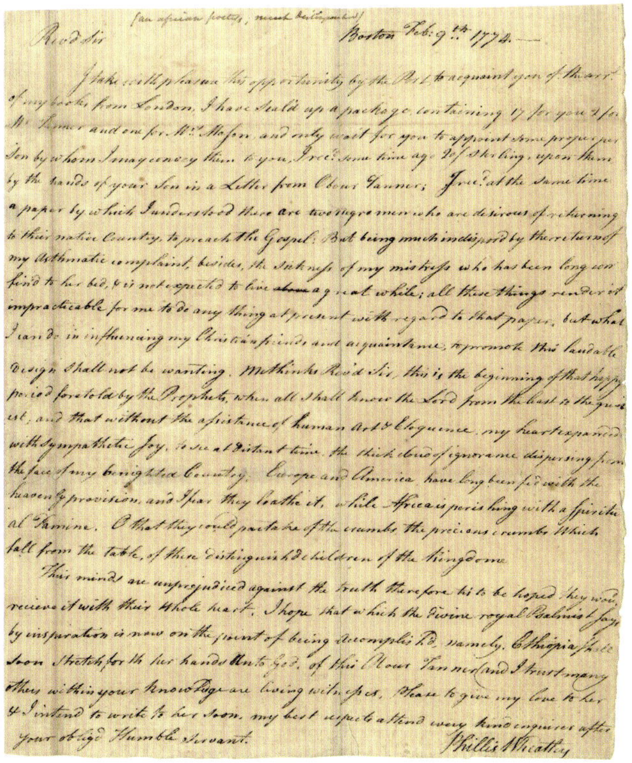

(an african poetess, much distinguished)

Revd Sir Boston Feb: 9th 1774 —

I take with pleasure this opportunity by the Post, to acquaint you of the arrl. of my books from London. I have sealed up a package containing 17 for you 2 for Mr Tanner and one for Mrs Mason, and only wait for you to appoint some proper person by whom I may convey them to you. I recd. some time ago 20/ sterling, upon them by the hands of your Son in a Letter from Obour Tanner; I recd. at the same time a paper by which I understood there are two negro men who are desirous of returning to their native Country, to preach the Gospel. But being much indisposed by the return of my Asthmatic complaint, besides, the sickness of my mistress who has been long confin'd to her bed, & is not expected to live ~~long~~ a great while; all these things render it impracticable for me to do any thing at present with regard to that paper, but what I can do in influencing my Christian friends and acquaintance, to promote this laudable Design shall not be wanting. Methinks Revd Sir, this is the beginning of that happy period foretold by the Prophets, when all shall know the Lord from the least to the greatest, and that without the assistance of human Art & Eloquence. my heart expanded with sympathetic Joy, to see at distant time, the thick cloud of ignorance dispersing from the face of my benighted Country. Europe and America have long been fed with the heavenly provision, and I fear they loathe it, while Africa is perishing with a spiritual Famine. O that they could partake of the crumbs, the precious crumbs Which fall from the table, of these distinguish'd children of the kingdom.

Their minds are unprejudiced against the truth therefore tis to be hoped they would recieve it with their Whole heart. I hope that which the divine royal Psalmist says by inspiration is now on the point of being accomplish'd, namely, Ethiopia shall soon stretch forth her hands unto God. of this Obour Tanner (and I trust many others within your knowledge) are living witnesses. Please to give my love to her & I intend to write to her soon. my best respects attend every kind enquirer after your oblig'd Humble Servant.

Phillis Wheatley

Phillis Wheatley's volume of poems, the first book published by an African or person of African descent in North America and the third by a woman, formed an important entry in emerging debates over slavery. The demonstration of learning, piety, and patriotism, as well as the forthright criticisms of racism and enslavement, found in Wheatley's poems challenged the racial proslavery arguments that plantation lobbyists like Edward Long (1734–1813) made in the wake of the decision in *Somerset v. Steuart* (1772), which saved the fugitive James Somerset from being shipped from London to Jamaica. Wheatley's pose in the frontispiece image, probably engraved from a painting by her fellow Afro-Bostonian Scipio Moorhead (b. 1750), depicts her as inspired to write from above and from books close at hand and evokes similar portrait prints of both Alexander Pope and that of Wheatley's patron, Selina Hastings, Countess of Huntingdon. This leader of the Methodist "Connexion" in England, who had underwritten the first published English slave narrative the previous year, had suggested a portrait as necessary to defuse skepticism that she had not actually written the verses.

For Wheatley, the publication of her book and the writing of letters served both personal and political ends. Wheatley had already achieved a significant degree of celebrity in New England and beyond. Her manuscripts circulated near Philadelphia as early as 1767. Reverend Samuel Hopkins, a critic of slavery who was involved in efforts to evangelize enslaved people in Newport, Rhode Island, and Africa, identified her at the top of this letter as "the African poetess, much distinguished." Wheatley's letter responds to his printed proposal to send African-born missionaries from his congregation to Cape Coast Castle to assist Phillip Quaque, an English-educated ordained minister already in residence there. Her endorsement of the scheme in this letter excited Hopkins so much that he included her extended blurb in his next publicity effort without her permission.

Yet Wheatley's letter is also testimony to her multiple agendas. She starts not with praise of missionaries but rather with business: Hopkins had assisted in the distribution of her books, which included cash payments that she hoped would finance her future as a free individual. She also refers to her African friend Obour Tanner (1750–1835), praising her and other members of Hopkins's congregation as "living witnesses" of what piety might do for Africans who may be "perishing with a Spiritual Famine" but who are also, she writes pointedly, "unprejudiced." She ends by asking Reverend Hopkins to "give my love" to Tanner and to convey that "I intend to write her very soon." This letter is a stunning demonstration of Black American politics at its inception, African American women's networks, and the efforts of individuals like Wheatley and Tanner to make Christianity their own.

DAVID WALDSTREICHER

# 20. **Charles Thomson** (1729–1824)

## *Secret Journal of Congress, Volume A*

---

1776
Manuscript; ink on laid paper
5 15⁄16 × 3 11⁄16 inches (15.1 × 9.4 cm)

Charles Thomson Papers [0658]

No single person was as much a witness to the American Revolution and the founding as Charles Thomson. As secretary of Congress from 1774 until 1789, Thomson had a front-row seat to the most formative years of the country's history. His tenure covered the arguments that surrounded the Declaration of Independence, the tumultuous war, the difficult first years of nationhood under the Articles of Confederation, and finally the Constitution. For those fourteen years, Thomson sat studiously listening to and recording the debates that riled and ultimately forged a new nation. Yet throughout all this tumult, Thomson remained a stalwart. He was a trusted and respected figure and a friend and confidante to many who passed through Congress's halls, no matter their political affiliation. He was also privy to all the petty squabbles between individuals and among colonies, the feuds and rifts that divided rather than united people, and the backroom dealings needed to make things work.

In fact, he saw and heard so much that as he neared the end of his life, he did the unthinkable. He burned many of his papers. He did so, he said, because he did not want to "contradict all the histories of the great events of the Revolution. Let the world admire the supposed wisdom and valor of our great men. Perhaps they may adopt the qualities that have been ascribed to them, and thus good may be done. I shall not undeceive future generations." In other words, Thomson knew the messy underpinnings of what made the country, and he preferred the cleaner story. According to Thomson's rationale, this more pristine and idealized version, with its great men pursuing principle and virtue over self-interest, would serve a better civic purpose for future generations who might try to emulate these tales. Better that they try to do that than pursue the real motivations he witnessed, Thomson reasoned. Perhaps much to his dismay, historians have been trying to recover the story he destroyed ever since.

One of the documents that escaped the flames was Thomson's "Secret Journals of the Continental Congress." Today, these manuscripts filled with Thomson's handwriting sit securely preserved in the vaults of the Historical Society of Pennsylvania. One would hope that they would give a hint of what Thomson saw and had expected to destroy for posterity. Unfortunately, they are not quite that. Instead, they contain minutes of congressional proceedings that Thomson deemed unsuitable for public consumption at the time of their writing.

As it turns out, the Continental Congress was committed to transparent government and ordered that their proceedings be published in a timely manner. They also knew, however, that some deliberations and actions needed to remain private, lest they betray military strategies or diplomatic secrets to their enemies. The secret journals contain

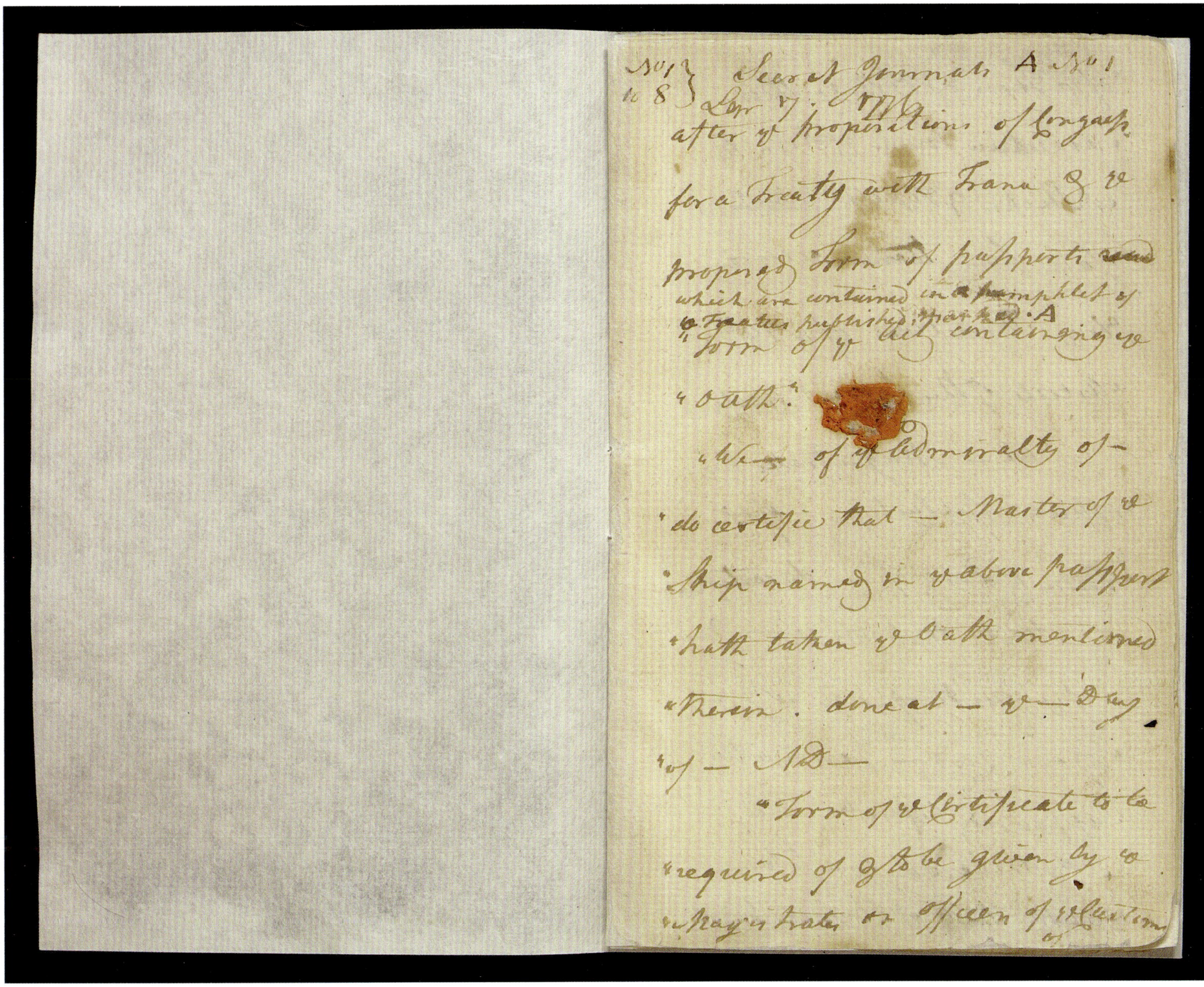


much of that classified material but also items deemed too mundane. These confidential minutes thus complement Thomson's official rough minutes of meetings that served as the basis for the printed volumes of *The Journals of Continental Congress* that the Congress commissioned and that Thomson oversaw. Congress authorized the publication of these "secret journals" in 1820 to add to what was made available earlier.

Scholars who have pored over these volumes, comparing them to the official versions published by Congress at the time and Thomson's own rough minutes, have found important omissions and changes. In 1897 HSP published a detailed comparison of the printed and manuscript versions of Thomson's various journals of Congress. The author wryly concluded that even though there have been numerous editions of Thomson's journals published, no complete account had yet been produced because of the selective editing that went into every version and their occasional contradictions. In fact, with so many editions and such heavy intervention, the original manuscripts, residing safely on the shelves of HSP, likely remain the best source for someone looking to understand the early government of the United States.

PATRICK SPERO

# 21. *Declaration of Independence, Printer's Proof*

1776
Printed by John Dunlap (1747–1812)
Broadside; letterpress on laid paper
9 5/16 × 14 3/4 inches (23.6 × 37.5 cm)

Historical Society of Pennsylvania Treasures Collection
Gift of Frank M. Etting, 1891

First printings of the Declaration of Independence are extremely rare and valuable. Of an estimated two hundred copies emanating from John Dunlap's press the evening after the final adoption of the text, only twenty-six are known to have survived. Rarer still is the printer's proof that was first pulled from the press to verify correct typesetting. Only a single copy of that exists, bequeathed to the Historical Society of Pennsylvania in 1891 by Frank M. Etting, a Philadelphia lawyer and collector.

The Declaration had culminated from actions that began with debate over Richard Henry Lee's Resolution of Independence, offered to Congress on June 7, 1776. The issue was tabled until July 1, partly to buy time to achieve unanimity among all the states. Assuming the resolution would be approved when debate resumed, and time being of the essence, on June 11 a committee of five was created to prepare a statement justifying the break. Benjamin Franklin, John Adams, Thomas Jefferson, Roger Sherman, and Robert R. Livingston began that task by choosing the thirty-three-year-old Jefferson to write the statement. Jefferson wrote several rough drafts and showed them to Franklin and Adams, both of whom suggested minor changes. The committee submitted the final version as its report on June 28. Lee's resolution was debated all day on July 1 and was approved the next day.

After considering Jefferson's draft for two days, deleting significant parts, Congress heard Jefferson's final reading of the revised report and approved it late in the afternoon of July 4. Desiring to spread the word with all due haste, Congress directed that it be printed immediately for widespread distribution to the states and the army. Evidence strongly suggests that Jefferson as chief author took it right away to Congress's official printer, the young John Dunlap. Witnesses recalled a frantic race to set type and complete a press run that produced perhaps two hundred copies overnight, all of which were then distributed over the signature of John Hancock, president of Congress. Newspapers throughout the new nation quickly reproduced the broadside, enabling it to be read by all citizens.

Jefferson's manuscript, consisting of four handwritten pages, doubtless was given to more than one typesetter for composition, contributing to the loss of the only copy of what Congress had approved. The single surviving proof page reveals that its typesetter did what good typesetters are supposed to do: set into type exactly what the copy contains. The proof shows only the first part of Jefferson's manuscript and contains scattered quotation marks that represented breath marks the author had penned as elocution aids, a practice found elsewhere in Jefferson's papers. Jefferson had these extraneous marks removed, and the press run of the broadside then produced an accurate copy of the approved text.

The manuscript from which type was set has been missing since the night it was taken to Dunlap's shop, resulting therefore in the partial proof at HSP being the only extant bridge between the original handwritten Declaration and Dunlap's printed broadside announcing the momentous news.

CHARLES T. CULLEN

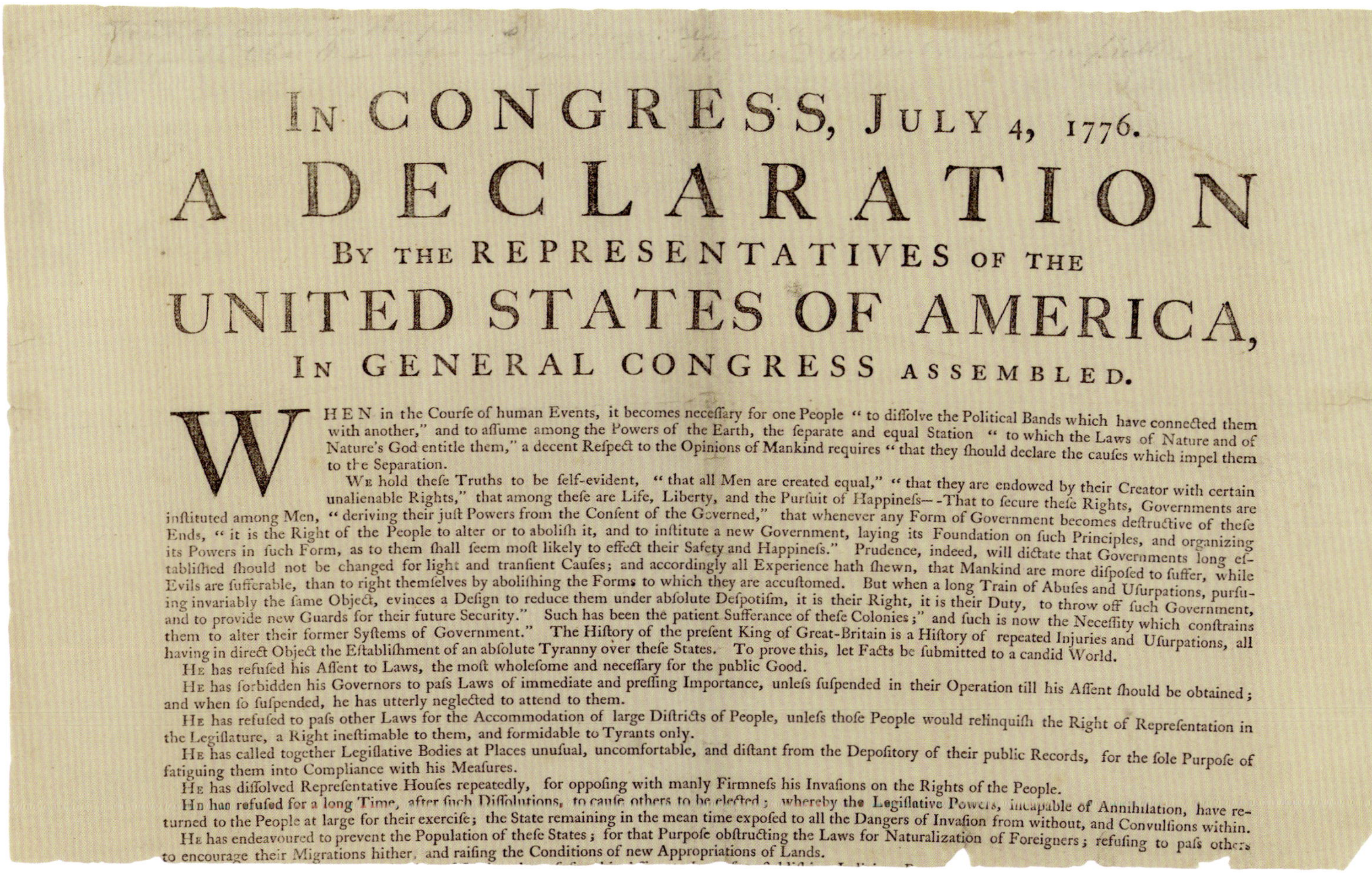

IN CONGRESS, JULY 4, 1776.

# A DECLARATION

BY THE REPRESENTATIVES OF THE

## UNITED STATES OF AMERICA,

IN GENERAL CONGRESS ASSEMBLED.

WHEN in the Courſe of human Events, it becomes neceſſary for one People "to diſſolve the Political Bands which have connected them with another," and to aſſume among the Powers of the Earth, the ſeparate and equal Station "to which the Laws of Nature and of Nature's God entitle them," a decent Reſpect to the Opinions of Mankind requires "that they ſhould declare the cauſes which impel them to the Separation.

WE hold theſe Truths to be ſelf-evident, "that all Men are created equal," "that they are endowed by their Creator with certain unalienable Rights," that among theſe are Life, Liberty, and the Purſuit of Happineſs--That to ſecure theſe Rights, Governments are inſtituted among Men, "deriving their juſt Powers from the Conſent of the Governed," that whenever any Form of Government becomes deſtructive of theſe Ends, "it is the Right of the People to alter or to aboliſh it, and to inſtitute a new Government, laying its Foundation on ſuch Principles, and organizing its Powers in ſuch Form, as to them ſhall ſeem moſt likely to effect their Safety and Happineſs." Prudence, indeed, will dictate that Governments long eſtabliſhed ſhould not be changed for light and tranſient Cauſes; and accordingly all Experience hath ſhewn, that Mankind are more diſpoſed to ſuffer, while Evils are ſufferable, than to right themſelves by aboliſhing the Forms to which they are accuſtomed. But when a long Train of Abuſes and Uſurpations, purſuing invariably the ſame Object, evinces a Deſign to reduce them under abſolute Deſpotiſm, it is their Right, it is their Duty, to throw off ſuch Government, and to provide new Guards for their future Security." Such has been the patient Sufferance of theſe Colonies;" and ſuch is now the Neceſſity which conſtrains them to alter their former Syſtems of Government." The Hiſtory of the preſent King of Great-Britain is a Hiſtory of repeated Injuries and Uſurpations, all having in direct Object the Eſtabliſhment of an abſolute Tyranny over theſe States. To prove this, let Facts be ſubmitted to a candid World.

HE has refuſed his Aſſent to Laws, the moſt wholeſome and neceſſary for the public Good.

HE has forbidden his Governors to paſs Laws of immediate and preſſing Importance, unleſs ſuſpended in their Operation till his Aſſent ſhould be obtained; and when ſo ſuſpended, he has utterly neglected to attend to them.

HE has refuſed to paſs other Laws for the Accommodation of large Diſtricts of People, unleſs thoſe People would relinquiſh the Right of Repreſentation in the Legiſlature, a Right ineſtimable to them, and formidable to Tyrants only.

HE has called together Legiſlative Bodies at Places unuſual, uncomfortable, and diſtant from the Depoſitory of their public Records, for the ſole Purpoſe of fatiguing them into Compliance with his Meaſures.

HE has diſſolved Repreſentative Houſes repeatedly, for oppoſing with manly Firmneſs his Invaſions on the Rights of the People.

HE has refuſed for a long Time, after ſuch Diſſolutions, to cauſe others to be elected; whereby the Legiſlative Powers, incapable of Annihilation, have returned to the People at large for their exerciſe; the State remaining in the mean time expoſed to all the Dangers of Invaſion from without, and Convulſions within.

HE has endeavoured to prevent the Population of theſe States; for that Purpoſe obſtructing the Laws for Naturalization of Foreigners; refuſing to paſs others to encourage their Migrations hither, and raiſing the Conditions of new Appropriations of Lands.

## 22. **John Dickinson** (1732–1808)

## *Articles of Confederation, Draft*

1776
Manuscript; ink on laid paper
12 3/4 × 7 15/16 inches (32.3 × 20.1 cm)

R. R. Logan Collection of John Dickinson Papers [0383]
Gift of Robert Restalrig Logan, 1928

## *Articles of Confederation, Draft Religious Liberty Clause*

1776
Manuscript; ink on laid paper
6 1/4 × 7 13/16 inches (15.9 × 19.8 cm)

R. R. Logan Collection of John Dickinson Papers [0383]
Gift of Robert Restalrig Logan, 1928

John Dickinson's draft of the Articles of Confederation from June 1776 is one of the most remarkable documents of the American Revolution. A chief reason Dickinson did not want independence was that he believed America was not ready. Among other deficiencies, it lacked a constitution providing a governing structure and protection of fundamental rights. As the leading member of the drafting committee, Dickinson crafted a document that included provisions necessary for the nation and individuals. He likely had Benjamin Franklin's 1775 version before him, and while he repeated some sections, his draft contained many significant departures. First, it created a strong central government with the states subordinate to the Union, providing that colonies would retain sovereignty "in all Matters that shall not interfere with the Articles of this Confederation." Second, using the Pennsylvania 1701 Charter of Privileges as a guide, he included protections for religious dissenters, freezing the laws of the colonies at their present state, so some would keep full religious liberty while others would retain toleration. This clause contained a striking novelty that was one of the most radical acts of the Revolution. For the first time in any Anglo-American constitution, gender-inclusive language ensured protection of women's religious rights. A draft of the provision, also at HSP, reveals that Dickinson first wrote "his or their," then changed it to "his or her" (line 2). Further, his use of the term "Practice" (line 3) in describing the religious rights to be protected meant that women's public speech would also

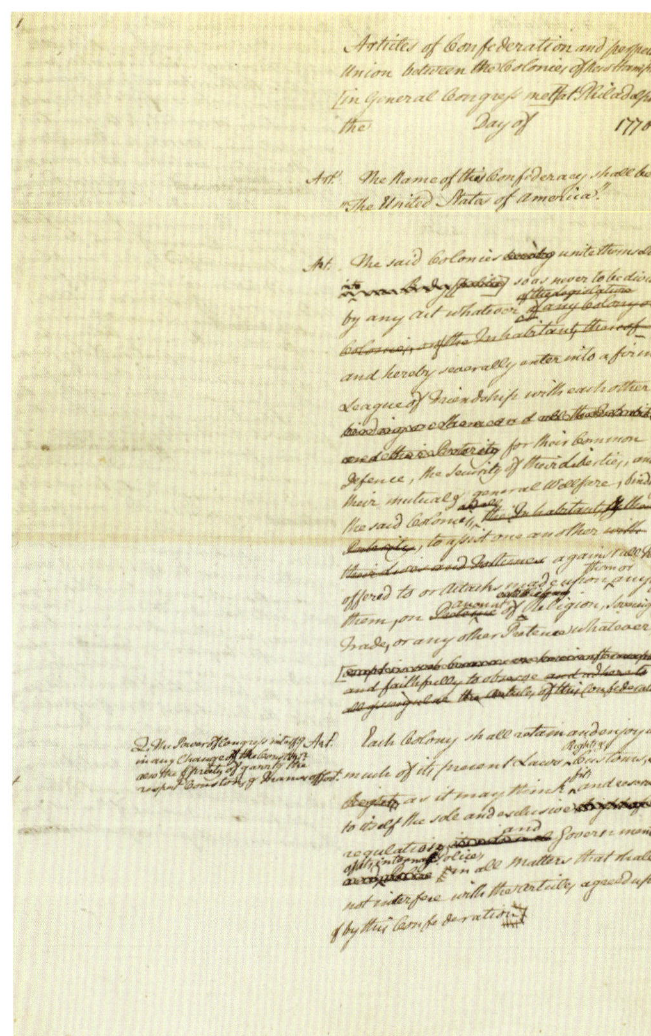

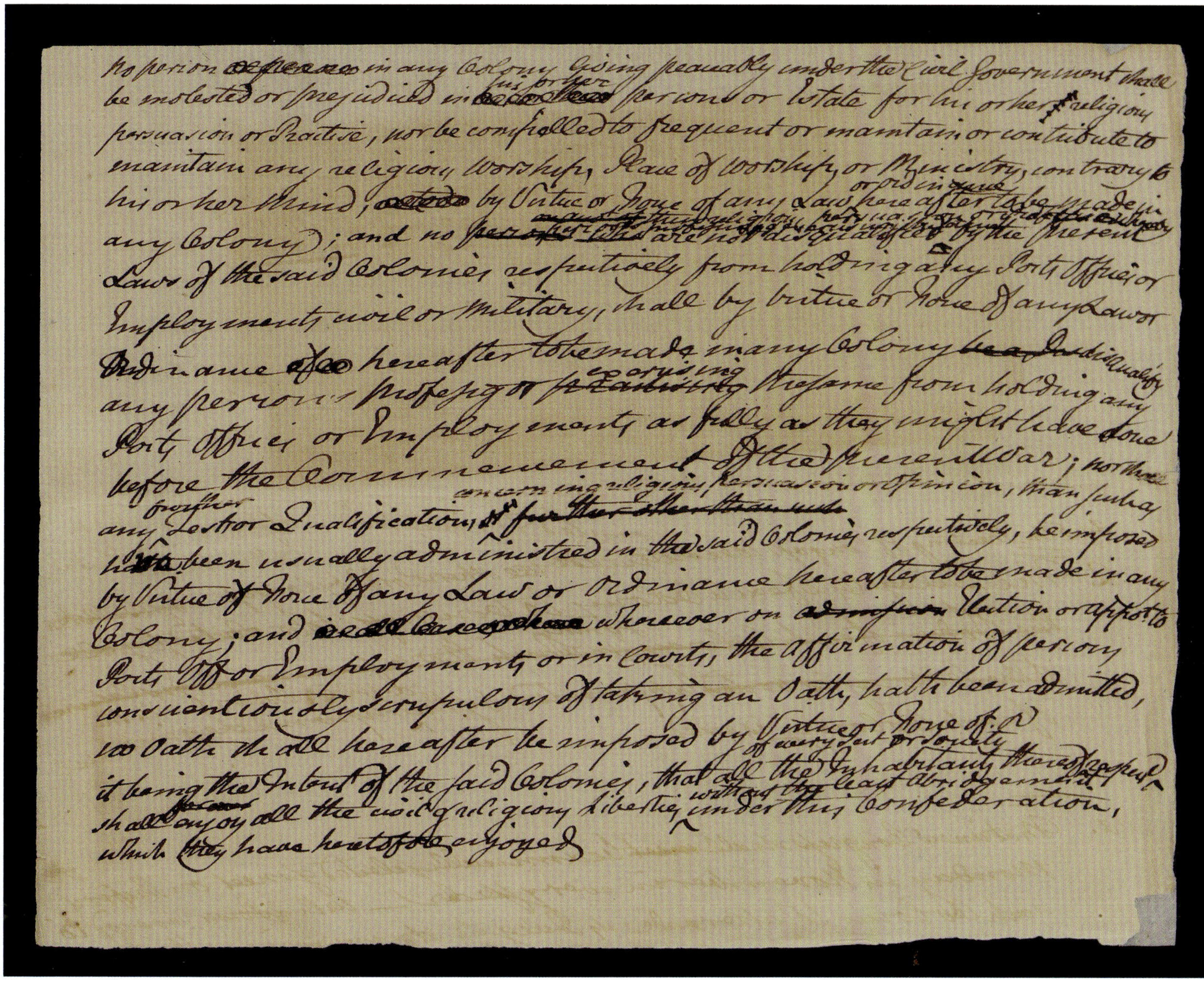

be guaranteed. Dickinson's female relatives were all Quakers, and Quaker women had always been ministers who preached publicly. Third, he would allow Congress to raise troops in a state without the aid or approval of the legislatures. None of these clauses were retained in the version ratified in 1781.

Other new provisions added by Dickinson that did appear include: prohibiting the acceptance of foreign emoluments by public officers; free trade between the states and foreign nations (though his ban on foreign exchange that interfered with the Union was not retained); prohibiting standing armies and requiring militias; prohibiting states from engaging in anything but defensive war upon imminent attack; and reserving to Congress the powers of emitting currency, establishing rules for prizes, and other maritime matters. He expressed myriad concerns in marginal queries, many of which were ignored, including whether states should be guaranteed their respective constitutions, how far states may interfere in Indian affairs, and whether Congress could assume powers held by Parliament, such as imposing duties to regulate trade or levying taxes to raise revenue. A topic that only Dickinson raised in any of the versions of the Articles throughout the process from 1775 to 1781 was slavery. He initially queried whether Congress ought to define and regulate the practice. In a subsequent draft, he asked, "Should there not be an Article to prevent those who are hereafter brought into these Colonies, from being held in Slavery within the Colonies?" Overall, Dickinson's draft of the Articles of Confederation would have protected rights of individuals and created national unity.

JANE E. CALVERT

A Diary of trifling Occurences

Volume the 2^d^ Begun 1^st^ M^o^ 12^th^ Day & concluded 5^th^ M^o^ 11^th^ 1777

1^st^ month 12^th^ Day 1777

Morning went to Meeting W^m^ Brown preached, Betty Morris prayd Dined & drank Tea with only my Tommy, evening went to Meeting which was silent supd with my Tommy

2^d^ Day. all Day at Home busy at Work, Sister Gilpin drank Tea with us, my Tommy reading to me in the Evening in Lyttelton's History of England. heard to Day that the Americans had retaken Elizabeth Town with a Sloop of Soldiers Cloaths & that Lord Cornwallis had sent to General Washington to desire a cessation of Arms for three Months, this News affected my mind as every little victory or even fancied

# 23. **Sarah Logan Fisher** (1751–1796)

## *Diaries*

1776–95
Manuscript; ink on laid paper bound in paste paper and marbled paper boards
6 5/16 × 4 1/8 inches (16.1 × 10.5 cm)

Sarah Logan Fisher Diaries [Am .06765]
Gift of Benjamin R. Cadwalader, 1965

Sarah Fisher's diaries, now neatly bound into twenty-four volumes, probably began as a series of homemade booklets made by folding small stacks of paper in half, turning them sideways, and adding a stitch or two at the crease. On January 12, 1777, on the first blank page of volume two, Fisher wrote: "A Diary of trifling Occurences [*sic*]." That title seems ironic given the fact that the American Revolution soon burst onto the opposite page. "Heard the Americans had retaken Elizabeth Town," Fisher wrote. That was not good news for her or her husband, Thomas, a Quaker pacifist who would soon be imprisoned for refusing to support the war.

The first five volumes of Fisher's diaries, which extend from October 1776 to August 1778, have been widely cited by historians, perhaps because they were transcribed and published in 1958. The remaining nineteen volumes have received scant attention. That may be because over time Fisher came to believe that public events were themselves "trifling Occurences." As a result, the entries in her late diaries move forward from "1st day" to "7th day" in spiraling loops that make it difficult to discern shifts from one month to another, let alone draw quick connections to landmark events in Philadelphia or Atlantic history. Yet for those willing to submit to her rhythms, the rewards are significant.

From 1776 onward, there are two constants in Fisher's diaries: the names of those with whom she "dined" and "drank tea" and daily reports on her own physical and mental health. She used these markers the way other diarists noted the weather. But together they highlight a central tension in Fisher's life between social duty and personal well-being. For historians, the consistency of such entries provides opportunities to map her changing social network, create a typology of Quaker obligation, and probe the connection between mind and body in eighteenth-century popular thought. As Fisher understood, "the mind & body are closely connected & my spirits are so weak that what affects the one greatly retards the recovery of the other."

Illness and the possibility of an early death were Fisher's constant companions, not only because she suffered from chronic ailments, including a recurring pain variously diagnosed as "a settled rheumatism" or "the flying gout," but because she lived in a setting plagued by both pestilence and war. In such a context, she constantly sought and failed to achieve Quaker "quietness." She came close in 1795 when she risked a difficult journey to the New York Society of Friends' Yearly Meeting. There, in whispered encounters that often occurred at dinner or teatime, she found a brief respite from anxiety in the earnest words of intrepid female ministers known as "traveling Friends," some from America, others from Britain. Their advice ultimately transformed the lives of at least two of her children, Hannah Logan Fisher Smith (1777–1846) and William Logan Fisher (1781–1862), whose writings provide a nineteenth-century context for understanding their mother's place in a larger religious and cultural transition.

LAUREL THATCHER ULRICH

# 24. **Antoine-Jean-Louis Le Bègue de Presle Duportail** (1743–1802)

## *Brouillion du Plan du Camp de Vallée Forge*

ca. 1778
Ink on laid paper
11 × 15 3/8 inches (28.0 × 39.1 cm)

Lewis Nicola Maps and Plans of the Revolution [Am .602]
Presented by the Willard Estate, 1908

For someone with a very precise name, Antoine-Jean-Louis Le Bègue de Presle Duportail, the Historical Society of Pennsylvania's description of the "Duportail map" is quite vague: "A detailed but unfinished manuscript map showing the encampment and earlier fortifications. Was probably prepared in December 1777."

What is known is that Duportail was a French engineer who served in the Continental Army as a colonel, brigadier general, commander, and major general with the Corps of Engineers from 1777 to 1781. The Vallée Forge map at HSP has long been attributed, by staff, to him—or at least has been known as the "Duportail map," though one history of the Society's collections indicates that the map was simply "owned by General Duportail." Authorship aside, there is no equivocation about the fine collection of HSP's French maps of the American Revolution: Camp of Valley Forge, Battle of Trenton, Attack on Fort Mercer, Forts Mercer and Mifflin on the Delaware, and Retreat from Barren Hill. Identifying the cartographers of these maps is only one aspect of the history of collecting at HSP. One interesting result of the process of creating this anniversary book is discovering all the idiosyncrasies of HSP's documentation practices.

Everywhere the Duportail map is listed (for example, in HSP's histories, card catalogues, or *Finding Philadelphia's Past* exhibition guide), it appears as "Plan Du Camp de vallié forge." But when one looks at the actual map, "Vallié" is clearly spelled "Vallée." How did HSP get something so simple so wrong? The actual written name is "Brouillion du plan du camp de Vallée Forge" (or Draft of the plan of Valley Forge).

Metadata aside, the history of the map's owner and possible cartographer, General Duportail, is worthy of note. While encamped at Valley Forge, he stayed at the home of Welsh Quaker John Harvard, returning to France after the

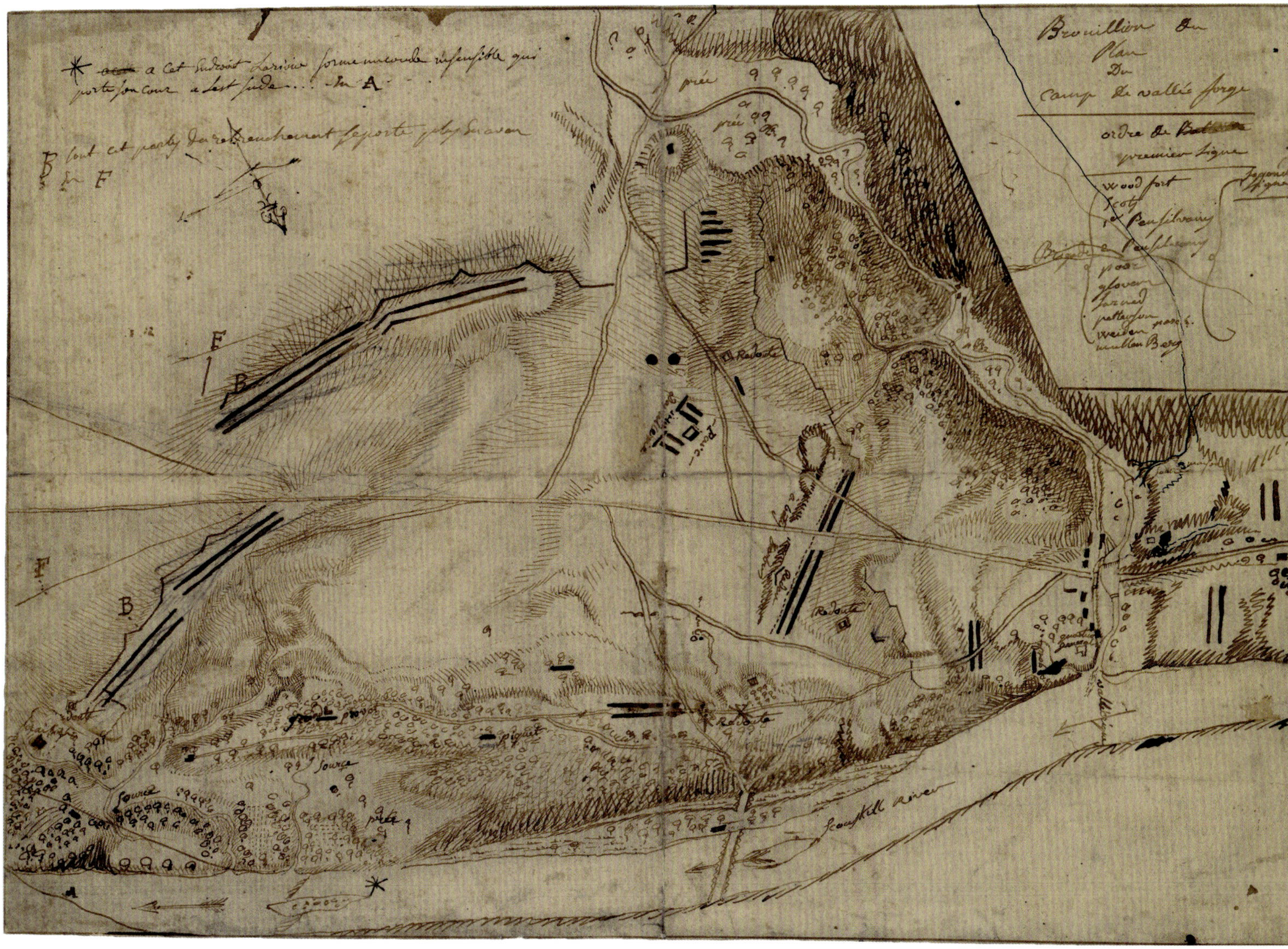


war ended. For a while he was a part of the French Revolution and then very much not part of it—returning to America to avoid the guillotine. He bought a house near the original encampment at Valley Forge. After Napoleon's rise to power, Duportail once more decided to return to France but died at sea on his way there.

Lawrence McCormick purchased the John Harvard family farm in 1903, renaming it Cressbrook. It was there that the Duportail map was discovered and eventually donated to HSP. However, even those seemingly simple statements have intrigue. A website promoting the "Duportail House" at Cressbrook Farm states that the map was "found in the rafters" during a renovation just after McCormick bought the property. While that does have a very *Antiques Roadshow* soundbite, like similar conclusions from the show, it may just remain a mystery. LEE ARNOLD

---

Other notable francophone American Revolutionary War manuscript maps at the Historical Society of Pennsylvania are *Plan de la bataille de Trenton,* 24 Nov. 1776 [Maps and Plans of the Revolution, Am .602 p. 6]; Ésquisse *du fort Mercer attaqué,* Oct. 1777 [Maps and Plans of the Revolution, Am .602 p. 29]; Ésquisse *des forts sur la Delaware, forts Mercer et Mifflin,* Nov. 1777 [Maps and Plans of the Revolution, Am .602 p. 28]; and *Plan de la retraite de Barrenhill en Pensilvanie,* 28 May 1778 [Maps and Plans of the Revolution, Am .602 p. 4].

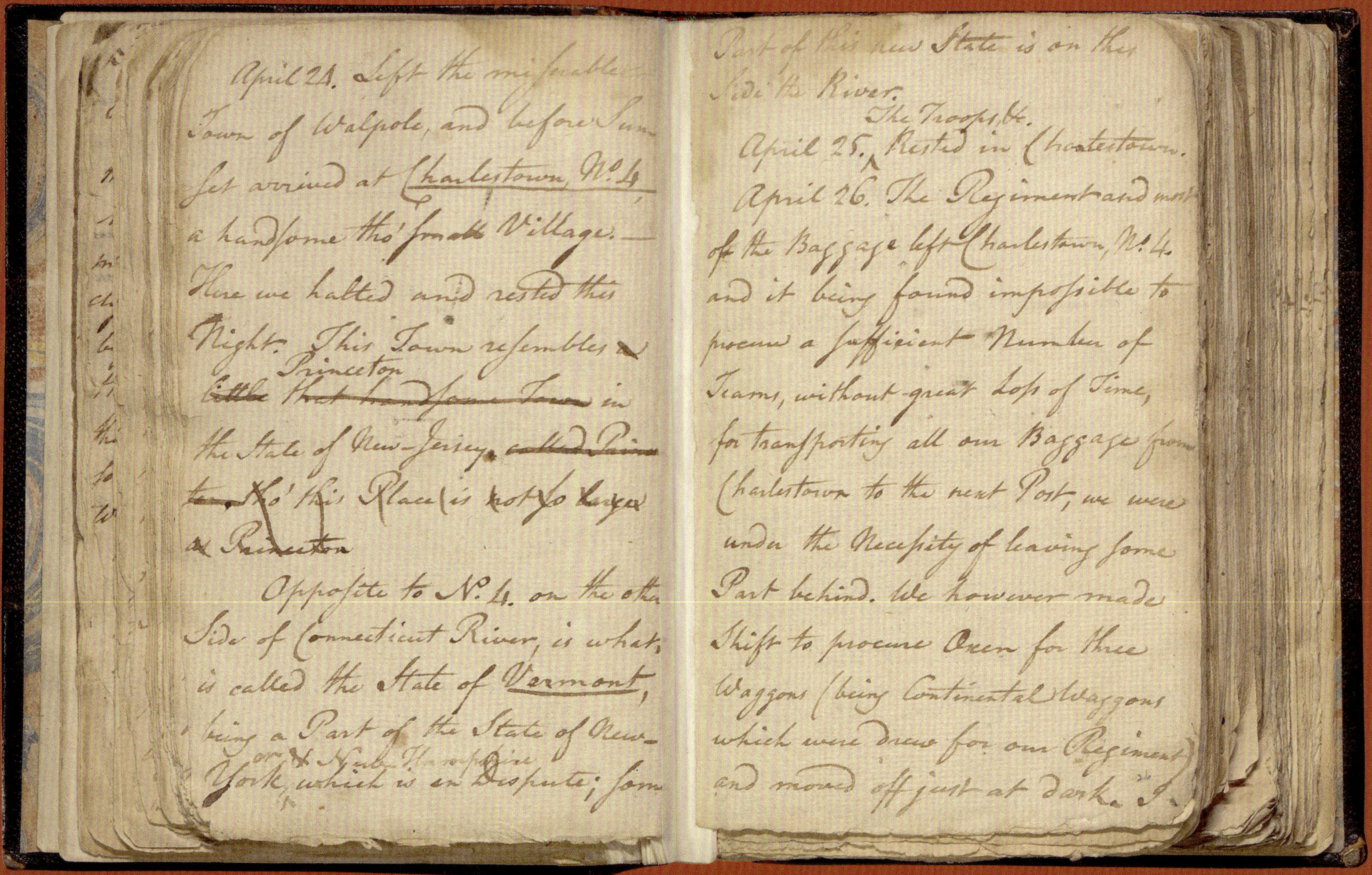
April 24. Left the miserable Town of Walpole, and before Sun-set arrived at Charlestown, No. 4, a handsome tho' small Village. — Here we halted and rested the Night. This Town resembles ~~a little that handsome Town~~ Princeton in the State of New-Jersey, ~~called Princeton~~ tho' this Place is not so large ~~as Princeton~~

Opposite to No. 4. on the other Side of Connecticut River, is what is called the State of Vermont, being a Part of the State of New-York or & New Hampshire which is in Dispute; some Part of this new State is on this Side the River.

April 25. The Troops, &c. Rested in Charlestown.

April 26. The Regiment and most of the Baggage left Charlestown, No. 4. and it being found impossible to procure a sufficient Number of Teams, without great Loss of Time, for transporting all our Baggage from Charlestown to the next Post, we were under the Necessity of leaving some Part behind. We however made Shift to procure Oxen for three Waggons (being Continental Waggons which were drew for our Regiment) and moved off just at dark. —

# 25. **John H. Hawkins** (b. ca. 1748)

## *Journal*

1777–82
Manuscript; ink on laid paper bound in half black leather and grain-cloth boards
6 7/8 × 4 5/16 inches (17.5 × 11.0 cm)

John H. Hawkins Journal [Am .0765]

A soldier's journal is a knapsack packed with ideas, observations, and experiences. John H. Hawkins made his by folding and cutting sheets into pages approximately 5 by 8 inches ("duodecimo"), which he filled while serving with the Second Canadian—Congress's Own—Regiment during the War for American Independence. His journal was a series of booklets, as were his copies of the regiment's orderly books. He carried them in a coat pocket or bundled with his stockings, knee buckles, pen, paper, ink, bits and bobs within the larger knapsack he slung over his shoulders. Someone later bound the booklets that survived the war into the leather-covered volume now at the Historical Society of Pennsylvania, preserved and ready to unpack.

Among the all-too-few journals and memoirs of those who marched with the Continental Army, the account by Hawkins is a standout for its descriptive passages. He did not record mileage but instead vignettes about the engaging people and events he encountered along those miles. He created a vivid travelogue that threaded through his more prosaic notes. Hawkins did not pen much about his personal affairs, but in a few of the tidbits and in editing his own writing—for he often crossed out and rewrote words and passages—he revealed something of himself.

A section from an earlier 1777 journal, tucked out of order into the bound volume, revealed Hawkins bemoaning the loss of his knapsack and its contents (including uniform items, a printed book, and memorandum with journal entries) as he vaulted fences to get away from "one of the ill-looking Highlanders" advancing on the regiment at the Battle of Brandywine. A 1778 snippet included a list of what was stolen from his pocket that March in Albany, New York: rosters, writings (one "by way of a journal"), a magazine and newspaper, and money. Those lists and other notes about visiting his "Typographical Brethren" in Philadelphia show us what was lost, but they also point to who and what he was. Likely born around 1748, Hawkins may have been a runaway printer's apprentice in 1768 who perhaps returned to complete his training. In January 1777, probably in Pennsylvania, he enlisted in the Second Canadian Regiment under an officer recruiting there and was ranked a sergeant until promoted to sergeant major in September 1778. He was with the regiment as it contributed to the victorious siege of Yorktown, Virginia, in 1781 and continued until furloughed at Pompton, New Jersey, in June or July 1783. Like so many other Continental Army veterans, Hawkins faded into the new nation, but unlike them, he left this record of his memories. HOLLY A. MAYER

Further related information in the Historical Society of Pennsylvania archives can be found in Hazen, Moses [Hawkins, John H. at Morristown] Orderly Books, 1 January–23 April 1780; 23 April–26 July 1780. Am .649, 2 vols., Second Canadian Regiment Orderly Books [Highland Dept.], 24 Feb. 1778–9 Sept. 1778; Sept. 1778–5 Aug. 1779. Am .632, 2 vols., and Hawkins, John H. "Memoranda, 1780." Am .6071.

# 26. *Benedict Arnold Paraded in Effigy in Philadelphia*

1780
Published by Steiner and Cist
Woodcut on laid paper
7 15⁄16 × 15 9⁄16 inches (20.2 × 39.5 cm) (open)

Foldout leaf in *Americanischer Haus- und Wirthschafts-Calender auf das 1781ste Jahr Christi Nach dem pennsylvanischen Horizont berechnet; jedoch in den angrenzenden Staaten ohne merklichen Unterscheid* [*sic*] *zu gebrauchen. Zum Zweytenmal heraus gegeben*

This Philadelphia woodcut from 1780 or 1781 by an unknown artist shows Benedict Arnold (1741–1801) on a cart, with the Devil seated behind him, being drawn toward his demise in the flames of a bonfire. Arnold's two-faced effigy rotates, and he holds a mask in his hand. Before him is an illuminated lantern with the names of Joshua Smith and Major John André, his co-conspirators, under a gallows (Arnold escaped to fight for the English, but André was hung, and Smith acquitted). In Arnold's hand is a letter of instructions from Beelzebub; the Devil himself is armed with a pitchfork and clutches a bag of gold. Militiamen on horseback and shouting boys join the parade while a fife and drum corps plays "The Rogues' March."

On September 27, 1780, news reached Philadelphia of Benedict Arnold's defection to the British. Arnold's command of the city had been controversial. He had profited personally from his garrison and maintained close relations with local Tories. Now he had been discovered trying to sell West Point to the English. On September 28, Philadelphians denounced Arnold's treachery by parading his effigy through the streets and burning it in a bonfire. To underline their repudiation, the city's revolutionaries organized a fuller, more elaborate procession for the night of September 30, featuring an illuminated float constructed by the artist and radical Charles Willson Peale.

Peale had witnessed similar performances singling out British officials for scorn and deprecation during the Stamp Act Riots in Boston. Effigy parades in the early Revolution grew out of the New England tradition of Pope's Night, which in turn descended from English Protestant celebrations of King James I's deliverance from the Guy Fawkes's Gunpowder Plot on November 5, 1605. On Pope's Night, crowds of working-class boys and young men dragged effigies of the Pope and the Devil through the streets on a cart, consigning them to flames amidst a night of brawling and drinking. Philadelphians accused Arnold of the most disgusting corruption by replicating this rough music and substituting him for the Pope. Peale's artistry enhanced the traditional refinements: the cart, devil, illumination, and the villain's double face.

Steiner and Cist's engraving was one of many similar depictions circulated by Philadelphia printers in their popular almanacs and broadsides. Printers may have hoped to mark September 30 as a new holiday celebrating loyalty and the ritual repudiation of traitors by including an engraving of Arnold's effigy in the indispensable calendars. Arnold was paraded and burnt in effigy in mid-Atlantic and New England states again in 1781, especially in cities that he attacked. As an annual custom, however, the degradation of Arnold was not added to the evolving calendar of national commemorations. SUSAN G. DAVIS

SPY
TRAYTOR.
I. SMITH
ANDRE

## 27. **William Bartram** (1739–1823)

### *Catalogue of American Trees, Shrubs and Herbaceous Plants, most of which are now growing, and produce ripe Seed in John Bartram's Garden, near Philadelphia*

ca. 1783
Broadside with manuscript verso; letterpress and ink on laid paper
16 5/16 × 20 ½ inches (41.5 × 52.3 cm)

Historical Society of Pennsylvania Poster and Broadside Collection [V94]

This broadside of North American plants from the Bartram family's botanic garden in Kingsessing, Pennsylvania, is undated but probably was printed in Philadelphia during the first half of 1783, after the signing of a preliminary treaty between the United States and Great Britain. A sheet of paper measuring 21 by 17 inches, the *Catalogue* lists 218 species for sale from the garden, which was the most important botanic collection on the continent. Unfortunately, neither the printer nor print run is known, and this copy is one of only two that seem to have survived, the other being held by the Library of Congress.

William Bartram prepared this list, preserving the common names and ordering used by his father, John Bartram (1699–1777), who founded the garden in 1728. But William also gave new Linnaean binomials, providing a key for translating John Bartram's older names to modern scientific nomenclature.

Primarily recording the woody species that formed the family business, the catalogue includes few edible, medicinal, or flowering herbaceous plants. And the list conveys little information on the uses of plants by Native Am cans, which William would provide elsewhere. Howe it does include environmental sorting as most species keyed to eight soil or situation types by letter codes.

Later in the decade, William drafted an antisla treatise on the blank verso of the catalogue, possibly to s valuable paper. The seemingly dissociated texts on eit side of the sheet actually form a suggestive pair, reflec a tension between William's evolving antipathy towa human bondage and the role of the garden as a commer enterprise, rooted in empire and linked to slavery.

While William directed his antislavery treatise "Americans" and the United States Congress, he proba never delivered his appeal. In fact, he may have writte in self-reproach for the years he spent on the slave pl tation of his uncle, William Bartram (1711–1770), in C Fear, North Carolina; his own enslavement of six peopl African descent, when he attempted to establish a rice indigo plantation in East Florida, in 1766; and his own ship of a woman named "Jenny," in the early 1770s.

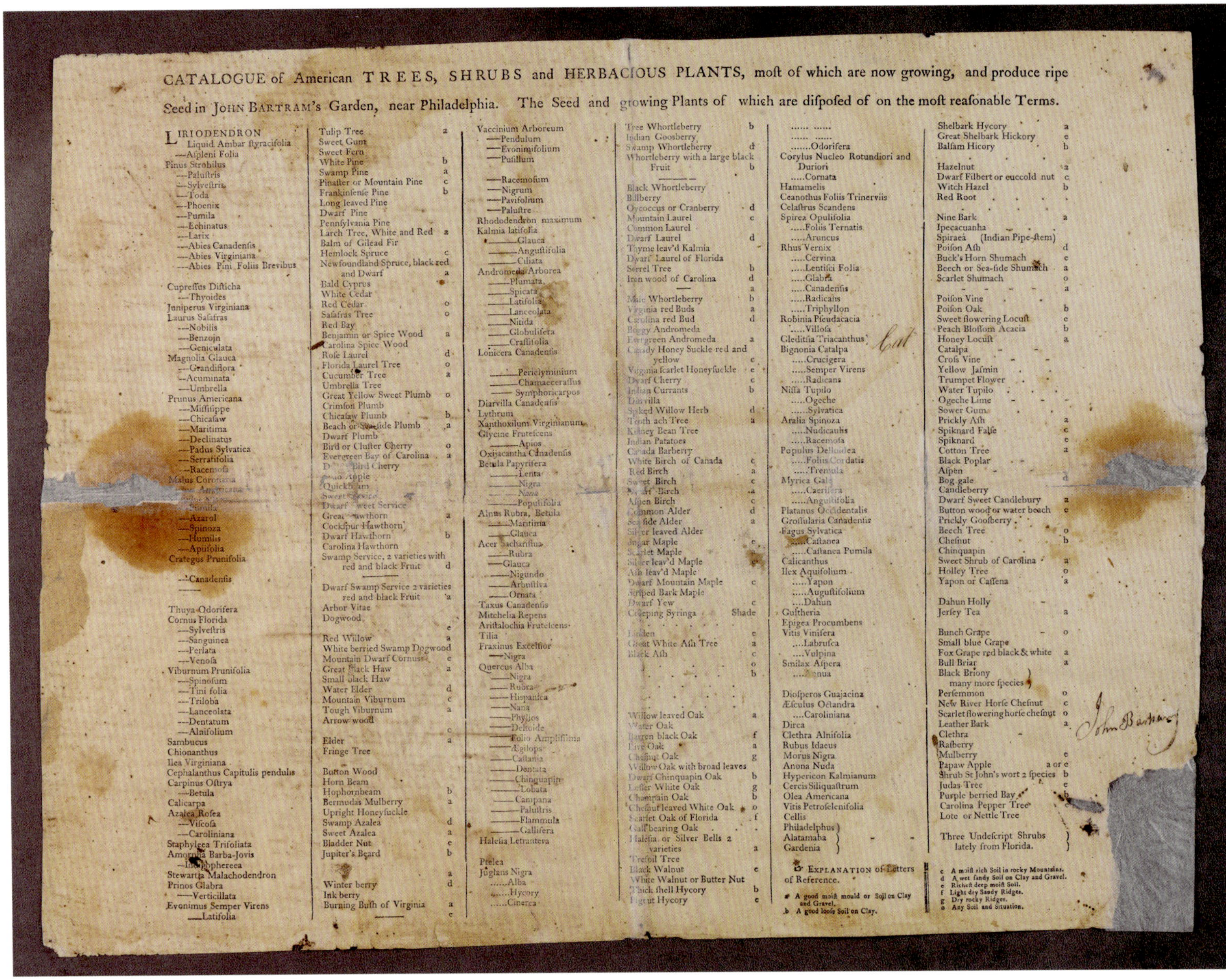

CATALOGUE of American TREES, SHRUBS and HERBACIOUS PLANTS, moſt of which are now growing, and produce ripe Seed in JOHN BARTRAM's Garden, near Philadelphia. The Seed and growing Plants of which are diſpoſed of on the moſt reaſonable Terms.

When William returned to his family's garden in 1777, following a four-year collecting expedition from the Carolinas through present-day Louisiana, he found himself part of a Quaker community that officially had prohibited slavery, and he joined Bartram family members in decrying the institution. Although his additional writings on slavery, particularly in his published *Travels*, would not equal his defense of the Indigenous Nations he feared would be lost to an expanding empire, he remained haunted by his past as a slave owner. Never explicitly acknowledging the association between the institution of slavery and the operation of the garden, he seems instead to have considered the site where he first learned about the balance of nature as a place where he could refine his sense of humanity. Ultimately, the garden served as a source for moral regeneration as he sought to contribute to the establishment of a nation that he hoped would rest on an ethical foundation.

JOEL T. FRY AND AMY MEYERS

# CATALOGUE of American TREES, SHRUBS and HERBACIOUS PLANTS, moſt

Seed in JOHN BARTRAM's Garden, near Philadelphia. The Seed and growing Plants of which a

| | | |
|---|---|---|
| LIRIODENDRON | Tulip Tree | a |
| Liquid Ambar ſtyracifolia | Sweet Gum | |
| ---Aſpleni Folia | Sweet Fern | |
| Pinus Strobilus | White Pine | b |
| ---Paluſtris | Swamp Pine | a |
| ---Sylveſtris | Pinaſter or Mountain Pine | c |
| ---Toda | Frankinſenſe Pine | b |
| ---Phoenix | Long leaved Pine | |
| ---Pumila | Dwarf Pine | |
| ---Echinatus | Pennſylvania Pine | |
| ---Larix | Larch Tree, White and Red | a |
| ---Abies Canadenſis | Balm of Gilead Fir | |
| ---Abies Virginiana | Hemlock Spruce | c |
| ---Abies Pini Foliis Brevibus | Newfoundland Spruce, black red and Dwarf | a |
| Cupreſſus Diſticha | Bald Cyprus | |
| ---Thyoides | White Cedar | |
| Juniperus Virginiana | Red Cedar | o |
| Laurus Saſafras | Saſafras Tree | o |
| ---Nobilis | Red Bay | |
| ---Benzoin | Benjamin or Spice Wood | a |
| ---Geniculata | Carolina Spice Wood | |
| Magnolia Glauca | Roſe Laurel | d |
| ---Grandiflora | Florida Laurel Tree | o |
| ---Acuminata | Cucumber Tree | a |
| ---Umbrella | Umbrella Tree | |
| Prunus Americana | Great Yellow Sweet Plumb | o |
| ---Miſſiſippe | Crimſon Plumb | |
| ---Chicaſaw | Chicaſaw Plumb | b |
| ---Maritima | Beach or Sea-ſide Plumb | a |
| ---Declinatus | Dwarf Plumb | |
| ---Padus Sylvatica | Bird or Cluſter Cherry | o |
| ---Serratifolia | Evergreen Bay of Carolina | a |
| ---Racemoſa | D[illegible] Bird Cherry | |
| Malus Coronaria | [illegible] Apple | |
| ---Americana | Quickbeam | |
| [illegible] | Sweet Service | |
| ---Pumila | Dwarf Sweet Service | |
| ---Azarol | Great Hawthorn | a |
| ---Spinoza | Cockſpur Hawthorn | |
| ---Humilis | Dwarf Hawthorn | b |
| ---Apiifolia | Carolina Hawthorn | |
| Crategus Prunifolia | Swamp Service, 2 varieties with red and black Fruit | d |
| ---Canadenſis | ——— | |
| ------ | Dwarf Swamp Service 2 varieties red and black Fruit | a |
| Thuya Odorifera | Arbor Vitae | |
| Cornus Florida | Dogwood | |
| ---Sylveſtris | | e |
| ---Sanguinea | Red Willow | a |
| ---Perlata | White berried Swamp Dogwood | |
| ---Venoſa | Mountain Dwarf Cornus | e |
| Viburnum Prunifolia | Great Black Haw | a |
| ---Spinoſum | Small black Haw | |
| ---Tini folia | Water Elder | d |
| ---Triloba | Mountain Viburnum | c |
| ---Lanceolata | Tough Viburnum | a |
| ---Dentatum | Arrow wood | |
| ---Alnifolium | | c |
| Sambucus | Elder | a |
| Chionanthus | Fringe Tree | |
| Ilea Virginiana | | |
| Cephalanthus Capitulis pendulis | Button Wood | |
| Carpinus Oſtrya | Horn Beam | |
| ---Betula | Hophornbeam | b |
| Calicarpa | Bermudas Mulberry | a |

| | | |
|---|---|---|
| Vaccinium Arboreum | Tree Whortleberry | b |
| —Pendulum | Indian Gooſberry | |
| —Evonimifolium | Swamp Whortleberry | d |
| —Puſillum | Whortleberry with a large black Fruit | b |
| —Racemoſum | ——— | |
| —Nigrum | Black Whortleberry | |
| —Pavifolium | Billberry | |
| —Paluſtre | Oxycoccus or Cranberry | d |
| Rhododendron maximum | Mountain Laurel | c |
| Kalmia latifolia | Common Laurel | |
| —Glauca | Dwarf Laurel | d |
| —Anguſtifolia | Thyme leav'd Kalmia | |
| —Ciliata | Dwarf Laurel of Florida | |
| Andromeda Arborea | Sorrel Tree | b |
| —Plumata | Iron wood of Carolina | d |
| —Spicata | ——— | a |
| —Latifolia | Male Whortleberry | b |
| —Lanceolata | Virginia red Buds | a |
| —Nitida | Carolina red Bud | d |
| —Globulifera | Boggy Andromeda | |
| —Craſſifolia | Evergreen Andromeda | a |
| Lonicera Canadenſis | Canady Honey Suckle red and yellow | c |
| —Periclyminium | Virginia ſcarlet Honeyſuckle | e |
| —Chamaeceraſſus | Dwarf Cherry | c |
| —Symphoricarpos | Indian Currants | b |
| Diarvilla Canadenſis | Diarvilla | |
| Lythrum | Spiked Willow Herb | d |
| Xanthoxilum Virginianum | Tooth ach Tree | a |
| Glycine Fruteſcens | Kidney Bean Tree | |
| —Apios | Indian Patatoes | |
| Oxijacantha Canadenſis | Canada Barberry | |
| Betula Papyrifera | White Birch of Canada | c |
| —Lenta | Red Birch | a |
| —Nigra | Sweet Birch | c |
| —Nana | Dwarf Birch | a |
| —Populifolia | Aſpen Birch | c |
| Alnus Rubra, Betula | Common Alder | d |
| —Maritima | Sea ſide Alder | a |
| —Glauca | Silver leaved Alder | |
| Acer Sachariſlua | Sugar Maple | c |
| —Rubra | Scarlet Maple | a |
| —Glauca | Silver leav'd Maple | e |
| —Nigundo | Aſh leav'd Maple | |
| —Arbuſtiva | Dwarf Mountain Maple | c |
| —Ornata | Striped Bark Maple | |
| Taxus Canadenſis | Dwarf Yew | c |
| Mitchelia Repens | Creeping Syringa | Shade |
| Ariſtalochia Fruteſcens | | |
| Tilia | Linden | e |
| Fraxinus Excelſior | Great White Aſh Tree | a |
| —Nigra | Black Aſh | c |
| Quercus Alba | | o |
| —Nigra | | b |
| —Rubra | | |
| —Hiſpanica | | |
| —Nana | | |
| —Phyllos | Willow leaved Oak | a |
| —Deltoide | Water Oak | |
| —Folio Ampliſſima | Barren black Oak | f |
| —Ægilops | Live Oak | a |
| —Caſtania | Cheſnut Oak | g |
| —Dentata | Willow Oak with broad leaves | |
| —Chinquapin | Dwarf Chinquapin Oak | b |
| —Lobata | Leſſer White Oak | g |
| —Campana | Champain Oak | b |

# 28. **Benjamin West** (1738–1820)

## *William Hamilton and His Niece, Anna Hamilton Lyle*

---

1785–1813
Oil on canvas
92 11⁄16 × 72 inches (235.4 × 182.8 cm)

Signed and dated lower right: *This picture was begun / in 1785 and completed in / 1813*[?] */ London Benjn West*

Historical Society of Pennsylvania Art and Artifact Collection [3137]
By descent in the family of Anna Hamilton (Mrs. James Lyle) to Charles Kuhn, by whom deposited with the Historical Society of Pennsylvania in 1873.

Born in Springfield, Pennsylvania, on what is today the campus of Swarthmore College, Benjamin West traveled to Italy, France, and England in 1760–63. Sponsored by Judge William Allen (1704–1780) of Philadelphia, West was supposed to study the works of the old masters, obtain formal instruction as an artist, and come home to Pennsylvania as the best-trained painter in the American colonies. Instead, West gained instant recognition and patronage in London; was among the founders of the Royal Academy of Arts in 1768 (later its second president); and became the court history painter to King George III. Aspiring American artists and wealthy travelers gravitated to his studio in London from the mid-1760s until his death in 1820.

Among those visiting Americans were William Hamilton and his niece Anna, not yet sixteen years old, who posed for a double portrait during a visit to London in 1785, and yet the painting was not completed until about 1813. By then, Anna had been dead for more than a decade, and William also may have died before seeing the finished work. The commission and its delayed completion are illuminated by a letter from West to William Hamilton's agent, Robert Barclay, in Surrey, England, in which the artist asks Barclay to inform his patron:

> That I have received his letter of instructions for finishing the picture which contains the Portraits of himself and Niece whole lengths. That I have a pride in rendering the picture as a finished work of art to the utmost of my abilities—and I am therefore repainting it all but the Faces—that it may possess the accumulated practice which twenty years study has added to the period since the picture was first undertaken; that it may honour—as far as my humble abilities will permit the memmory [*sic*] of Hamilton, that of my native country—and myself as the painter of it. For the additional painting and inrichments [*sic*] which I am making to the picture I shall not increase the charge for it; but shall charge the same I had for whole length Portraits when the picture was begun—which was Sixty Guineas a figure whole lengths.

A drawing in black-and-white chalk, now in the British Museum, preserves the original composition, and the finished painting shows the many changes that West made when he returned to complete the canvas that had languished for many years in his studio. For example, West shifted William's gaze away from the viewer and towards Anna. He also removed Anna's hat to reveal her lush, dark-brown hair and embellished her neoclassical, high-waisted dress with flowing drapery that cascades over her shoulder. The drawing also shows the artist considered positioning Anna's right arm hanging at her side rather than reaching out to her uncle's right arm, as seen in the final version.

The finished painting was intended to adorn Hamilton's neoclassical home, Woodlands, where he collected art and books. Hamilton avidly populated his gardens with thousands of botanical specimens purchased from his neighbors, the Bartrams, as well as exotics imported from Europe, Asia, Australia, and Africa. Not surprisingly, William inherited Woodlands from his cousin Andrew Hamilton, whose father, Andrew, was also Judge Allen's father-in-law. These were tight circles of wealth, power, and influence.

DAVID R. BRIGHAM

---

The Historical Society of Pennsylvania is a necessary destination for any student or scholar researching Benjamin West. The collection includes correspondence, business records, and drawings from about 1764 to 1820. A unique, seven-volume, extra-illustrated copy of West's first biography by John Galt, *The Life, Studies, and Works of Benjamin West* (1820), includes letters, deeds, and engravings. HSP also has a rare drawing manual based on West's paintings (1814) and an illustrated exposition of West's monumental work, *Christ Rejected* (1821), both with engraved illustrations by Edward Scriven and published in London. The papers of Helmut Von Erffa and Allen Staley, the authors of West's catalogue raisonné, also reside at HSP and preserve the detailed research on the 739 paintings they catalogued.

## 29. **James Wilson** (1742–1798)

## *United States Constitution, First Manuscript Draft*

1787
Manuscript; ink on laid paper
15 ⅛ × 18 ¾ inches (37.8 × 47.8 cm)

Historical Society of Pennsylvania Treasures Collection
Gift of Emily Hollingsworth, 1876

In 1876–77 the papers of James Wilson, a Pennsylvania attorney and delegate to the Constitutional Convention, were donated to the Historical Society of Pennsylvania. More than twenty years later, the eminent historian J. Franklin Jameson discovered among them two handwritten early drafts of the Constitution in Wilson's hand. These and other founding-era notes and documents in his writings provided new insights into how the Constitution moved beyond the weak Articles of Confederation to the enduring founding document by which the United States has been governed ever since. They also reveal that Wilson ranks with James Madison (1751–1836) as a prime player in the creation of our national government.

Jameson was one of several scholars focusing on the history and documentation of the Convention in the wake of its centennial celebration, and historians recognized that sources for studying it were limited. Knowing of the rich collections at HSP, Jameson hoped to find documents related to Wilson's work as a delegate to the Convention, but potentially more significantly as secretary to the Committee of Detail that produced a printed draft that became the US Constitution after modifications and ratification by the states. What he found exceeded his highest hopes.

The Constitution was the product of a meeting called by the former colonies—now states—that needed to work together if they were to retain their independence from Britain and prosper as a nation. The Convention met in Philadelphia in the summer of 1787, and discussions and debates were held behind closed doors with delegates sworn to secrecy outside of Independence Hall. The states ratified the Convention's draft in 1789.

For more than fifty years after ratification, nothing was known about how the Constitution was actually formed. Ultimately, the chief source of information about its origins became the journals and notes James Madison had kept during the Convention, confidential writings that he heavily edited after he left the presidency in 1816. In 1840, four years after his death, the government published these documents, revealing Madison's version of a "behind-the-scenes" view into the making of the Constitution. But in the absence of extant notes or journals in others' hands, scholars' reliance on Madison's account led to his becoming regarded as the "father" of the Constitution. Notably, Madison was not a member of the drafting committee.

During the Convention, much attention was consumed by a serious disagreement over the single topic of the states' representation in the new Congress. After settling on a series of resolutions outlining the new government, a five-member Select Committee of Detail, for which Wilson served as secretary, produced a draft that was printed and

Each House of the Legislature shall possess the Right of originating any Bills, except in the Cases beforementioned of the Legislature

The Senate shall chuse its own President and other Officers

The Members of each House shall be ineligible to and incapable of holding any Office under the Authority of the United States during the Time for which they shall be respectively elected: And the Members of the Senate shall be ineligible to and incapable of holding any such Office for one Year afterwards.

The Stile of the Laws of the United States shall be "be it enacted and it is hereby enacted by the House of Representatives, and by the Senate of the United States in Congress assembled"

The Members of each House shall receive a Compensation for their Services, to be ascertained and paid by the State in which they shall be chosen

The House of Representatives and the Senate when it shall be acting in a legislative Capacity shall keep a Journal of its Proceedings, and shall from Time to Time publish them; And the Yeas and Nays of the Members of each House on any Question shall at the Desire of any Member be entered on the Journal

for disorderly Behaviour

Freedom of Speech

be applied to the Senate only in its legislative Capacity.

In each House a Majority of the Members shall constitute a Quorum to do Business; but a smaller Number may adjourn from Day to Day

Each House of the Legislature shall be the Judge of the Elections, Returns and Qualifications of its own Members.

The Times and Places and the Manner of holding the Elections of the Members of each House shall be prescribed by the Legislature of each State; but their Provisions concerning them may, at any Time be altered and superseded by the Legislature of the United States.

The Legislature of the United States shall have Authority to establish such Qualifications of the Members of each House with Regard to Property as to the said Legislature shall seem proper and expedient

A Majority of the Members of each House shall constitute a Quorum to do Business; but a smaller Number than a Majority of them may in each House, adjourn from Day to Day.

Each House shall have Authority to determine the Rules of its Proceedings, and to punish its own Members

Each House may expel a Member, but not a second Time for the same Offence.

Neither House shall adjourn for more than three Days without the Consent of the other; nor, with such Consent, to any other Place than that at which the two Houses are sitting. But this Regulation shall

The Members of each House shall, in all Cases, except Treason, Felony & Breach of the Peace, be privileged from Arrest during their Attendance at Congress, and in going to and returning from it.

The

1

The Qualifications of the Electors

We the People of the States of New-Hampshire, Massachusetts, Rhode-Island and Providence Plantations, Connecticut, New-York, New-Jersey, Pennsylvania, Delaware, Maryland, Virginia, North-Carolina, South-Carolina and Georgia do ordain declare and establish the following Constitution for the Government of ourselves and of our Posterity.

1.

The Stile of this Government shall be the "United People and States of America"

2.

The Government shall consist of supreme legislative, executive and judicial Powers.

3.

The legislative Power shall be vested in a Congress to consist of two separate and distinct Bodies of Men, a House of Representatives, and a Senate; each of which shall in all Cases, have a Negative on the other.

4.

The Members of the House of Representatives shall be chosen every second Year by the People of the several States comprehended within this Union. The Times and Places and the Manner of holding the Elections shall be prescribed by the Legislatures of the several States; but their Provisions concerning them may at any Time be altered and superseded by the Legislature of the United States.

Every Member of the House of Representatives shall be of the Age of twenty five Years at least; shall have been a Citizen in the United States for at least three Years before his Election; and shall

sent to the delegates for consideration. The century-long loss of Wilson's manuscript drafts and the alacrity with which the committee produced them likely contributed to the comprehensive paucity of scholarly attention given to the work of the committee.

Their efforts over a hot week in July remained in the dark. The printed draft they produced for consideration was thought to be the only source of their work for more than a century. Only Madison's notes of the ensuing floor debate left hints to the drafting process. The committee's printed report was regarded as the first draft, which, after modifications, led to a second printed draft that served for continuing debate before a final version received approval with a recommendation that the Confederation Congress submit it to the states for ratification. What was not known until the twentieth century (and what Madison himself might not have known) was that the Committee of Detail prepared and edited two preliminary versions before sending a copy to the printer as their recommended charter. The two manuscript copies, in James Wilson's hand and filled with emendations, are the only copies of these preliminary drafts known to exist.

The differences between these first handwritten copies and the first printed (third draft) copy are not many, but they add greatly to our understanding of the committee's work while helping illuminate the later floor debate. Given the short time the group met, it appears Wilson immediately penned a draft following the outline approved by resolution of the Convention. But his drafts reveal that from the first day these five delegates went beyond what the Convention had agreed upon as the basis of their work. They added an enumeration clause limiting the federal government's power to the specific provisions in the draft. In addition, they included passages favored by the Southern states protecting slavery and limiting Congress's power to pass navigation acts. A striking difference between the first and subsequent drafts was what the government would be called. In the first draft, "The United People and States of America" appeared, but after much further editing by the committee, Wilson's second draft dropped "People and." That draft received more editing before becoming copy for the printed version distributed to each delegate as they reconvened at the end of their ten-day recess to consider its adoption.

The concept that power emanated from "the people" rather than the states was in the preamble of each draft, but only obliquely. It consisted entirely of "We the people of" and a list of each state then existing, followed by a simple statement of ordination and declaration. In the final draft adopted by the Convention, Gouverneur Morris (1752–1816) changed this rather drab (and cumbersome, if new states were to be formed) preamble to "We the People of the United States," and followed it with the elegant "in order to form a more perfect union," and words of purpose that added grace to an otherwise technical document.

After playing an active role in ratification, Wilson's influence was relatively short lived. He died in 1798, having spent his post-Convention years as an inaugural Supreme Court justice and the University of Pennsylvania's first law professor. His drafts passed to his son and then his granddaughter, who apparently remained unaware of the importance of these and other seminal notes and papers in the collection.

When Emily Hollingsworth offered them to HSP in 1876, she told the Society's president that the only item of importance she was aware they contained was a letter by George Washington. Jameson's research changed that impression dramatically, and subsequent scholars who have delved into the collections at HSP have suggested Wilson should be recognized with Madison as co-father of the Constitution. Study of these drafts and other notes and documents in Wilson's papers strengthens that view and continues to enhance our knowledge and understanding of our nation's founding.

CHARLES T. CULLEN

---

For an edited transcription of Wilson's two drafts and other manuscripts the Committee of Detail considered in the process of drafting a constitution, see the brilliant work of William Ewald and Lorianne Updike Tyler that occupies the entire issue of *The Pennsylvania Magazine of History and Biography* (July 2011), and the creative online Interactive Constitution prepared by the National Constitution Center using these manuscripts: https://draftingtable.constitutioncenter.org/item/drafting-the-united-states-constitution. See also William Ewald, "The Committee of Detail," *Constitutional Commentary* 28 (Fall 2012): 197–285, online at https://hdl.handle.net/11299/163466.

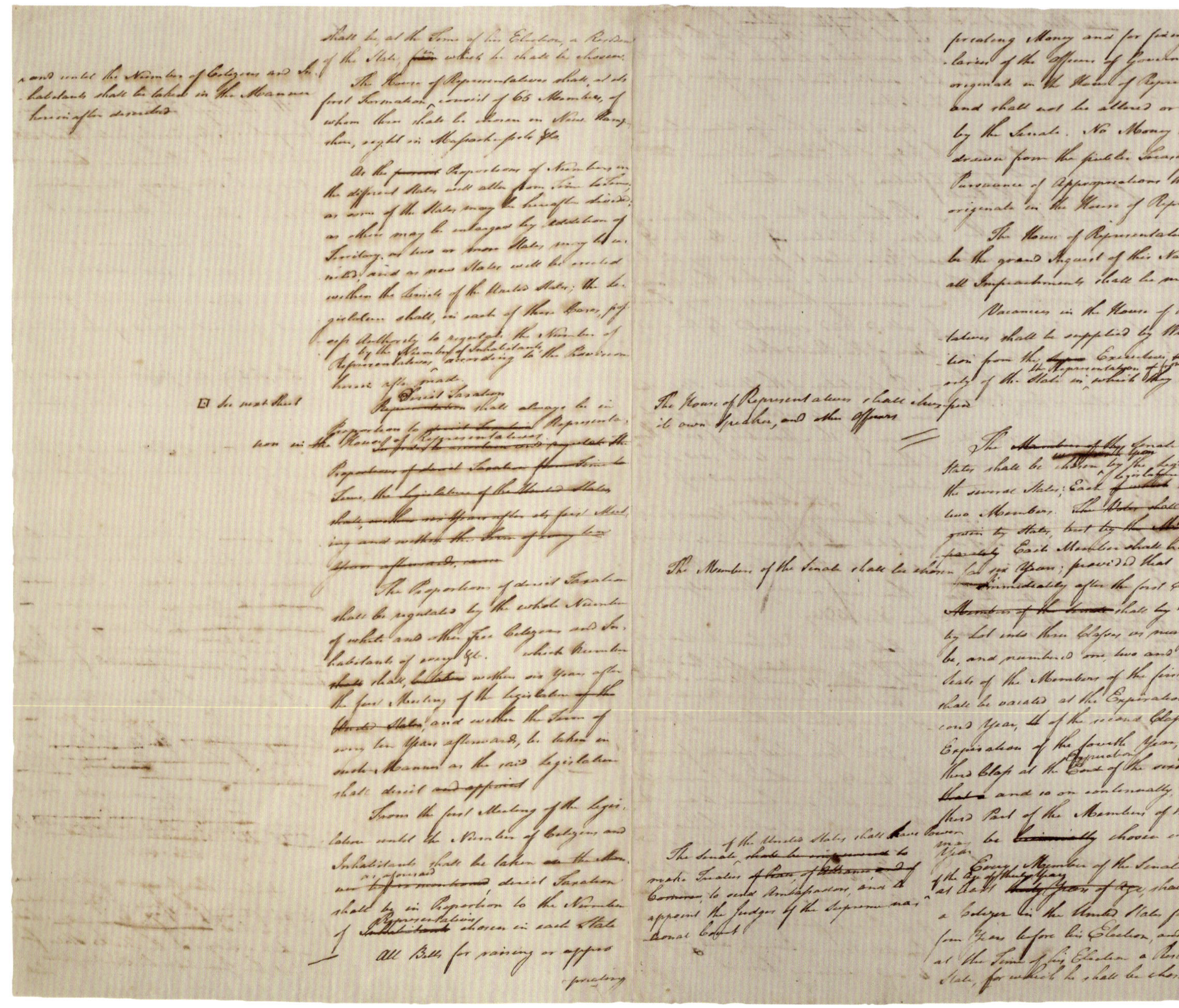

An Appeal for the Correction of all Errors both in Law and Fact

That the United States in Congress be authorised — to pass Acts for raising a Revenue, by levying Duties on all Goods and Merchandise of foreign Growth or Manufacture imported into any Part of the United States — by Stamps on Paper Vellum or Parchment — and by a Postage on all Letters and Packages passing through the general Post-Office, to be applied to such federal Purposes as they shall deem proper and expedient — to make Rules and Regulations for the Collection thereof — to pass Acts for the Regulation of Trade and Commerce as well with foreign Nations as with each other

to lay and collect Taxes

That the Executive direct all military Operations

That the Judiciary have Authority to hear and determine all Impeachments of federal Officers; and, by Way of Appeal in all Cases touching the Rights of Ambassadors — in all Cases of Captures from an Enemy — in all Cases of Piracies and Felonies on the high Seas — in all Cases in which Foreigners may be interested in the Construction of any Treaty, or which may arise on any Act for regulating Trade or collecting Revenue

in all Cases of Revenue

or on the Law of Nations, or general commercial or marine Laws

If any State, or any Body of Men in any State shall oppose or prevent the carrying into Execution the Acts or Treaties of the United States; the Executive shall be authorised to enforce and compel Obedience by calling forth the Powers of the United States.

That the Rule for Naturalization ought to be the same in every State

The Legislature shall consist of two distinct Branches — a Senate and a House of Delegates, each of which shall have a Negative on the other, and shall be stiled the U. S. in Congress assembled.

Each House shall appoint its own Speaker and other Officers, and settle its own Rules of Proceeding; but neither the Senate nor H. D. shall have the Power to adjourn for more than Days, without the ~~other~~ Consent of both.

There shall be a President, in whom the Ex. Authority of the U. S. shall be vested. It shall be his Duty to inform the Legislature of

of the Condition of U. S. so far as may respect his Department — to recommend Matters to their Consideration — to correspond with the Executives of the several States — to attend to the Execution of the Laws of the U. S. — to transact Affairs with the Officers of Government, civil and military — to expedite all such Measures as may be resolved on by the Legislature — to inspect the Departments of foreign Affairs — War — Treasury — Admiralty — to reside where the Legislature shall sit — to commission all Officers, and keep the Great Seal of U. S. — He shall, by Virtue of his Office be Commander in Chief of the Land Forces of U. S. and Admiral of their Navy — He shall have Power to convene the Legislature on extraordinary Occasions — to prorogue them, provided such Prorogation shall not exceed Days in the Space of any — He may suspend Officers, civil and military

The Legislature of U. S. shall have the exclusive Power — of raising a military Land Force — of equipping a Navy — of rating and causing public Taxes to be levied — of regulating the Trade of the several States as well with foreign Nations as with each other — of levying Duties upon Imports and Exports — of establishing Post-Offices, and raising a Revenue from them — of regulating Indian Affairs — of coining Money — fixing the Standard of Weights and Measures — of determining in what Species of Money the public Treasury shall be supplied

The federal judicial Court shall try Officers of the U. S. for all Crimes &c. in their Offices — ~~and to this Court an Appeal shall be allowed from the Courts of~~

The Legislature of U. S. shall have the exclusive Right of instituting in each State a Court of Admiralty for hearing and determining maritime Causes.

The Power of impeaching shall be vested in the H. D. — The Senators and Judges of the federal Court, be a Court for trying Impeachments

The Legislature of U. S. shall possess the exclusive Right of establishing the Government and Discipline of the Militia of — and of ordering the Militia of any State to any Place within U. S.

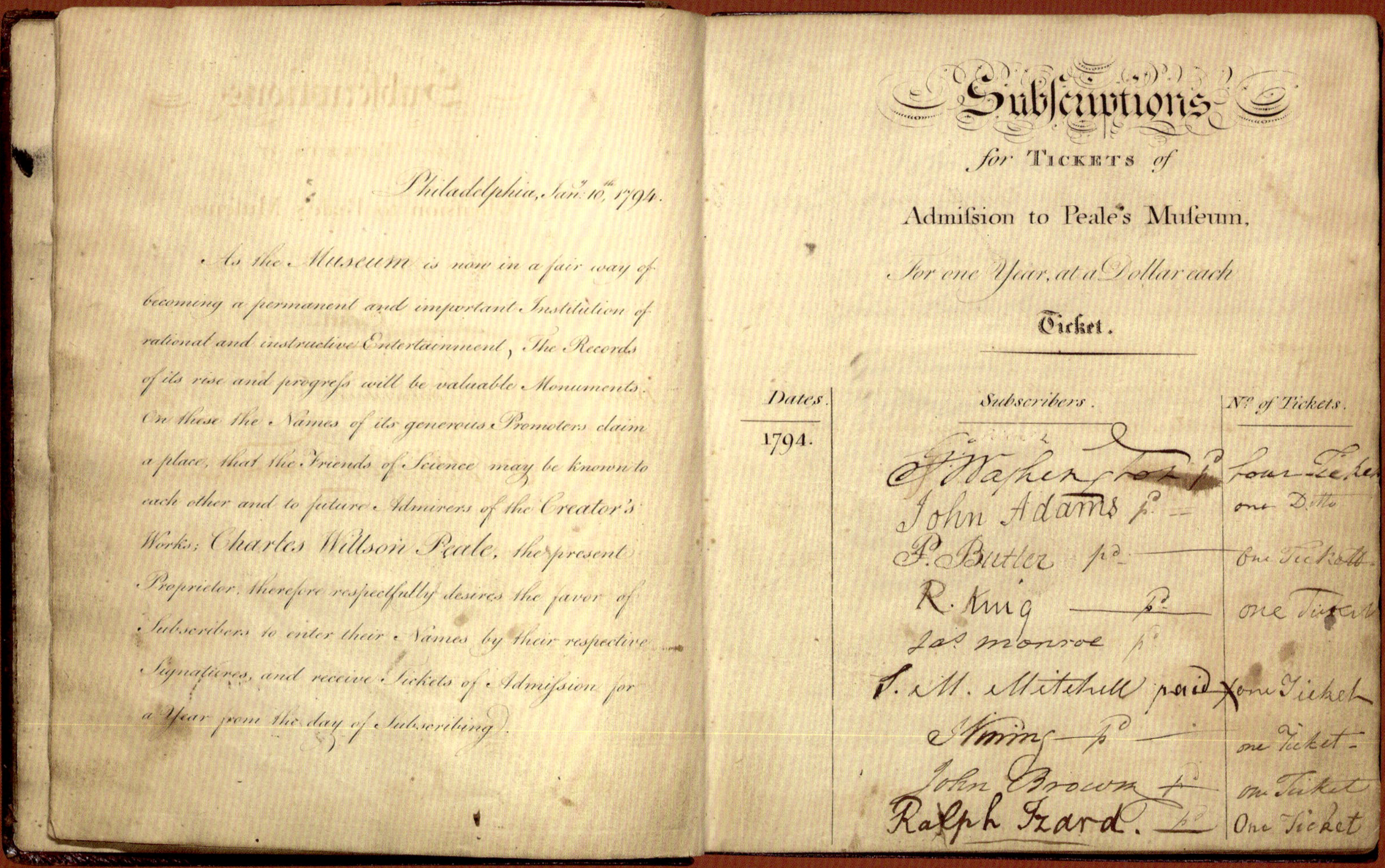

Philadelphia, Jan.^y 10th 1794.

As the Museum is now in a fair way of becoming a permanent and important Institution of rational and instructive Entertainment, The Records of its rise and progreſs will be valuable Monuments. On these the Names of its generous Promoters claim a place, that the Friends of Science may be known to each other and to future Admirers of the Creator's Works; Charles Willson Peale, the present Proprietor, therefore respectfully desires the favor of Subscribers to enter their Names by their respective Signatures, and receive Tickets of Admiſsion for a Year from the day of Subscribing.

Subscriptions

for Tickets of

Admiſsion to Peale's Muſeum,

For one Year, at a Dollar each

Ticket.

| Dates. | Subscribers. | No. of Tickets. |
|---|---|---|
| 1794. | G. Washington pd | four Tickets |
| | John Adams pd | one Ditto |
| | P. Butler pd | One Ticket |
| | R. King pd | one Ticket |
| | Jas. Monroe pd | |
| | S. M. Mitchell paid | one Ticket |
| | [illegible] pd | one Ticket |
| | John Brown pd | one Ticket |
| | Ralph Izard. pd | One Ticket |

# 30. **Charles Willson Peale** (1741–1827)

## *Peale's Museum Subscription Book*

1794–1833
Laid paper bound in full red morocco with gilt border and lettering
9 7/8 × 8 inches (25.1 × 20.3 cm)

Peale Family Papers [0481]
Presented by the Peale Family

Founded in 1786, Peale's Museum in Philadelphia was the first museum of art and science in the United States and a precursor to the Smithsonian Institution in its ambitions to serve as an encyclopedic national repository. Charles Willson Peale envisioned that his museum would serve as a university for the benefit of the "learned and the unwise" and would include a collection that was global in scope and encompass one of every kind of human and natural production.

This manuscript volume documents the purchasers of annual tickets to Peale's Museum who paid one dollar for the privilege of free admission. Beyond being an innovator who wanted to make knowledge accessible to a wide range of people, Peale was also a pioneer in marketing, membership, public programming, and other aspects of museum management. Not only does the subscription book serve as a roster of members, its first page was clearly the product of Peale's thoughtful outreach to the most prominent citizens of Philadelphia, and it was used to promote membership to the general audiences who visited his galleries. Indeed, the first signature is that of George Washington, who purchased four annual tickets. In addition to the sitting president of the United States, Peale also secured membership subscriptions from John Adams, then vice president, and four United States senators: James Monroe, Pierce Butler, Rufus King, and Ralph Izard. In 1794, Peale's Museum had moved to Philosophical Hall, less than a block from Congress Hall, where the Senate met at that time, giving Peale ready access to the nation's political leaders. The pages that follow memorialize the names of people from a broad spectrum of occupations and social positions: bankers, scientists, attorneys, merchants, doctors, apothecaries, ironmongers, clergymen, printers, booksellers, innkeepers, leather workers, cabinetmakers, metal workers, grocers, and more.

The Historical Society of Pennsylvania also owns Peale's book of accessions, which records the items that came into the museum by gift and exchange between 1803 and 1842. This volume includes notes on natural history specimens, curiosities donated by ship's captains and seamen from their world voyages, historical relics, patents and inventions, Native American artifacts, and ancient coins. Peale arranged his natural history collections according to Linnaean order and placed them in dioramas that suggested their natural habitats. Peale also painted oval, bust-length portraits of the leading figures of his day, which he displayed as exemplars of achievement within a meritocracy. A printed catalogue was available to help guide visitors, and Peale presented lectures that spoke of animals in anthropomorphic terms as a natural model for the development of a harmonious republic.

The museum moved in 1802 to the upper floor of the State House, now known as Independence Hall, and later relocated to a commercial block called The Arcade. It operated until 1849, after which its collections were sold. HSP's holdings of Peale Family Papers include drawings by Titian Ramsay Peale (1799–1885), Titian's correspondence (1827–54) with ornithologist George Ord (1781–1866), and a daguerreotype of Rembrandt Peale (1778–1860) taken in 1855.

DAVID R. BRIGHAM

# 31. **Moses Williams** (1777–ca. 1825)

## *Patience Marshall Tyson*

ca. 1815
Hollow-cut cream wove paper mounted on blue stock
4 ½ × 4 inches (11.5 × 10.3 cm) (silhouette)

Inscribed in graphite, lower left: *B Sept 21, 1771 / M June 8, 1814 Isaac Tyson / D at Baltimore Dec. 15. 1834*; in graphite and ink, lower right: *Patience Marshall / Tyson*

From Mary Ann Marshall Silhouettes, book C, Perot Family Papers [no. 1886]. In Historical Society of Pennsylvania Collection of Silhouettes, ca. 1790–ca. 1900 [no. V87].

Patience Marshall Tyson (1771–1834), the likely creator of this album, assembled cut-paper portraits of family and friends that speak to these individuals' activities in the public and private spheres. Many of the silhouettes bear one of two embossed Peale's Museum stamps, indicating that they were taken at either Peale's Museum in Philadelphia or Baltimore. Moses Williams cut many of the silhouettes at Charles Willson Peale's Philadelphia Museum, and the images are a testament to individuals' patronage of a Black profilist during the first two decades of the nineteenth century.

Silhouettes were quick, inexpensive, novel, and could be produced in multiples. Introduced in France in the 1700s, they were taken up by Peale in Philadelphia in 1802. Peale, Williams, and others at Peale's museums used a physionotrace to outline the sitter's head; a connected bar impressed a smaller version of the image onto paper that was then cut. In a disdainful letter, Rembrandt Peale describes Williams:

> It is a curious fact that until the age of 27, Moses was entirely worthless: but on the invention of the Physiognotrace, he took a fancy to amuse himself in cutting out the rejected profiles made by the machine. . . . This soon became so profitable that my father insisted upon giving him his freedom one-year in advance. In a few years he amassed a fund sufficient to buy a two storey [*sic*] brick house, and actually married my father's white cook, who during his bondage, would not permit him to eat at the same table as her.

Many of the thousands of silhouettes by Williams and others at the Historical Society of Pennsylvania and other area collections are of Quakers, suggesting that these types of images met their unwritten mores about portrayal. Albums of silhouettes, largely compiled by young, well-to-do Quaker women, reinforced social, business, and kinship ties among Quakers and selected others in their circles. The Baltimore-based Tysons intermarried with Philadelphia families such as the Marshalls, retained strong ties to that city, and were active in antislavery activities. The album begins with Patience Marshall Tyson; silhouettes of family members follow; and several important Quaker figures are interspersed. The album includes a pencil sketch of "'Bill' Waiter of P. Marshall," a Black man, glued inside the front cover. Like the inclusion of antislavery proponents in this and other albums and the profiles by Williams, this portrait alludes to specific families' sentiments about race. ANNE A. VERPLANCK

Patience Marshall
Tyson
Elisha E Tyson
& Lady

## 32. **Peter Charles Varlé** (ca. 1770–1835)

### *Plan of Philadelphia*

1802
Engraving on wove paper
17 15⁄16 × 24 ½ inches (45.5 × 62.3 cm)

Inscribed upper left: *TO THE / CITIZENS OF / PHILADELPHIA / THIS NEW / PLAN OF THE CITY AND ITS / ENVIRONS / Is respectfully dedicated / By the / Editor / 1802.*; lower left: *P. C. Varlé Geographer & Engin*[r]*, Del.*

Historical Society of Pennsylvania Map Collection

Peter Charles Varlé trained as a civil engineer in France and worked in Haiti before arriving in Philadelphia in 1794. His stay in the city was interrupted by projects in Maine and Massachusetts, and in 1798, he moved permanently to Maryland when he was appointed superintendent of the Susquehanna Canal Company. However, Varlé did find time, in 1796, to publish a map of Philadelphia and its vicinity that documented the city's growth eastward from the Delaware River and to the north and west along the Schuylkill River, where many wealthy Philadelphians maintained country houses. In 1802 Varlé revised the map by adding a prospective extension of the street grid across the Schuylkill into Blockley Township. The new neighborhood featured two public squares, labeled Market and Washington, and an unnamed elliptical plaza. The street layout repeated the eastern grid, now elaborated with four diagonal avenues (one of which followed the existing road to Columbia and Lancaster), perhaps indicating Varlé's familiarity with Pierre Charles l'Enfant's (1754–1825) 1791 plan for Washington. Though most of the major streets in the city had not yet been opened all the way to the Schuylkill, Varlé drew these across to the western bank to indicate that the locations and names of major east-west streets would extend across the river. New north-south streets were named for Revolutionary War leaders: Adams, Green, Mercer, Montgomery, and Warren.

Varlé developed both the 1796 and 1802 maps by copying earlier examples, notably the frequently reprinted 1752 Scull and Heap map of *Philadelphia and Parts Adjacent* and A. P. Folie's 1794 map of the city, from which Varlé also copied the ships in the harbor and the vignette of the State House. However, Varlé rendered topography more accurately and in greater detail. He also added vignettes of Library Hall and the Bank of the United States and identified noteworthy landmarks, including the recently erected waterworks in Centre Square, the Navy Yard, and a dotted line showing the entrenchments built during the British occupation in 1777. Like Scull and Heap, and several other mapmakers, Varlé added the names of many country estate owners, perhaps in hopes of persuading them to purchase copies of the map. The roads shown in surrounding districts document that Penn's street grid was conveniently ignored beyond the city limits—many county roads simply followed existing paths opened by the native Lenni Lenape. Varlé's rectangular tracts also were only rough estimates of the boundaries of the country estates, which varied widely in size. North of the city, he included another important but abortive public works project: the canal running along the east bank of the Schuylkill River, excavated during the 1790s in what would prove to be a failed attempt to connect to the Delaware River.

Varlé's proposed subdivision west of the Schuylkill was similarly unsuccessful. Any plan to extend urban development could not proceed because Philadelphia was constrained politically by the boundaries set out in Penn's original plan. Not until 1854, when the Pennsylvania state legislature passed the Consolidation Act, which united the city and county, did Philadelphia's civic and business leaders gain the authority to pursue concerted development into the surrounding districts. ELIZABETH MILROY

# 33. *A Booke of Cookery* and *A Booke of Sweetmeats*

Late seventeenth century
Manuscript; ink on laid paper bound in full brown leather
7 15/16 × 6 1/4 inches (20.2 × 15.9 cm)

Historical Society of Pennsylvania Collection of George Washington Family Papers [Am .001]
Gift, 1892

This book is known as Martha Washington's cookbook, but it is unlikely that she cooked from it. Martha would have done little cooking in her life, having been born into the class that managed other cooks, such as men and women enslaved by her family. The book was also several generations old when she acquired it and was created in England, distant from her Virginia environs. There are hundreds of recipes in the book but none for corn, pumpkins, tomatoes, or peppers, foods indigenous only to the Americas. While some of the materials and methods would have been familiar to Martha, the flavors would have been out of fashion.

Culinary historian Karen Hess made a solid argument that the book was created in the late seventeenth century in England for Lady Berkeley, who was connected with the family of Daniel Custis, Martha's first husband. Berkeley might have written out the recipes herself, but it was also common practice to hire a scribe to do this, reflecting, as cookbook historian Janet Theophano has argued, how much families valued culinary knowledge.

The book was not only handed down through generations but also carried across the ocean when members of the family settled in the English colonies. It helped them to maintain cultural and class expectations in the most tangible way, easing the passage from England to Virginia. Because the colonies were so far away and had few institutions that replicated English society, maintaining foodways took on extra importance. However, if Martha requested these recipes from her staff, Mount Vernon cooks Hercules and Doll interpreted them through a different culinary tradition. They worked with intellectual habits and embodied knowledge of food preparation handed down from African cooks. This might have resulted in a more generous use of flavorings and a different interplay between starches, sauces, and meats. The cooks would have brought to the recipe art and skill honed through analysis and practice, elements that Martha herself could not bring to the task because class and race expectations of her era mostly kept her out of the kitchen.

The most intriguing parts of this book are those in which culinary knowledge overlaps with other kinds of thinking and learning. The book is rich with references to plants and animals of every kind known in England and of spices and other flavorings imported from Asia and Africa. Some of this knowledge is applied for culinary pleasure and some for healthcare. Recipes for cordials tell us what kinds of plants the author knew of and what types of treatments she had faith in. Spirits of Cinnamon, for example, were good for combating "spirits oppressed with heaviness" as well as fainting fits. Several pages without recipes are filled with notes written by one of the book's owners that explain mathematical principles relevant to cooks. In these pages, readers can see clearly how much domesticity engages the intellect and where it intersects with the world beyond the kitchen.

MEGAN J. ELIAS

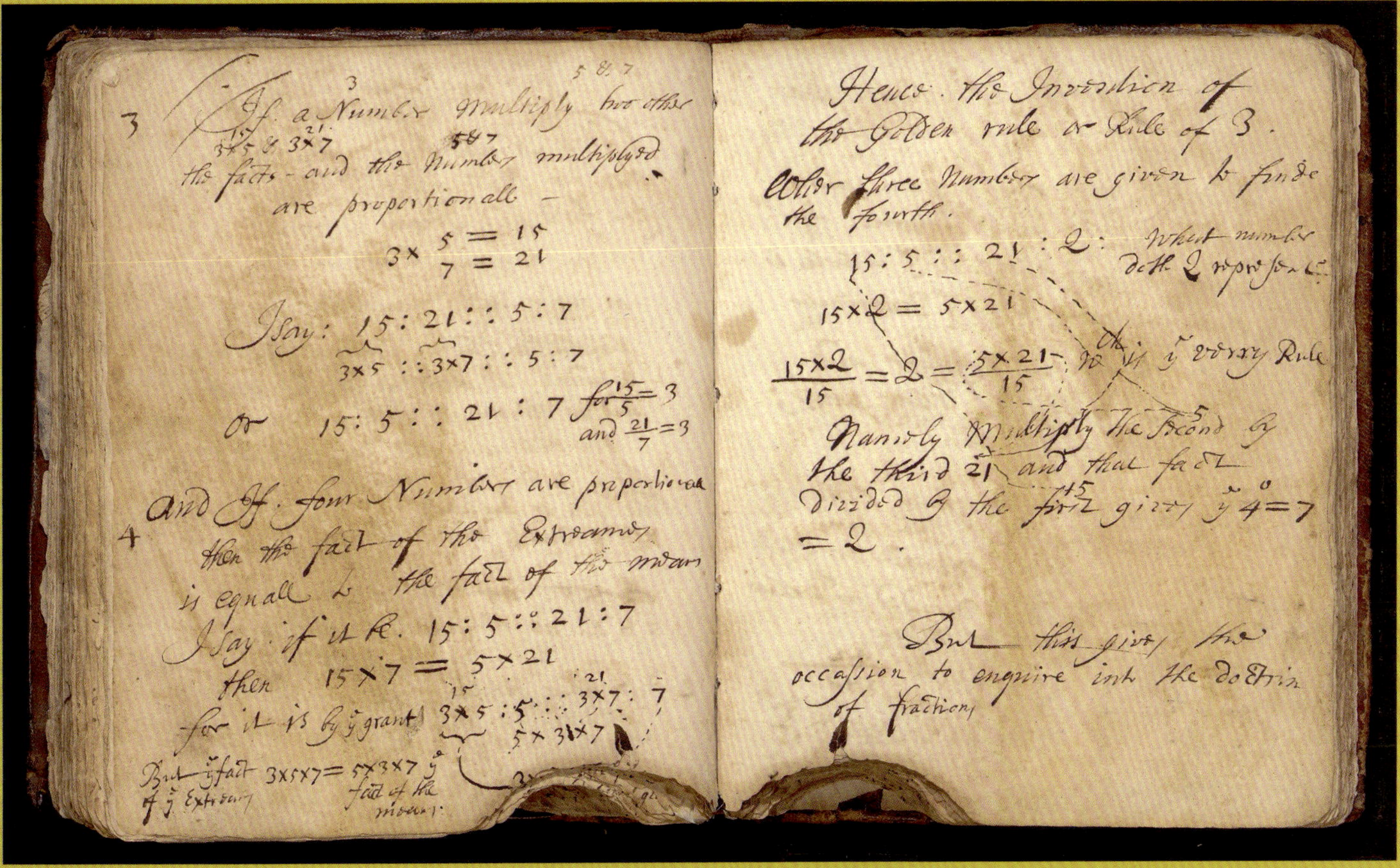
3 If a Number multiply two other[s] the facts and the Number multiplyed are proportionall —
3 × 5 = 15
7 = 21
I say: 15 : 21 : : 5 : 7
3×5 : : 3×7 : : 5 : 7
Or 15 : 5 : : 21 : 7 for 15/5 = 3 and 21/7 = 3
4 And If four Numbers are proportionall then the fact of the Extreames is equall to the fact of the meanes
I say if it be 15 : 5 : : 21 : 7
then 15×7 = 5×21
for it is by y grant 3×5 : 5 : : 3×7 : 7
5 × 3×7
But y fact of y Extreams 3×5×7 = 5×3×7 y fact of the meanes.
Hence the Invention of the Golden rule or Rule of 3.
Where three Numbers are given to finde the fourth.
15 : 5 : : 21 : 2 : what number doth 2 represent.
15×2 = 5×21
15×2/15 = 2 = 5×21/15 to wit y every Rule
Namely Multiply the second by the third 21 and that fact divided by the first 15 giv y 4 = 7 = 2.
But this gives the occasion to enquire into the doctrin of fractions

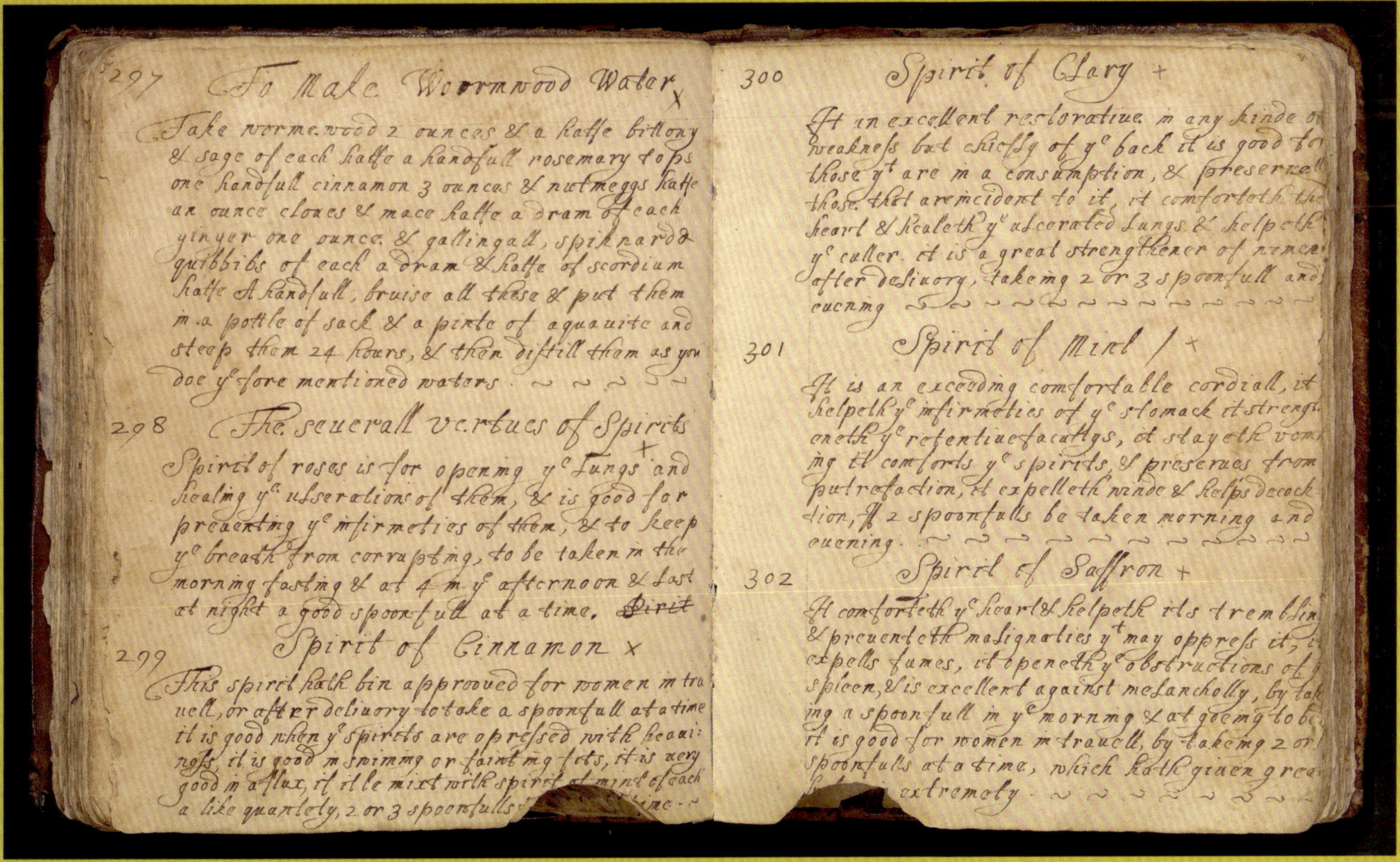
297 To Make Wormwood Water x
Take wormewood 2 ounces & a halfe bittony & sage of each halfe a handfull rosemary tops one handfull cinnamon 3 ounces & nutmeggs halfe an ounce cloves & mace halfe a dram of each ginger one ounce & gallingall, spiknard & quibbibs of each a dram & halfe of scordium halfe A handfull, bruise all these & put them in a pottle of sack & a pinte of aquavite and steep them 24 hours, & then distill them as you doe y fore mentioned waters
298 The severall vertues of Spirits
Spirit of roses is for opening ye Lungs and healing ye ulserations of them, & is good for preventing ye infirmeties of them, & to keep ye breath from corrupting, to be taken in the morning fasting & at 4 in y afternoon & last at night a good spoonfull at a time. Spirit
Spirit of Cinnamon x
299 This spirit hath bin approoved for women in travell, or after deliuory to take a spoonfull at a time it is good when ye spirits are opressed with heaviness, it is good in swiming or fainting fets, it is very good in a flux, if it be mixt with spirit of mint of each a like quantety, 2 or 3 spoonfulls [illegible]
300 Spirit of Clary +
It in excellent restorative in any kinde of weakness but chiefly of ye back it is good for those yt are in a consumption, & preserves those that are incedent to it, it comforteth the heart & healeth ye ulcerated lungs & helpeth ye caller. it is a great strengthener of women after deliuory, takeing 2 or 3 spoonfull and evening
301 Spirit of Mint / x
It is an exceeding comfortable cordiall, it helpeth ye infirmeties of ye stomack it strengtheneth ye retentive facultys, it stayeth vomiting it comforts ye spirits, & preserves from putrefaction, it expelleth winde & helps decoction, if 2 spoonfuls be taken morning and evening
302 Spirit of Saffron +
It comforteth ye heart & helpeth its trembling & preventeth malignaties yt may oppress it, it expells fumes, it openeth ye obstructions of ye spleen, & is excellent against melancholly, by taking a spoonfull in ye morning & at going to bed it is good for women in travell, by takeing 2 or 3 spoonfuls at a time, which hath given great [illegible] extremoly

# 34. **Tobias Lear** (1762–1816)

## *Diary*

---

1799–1801
Manuscript; ink on laid paper bound in quarter brown leather and paste paper boards
7 3/8 × 4 3/4 inches (18.3 × 12.3 cm)

Tobias Lear Diary [Am .09238]
Bequest of John Gribbel estate, 1947

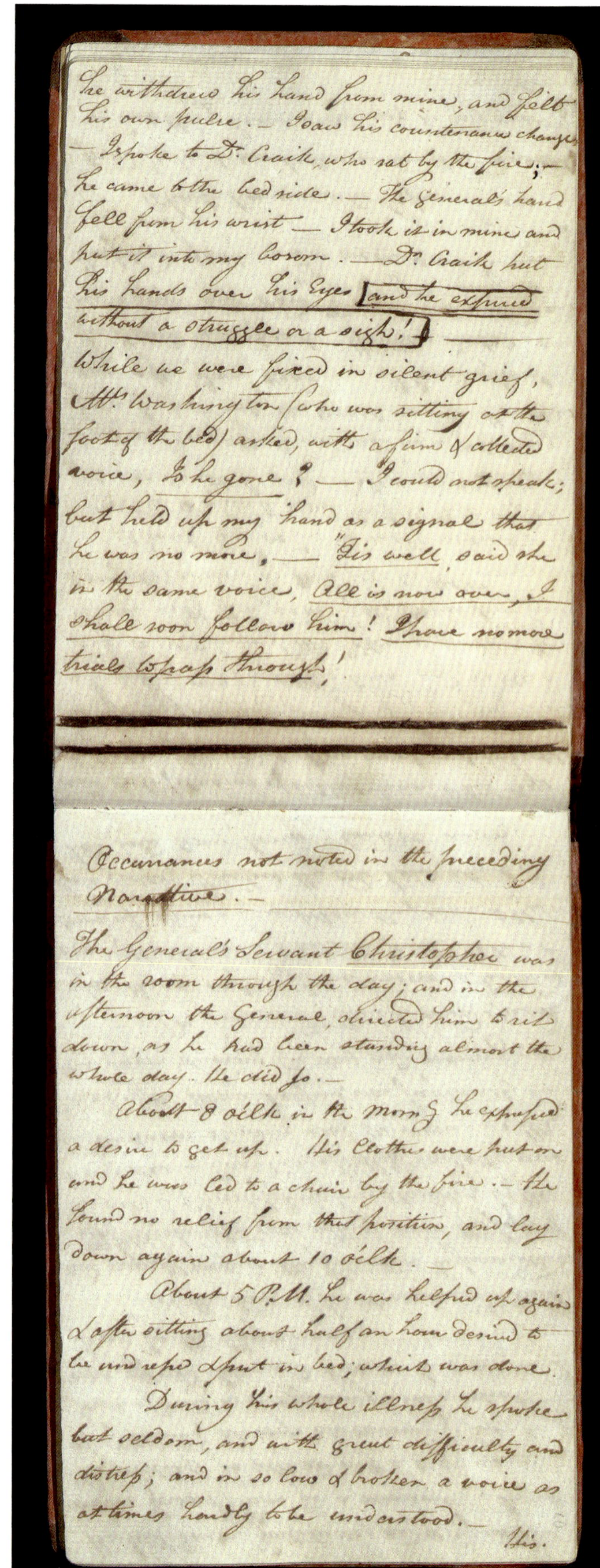
he withdrew his hand from mine, and felt
his own pulse. — I saw his countenance change
— I spoke to Dr. Craik, who sat by the fire; —
he came to the bed side. — The General's hand
fell from his wrist — I took it in mine and
put it into my bosom. — Dr. Craik put
his hands over his Eyes and he expired
without a struggle or a sigh! —
While we were fixed in silent grief,
Mrs. Washington (who was sitting at the
foot of the bed) asked, with a firm & collected
voice, Is he gone? — I could not speak;
but held up my hand as a signal that
he was no more. — 'Tis well, said she
in the same voice, All is now over, I
shall soon follow him! I have no more
trials to pass through!

Occurrences not noted in the preceding
Narrative. —
The General's Servant Christopher was
in the room through the day; and in the
afternoon the General directed him to sit
down, as he had been standing almost the
whole day. He did so. —
About 8 o'clk in the morng he expressed
a desire to get up. His Clothes were put on
and he was led to a chair by the fire. — He
found no relief from that position, and lay
down again about 10 o'clk. —
About 5 P.M. he was helped up again
& after sitting about half an hour desired to
be undressed & put in bed; which was done.
During his whole illness he spoke
but seldom, and with great difficulty and
distress; and in so low & broken a voice as
at times hardly to be understood. —
His.

Perhaps the most important words from the only eyewitness account of the death of George Washington are the ones Tobias Lear highlighted within a rectangle: "and he expired without a struggle or a sigh!" He added two thick mourning lines at the bottom of the page to emphasize the point.

New Hampshire-born Tobias Lear became George Washington's private secretary in 1786. Not only was he treated as a member of the family early on, he eventually became one—marrying not one but two Washington relatives. After his first wife died of yellow fever in 1793, Lear married Frances Bassett Washington, widow of George's nephew, George Augustine Washington. When Frances passed from tuberculosis in 1796, he married Frances Dandridge Henley, niece of Martha Washington. Lear served the Washingtons in the official presidential residence in Philadelphia as well as at their beloved Mount Vernon. Under Thomas Jefferson he served as the US envoy to Saint-Domingue (now Haiti). He later served as a counsel general in North Africa.

But it was Lear's detailed descriptions of Washington's initial symptoms, his various treatments by three physicians, deathbed interactions with Mrs. Washington and others in the household, and eventually Washington's demise that will be his lasting legacy. Washington was out in a cold December storm and began to complain of a sore throat. He kept getting worse, and doctors were called. Among their treatments, "a mixture of Molasses, Vinegar

& butter was prepared to try its effects in the throat." Then came the bloodletting. Mrs. Washington worried that too much was being let. Washington ignored her protests and urged for "more, more!"

After a point Washington knew it was a battle he couldn't win. Lear records Washington instructing them, "Have me decently buried; and do not let my body be put into the vault in less than three days after I am dead." After Dr. Craik closed Washington's eyes, Mrs. Washington asked Lear if her husband was "gone." Lear indicated that he was. "'Tis well," said she in the same voice, "All is now over, I shall soon follow him! I have no more trials to pass through!'"

The diary, as an artifact, is also interesting. The day after Washington's death, Lear had Dr. Craik read what he recorded and attest to its accuracy—Craik signed and dated the page. Lear records measuring the cadaver for the coffin (Washington was: "6 feet 3 ½ inches exact"; 1 foot 9 inches across the shoulders and 2 feet 9 inches across the elbows). Later in the diary, Lear switches to the 1801 voyage to Haiti to begin his post as an envoy. Besides taking his son, Lincoln, with him, he gives details about packing, among other things, clothes, books, pistols, glassware, chinaware, stationery, and "2 barrels containing Hams."

The diary has its original boards, covered in comb-etched paste paper. Over the years those two heavy iron gall ink mourning lines on the December 14, 1799, "death page," started to eat through the paper, nearly perforating it. The Historical Society of Pennsylvania had the entire volume conserved (paper, binding, and boards) so that the words of Lear, stated at the diary's beginning, would be realized: "This day being marked by an event which will be memorable in the History of America, and perhaps of the World."

LEE ARNOLD

---

Other notable Washington family/Tobias Lear material at the Historical Society of Pennsylvania include *A Booke of Cookery* and *A Booke of Sweetmeats* (Martha Washington's Cookbook), seventeenth century **(no. 33)** [Washington Family Papers, 696]; Henri Christophe, *Letter to Tobias Lear* (from the Haitian king while Lear was US envoy to Haiti under Jefferson), Dec. 19, 1801 [Simon Gratz autograph collection, 250A]; Howard Edwards, *Washingtoniana case* (personal letter from George Washington, images, and locket of Washington's hair), 1882 **(no. 35)** [Washington Family Papers, 696]; George Washington, *Pocket diary* (kept while at Mount Vernon), Jan. 1–June 21, 1796 [Washington Family Papers, 696]; and *Washington household journal* (presidential residence in Philadelphia), 1793–1797 [Washington Family Papers, 696].

# 35. **Howard Edwards** (1833–1925)

## *Washington Relic Case*

1882
Manuscript; ink on laid paper; watercolor on wove paper; engraving on wove paper; hair encased in glass
8 5/16 × 7 inches (21.2 × 18.0 cm) (manuscript); 9 3/4 × 8 inches (24.8 × 20.3 cm) (engraving); 3 3/4 × 2 5/8 (9.5 × 6.7 cm) (watercolor); 1 1/8 × 1 1/8 inches (2.8 × 2.8 cm) (hair encasement); 17 5/16 × 11 13/16 × 1 3/4 inches (44.0 × 30.0 × 4.5 cm) (case)

Dated and signed under encapsulated hair, lower right panel: *Philada. Nov 30. 1882 / Howard Edwards.*
Inscribed in plate of engraving of George Washington on right panel: *Fairmen*; lower right panel, under encapsulated hair: *Presented by John Perrie, son of Martin Perrie, / Washington's Hair Dresser, in 1781 – to my Relative, / the late Anthony M. Buckley.*

Washingtoniana Case [Am .00151]

In the decades following his death in 1799, George Washington came as close to assuming sainthood as anyone in the United States. Just as Europeans had sought saintly relics in the Middle Ages, the American public revered physical vouchers of their fallen heroes. As those who had personally experienced the American Revolution faded from the scene, their descendants turned to images and relics of the country's most beloved founding father to remind themselves of his greatness and the imagined happier times he represented. In 1882, the 150th anniversary of Washington's birth, Historical Society of Pennsylvania member Howard Edwards reverently collected and mounted in a leather-bound bookbox two printed portraits of Washington and a handwritten letter from the president to his brother-in-law Burwell Bassett. Edwards capped this assemblage with a small, round locket containing the president's hair, thus creating for his own descendants a personal shrine of patriotic significance.

While the public display of hair from a beloved friend, an admired figure, or a member of one's own family was widespread in the nineteenth century, it was a practice that had had its start among well-to-do families almost a century before. Martha Washington was said to have "always" worn a locket with a portrait of her husband on one side and a lock of his hair on the other. Nor did the Washingtons keep such mementos to themselves. As early as 1770, George and Martha were sending hair samples overseas to have them put into lockets that they could give to their family and friends.

Until Washington's hair began to change hands commercially in the twentieth century, most examples could be traced by descent from someone who had received clippings directly from the president and first lady or from Washington's secretary and aide, Tobias Lear, who was assigned the job of distributing presidential relics to friends and admirers after Washington's death. Another understandable, if slightly less revered, source was Martin Pierie, the barber who groomed the president during the years in which he lived in Philadelphia. (Pronounced "Perry," his name was spelled in a variety of ways.)

According to his son John, the elder Pierie snipped a good supply of the coveted strands directly from the president while administering to his hairdressing needs in the 1780s. When the younger Pierie followed in his father's barbering footsteps, he used Martin's trove of presidential hair to curry favor with friends or advertise his own hair-cutting services to those who wished to bathe in the reflected glory of the nation's first president. It was through John that Edwards obtained his Washington relic, noting that it had been given "to my Rclative, the late Anthony M. Buckley" in 1781 by the barber's son. Edwards's locket is one of two Washington hair samples of Pierie family origin in HSP's collections. The other was given to Eli Kirk Price by John Pierie in February 1854. While less elaborately preserved, it reflects the same reverence for America's sainted hero.

ROBERT MCCRACKEN PECK

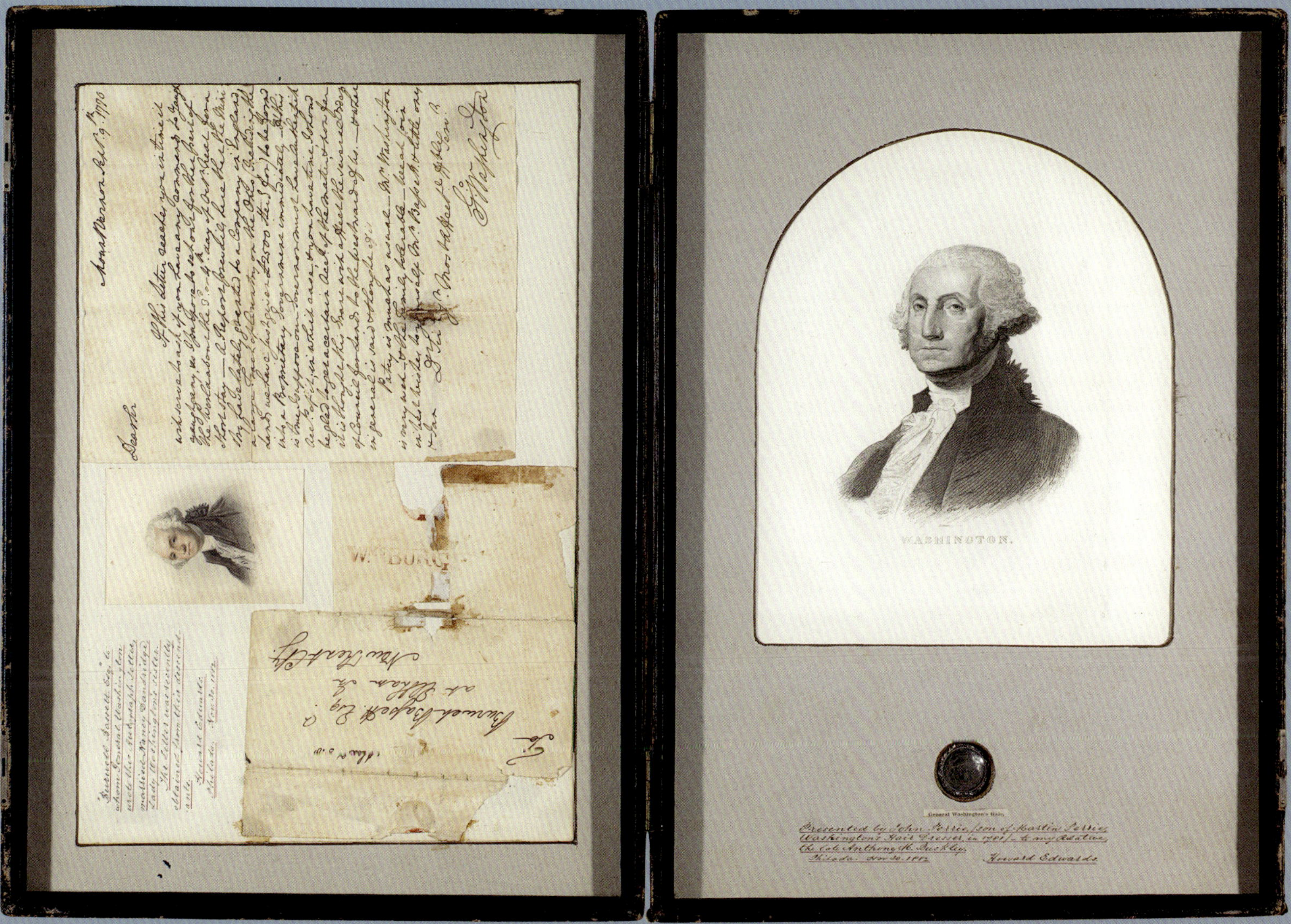
WASHINGTON.

## 36. **Benjamin Henry Latrobe** (1764–1820)

### *Section from West to East, Looking Northward*

1799
Graphite, ink, and wash on wove paper
11 1⁄8 × 13 11⁄16 inches (28.2 × 34.7 cm)

p. 9 of *Designs of Buildings erected in the Year 1799 in Philadelphia, by Benjamin Henry Latrobe Archt. & Engineer, Presented as a token of Sincere affection to his Brother C. J. Latrobe*

Historical Society of Pennsylvania Bound Graphics Collection [V66]

## **Cornelius Tiebout** (ca. 1773–1832), after **John James Barralet** (ca. 1747–1815)

### *View of the Water Works at Centre Square Philadelphia*

1812
Engraving on wove paper
13 11⁄16 × 21 inches (34.8 × 53.5 cm) (plate); 17 15⁄16 × 23 inches (45.5 × 58.3 cm) (sheet)

Inscribed below image: *VIEW OF THE WATER WORKS AT CENTRE SQUARE PHILADELPHIA*; below image, lower left: *J.J.Barralet del[t]*; below image, lower right: *C.Tiebout sculp[t]*

Historical Society of Pennsylvania Large Graphics Collection [V65]

Section drawings, cutting across buildings, are not typically the most recognizable images even of well-known sites, but this particularly well-rendered section helps explain a complicated structure that operated in multiple dimensions: as a functional work of engineering, distributing water to the city; as an ambitious work of monumental architecture, ushering in a new aesthetic; and as the centerpiece of a work of civic embellishment that celebrated the meeting of Philadelphia's ordering axes.

In the wake of the recurring yellow fever epidemics of the 1790s, the city was eager to secure a supply of clean water in place of a prior dependence on local wells too close to household privies, particularly in the densely built parts of the city. To that end, Philadelphia's "Watering Committee" engaged Benjamin Latrobe for the task. Latrobe had arrived from England only a few years before, bringing to the young country an unmatched level of training and experience in both engineering and architectural practice.

Latrobe's plan was to raise and distribute fresh river water conducted from the Schuylkill via a tunnel, shown at the bottom of the drawing as a blue rectangle. Above was a steam engine, with its firebox, boiler, and cylinder below a wooden framework supporting a large flywheel. Heat would produce steam power translated into up-and-down motion. An eccentric connection to the flywheel would convert that into rotary motion powering a pump that raised water up into wooden tanks within the dome. From there, gravity would feed the water through underground pipes to public hydrants and subscribing households.

Latrobe housed all this within a container of local marble and brick whose exterior revealed very little of its inner workings. Instead, his design offered an essay in architectural modernity, fresh from London and Paris, that employed enlarged, simplified classical elements to ennoble a composition of large geometric volumes—a half-cube base supporting a broad cylinder capped by a low-rising dome. Monolithic Doric columns and moldings of an early Greek form marked entrances that led to offices at the corners lit by large arched windows. In operation, plumes of smoke emerged incongruously from the apex of the dome, as if evidence of some sort of ancient ritual, though that idyll was probably accompanied by the modern hissing and banging of the engine and the storage of ready piles of fuel that fed it. This startlingly new, monumental object at the city's ordained center was set within an expansive green park, inscribed within a circular roadway that reinforced its symbolic centrality.

Latrobe's building persisted until 1827, well after a new waterworks was completed in 1815 along the Schuylkill River's edge just below today's Philadelphia Museum of Art. His pupils William Strickland and Robert Mills continued his hybrid form of monumental neoclassicism, which soon yielded to the more literal embrace of the Greek Revival in the second quarter of the nineteenth century. A generation later, though, the symbolic centrality of Latrobe's waterworks was echoed at a far greater scale for a far larger city with the construction of City Hall—whose tower's base subtly recalls the old waterworks that stood just to its south within the present courtyard. JEFFREY A. COHEN

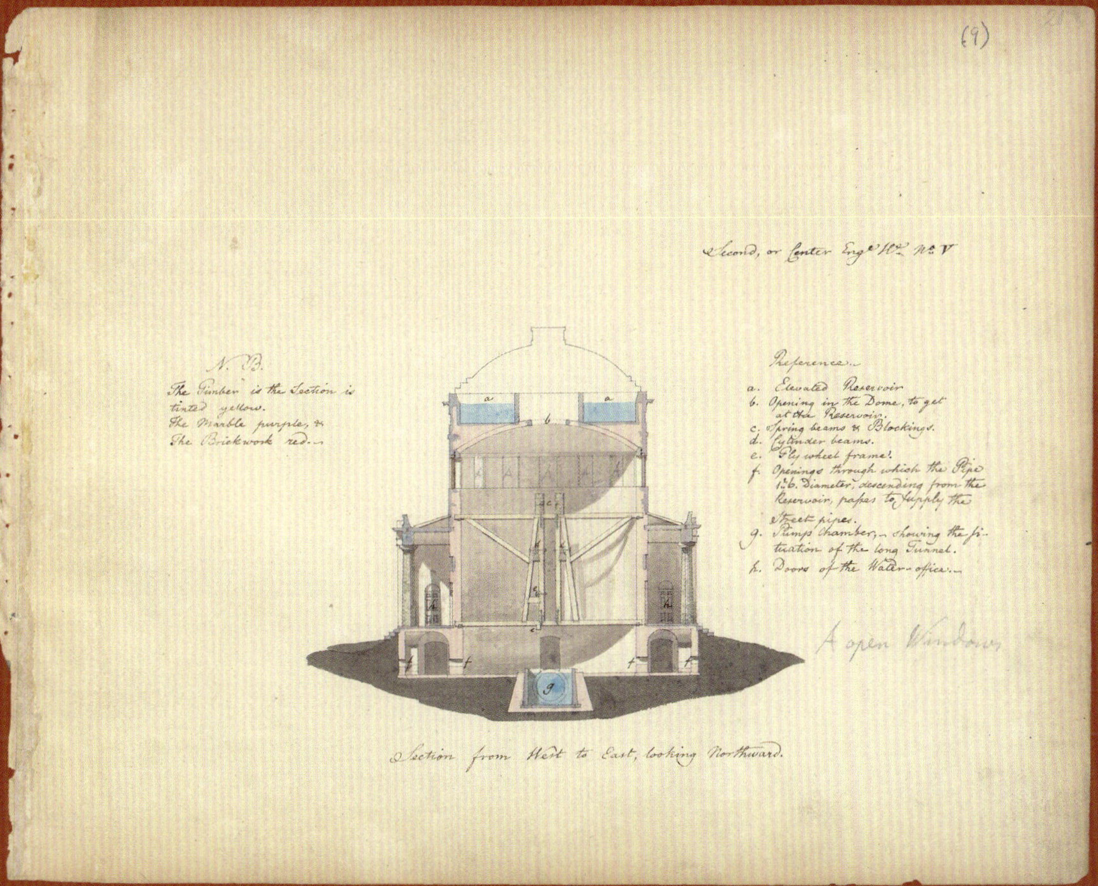

J.J. Barralet del. C. Tiebout sculp.

VIEW OF THE WATER WORKS AT CENTRE SQUARE PHILADELPHIA.

## 37. **William Birch** (1755–1834)

### *High Street, From the Country Market-place Philadelphia*

1798
Published by R. Campbell & Co.
Etching and engraving with watercolor on wove paper
10 15/16 × 13 3/8 inches (27.8 × 34.0 cm) (plate);
16 1/4 × 18 11/16 inches (47.5 × 41.2 cm) (volume)

pl. 12 of *The City of Philadelphia: in the State of Pennsylvania, North America; as it appeared in the Year 1800, consisting of twenty eight plates*
Inscribed below image: *HIGH STREET, From the Country Market-place* PHILADELPHIA.; below image, lower left: *Drawn & Engraved by W.Birch & Son.*; below image, lower right: *Published by R. Campbell & C° N° 30 Chesnut* [*sic*] *Street Philad*[a] *1798.*

Historical Society of Pennsylvania Bound Graphics Collection [V66]

### *High Street, From the Country Market-place Philadelphia: with the Procession in Commemoration of the Death of General George Washington, December 26th, 1799*

1800
Published by R. Campbell & Co.
Etching and engraving with watercolor on laid paper
10 15/16 × 13 3/8 inches (27.8 × 34.0 cm) (plate);
16 1/4 × 18 11/16 inches (47.5 × 41.2 cm) (volume)

pl. 13 of *The City of Philadelphia: in the State of Pennsylvania, North America; as it appeared in the Year 1800, consisting of twenty eight plates*
Inscribed below image: *HIGH STREET, From the Country Market-place* PHILADELPHIA: / *with the Procession in Commemoration of the Death of* GENERAL GEORGE WASHINGTON, *December 26*[th] *1799.*; below image, lower left: *Drawn & Engraved by W.Birch & Son.*; below image, lower right: *Published by R. Campbell & C° N° 30 Chesnut* [*sic*] *Street Philad*[a] *1800.*

Historical Society of Pennsylvania Bound Graphics Collection [V66]

It has been over two hundred years since William Birch published a bound book of hand-colored engraved prints titled *The City of Philadelphia, in the State of Pennsylvania North America as it appeared in the Year 1800*. It would be hard to overstate how well known these prints are today in American art and to the public. They are as appealing an artistic achievement as they are an important historical record of Philadelphia at the end of the eighteenth century. Birch arrived in Philadelphia with his family in 1794 from England. He was thirty-nine years old and a successful miniature enamel painter and printmaker. His decision to reestablish himself in Philadelphia was partly based on the reports of opportunities in that city. Birch was not to be disappointed. He was energetic and outgoing in personality. He advertised in the newspapers and met the commercial, professional, and political leaders of Philadelphia, which was then the seat of the federal government. Birch recognized in this city a special subject matter to record in engraved prints similar to those he had published in 1791, which were primarily of paintings by English artists. In Philadelphia, he was inspired to make a major departure with the prints by using a larger paper size and a subject matter based on original drawings and watercolors drawn from the actual street locations.

Birch was ambitious and commercially astute in how he envisioned this project to succeed. The original 1800 publication of twenty-nine engraved prints plus two typeset pages was composed of twenty-six city views, a title page, frontispiece, introduction with print titles, city plan, and subscribers list. He stated in his introduction that the bound book would tell the story of the city's architecture and sophisticated lifestyle almost as a tour from the ships at the docks to the center of William Penn's original city plan. Birch intended to show how Philadelphia was a commercially active city for investors abroad and an opportunity for more settlers to help grow the population.

*Drawn & Engraved by W. Birch & Son.*

*Published by R. Campbell & Co. No. 30 Chesnut Street Philada. 1798.*

*HIGH STREET, From the Country Market-place* PHILADELPHIA.

*Drawn & Engraved by W. Birch & Son.* *Published by R. Campbell & Co. No. 30 Chesnut Street Philada. 1800.*

*HIGH STREET, From the Country Market-place* PHILADELPHIA:

*with the procession in commemoration of the Death of* GENERAL GEORGE WASHINGTON, *December 26th 1799.*

He conceived the original publication as one that could be added to as new prints were engraved and available to be sold both with and without color. The most expensive hand-colored bound book of plates sold for $44.50, the equivalent of hundreds of dollars in today's currency. Over half of the subscribers for the book were business people who saw its potential as an advertising tool for their locale and products. He took pride in the more notable subscribers, like then–Vice President Thomas Jefferson, Senator John Rutherford, and Representative Samuel Smith, as well as the admired artist Gilbert Stuart and architect Benjamin Henry Latrobe.

After the 1800 edition, Birch published three more editions in 1804, 1809, and 1827–28. There are differences between the editions in the number of plates, choice of images, and size of the paper. The Historical Society of Pennsylvania's 1800 copy has two additional plates plus two blank pages. Copper plates were expensive, and Birch reworked used plates to alter or improve an image. Such a change was made in the 1798 print of *HIGH STREET, From the Country Market-place PHILADELPHIA* with its open view through the arch. After the death of General George Washington on December 14, 1799, Birch made the decision to rework the marketplace plate and created a second print from it that included Philadelphia's symbolic funeral procession for Washington as it passed by the market's entrance on December 26, 1799. Both these prints are in the book at HSP, as well as the first and second compositions for the Bank of the United States print, giving it a total of twenty-eight street views.

Birch oversaw every aspect of the 1800 edition. The title page proudly announces the book was published by W. Birch & Son. Thomas Birch was trained by his father to be a painter and printmaker. William Birch acknowledged in his autobiography that his son made the drawings and watercolors for the prints, and the project was aided by the engraver Samuel Seymour (ca. 1775–1823) and the script engraver William Barker. These four men united to produce a masterpiece of American printmaking, the first of its kind to be created in the United States.

MARTHA HUTSON-SAXTON

The Birch Collection at the Historical Society of Pennsylvania contains the original publications of *The Philadelphia Views* in 1800 and *The Country Seats* (18 plates) in 1808–1809, plus original letters by the Birch family, William Birch's subscription book, business correspondence, and his unpublished autobiography with notes on his enamel painting. The collection also contains watercolors and prints pertaining to the 1800 publication as well as over 122 drawings by Thomas Birch.

# 38. **Thomas Birch** (1779–1851)

## *Penn's Treaty Tree*

---

1800–1801
Oil on canvas
38 3/8 × 48 7/16 inches (97.5 × 123.0 cm)

Historical Society of Pennsylvania Art and Artifact Collection
[3137]
Presented by Mrs. Edward S. Buckley, 1924

The stars were aligned for Thomas Birch to be so young when he created his first major painting, *Penn's Treaty Tree*, in 1800–1801. Thomas arrived in Philadelphia from England with his family at the age of fifteen in 1794. He had already started his artistic training with his father, William Birch, a respected painter of miniature portraits on enamel and a printmaker. William recognized his son's artistic talent and encouraged him to participate in studio projects. Thomas was soon involved with his father's dream of a collection of prints published as *The City of Philadelphia, in the State of Pennsylvania North America, as it appeared in the Year 1800*. Included in the book were twenty-six images of street scenes inside the city and Thomas's frontispiece showing the city's harbor from across the Delaware River. He was twenty-one years old in 1800 and about to begin a long artistic career.

Thomas completed the painting *Penn's Treaty Tree* only months after the publication of the same composition in the frontispiece print entitled *The City and Port of Philadelphia, on the River Delaware from Kensington.* This site in the village of Kensington was well known due to the famous elm tree considered by oral tradition to be where the Quaker William Penn met with the Lenni Lenape tribe in 1682 to sign a treaty. The Quaker theme of peaceful coexistence with the local tribes had been memorialized previously by Benjamin West in his painting *Penn's Treaty with the Indians,* 1771–72. Thomas's painting recorded the same location as West's work, but now with an enhanced view of the Delaware River as it appeared in 1800, filled with shipping vessels and Philadelphia in the distance. It was a statement of historical change over a hundred years and the dynamic commercial success of Penn's dream for Pennsylvania.

In 1791 William had published a book of engravings after primarily English landscape scenes, and it was from this stylistic tradition that Thomas based his painting. The view of Philadelphia from across the river is directly related to the popular British prints of London seen across the Thames River and was meant to show a comparable metropolis with a worldwide shipping port. In preparation for the painting, Thomas made drawings of the city and the coastline, plus dozens of sketches of boats and large ships on the river, as well as being repaired on the shore and in dockyards. These studies helped him create a dynamic river scene under the protection of the Treaty Tree, whose branches stretch across the top of the composition. Directly below the tree's dense foliage, men are at work or relaxing in the shade, while a well-dressed couple looks out at the brightly lit river and the impressive silhouette of the city on the horizon. The message of paradise achieved was clearly meant to convey the successful future of the city.

The painting of *Penn's Treaty Tree* was very likely a private commission brought about by the public success of the frontispiece print. The canvas size alone makes it an ambitious endeavor for a young and inexperienced painter in oils, who accomplished a major step forward in his desire to be known as a landscape artist. By 1802, Thomas had set up his own studio and was advertising for clients. His relationship with his father continued to be pivotal to his career. William's next project of engraved prints was *The Country Seats of the United States of North America,* 1808–1809. He used a watercolor composition by Thomas for a print in the book and created an opportunity as well for his son to paint commissioned landscapes of the country homes located just outside of Philadelphia, like *South-East View of Sedgeley Park, Seat of James Cowles Fisher, Esq.* (ca. 1819, SAAM).

*Penn's Treaty Tree* and the country estate works display an aesthetic philosophy in landscape design that successfully advanced Thomas's early career. By 1811, he was exhibiting at the Pennsylvania Academy of the Fine Arts, where he continued to have an active role. Throughout his career, Birch was a prolific and widely exhibited artist on the eastern seaboard. He played an important part in the American landscape tradition before the advent of the Hudson River School in the 1820s. These early landscape paintings of American scenes left a record of not only historical importance but of the ambitions and ideals of a young nation. MARTHA HUTSON-SAXTON

---

The Historical Society of Pennsylvania holds in the Birch Collection over 122 drawings, mainly by Thomas Birch, as well as watercolors and prints by him. There is also a collection of Birch family letters and other material associated with his father, the artist William Birch.

## 39. Magdalen Society of Philadelphia

*Seal Die*

---

ca. 1850
Steel
2 3⁄16 × 2 3⁄16 × 1 inches (5.5 × 5.5 × 2.5 cm)

Engraved around edge of die, mirrored: *THE MAGDALEN SOCIETY OF PHILADELPHIA / COME RETURN TO VIRTUE*; lower center, mirrored: *INCORPORATED / 1802*

Magdalen Society of Philadelphia Records [2016]
Gift of the White-Williams Foundation, 1973

In its early days, Philadelphia, like London and other cities, felt a need to deal with its so-called fallen women. Victorian England eventually created what came to be known as the Magdalen Movement, which was part of their penal system.

In Philadelphia, the Magdalen Society Asylum, the first of its kind in America, was founded in 1800. Bishop William White (1748–1836), the first bishop of the Episcopal Church of the United States as well as the first bishop of the Diocese of Pennsylvania, served as the society's president until his death.

The goal of the society was to help women who had strayed from the path of virtue and wished to return to a moral life. Over the years, however, it became evident that most of the women who entered the asylum did not feel the need for reform but sought sanctuary from circumstances such as disease, the almshouse, abusive men, or economic troubles. It should be noted that pregnant women and African Americans were barred from the asylum.

The original Philadelphia asylum was on North 20th Street, now the site of the Franklin Institute Science Museum Futures Center. Historian Lu Ann DeCunzo observed that this put it on the outskirts of the city, effectively separating the women from their former lives and identities. Eventually, an eleven-foot wall was built around the property, and a new building was constructed in the 1840s.

Records housed in the Historical Society of Pennsylvania include annual matrons' reports, as well as lists of dismissals, monies received and spent, and letters received. The report for 1916, for example, discussed the previous year's move from the city to the country and noted various reasons that some of the women were discharged, including: being returned to relatives; entering the hospital for training or operations; or being sent to other institutions.

In 1847, a group of Philadelphia women founded the Rosine Association. It rejected the reform program of the Magdalen Society, blaming its lack of effectiveness on the men in charge. The founders of the Rosine Association believed that only women could truly care for other women. The association determined that these women needed marketable skills and training in household management, so its approach included education with no emphasis on moral regeneration.

Eventually, the Magdalen Society followed the lead of the Rosine Association and changed its procedures, sheltering, caring for, and even educating homeless girls rather than attempting to reform prostitutes.

In 1918, the Philadelphia Magdalen Society became the White-Williams Foundation for Girls. (The name honored Bishop White and Quaker philanthropist George Williams). In 1920, having decided to include boys, the name was changed to William-White Scholars. In 2011, it merged with Philadelphia Futures, a nonprofit organization that provides Philadelphia's low-income, first-generation-to-college students with the tools and resources necessary for admission to and success in college. MARIE A. CONN

## 40. **Thomas Jefferson** (1743–1826)

### *Draught of Garden Plan and Key to Plants*

---

1807
Ink on laid paper
7 11⁄16 × 5 15⁄16 inches (19.5 × 15.1 cm)

Ferdinand J. Dreer Autograph Collection [0175]
Gift of Ferdinand J. Dreer, 1890

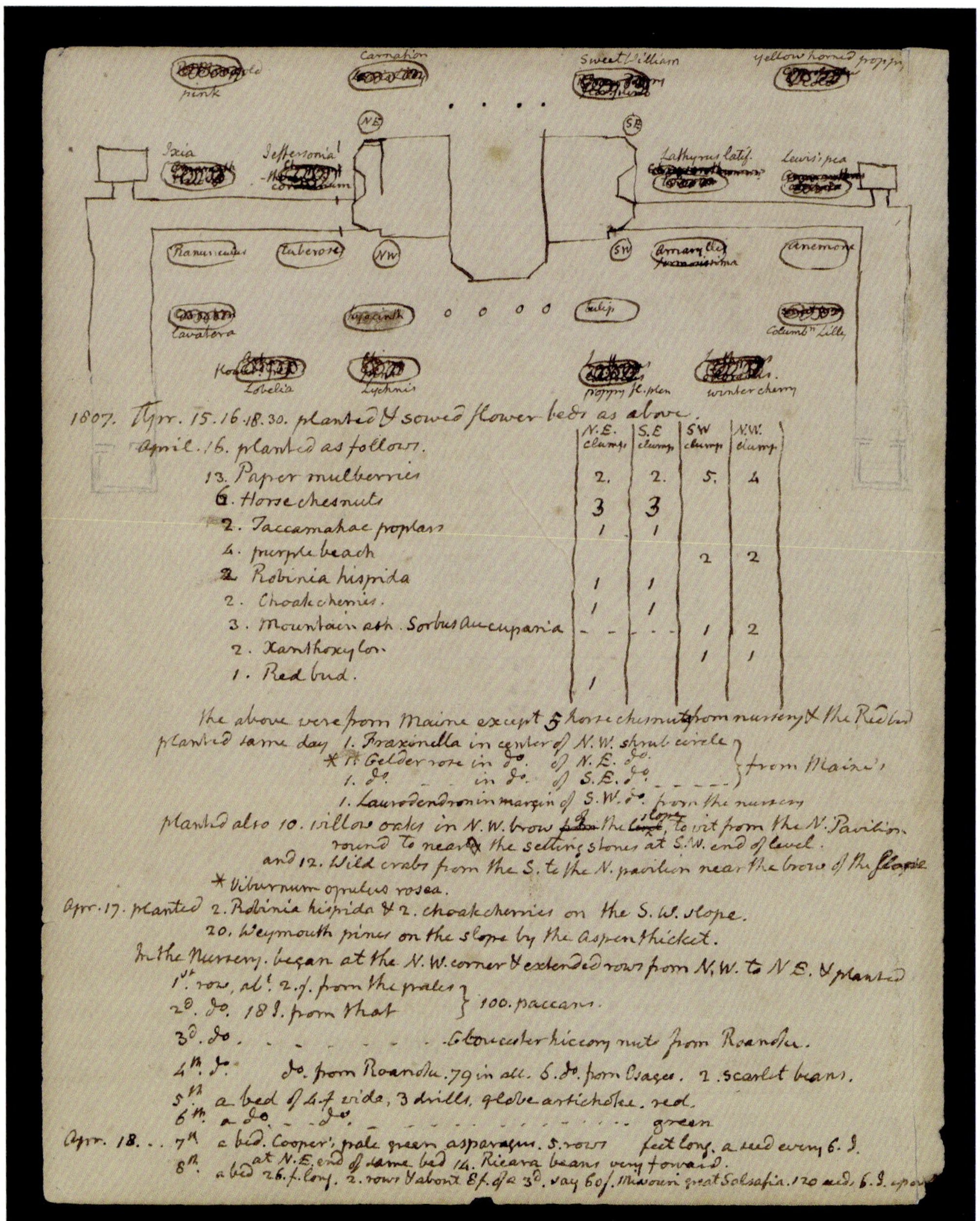

In late March 1807, President Thomas Jefferson left Washington, DC, to oversee the spring planting at his Virginia plantation, Monticello. He recorded in detail the work as it proceeded. This sheet is detached from one of his meticulously kept memorandum books, in this case, his *The Weather Record, 1776–1818*, now at the Library of Congress. Usually, Jefferson kept his notes on gardening and agriculture in his garden or farm books, so it is exceptional that this page was written in his weather notes. Separated at least since the mid- to late nineteenth century, it was rediscovered and transcribed by Jefferson scholar Edwin M. Betts in the early 1940s at a time when Monticello's gardens, long effaced by time and neglect, were undergoing restoration. Densely written on both sides, this sheet records a period in which Jefferson was intensely improving his plantation in anticipation of retirement from public office. It is recognized as a key document because it notes specifically what was planted, where, in what shape (clump, oval bed, rows of eight feet, etc.), and the date of the work. The richness of this information refocused the 1940s restoration campaign away from speculation and ahistorical imaginings toward archivally and ultimately archaeologically supported efforts. Thus, it played a role in establishing good practice in the newly emerging field of landscape preservation.

The sheet, supported by hundreds of related documents, illuminates a history of the gardening endeavors of Jefferson and his contemporaries. His notes mention those individuals who provided him with plants, seeds, advice, and labor, including family members, nurserymen, enslaved and paid gardeners, and fellow landowners. The sense of local, national, and indeed international networks emerge from his logs in phrases such as: "seeds of the chaste tree from Doctr Gouan at Montpelier"; "Genl. Jackson's peaches"; or "trees from [Thomas] Main[e]." These notes provide the evidence for a fuller history of Jefferson's landscape world.

The earliest entry on this sheet begins with the terraced slope along the plantation road, Mulberry Row. Jefferson listed the plants on each level: fruit and berry beds, fifteen "terrasses" of wine and table grapes, another of trees and shrubs, and finally, Bailey's alley, bearing the name of Monticello's Scottish gardener Robert Bailey. This page testifies to Jefferson's deep interest in and commitment to the cultivation of grapes and lists dozens of European cultivars as well as native grapes. Although he was frustrated in making wine from European grapes due to pests and disease, he continued to plant and replant his vineyards, experimenting as he laid the foundation for an American wine industry.

The reverse of the sheet, dated from April 11 to 30, shows a plan of oval and round beds on the lawns surrounding the house. Jefferson scribbled within each bed the flower or shrub name and "planted & sowed." Below the sketch, he recorded the planting of an arboretum he called the Grove that extended beyond the lawn, specifying tree species, how many, and where they were planted: "in the center . . . of the shrub circle," or "on the brow of the slope." The last section listed shrubs, fruit and nut trees, vegetables, and hundreds more trees, all planted in the "Nursery."

What is notable about the plants Jefferson identified on this sheet is the range of native and non-native species. He planted those recently collected from Northern Plains Indigenous tribes, including *Fritillaria pudica*, which he described as a "food of the native." There were Ricara beans and Missouri Great Salsafia, fresh from the Lewis and Clark expedition and brought directly to Jefferson. He planted *Jeffersonia binata* (diphylla), which had been named in his honor just a few years earlier. These native plants were intermingled throughout the plantation with imported non-native flowers, fruits, and woody plants.

Importantly, Jefferson recorded his failures as often as his winners. His efforts were experimental and productive, and all contributed to the knowledge-making to which he was committed. Monticello was a true botanical garden—one intended to promote and celebrate New World plants as well as introduce to the new United States imported plants for economic, scientific, and ornamental use. This sheet has motivated expansive studies by plant experts Peter J. Hatch, Peggy Cornett, and others, whose examination of original sources and debates over taxonomic classification have yielded a wealth of information on the art, science, and culture of plants in the early years of the American Republic.

THERESE O'MALLEY

Further related information in the Historical Society of Pennsylvania archives can be found in the Jefferson Papers, Bartram Family Papers, Benjamin Smith Barton Papers, Henry Muhlenberg Papers, and Peale Family Papers.

## 41. **William Charles** (1776–1820)

### *The Cock Fight—or Another Sting for the Pride of John Bull*

ca. 1813
Hand-colored etching on wove paper
10 × 14 inches (25.5 × 35.5 cm)

Inscribed below image: *The Cock Fight—or Another Sting for the Pride of John Bull.*; below image, lower right: *Charles del et Sculp*

Historical Society of Pennsylvania Large Graphics Collection [V65]

Improbably, on June 18, 1812, the United States declared war against Great Britain over territorial issues on the northwestern frontier and maritime rights, providing artist William Charles, who was born in Scotland and had emigrated to the United States in about 1805, an outlet for his talents. Working first in New York and then in Philadelphia after 1808, Charles continued to produce social and political graphic satires and later illustrated children's books. He came to the US as a mature and experienced artist and was by far the best and most prolific caricaturist during the War of 1812. British political satire at the time had reached a high point in the work of Thomas Rowlandson, James Gillray, and George Cruikshank. Charles would have been well aware of their prints. Indeed, Gillray, proclaimed by one contemporary as "the foremost living artist in the whole of Europe," provided inspiration for *The Cock Fight*.

*The Cock Fight* is one of about two dozen cartoons that Charles produced during the War of 1812. In this rare print, of which just two impressions are recorded, Charles celebrates the victory of the American *Hornet* commanded by Captain James Lawrence over the British *Peacock* under the command of Captain Peake with a caustic satire of King George III. To vivify the battles, Charles has represented the two naval vessels as their visual equivalents. King George watches in horror as the hornet tears the peacock's tail apart. He has already pierced the peacock's body with an elongated and massive stinger shaped as a saber, a device Charles used earlier in *A Wasp Taking a Frolick Or a Sting for Johnny Bull* (1812). In a caption to *The Cock Fight*, the hornet exclaims to the peacock: "I'll make you rue the day that 'ever you fixed your Argus eyes [referring to the pattern on a peacock's tail] on me. I'll rake you fore and aft my boy. I'll send you to davy's locker." A few more thrusts and the peacock will sink to the bottom of the sea, as *the Peacock* did after the battle off the Brazilian coast on February 24, 1813. The peacock wishes he "had stayed home and struted [*sic*] on my own Dunghill" rather than be consigned to the ocean's depths. King George is stunned: "Brother Jonathan's Hornet killed my Peacock!!! In fifteen minutes too! Not possible. Fine bird, well fed, I fear he was too fond of showing his tail."

Charles derived the figure of George III from a print conceived by Lieutenant Colonel Bradyll and James Gillray, *The King of Brobdingnag and Gulliver*, published in London in 1803. That print shows King George holding a miniature Napoleon Bonaparte in his hand while examining him with a monoscope. A similar elongated stinger appeared in Charles's *A Wasp Taking a Frolick* etched a year earlier. Amos Doolittle, a general engraver working in New Haven, Connecticut, produced *The Hornet and Peacock, or, John Bull in Distress,* creating a half bull and half peacock pierced by a hornet's stinger. Doolittle probably had seen one or both of Charles's cartoons. In any event, the reuse of imagery was common on both sides of the Atlantic, as the etching by Charles demonstrates.

GEORGIA B. BARNHILL

Charles del et Sculp

THE COCK FIGHT — or another sting for the Pride of JOHN BULL.

Robert Jones son of David Jones (now living) was born in the parish of Llanfair Dalhaiarn, Denbighshire North Wales, Augst 1800. was married to Phoebe Hughes, of the parish of Llangernew, Denbighshire North Wales, on the 24th Dec 1826; their eldest son Thomas was born in the parish of Eglwysfach, township of Maenan, Caernarvonshire, North Wales Sept 1827. The said Robert Jones, wife and child left Wales for America on the 19th June 1829; arrived in the city of New York on the 19th August same year, after a few days left that city for the state of Pennsylvania and settled at New Philadelphia Schuylkill county, in that state; in which place Robert Jones died on the 1st Oct 1830, and his wife Phoebe Jones on the following 9th Nov.

New York Feb 9th 1831

## 42. Orphan Society of Philadelphia

### *Life and Family of Robert Jones*

February 9, 1831
Manuscript; ink on wove paper
7 7/8 × 4 3/4 inches (20.0 × 12.0 cm)

Orphan Society of Philadelphia Records [1913]
Gift of Orphan Society of Philadelphia, 1965

All genealogists dream of finding that one document that knocks down a long-standing brick wall and connects a known ancestor to the previous generation. Locating that unique document often requires research into private manuscript collections, most of which are not available online.

The Historical Society of Pennsylvania's extraordinary manuscript collections hold one such group that contains 150 years of organizational records documenting admissions and indentures for the thousands of young children in the care of the Orphan Society of Philadelphia. Founded in 1814, their earliest record book related the stories of destitute, fatherless children transferred from the almshouse, an institution under the jurisdiction of the Guardians of the Poor.

Officially incorporated on January 29, 1816, the society's first constitution was prefaced with words that established its founding principles: "To rescue from ignorance, idleness and vice, destitute, unprotected and helpless children, and to provide for them that support and instruction which may eventually render them valuable members of the community." However, to be admitted, the child needed to be white, fatherless, and born to legally married parents.

Notable treasures in this collection are the marriage certificates signed by a minister from the church where the ceremony occurred. Whether the family surrendered them with the child, or a society representative had to request a duplicate from the church, the Orphan Society retained these vital records in their files.

Letters written to support a child's eligibility as an orphan can often reveal extensive details of a family's history: a father lost at sea, a mother's illness, abandonment, or the untimely death of both parents. Names of children as young as eleven months were recorded in the admittance books, and importantly, for many of these children, their birth dates were recorded, too. Dates for any of these life events for the parents or the child will often prove to be the key to documenting a genealogy, especially when the birthplace was recorded from another state.

To control the cost of maintaining a child, orphans were indentured to people not only in Philadelphia but in all the surrounding Pennsylvania counties, as well as to families living in distant counties such as Bradford, McKean, Mifflin, and Susquehanna, and from the states of Delaware, New Jersey, and New York. Occasionally, fortunate children were adopted by the families they were initially bound to serve, and notably, adoptive parents traveled from Massachusetts and Illinois to bring home a child.

The society's first board reflects the strength behind the organization from its inception. Three of the initial board members were Mrs. Sarah Ralston, the first directress of the society; Mrs. Julia Rush, the second directress and the wife of Dr. Benjamin Rush, a physician and signer of the Declaration of Independence; and Miss Rebecca Gratz, the society's secretary for forty years, well known for her charitable work within the local Jewish community. Within a year of its inception, the society had been donated land by wealthy Philadelphians for the construction of its first home located at "Schuylkill Fifth [18th Street] and Cherry Streets."

On the society's 100th anniversary in 1915, it could celebrate its accommodation of 1346 orphan children: 566 girls and 780 boys. The stories of so many of these children can be gleaned from the Orphan Society of Philadelphia Records at HSP. SANDRA M. HEWLETT

## 43. Samuel Honeyman Kneass (1806–1858)

### *Front Elevation of the Bank of the U.S.*

1819
Engraving on wove paper
10 × 13 inches (25.4 × 33.0 cm)

Inscribed below image: *FRONT ELEVATION OF THE BANK OF THE U.S. / Design'd by W. Strickland Arch*[t]; below image, lower right: *Engrav'd by Kneass, Young & C*[o]

Historical Society of Pennsylvania Medium Graphics Collection [V64]

### *United States Bank, Philadelphia*

1824
Ink and colored wash on wove paper
19 ⅞ × 27 ⅞ inches (50.5 × 70.8 cm)

Inscribed below image: *United States Bank, Philadelphia. / Presented to Mr. John Struthers, Marble Mason, by his Friend S.H. Kneass.*; below image, lower left: *Designed & executed by Wm. Strickland Arch*[t] *& Engineer.*; below image, lower right: *Drawn by his Pupil Samuel H. Kneass 182*[*4*]

Historical Society of Pennsylvania Large Graphics Collection [V65]

This engraving and drawing unite several important figures in the creation of the Second Bank of the United States—architect William Strickland (1788–1854); his assistant, Samuel Honeyman Kneass, and Kneass's father, William (1780–1840); and marble mason John Struthers (1786–1851).

The bank was fraught with controversy from its inception. It was chartered in 1816 against strong opposition, five years after Congress failed to renew the charter of the first Bank of the United States. In May 1818 the bank's directors announced a competition for the design of their new building, calling for an edifice "exhibiting a chas[t]e imitation of Grecian architecture, in the simplest and least expensive form." Among the many competitors were Benjamin Henry Latrobe, America's first professionally trained architect and engineer whose Bank of Pennsylvania had already established him as a successful designer of the neoclassical, temple-form building, and his then-inexperienced former pupil, Strickland. The pupil bested the mentor when Strickland won the commission and Latrobe placed second. Latrobe, however, claimed that Strickland had submitted a design for an Ionic temple before he was shown Latrobe's competition drawings for a Doric temple, at which point he withdrew his plan and presented a new building in the Doric style. Some contemporaries, however, attributed the board's decision to favoring a Philadelphian who had performed exemplary service for the city during the War of 1812. Nevertheless, circumstantial evidence and Latrobe's numerous competition drawings, nine of them in the Historical Society of Pennsylvania collections, do show a Doric temple design similar to that ultimately championed by Strickland; indeed, Latrobe's suspicions may have been well founded.

The later history of the bank was just as contentious, as its president, Nicholas Biddle (1786–1844), many of whose papers are housed at HSP, battled with President Andrew Jackson over the nation's financial policies—the so-called Bank War. In the event, Jackson vetoed the renewal of the bank's charter in 1832, and Biddle resigned from the state-chartered institution in 1839.

The imposing building, now a National Historic Landmark, was constructed between 1819 and 1824 on the south side of Chestnut Street between Fourth and Fifth Streets and, with Latrobe's nearby Bank of Pennsylvania, spawned a Greek Revival that swept the nation in subsequent decades. The bank building now houses a permanent collection of over 150 portraits of eighteenth- and nineteenth-century political leaders, military officers, explorers, and scientists, many of them by Charles Willson Peale.

Kneass is remembered mostly as the chief coiner of the US Mint but also as an engraver who rendered some of Strickland's paintings into prints. His engraving of the Second Bank of the United States first appeared in the *Analectic Magazine* in March 1819 and then as a separate print. The two families were close, and William's son Samuel was taken into Strickland's office in 1821 at the age of fifteen while the bank was under construction. At some point in the 1820s, Samuel presented the drawing to Struthers, a stonecutter and marble mason who worked on the bank and many other Strickland projects. Struthers also carved the marble sarcophagus that houses the coffin of George Washington. Samuel later assisted Strickland with reports on canals and railroads and went on to have a distinguished career as a railroad and civil engineer and diplomat.

JOHN C. VAN HORNE

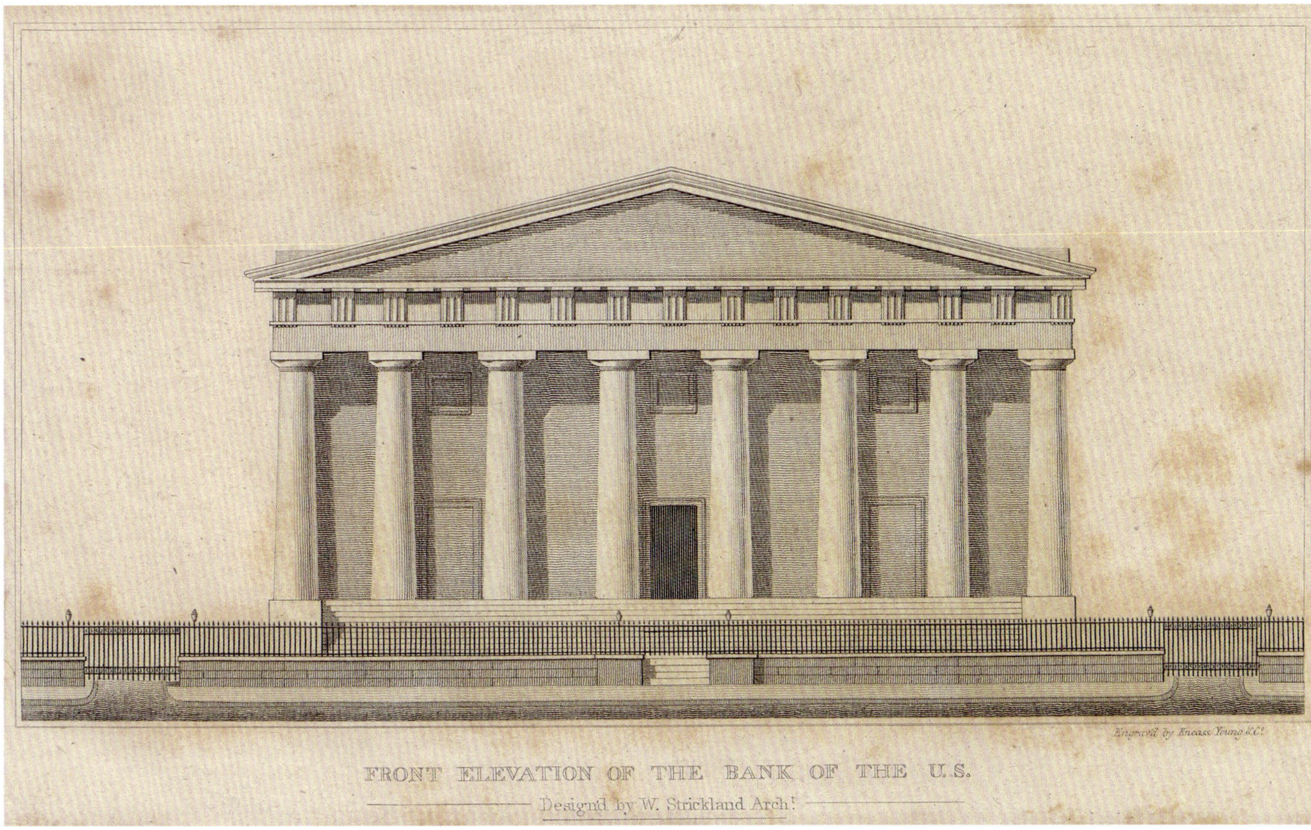
Engrav'd by Eneass Young & C°.
FRONT ELEVATION OF THE BANK OF THE U.S.
Design'd by W. Strickland Arch^t.

United States Bank, Philadelphia

# 44. *James Forten*

ca. 1825
Gouache on laid paper
8 5⁄16 × 6 15⁄16 inches (21.1 × 17.6 cm)

Leon Gardiner Collection of American Negro Historical Society Records [0008]
Gift of Leon Gardiner, 1933

When Black abolitionist and Philadelphia sailmaker James Forten died in 1842, thousands of Philadelphians, regardless of race, attended his funeral. They paid their respects to a man who committed his life to advancing the promise of equality stated in the Declaration of Independence. This small portrait of an African American gentleman is thought to depict Forten. It is unlabeled, unsigned, and undated, but the sitter's clothing and hairstyle suggest that it was created in the 1820s or 1830s, which corresponds with the height of Forten's career. Leon Gardiner (1892–1945), a Philadelphia-based collector of African American ephemera and member of the American Negro Historical Society, donated the portrait to the Historical Society of Pennsylvania in late 1933.

Born free in Philadelphia on September 2, 1766, Forten grew up as his native city stirred over debates about American liberties. He watched and listened as the Declaration of Independence was read to the public for the first time in 1776. Five years later, he signed up to serve aboard the privateer ship *Royal Louis* and survived seven months of suffering aboard a British prison ship. Forten's Revolutionary War service solidified his commitment to the young United States of America and its ideals of equality.

Trained as a sailmaker, Forten ran a successful sailmaking business from 1798 until his death in 1842, employing Black and white workers. His accumulated wealth allowed him the opportunity to own a substantial home on Lombard Street, purchase fine clothing and furniture, make investments, lend money, and pay for his children's education.

Forten, though, did not take his wealth, nor his freedom, for granted. Instead, he devoted himself to antislavery efforts and halting the unequal treatment of African Americans. He did not abandon his enslaved "brethren." Armed with his pen, Forten became a voice for Philadelphia's growing Black community, notably with the 1813 pamphlet *Letters from a Man of Colour on a Late Bill Before the Senate of Pennsylvania*. Forten routinely served as an officer of the American Anti-Slavery Society during the 1830s and helped establish the Philadelphia Anti-Slavery Society. He and his wife, Charlotte Vandine Forten, passed on their dedication to reform causes to their eight surviving children. In 1848, one group of Black Pennsylvanians, inspired by the late-Forten's work, declared, "if we imitate his virtues, our influence will dissolve mountains of prejudice."

The portrait here shows a confident gentleman and veteran businessman in a finely tailored suit. It is a respectful image that stands in stark contrast to other prejudice-filled portrayals of African Americans of the period, notably Edward Clay's *Life in Philadelphia* series (1828–30), which satirized wealthy Black Philadelphians like Forten. Forten's picture is among a handful of surviving works from the Antebellum Period that communicate the achievement and dignity of elite Black Philadelphia businessmen.

This portrait, however, may not be the only surviving depiction of Forten created during his lifetime. Another example, an "oil painting," has yet to be located. Writing to William Lloyd Garrison Jr. in 1882, Robert Purvis, Forten's son-in-law, remembered that Charlotte, then ninety-seven years old, owned a picture of her late husband in Philadelphia. Purvis, who had great respect and admiration for his father-in-law, added a caveat: "In my judgment, I believe, you can paint with your pen, a more satisfactory likeness, of that excellent man, than any you may get from the very poor one Mrs. F[orten] has." Perhaps this portrait will someday be found and add to our understanding of Forten's storied life.

MATTHEW SKIC

## 45. *The New Theatre in Chesnut Street Philadelphia*

1823
Engraving on wove paper
9 ½ × 10 ¾ inches (24.3 × 27.3 cm) (plate); 11 7⁄16 × 14 6⁄16 inches (29.0 × 36.4 cm) (sheet)

Inscribed below image: *The New Theatre in / Chesnut Street Philadelphia. / Published by Wm Birch 1823.*

Historical Society of Pennsylvania Medium Graphics Collection [V64]

## *New Theatre, Wood Dæmon; or, the Clock has Struck*

1822
Broadside; woodcut and letterpress on wove paper
15 ⅜ × 6 ⅜ inches (39.0 × 16.0 cm)

Historical Society of Pennsylvania Playbill Collection [3131]

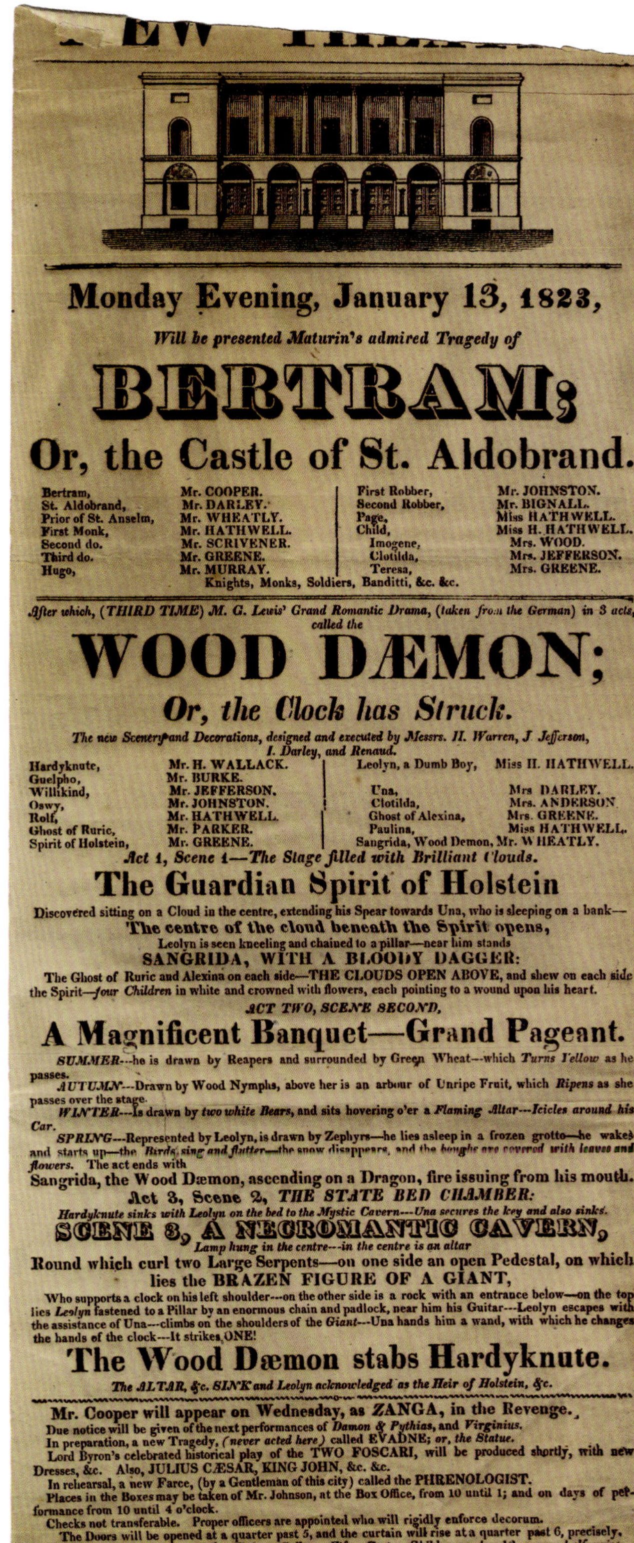

N EW THEATRE.

Monday Evening, January 13, 1823,

*Will be presented Maturin's admired Tragedy of*

# BERTRAM;

## Or, the Castle of St. Aldobrand.

| | | | |
|---|---|---|---|
| Bertram, | Mr. COOPER. | First Robber, | Mr. JOHNSTON. |
| St. Aldobrand, | Mr. DARLEY. | Second Robber, | Mr. BIGNALL. |
| Prior of St. Anselm, | Mr. WHEATLY. | Page, | Miss HATHWELL. |
| First Monk, | Mr. HATHWELL. | Child, | Miss H. HATHWELL. |
| Second do. | Mr. SCRIVENER. | Imogene, | Mrs. WOOD. |
| Third do. | Mr. GREENE. | Clotilda, | Mrs. JEFFERSON. |
| Hugo, | Mr. MURRAY. | Teresa, | Mrs. GREENE. |

Knights, Monks, Soldiers, Banditti, &c. &c.

*After which, (THIRD TIME) M. G. Lewis' Grand Romantic Drama, (taken from the German) in 3 acts, called the*

# WOOD DÆMON;

## *Or, the Clock has Struck.*

*The new Scenery and Decorations, designed and executed by Messrs. H. Warren, J. Jefferson, I. Darley, and Renaud.*

| | | | |
|---|---|---|---|
| Hardyknute, | Mr. H. WALLACK. | Leolyn, a Dumb Boy, | Miss H. HATHWELL. |
| Guelpho, | Mr. BURKE. | | |
| Willikind, | Mr. JEFFERSON. | Una, | Mrs DARLEY. |
| Oswy, | Mr. JOHNSTON. | Clotilda, | Mrs. ANDERSON |
| Rolf, | Mr. HATHWELL. | Ghost of Alexina, | Mrs. GREENE. |
| Ghost of Ruric, | Mr. PARKER. | Paulina, | Miss HATHWELL. |
| Spirit of Holstein, | Mr. GREENE. | Sangrida, Wood Demon, | Mr. WHEATLY. |

*Act 1, Scene 1—The Stage filled with Brilliant Clouds.*

**The Guardian Spirit of Holstein**

Discovered sitting on a Cloud in the centre, extending his Spear towards Una, who is sleeping on a bank—

**The centre of the cloud beneath the Spirit opens,**

Leolyn is seen kneeling and chained to a pillar—near him stands

**SANGRIDA, WITH A BLOODY DAGGER:**

The Ghost of Ruric and Alexina on each side—THE CLOUDS OPEN ABOVE, and shew on each side the Spirit—*four Children* in white and crowned with flowers, each pointing to a wound upon his heart.

*ACT TWO, SCENE SECOND,*

**A Magnificent Banquet—Grand Pageant.**

*SUMMER*---he is drawn by Reapers and surrounded by Green Wheat---which *Turns Yellow* as he passes.

*AUTUMN*---Drawn by Wood Nymphs, above her is an arbour of Unripe Fruit, which *Ripens* as she passes over the stage.

*WINTER*---Is drawn by *two white Bears*, and sits hovering o'er a *Flaming Altar---Icicles around his Car.*

*SPRING*---Represented by Leolyn, is drawn by Zephyrs—he lies asleep in a frozen grotto—he wakes and starts up—the *Birds sing and flutter*—the snow disappears, and the *boughs are covered with leaves and flowers.* The act ends with

**Sangrida, the Wood Dæmon, ascending on a Dragon, fire issuing from his mouth.**

**Act 3, Scene 2, *THE STATE BED CHAMBER:***

*Hardyknute sinks with Leolyn on the bed to the Mystic Cavern---Una secures the key and also sinks.*

**SCENE 3, A NECROMANTIC CAVERN,**

*Lamp hung in the centre---in the centre is an altar*

**Round which curl two Large Serpents—on one side an open Pedestal, on which lies the BRAZEN FIGURE OF A GIANT,**

Who supports a clock on his left shoulder---on the other side is a rock with an entrance below—on the top lies *Leolyn* fastened to a Pillar by an enormous chain and padlock, near him his Guitar---Leolyn escapes with the assistance of Una---climbs on the shoulders of the *Giant*---Una hands him a wand, with which he changes the hands of the clock---It strikes ONE!

**The Wood Dæmon stabs Hardyknute.**

*The ALTAR, &c. SINK and Leolyn acknowledged as the Heir of Holstein, &c.*

**Mr. Cooper will appear on Wednesday, as ZANGA, in the Revenge.**

Due notice will be given of the next performances of *Damon & Pythias*, and *Virginius.*

In preparation, a new Tragedy, *(never acted here)* called EVADNE; *or, the Statue.*

Lord Byron's celebrated historical play of the TWO FOSCARI, will be produced shortly, with new Dresses, &c. Also, JULIUS CÆSAR, KING JOHN, &c. &c.

In rehearsal, a new Farce, (by a Gentleman of this city) called the PHRENOLOGIST.

Places in the Boxes may be taken of Mr. Johnson, at the Box Office, from 10 until 1; and on days of performance from 10 until 4 o'clock.

Checks not transferable. Proper officers are appointed who will rigidly enforce decorum.

The Doors will be opened at a quarter past 5, and the curtain will rise at a quarter past 6, precisely.

*Box, One Dollar—Pit, Seventy-five Cents—Gallery, Fifty Cents—Children under 12 years, half price—Thirty-five Seats in the Orchestra, for Sale nightly, at Box price.*

The Chestnut Street Theatre was the leading playhouse in the early United States. Established in 1794, it featured a repertory of British and American plays performed by a cast hailing primarily from England, including a wide range of melodramas and comedies, afterpieces and pantomimes, patriotic tributes and panorama paintings. Over two thousand people attended performances nightly, and the stock company traveled to perform in cities from New York to Alexandria, Virginia. It succeeded in drawing crowds even as newer entertainments surged, such as circuses and equestrian spectacles.

But in April 1820, the Chestnut Street suffered the fate that routinely spelled the end of theaters when candles came too close to costumes and sets: fire consumed the building, just as it had done a decade earlier to London's great playhouses of Covent Garden and Drury Lane. However, just as quickly as the managers of those theaters rebuilt, so did the Chestnut Street. The company temporarily relocated to the newest stage in town: the Olympic, soon to be renamed the Walnut Street Theatre. Meanwhile, it hired architect William Strickland to design a new building in the old location at Chestnut and Sixth Streets. The Chestnut Street triumphantly reopened for business in 1822 with a production of *The Wood Dœmon*, a popular pantomime.

William Birch, the British-born artist responsible for the landmark portfolio of colored engravings called *City of Philadelphia* (colloquially known as the *Philadelphia Views*) **(no. 37)**, was the first to depict the exterior of the Chestnut Street in 1800 and capture its updated look after a remodel by architect Benjamin Henry Latrobe in 1804. In 1823, Birch returned to the scene of the rebuilt playhouse to document its new appearance.

Viewed together, the three images chronicle the changes in architectural style and form that matched the cultural ambition of the theatre itself. From its modest appearance in 1800, when a wooden lean-to marked the entrance to the building, the theatre had swelled in proportion and grandeur under Latrobe's direction to include a graceful colonnade, a nod to the Greek Revival style Latrobe was popularizing, as well as pavilion wings and niches for allegorical sculptures of Comedy and Tragedy fashioned by the city's leading sculptor, William Rush. Strickland's design reproduced aspects of Latrobe's façade, including the wings and sculptures, but replaced the grand Georgian pediment of the earlier building with a horizontal scheme of arches and columns.

Although "Old Drury," as the Chestnut Street was locally known, never recovered the cultural luster it had enjoyed for its first three decades, Birch's engraving achieved something important of its own. It made visible the interdependent relationships of artists, architects, and actors in the early American Republic, when pictures and playhouses together animated a dynamic and expanding visual culture in the nation's largest city. WENDY BELLION

# 46. **David J. Kennedy** (1816–1898), after **Thomas Sully** (1783–1872)

## *Grand Civic Arch erected on Chestnut Street opposite Independence Hall in honor of the arrival of General Lafayette in the City of Philadelphia on September 28th, 1824*

ca. 1867
Watercolor on wove paper
9 1/4 × 8 3/16 inches (23.5 × 20.9 cm)

Signed in purple ink, lower center: *Painting & figures by Thomas Sully Artist.*
Inscribed in purple ink, below image: *Grand Civix Arch erected on Chestnut street opposite Independence / Hall in honor of the arrival of General Lafayette in the City of Phil. / -adelphia on September 27th 1824.—45 feet front, 12 ft. deep, & 24 ft. high.*; in red ink, lower left: *Des. P. 30._2_3._4*

David J. Kennedy Watercolors [V61]
Purchase, 1901

In this delicate watercolor, David J. Kennedy preserved the work of two important fellow Philadelphians, painter Thomas Sully and architect William Strickland. The original by Sully depicted Strickland's Grand Triumphal Arch, constructed as the centerpiece of the 1824 visit of Gilbert du Motier, Marquis de Lafayette, to Philadelphia.

Sully and Kennedy recorded the arch and, in doing so, marked 1824 as a momentous year. There were continuous commemorations, as nearly every significant American city and town in every state arranged to honor Lafayette and his contributions to the American Revolution. As a young man, Lafayette had helped lead the fight against the British and raised funds in France for the war effort. Nearly fifty years later, he was one of the last living heroes of the war; the tour would be his farewell to the new nation and a final salute to his old soldiers.

As Lafayette's itinerary mapped the history of the war, taking him to every important battleground, his visits prompted the retelling of old stories, the recording of memories, and the plans to create new monuments. Lafayette's tour and the artifacts created for it captured a moment when many Americans had started to consider how to remember and preserve the Revolution's past rather than allow it to fade and had begun to weave remarkable past events into a national origin story.

At every stop, Lafayette was greeted by dignitaries who accompanied him in a military procession and feted him with speeches, dinners, and balls. Not to be outdone by New York or Boston, Philadelphia's arrangements committee planned a full week of honors, blending egalitarian mass gatherings with elegant receptions, especially at that notable old building, the State House, which Strickland refurbished for the occasion. Central to the city's ceremonial language were the grand civic procession and the classical arch.

Philadelphia's parade was enormous and represented the industry and progress of the city. Three miles of military men, dignitaries, merchants, craftsmen, and farmers brought Lafayette through the town, passing under twelve ceremonial arches, to arrive at the thirteenth and largest

one, built across Chestnut Street from the State House. Here his carriage stopped, surrounded by dense crowds, to be greeted by Revolutionary veterans, the mayor, and the city council. He was ushered into the room where the Declaration of Independence had been written to receive thousands of well-wishers.

Strickland modeled his grand arch on Roman stone triumphal arches, which marked the military conquest of a city or territory. It was impermanent street furniture, made of lathe and canvas and painted to look like stone, decorated with plaster urns and figures of the goddesses of Peace and Plenty. Sully and, later, David Kennedy recorded the arch's image to memorialize 1824's extravagant moment of recognition and remembrance for the future. It is no surprise, then, that in this same year, prominent Philadelphians founded the Historical Society of Pennsylvania and began to ponder how to preserve the old State House, to be known later as Independence Hall. SUSAN G. DAVIS

12

Philadelphia Monday August 1. 1825.

A quarterly meeting of the Society was held this day at the apartments of the Phrenological Society. Wm Rawle, President, in the chair, G. W. Smith, Secretary.

Application to Deborah Logan.

Resolved That a committee of three be appointed to consider the propriety of making an application to Deborah Logan for the manuscript correspondence of Wm. Penn and James Logan, which she has collected and arranged, in order for its publication by this society, and that the committee have authority to take order on this subject if it be deemed adviseable.

Whereupon Roberts Vaux, Charles J. Ingersoll and Isaac Norris were appointed the Committee.

Consideration of amendments to Constitution postponed.

On motion the consideration of the proposition of Wm Rawle submitted at the last quarterly meeting, to make sundry alterations in the constitution, as set forth on the minutes of that meeting, was postponed to the 19. day of September 1825.

On motion the Society pro-

# 47. History, Genealogy, and the Origins of the Historical Society of Pennsylvania

## *Historical Society of Pennsylvania Minute Book*

1824–43
Manuscript; ink on wove paper bound in half brown leather and marbled paper boards
12 11⁄16 × 8 inches (32.3 × 20.5 cm)

Historical Society of Pennsylvania Institutional Archives [3136]

At its quarterly meeting in August of 1825, the Historical Society of Pennsylvania voted to approach one of Philadelphia's most venerable ladies with the early nineteenth-century version of a "big ask." They would send a delegation that included one of her close relations as well as two other men she would later describe as "good and sensible."

But she would not give them what they asked for—or at least, not yet. For the time being, Deborah Norris Logan would hold onto the manuscripts she had inherited and organized and the transcripts she had made of the extensive letters between Pennsylvania's founder William Penn and the colony's secretary, James Logan. For now, these would remain at Stenton, the home that James had built and, two generations later, Deborah's home. It was where she had long cultivated both interest and expertise in the entwined history of Pennsylvania and her family.

Born and married into families with roots in Pennsylvania's colonial founding, Deborah was the granddaughter of Isaac Norris I and the granddaughter-in-law of James Logan with multiple other familial connections as befitted her Quaker and elite ancestry. She became an enthusiastic preserver and interpreter of the mutual histories of family, society, and government. Her range of antiquarian, genealogical, and historical interests was astonishing, including architecture, manuscripts, material culture, and landscape. She wrote a series of diaries that married these subjects; she was not unusual in thoroughly combining genealogy and history, though she was both exemplary and energetic and had an elite perch from which to work. She and her contemporaries both encouraged more genealogical exploration and drew on the family histories that their ancestors had produced.

Logan shared plenty of information publicly about how her family history and the early history of Pennsylvania combined, publishing pieces in magazines as well as continuing to collaborate with some of Philadelphia's most prominent antiquarians and historians. The idea that an elite family's history was integral to the history of a place was shared across British America and reverberated through the early historical collections and societies. The idea that understanding many family histories together was a form of community history was equally potent.

Thus History and Genealogy, two pillars of HSP, were twinned from the beginning. Like the founders of HSP, Deborah Norris Logan was interested in how the lineages of "founding families" intersected with the early American history she was organizing to preserve and promote. The Logan-Penn letters came to the HSP after Deborah's death; in 1870–72 the Society published *The Correspondence Between William Penn and James Logan, Secretary of the Province of Pennsylvania, and others, 1700–1750. From the Original Letters in Possession of the Family Logan Family, with Notes by the Late Mrs. Deborah Logan.*

KARIN WULF

# 48. **John Neagle** (1796–1865)

## *Mr. Sully's Palette for a Lady*

June 1827
Manuscript with color palette; ink and oil on wove paper bound in quarter brown leather and marbled paper boards
7 7/8 × 6 ½ inches (20.0 × 16.6 cm)

p. 19 of student notebook

John Neagle Papers and Related Items [2112]
Purchase, 1984

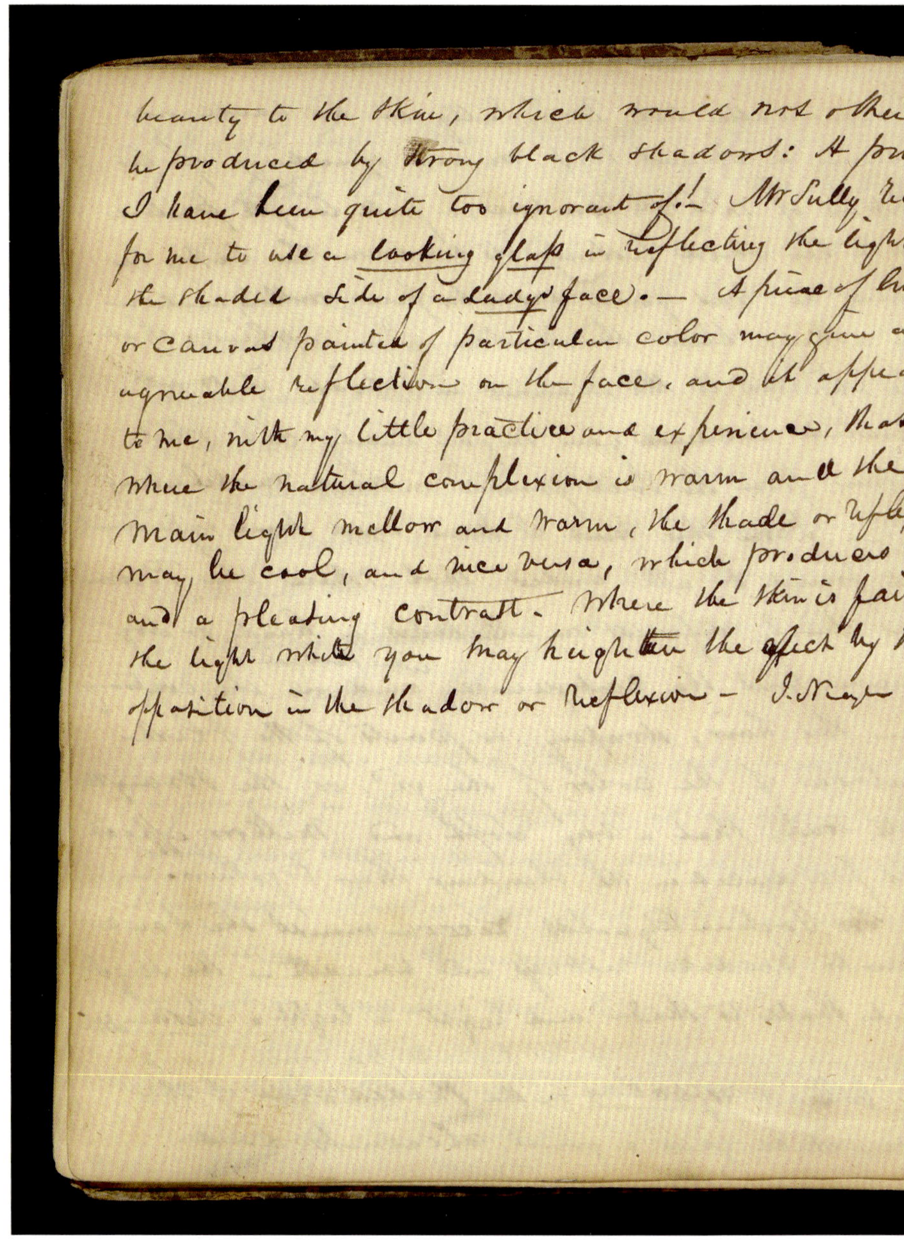
beauty to the skin, which would not other
be produced by strong black shadows: A poi
I have been quite too ignorant of.– Mr Sully rec
for me to use a looking glass in reflecting the light
the shaded side of a ladys face.— A piece of lin
or canvas painted of particular color may give a
agreeable reflection on the face, and it appea
to me, with my little practice and experience, that
where the natural complexion is warm and the
main light mellow and warm, the shade or reflex
may be cool, and vice versa, which produces a
and a pleasing contrast. Where the skin is fair
the light white you may heighten the effect by th
opposition in the shadow or reflexion – J. Neagle

In neat cursive lettering drafted with thick black ink, John Neagle heads a page of his notebook with the title "Mr. Sully's palette for a lady, June 1827." Below this he notes "Finishing palette" and includes dollops of oil paint with corresponding numbers 1 through 21. These are the colors of the palette, and they range from "Brown oker [*sic*] Vermillion" to "Carmine." Although somewhat faded over time, the warm, rich colors shine forth in Neagle's notes, particularly in the shocking vibrance of his reds.

Painter Thomas Sully was an advocate for the professional arts education of women. His daughters Jane Cooper Sully Darley (1807–1877) and Rosalie Kemble Sully (1818–1847) were both accomplished portrait painters who were instructed in the art by their father. Jane professionally exhibited her paintings, mostly of children, at the Pennsylvania Academy of the Fine Arts from 1825 to 1869. Since Neagle married Sully's stepdaughter Mary Chester Sully (1802–1845), one might imagine that this "palette for a lady" was prepared for women artists.

However, close examination of the right side of the page reveals another note from Neagle, "For Mrs Nicholas Biddle's portrait painted by T. Sully who favored me with this list." This palette, then, is a companion to the painting Sully did of Mrs. Nicholas Biddle (Jane Margaret Craig Biddle, 1796–1856), which still hangs in the Biddle family home, Andalusia, outside of Philadelphia. Like other color

schemes, such as “Palette for a Fair Complexion” and “Palette for a Dark Complexion” copied in Neagle’s sketchbook, it is a study in how to reflect the varied skin tones of an elite Philadelphia woman, one wealthy enough to pay for the services of Neagle or Sully.

Sully in particular was one of the most sought-after portraitists of the early republic, known for his soft, romantic, and theatrical portraits of Philadelphia’s women. His portrait of Jane Biddle is no exception. She wears a fabulously fashionable brown velvet hat decorated with white feathers and lace, an empire waist gown of cream silk, and a golden cloak. Her skin is fair, her hair and eyes dark. She materializes out of thin air like a Grecian goddess descending from Mount Olympus. This is apt since this painting was meant to hang at Andalusia, the Biddle family’s Greek Revival mansion outside of Philadelphia on the Delaware River. It is easy to see why women sought out Sully to capture their portraits and why Neagle took such care in documenting how his teacher and father-in-law instructed him to paint women at their most elevated. Indeed, Neagle’s painting of Anna Gibbon Johnson (1828) in the Pennsylvania Academy of the Fine Arts shows exactly what he learned from Sully and how he took his painting of another elite Philadelphian to an even more lofty plain.

ANNA O. MARLEY

# 49. Baldwin Locomotive Works

## **William H. Rau** (1855–1920)

## *The Erecting Shop at Baldwin Locomotive Works*

1896
Albumen print mounted on card
9 × 10 ⅞ inches (22.8 × 27.7 cm)

Inscribed lower left of card: *WILLIAM H RAU*; lower right of card: *1324 Chestnut Street, Phila.*

Boies Penrose Pictorial Philadelphia Collection [V60]
Purchased through the Historical Society of Pennsylvania's Boies Penrose Fund. Portions of the collection were donated to HSP by Boies Penrose II.

Frederick Gutekunst (1831–1917) and Phares F. Goist (1841–1913), *Matthias W. Baldwin. Inventor and Builder of Locomotive Old Ironsides*, 1883; lithograph on wove paper, 14 ⅞ × 11 ⅛ inches (37.8 × 28.3 cm). Historical Society of Pennsylvania Portrait Collection [V88]

Matthias Baldwin (1795–1866) was born in Elizabethtown, New Jersey, where he served as a jeweler's apprentice in his teen years, subsequently opening his own business. Relocating to Philadelphia in 1825, Baldwin and a partner shifted to the manufacture of bookbinders' tools. An inveterate tinkerer, he developed a hydraulic book press and built a stationary steam engine; the latter led him to create a miniature prototype steam locomotive in 1831. Word spread, and he received an order from the fledgling Philadelphia and Germantown Railroad to construct a full-scale train engine. Baldwin soon became inundated with orders as railroad construction and operations rapidly expanded. From these beginnings, Baldwin, with several associates, established an internationally renowned locomotive works. By the late nineteenth century, Baldwin's firm had become by far the largest employer in Philadelphia, and its sprawling facilities stretched from Broad Street west to 28th Street, two-and-three blocks deep, with Spring Garden Street as its northern border.

Baldwin's company never produced standard locomotives. From its inception, the firm always made engines to order, filling the specifications and needs of the large number of railroads that became its customers. They were singularly designed, and then blueprints of components were sent to the pattern, foundry, forge, boiler, and tinsmith shops, where skilled mechanics produced parts for assembly. Engineering expertise and highly skilled labor were crucial aspects in the production of Baldwin locomotives.

The Historical Society of Pennsylvania holds several remarkable collections illuminating the history of the Baldwin Locomotive Works. The core collection contains complete office records for the period 1831–69 and business papers of Baldwin dating back to 1825. The unusual holdings of incoming and outgoing correspondence provide insight into deliberations between the firm and railroad companies, including a growing number in Europe; financial challenges faced during economic downturns and efforts to expand operations (in the latter case, Baldwin brought in new partners); experiences of skilled mechanics who went with the new engines to customer railroads, driving and repairing the locomotives and training their successors; lost business from southern railroads before and during the Civil War with Baldwin's ardent support for the abolition of slavery; and labor unrest on the shop floor. There are also full ledger books that provide information on cash flows, productivity, and technological innovation. With a great need for skilled labor, Baldwin began a factory apprenticeship program, and

the collection includes a registry of apprentices with names, dates, and places of birth, trades being taught, length of service, and causes of absences and terminations (in correspondence files, letters appear from parents who were unhappy with the treatment of their sons).

Another prime Baldwin-related collection offers information on established foreign operations. Wallace Rogers Lee oversaw production of Baldwin locomotives in Latin America, and his papers at HSP are of interest as Baldwin Locomotive was one of the first US multinational companies. Other valuable records can be found in the collection of Samuel Matthew Vauclain, who served as a top executive at Baldwin from 1911 to 1929. Vauclain presided over the demolition of facilities in Philadelphia as the firm relocated to a new site south of the city and during an intense production period during World War I. His papers are particularly revealing on foreign contacts and sales, administrative structuring of the firm, and personnel relations and labor strife. This collection also contains striking photographs of the manufacture of Baldwin engines.

For students of US economic history and industrialization, the Baldwin Locomotive Company Collections at HSP are a vital resource.

WALTER LICHT

# 50. Philadelphia Female Anti-Slavery Society

## *Minute Book*

---

1838–39
Manuscript; ink on wove paper bound in quarter brown leather and marbled paper boards
7 3/4 × 6 3/8 inches (19.8 × 16.3 cm)

Pennsylvania Abolition Society Papers [0490]
Gift of the Philadelphia Pennsylvania Abolition Society, 1992, 2001, 2015

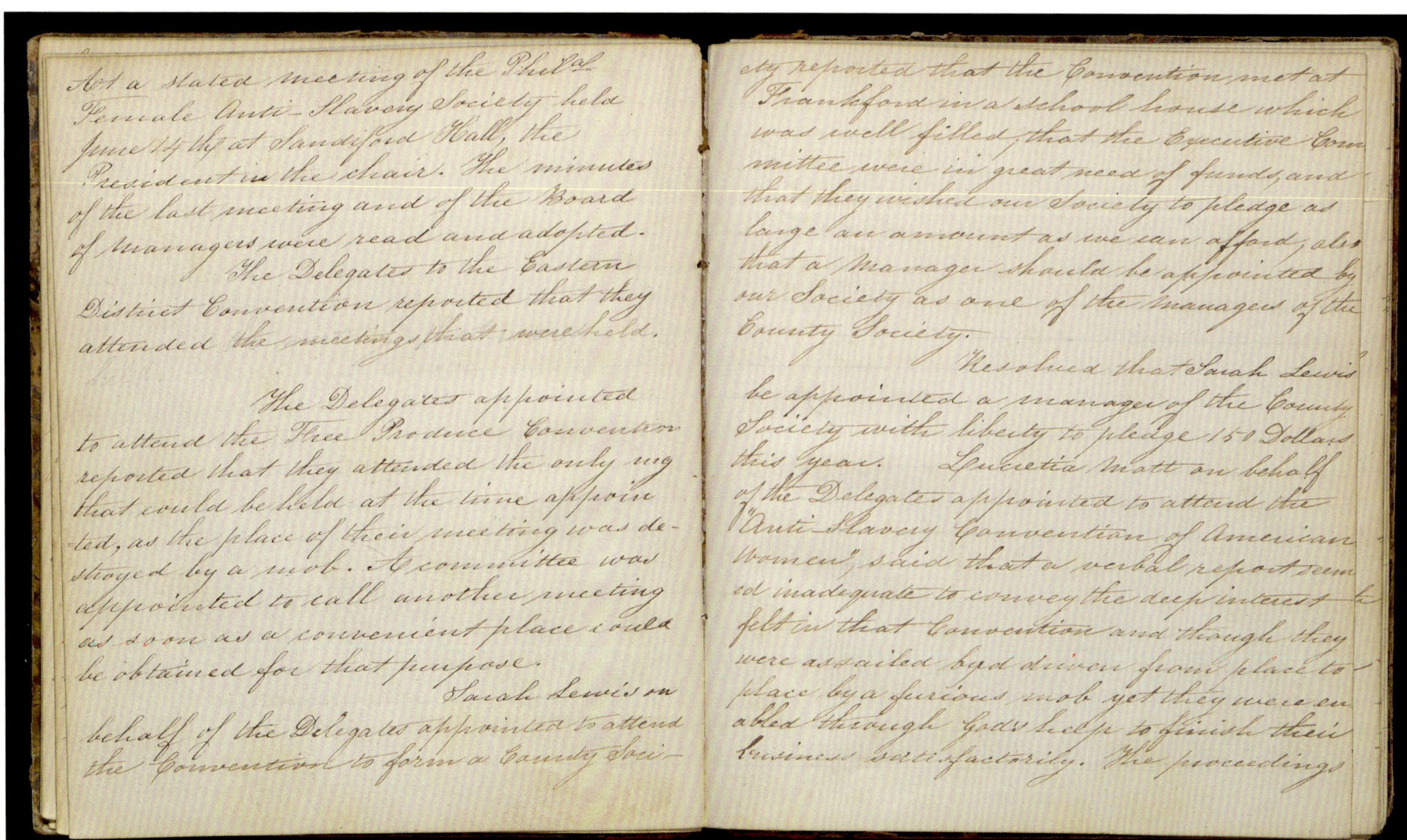

At a stated meeting of the Phil^a^ Female Anti-Slavery Society held June 14th at Sandiford Hall, the President in the chair. The minutes of the last meeting and of the Board of managers were read and adopted.

The Delegates to the Eastern District Convention reported that they attended the meetings that were held.

The Delegates appointed to attend the Free Produce Convention reported that they attended the only mtg that could be held at the time appointed, as the place of their meeting was destroyed by a mob. A committee was appointed to call another meeting as soon as a convenient place could be obtained for that purpose.

Sarah Lewis on behalf of the Delegates appointed to attend the Convention to form a County Society reported that the Convention met at Frankford in a school house which was well filled, that the Executive Committee were in great need of funds, and that they wished our Society to pledge as large an amount as we can afford, also that a Manager should be appointed by our Society as one of the managers of the County Society.

Resolved that Sarah Lewis be appointed a manager of the County Society with liberty to pledge 150 Dollars this year. Lucretia Mott on behalf of the Delegates appointed to attend the "Anti-Slavery Convention of American Women", said that a verbal report seemed inadequate to convey the deep interest felt in that Convention and though they were assailed and driven from place to place by a furious mob yet they were enabled through God's help to finish their business satisfactorily. The proceedings

Six brown leather-bound volumes document the Philadelphia Female Anti-Slavery Society's (PFASS) thirty-seven years of activism against slavery. In December 1833, a group of forty-one white and African-descended women became signatories of PFASS. Members embraced radical propositions about female activism, consumer boycotts, racial and gender equality, the Fugitive Slave Law, and the moral necessity of disunion from Southern enslavers. Although white members jeopardized the organization's unique interracial coalition with condescending presumptions about the value of their own leadership, PFASS sustained an interracial membership into its final decade.

PFASS founders were committed to undermining markets for slave-produced goods by consuming only those products made by free labor. Ethical consumerism, believed by participants to be especially well suited to women, also framed PFASS's annual antislavery fair, in which members sold free-produced goods to raise funds for numerous PFASS projects such as free Black education, most notably the school run by member Sarah Mapps Douglass (1806–1882). Other PFASS activities included the State Abolition Society and collaboration with the city's Vigilance Committee, a semiclandestine network that facilitated the escapes of enslaved people into Philadelphia and beyond.

One of PFASS's biggest setbacks came in 1838 with the destruction of Pennsylvania Hall **(fig. 10)**. Built with the financial assistance of groups like PFASS to establish a non-denominational meeting space for reformers, the hall was a material expression of abolitionist hopes for ending slavery through reasoned public debate. Unfortunately, the newly constructed building was destroyed by arson three days after it opened its doors. PFASS had invested $400 in the hall, most of which they never recouped. The day after the fire, several members attended the Requited Labor Convention held next to the building's still smoldering ruins.

But PFASS members, led by the intrepid Lucretia Mott (1793–1880), were in the fight against slavery for the long haul. Following the attack on Pennsylvania Hall, they toned down their formal political engagement but continued to apply domestic and organizational skills to fundraising and petitioning. PFASS submitted scores of antislavery petitions to the Pennsylvania state legislature and the US Congress. The petitions ranged from denunciations of the state's so-called sojourner loophole allowing enslavers to enter the state without jeopardizing their ownership of enslaved people, to demands for immediate Congressional action to end slavery.

PFASS members also provided funds for the Philadelphia Vigilance Committee to protect both enslaved refugees and the free Black people erroneously targeted as fugitives. PFASS members filled the city's courtrooms to witness proceedings that determined the fate of refugees. As abolitionist politics became more militant during the 1840s, PFASS members joined ultraist denunciations of the continued union of free states with slave states.

Hardly a perfect model of political activism or interracial organizing, PFASS nonetheless demonstrated remarkable persistence. Although longtime member Mott expressed the fatigue that many activists felt by the 1850s, PFASS remained active during the Civil War, providing financial support and hands-on assistance to freed people. The society finally disbanded in 1870 after passage of the Thirteenth and Fourteenth Amendments marked slavery's demise. As PFASS meeting minutes reveal, even an organization with flawed interracial politics among its own members might accomplish significant work to end slavery.

KATHLEEN M. BROWN

## 51. **Joseph Saxton** (1799–1873)

### *Philadelphia Central High School for Boys and Pennsylvania State Arsenal*

---

1839
Silver-coated copper plate
2 ¼ × 2 ⅞ inches (5.7 × 7.2 cm) (plate)

Historical Society of Pennsylvania Treasures Collection

The indistinct image on this small metal rectangle constitutes one of America's most treasured pieces of photographic history. Taken in the fall of 1839 and publicly announced on October 24, 1839, Joseph Saxton's view of Philadelphia's Central High School and the nearby Pennsylvania Arsenal is the oldest existing American daguerreotype.

In August 1839 Frenchman Louis-Jacques-Mandé Daguerre (1787–1851) publicly declared his success in capturing a permanent image on a silver-coated copper plate through the use of light and chemicals, and the news reverberated around the world. Saxton, an inventor and instrument maker at the United States Mint in Philadelphia, typified the early experimenters who attempted to replicate the daguerreotype process as explained in newspaper and periodical articles. He had apprenticed as a watchmaker, worked as an engraver, and applied his scientific knowledge and curious mind to improving and inventing a multitude of apparatuses.

According to his contemporaries, Saxton built a camera from a cigar box and a spectacle lens and constructed a sensitizing box and mercury bath from repurposed containers and scraps of wood and metal. He pointed his device out the second-story window of the US Mint, capturing the recently opened Central High School with its distinctive turret and the Pennsylvania State Arsenal, located on the east side of Juniper Street between Market and Chestnut Streets.

Saxton's interest in daguerreotypes seems short-lived and focused on the technical aspects of affixing the image to the plate rather than the creation of aesthetically pleasing images. Fellow Philadelphian Robert Cornelius **(no. 52)** supplied him with metal plates, and a few references to other Saxton daguerreotypes can be found in nineteenth-century sources, but no other examples of his work exist today. By 1844 Saxton moved to Washington, DC, to become Superintendent of Weights and Measures for the United States Coast Survey and apparently gave up his daguerreotype experimentation.

Saxton was a member of the Franklin Institute and the American Philosophical Society, organizations that were keenly interested in the new daguerreotype process, but according to tradition, he chose to donate this daguerreotype to the Historical Society of Pennsylvania in 1839. This information, however, cannot be confirmed and is probably incorrect because in a letter dated May 19, 1840, George D. Bruce of Pittsburgh thanked his brother-in-law William Y. McAllister of Philadelphia for sending him "a very great curiosity. . . . the Daguerreotype of the High School," undoubtedly Saxton's image. Bruce described it as only the second daguerreotype ever seen in Pittsburgh, declaring, "We have been perfectly charmed with it." A McAllister family member may have donated the Saxton daguerreotype to HSP upon its return to Philadelphia, or it may have entered HSP's collection on April 28, 1864, when a Dr. Ash was recorded in the accession book as giving "[o]ne of the first daguerreotypes taken in Philadelphia." Regardless of its provenance, the daguerreotype is a national treasure.

SARAH J. WEATHERWAX

## 52. **Robert Cornelius** (1809–1893)

### *Martin Hans Boyè*

December 1843
Cased sixth-plate daguerreotype
3 3⁄8 × 2 3⁄4 inches (8.6 × 7.0 cm) (plate); 3 3⁄4 × 3 1⁄8 × 3⁄4 inches (9.5 × 7.9 × 2.0 cm) (case)

Inscribed in ink, on paper liner of case tray beneath image package: *Daguerreotype / restored 1939 / by Louis W. Sipley / from / Historical Society / of / Pennsylvania*

Historical Society of Pennsylvania Art and Artifact Collection [3137]
Possibly gift of Martin Boyè

Danish-born chemist, physicist, and geologist Martin Hans Boyè (1812–1909) sat for at least six portraits taken by Philadelphian Robert Cornelius during the earliest years of daguerreotyping. Unlike most daguerreotype portraits, which were taken as personal mementos meant to be shared with family and friends, this portrait, and another from the same sitting, served as the basis for wood engravings in an essay by Boyè published in a chemistry book in 1850.

Cornelius was working in his family's Philadelphia lamp manufacturing business when the news of Louis-Jacques-Mandé Daguerre's discovery reached the United States from France in the fall of 1839. An economic downturn probably gave Cornelius time away from the family business to apply his metallurgy knowledge to experimenting with daguerreotyping. In October or November 1839, he took the first known daguerreotype self-portrait, now in the possession of the Library of Congress. Cornelius and his partner Dr. Paul Beck Goddard (1811–1866), a chemist at the University of Pennsylvania, greatly shortened the exposure time needed for a successful image to as little as ten to sixty seconds by introducing bromine into the process, making studio portraiture feasible. On May 6, 1840, Cornelius opened the first daguerreotype studio in Philadelphia but remained in business for less than three years. Located initially on Eighth Street just south of Market Street and later moving around the corner to Market Street, Cornelius charged $5.00 for a portrait. Only fifty-three Robert Cornelius daguerreotypes are known to still exist. Most are in different institutional collections, but some are still in private hands, including the descendants of Cornelius.

In a typical studio portrait, the sitter usually looks at the camera or engages unconvincingly with a prop, such as a book. In this portrait, however, Boyè's face is only partially visible, and his attention is totally directed at the scientific equipment on the table in front of him. He keeps his pose steady by placing one elbow on the table and resting the pinky finger of the other hand against the support stand's bracket rod as he prepares to pour liquid into a beaker. Boyè's scientific expertise is the subject of this daguerreotype, not Boyè, the man. Cornelius struck a similar pose for his own portrait during the same session, but the scientific equipment completely obscured his face. When reproduced as engravings in James C. Booth's *Encyclopedia of Chemistry*, only the men's hands and the scientific equipment were illustrated.

This daguerreotype is not only an example of work by one of America's earliest daguerreotypists, it also represents Philadelphia's role as a center of scientific knowledge, innovation, and experimentation. Philadelphia supported the exchange of these ideas at organizations such as the American Philosophical Society, of which Cornelius, Boyè, Booth, Goddard, and Saxton **(no. 51)** were all members. The Historical Society of Pennsylvania recognized the historical significance of these advances and, by adding daguerreotypes such as this and Saxton's to the collection, preserved them for the future.

SARAH J. WEATHERWAX

## 53. **Albert Newsam** (1809–1864)

# *P. S. Duval Lithography Trade Card*

1843
Lithograph with watercolor on wove paper
16 5/16 × 15 3/4 inches (41.5 × 40.0 cm)

Inscribed above image: *Lithography*; below image: *P.S. Duval Philadelphia / 7 BANK ALLEY.*; within image, lower center: *A. NEWSAM / Artist. / No. 7 Bank Alley*

Albert Newsam Print Collection [V100]
Acquired by gift and purchase. Albert Newsam's own portfolio of prints (162 pieces) were donated by John A. McAllister in April 1881.

"LITHOGRAPHY," declares an advertisement for the prominent Philadelphian lithographic establishment of Peter S. Duval. The title does not disappoint. Over two dozen lithographed papers appear to be scattered over an indistinct black background; maps, portraits, checks, sheet music, billheads, landscapes, cityscapes, bills of laden, and business cards reveal and obscure one another. Executed in an exacting trompe l'oeil style by Albert Newsam, the lithograph exhibits the medium's growing versatility and reach at midcentury.

This trade card is an important artifact in the history of printing and American lithography. Hailing from Paris, Duval transformed the business of lithography in the United States by employing skilled European artists, sourcing superior stones and printing paper, and introducing technological advances such as steam power and, later, color printing to his practice. The trade card displays the broad range of products printed by Duval's firm. Lithographs of popular tourist sites, well-known figures, as well as business documents like visiting cards and circulars, appealed to an expansive audience. Reproduced advertisements and letters within the trade card remind the viewer that lithographs could be made "at the shortest notice," noting the "cheapness of the work." The print also cleverly locates Duval's business near the Merchants' Exchange through two lithographic views. Anchoring the composition is a portrait of the inventor of lithography, Aloys Senefelder (1771–1834), centered among the network of papers below. The trade card thus functions as an advertisement for both Duval's firm and lithography itself, pointing to the practice's pervasiveness in nineteenth-century visual culture.

Newsam, the artist behind the trade card, was the most esteemed lithographic artist in the United States. Born deaf, Newsam displayed a natural gift for drawing and copying while at the Pennsylvania Institution for the Deaf and Dumb. He apprenticed with well-known engraver Cephas G. Childs, a proprietor in the lithographic firm over which Duval would eventually assume ownership. A renowned portrait artist, Newsam had a prolific career, creating over five hundred portraits. "He was so faithful in reproducing the original," Duval wrote of Newsam's pictures, "[i]t was with difficulty he could avoid copying minutely."

The trade card evinces Newsam's exceptional skill in reproduction. His depictions of curled corners and shadows convincingly create the impression that one is looking at a real arrangement of layered papers, inciting feelings of disbelief and tactility commonly associated with trompe l'oeil. While Newsam was not alone in engaging with trompe l'oeil in this period, his commitment to the style within a lithographic advertisement appears unique. The trade card compellingly exhibits Newsam's artistic and reproductive prowess: it is a lithograph of lithographs, one that celebrates lithography, and positions it squarely at Duval's lithographic firm. KRISTEN NASSIF

LITHOGRAPHY
P. S. Duval,
Executes on Stone at the shortest notice
all kinds of Drawings, Portraits, Landscapes, Historical Subjects, Animals &c.
Also all kinds of Writings: Maps,
Charts, Plans, professional and
visitings Cards, Circulars,
Billheads
PHILADELPHIA
Delaware
Shipped
ALOYS SENEFELDER
Inventor of Lithography. Munich A.D.1796.
MERCHANTS' EXCHANGE.
PHILADELPHIA.
London
Artist.
No. 7 Bank Alley
P. S. Duval
7
BANK ALLEY.
Philadelphia.

# 54. **Francis Scott Key** (1779–1843)

## *Handwritten Souvenir Copy of the Lyrics to "The Star-Spangled Banner"*

1842
Manuscript; ink on wove paper
9 15⁄16 × 7 7⁄8 inches (25.2 × 20.0 cm)

George May Keim Collection of autographed copies of "The Star-Spangled Banner" and "Home Sweet Home" [Am .838]
Gift to George May Keim by author. Given to the Historical Society of Pennsylvania by Keim's heirs, 1876.

Despite the immediate and broad popularity of "The Star-Spangled Banner" during his lifetime, its author Francis Scott Key is known to have made only five handwritten copies of the lyrics: the 1814 original and four later souvenirs given to friends and colleagues. Key never made copies for any of his eleven children; they were expected to memorize it.

Likely made in 1842, the copy held by the Historical Society of Pennsylvania is inscribed to General George May Keim, who was born in Reading and had served as a major general in the Pennsylvania State Militia. Key, who lived in the nation's capital, likely met Keim when he served as a representative in Congress from 1838 to 1843.

Key wrote "The Star-Spangled Banner" in September 1814, after witnessing the surprising and successful defense of Baltimore from British attack during the War of 1812. He did not write a poem, as most Americans think, but crafted a lyric to fit an already well-known melody. His creation is and has always been a song, an emotion-driven alloy of words and music intended to inspire hearts and change minds. Key's goal was to unite a divided nation.

Yet for General Keim's copy, Key made a few changes. Most are inconsequential variations of the pen, except for one edit he made consistently in each of his four souvenir editions. He replaced the phrase "through the perilous fight," with the words "through the clouds of the fight." It seems that for Key, the peril he felt in 1814 had faded somewhat over the three decades since the battle, but his memory of the smoky clouds created by the bombardment's 1500 exploding mortars and rockets, as well as the cannon that launched them, remained vivid.

Detained at anchor aboard his own American truce ship during the bombardment, Key was positioned behind the British navy cannon. "The clouds of the fight" thus made it impossible for him to see the fort and its flag. Yet while the bombing persisted, he knew his countrymen continued to resist. Even through the night, the rockets and bombs "gave proof" that the US held the fort, that the "flag was still there." At around 4 a.m., however, the bombing ceased. A terrifying silence asked the questions: Why had the bombing stopped? Had the British decided to pause their guns, had they given up, or had they taken the fort?

At daybreak, Key's anxious concerns were answered. The Stars and Stripes still flew over the fort. Not only had Baltimore been saved, but the nation itself was preserved. With both relief and exhilaration, Key penned his lyrics to celebrate the heroism of Fort McHenry's defenders.

Today Key's words are still sung as originally conceived—they are simply too well known to permit revision. Yet for its author, the song—like the nation—was still a work in progress. In that vein, it remains significant that the US anthem as sung today closes with a question mark. This question remains, as it did for Key, both literal and existential. The anthem is a statement of patriotic devotion and a call to citizenship. Every time it is sung, it asks Americans—will they live true to the nation's ideals? Their task is to answer.

MARK CLAGUE

O say can you see by the dawn's early light
What so proudly we hail'd at the twilight's last gleaming,
Whose broad stripes and bright stars, through the clouds of the fight,
O'er the ramparts we watch'd were so gallantly streaming?
And the rocket's red glare – the bomb bursting in air
Gave proof through the night that our flag was still there?
O say, does that star-spangled banner yet wave
O'er the land of the free & the home of the brave? –

On that shore, dimly seen through the mists of the deep,
Where the foe's haughty host in dread silence reposes,
What is that, which the breeze, o'er the towering steep
As it fitfully blows, half conceals, half discloses?
Now it catches the gleam – of the morning's first beam,
In full glory reflected, now shines on the stream,
'Tis the star-spangled banner – O long may it wave
O'er the land of the free & the home of the brave!

And where are the foes that so vauntingly swore
That the havoc of war & the battle's confusion
A home and a Country should leave us no more?
Their blood has wash'd out their foul footstep's pollution.
No refuge could save – the hireling & slave
From the terror of flight, or the gloom of the grave,
And the star-spangled banner in triumph doth wave
O'er the land of the free & the home of the brave.

(2)

# 55. **Henry R. Robinson** (d. 1850)

## *View of the City of Brotherly Love*

---

1842
Lithograph on wove paper
12 ½ × 18 ¾ inches (31.8 × 47.6 cm)

Inscribed below image: *A VIEW OF THE CITY OF BROTHERLY LOVE*; below image, lower right: *Published by H.R. Robinson, Lith^o H [2 Nassau St]*; below image of William Penn: *Wise Laws and a promt* [*sic*] *and / just administration of them*

Historical Society of Pennsylvania Large Graphics Collection [V65]

The 1830s and 1840s were rocked by social, political, and economic turmoil in Philadelphia, as in the rest of the United States. These events were marked by labor strikes exacerbated by financial crises, as well as racial, ethnic, and religious conflict fed by the growing anti-immigrant Nativist movement. New York–based caricaturist and lithographer Henry R. Robinson published this slyly titled commentary on the city's tribulations probably in 1842. William Penn hovers sadly above the fray, holding a calumet and scroll inscribed, "Wise Laws and a promt [*sic*] and just administration of them," as mobs swarm around haphazardly arranged buildings that identify the sites or circumstances of recent unrest. Volunteer firemen crowd around a fire engine dubbed "Goodwill" while their comrades "water" the riot. Signs on a nearby building—"Irish Repeal Meeting" and "Best of liquors at 3 [cents] a glass"—reinforce ethnic stereotypes. The financial panic of 1837 is signaled by the pillared "U. S. Bank," Penn Township Bank, and Manual Labor Bank, all of which failed in the economic collapse. On the right, Pennsylvania Hall is shown engulfed in flames, memorializing the notorious 1838 assault on an abolitionist meeting there.

Historian Gary Nash has dated the cartoon to 1842 because Robinson includes the anti-abolitionist attack on Black and Quaker bandsmen celebrating the eighth anniversary of the end of slavery in Britain's West Indies colonies that went into effect on August 1, 1834. During the riot that ensued, Smith's Beneficial Hall, shown in the middle of the cartoon, was set on fire. Further evidence of misrule in Philadelphia is signaled by "Bush Hill" in the background. This was a former private estate near Fairmount, north and west of the city center, a parade ground and popular gathering place since the late eighteenth century. However, even this once-genteel landscape was disrupted. On July 4, 1842, at Bush Hill, "where there were about two hundred tents pitched and gambling of all kinds was extensively carried on, a general quarrel took place, and broken heads and bloody noses in great profusion were the consequence." Robinson depicts the city's racial divisions at the center of the cartoon, personified by a Black woman, a white woman, and their offspring, who spar in the foreground. A third boy, who opens a hydrant on the battling women, adds a touch of irony: could Philadelphia's much-admired municipally administered water system cool these disruptions?

ELIZABETH MILROY

Further information to be found at the Historical Society of Pennsylvania includes the Bush Hill Estate Papers, Cadwalader Family Papers, Fire Company Records (various), and the Pennsylvania Abolition Society Papers.

# 56. William H. Horstmann & Sons

## *Ribbon Sample Book*

1850–72
Cotton ribbon mounted on wove paper
12 × 8 15⁄16 inches (30.6 × 22.7 cm)

Horstmann-Lippincott Family Papers [1899]
Gift of Mrs. Coles Langhorne, 1964

Sarah Cain had been employed for sixteen years at the William H. Horstmann Company sewing specialty silk items when she was fired for failure to conform to moral standards: "it was heard she was living with another woman's husband." Two other employees at the firm, sisters Mary and Alice Brennan, were also discharged for a "disturbance with Mr. Sichnel"; their ousting for insubordination prompted a walkout by coworkers in a show of solidarity. These traces of the employment experiences of working people in Philadelphia in the mid-nineteenth century appear in an unusual and intriguing registry of employees contained in the William H. Horstmann Company Papers at the Historical Society of Pennsylvania.

Horstmann (1785–1850), a German immigrant and skilled silk weaver, established a small silk-weaving workshop in Philadelphia in 1815. Then in 1824 he introduced Jacquard looms to his shop, the first textile firm in the country to do so; the event transformed the nature of his business. The company continued to process raw silk and produce colorful braided and woven specialty items, such as tassels, dress fringe, lace, military regalia, and flags, but now on a larger scale. In 1854, the firm moved its operations to a newly built, five-story factory at Fifth and Cherry Streets, with over three hundred workers on the payroll, eighty-five percent of whom were women. Company managers largely recruited workers from the expanding German immigrant community in Philadelphia. After 125 years of operation, the Horstmann Company closed its doors in 1940.

The company records at HSP span the years 1845–88. The collection includes sample books of colorful silk ribbons and labels, ledgers of cash transactions, an inventory of machine purchases and installation, and a scrapbook of newspaper clippings; the latter trace the growing reputation of the firm and its products.

Information found in the roster of employees reveals that turnover was high; fifty percent of those hired remained with the firm for less than five months. Tenure at Horstmann varied by gender, occupational position, and family connections. Male employees stayed far longer than women, skilled mechanics longer than unskilled machine tenders, and employees who labored alongside kin had longer ties to the company than those who did not.

The Horstmann Company employee register is unusual because it includes notations explaining why workers left the firm. Eight of these employees died through injury on the job (at least one gruesomely, as noted for Louis Lamind, he "died in our blade at 2:20"). A large number, thirty-six percent of the total, were laid off during short- and long-term periods of economic downturn. For forty-eight percent of the workers, leave-taking was a voluntary act. They quit to take other jobs, start businesses, learn new trades,

go to school, get married, attend to family matters, or move, with a few noted as returning to their countries of origin. Dissatisfaction with conditions of employment drove others to leave. James Lindsey quit his job in the machine shop "because he did not want to clean oil cups, said it was colored work."

Sixteen percent of Horstmann employees exited the rolls because they were fired. Annie Smith, who held an office job, was deemed "too lively." Paul Volker, after six months in the sword shop (making silk scabbards), was shown the door because he "paid no attention to his work and too much to the girls." Alexander Smith, in a training program for supervisors, was dismissed because he was "not a suitable person to take charge of girls." Overt resistance to managerial authority served as grounds for quick discharge. Two women were fired when it was learned that they planned to lead a "strike for $7.00 per week" pay. More cryptic is the case of Margaret Crocke, who was let go for "raising disturbances with the hands."

The whole collection is a remarkable resource for students of US business enterprise, technological innovation, specialty production, and immigration. The employee registry itself provides a rare view and insight into the employment experiences of industrial workers, both men and women, in mid-nineteenth-century America.

WALTER LICHT

## 57. Franklin Fire Insurance Company of Philadelphia

### *Policy No. 1054, Survey and Plan of Row Houses for Jefferson H. Brolaskey*

October 10, 1834
Ink on wove paper
12 ⅝ × 8 inches (32.0 × 20.5 cm) (plan); 8 × 3 3⁄16 inches (20.5 × 8.1 cm) (folded)

Franklin Fire Insurance Records [3269]

### *Policy No. 67731, Survey and Plan of House for George A. Heyl*

June 4, 1888
Red and black ink on paper (plan); collotype
8 ½ × 3 11⁄16 inches (21.6 × 9.3 cm) (folded); 13 15⁄16 × 17 inches (35.4 × 43.3 cm) (unfolded); 6 ¾ × 8 inches (17.2 × 20.3 cm) (plan); 4 ⅝ × 6 inches (11.8 × 15.2 cm) (collotype)

Franklin Fire Insurance Records [3269]

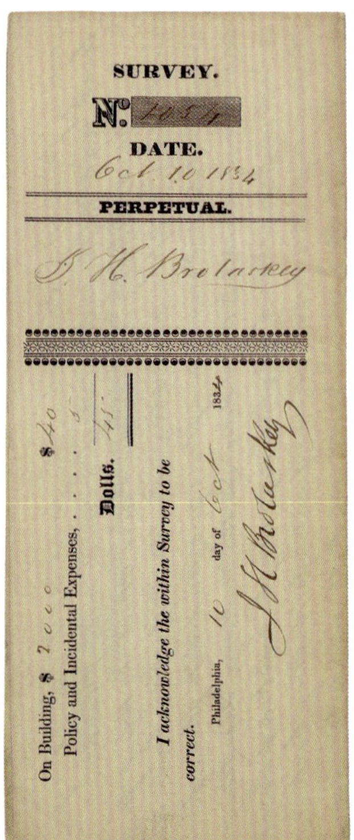


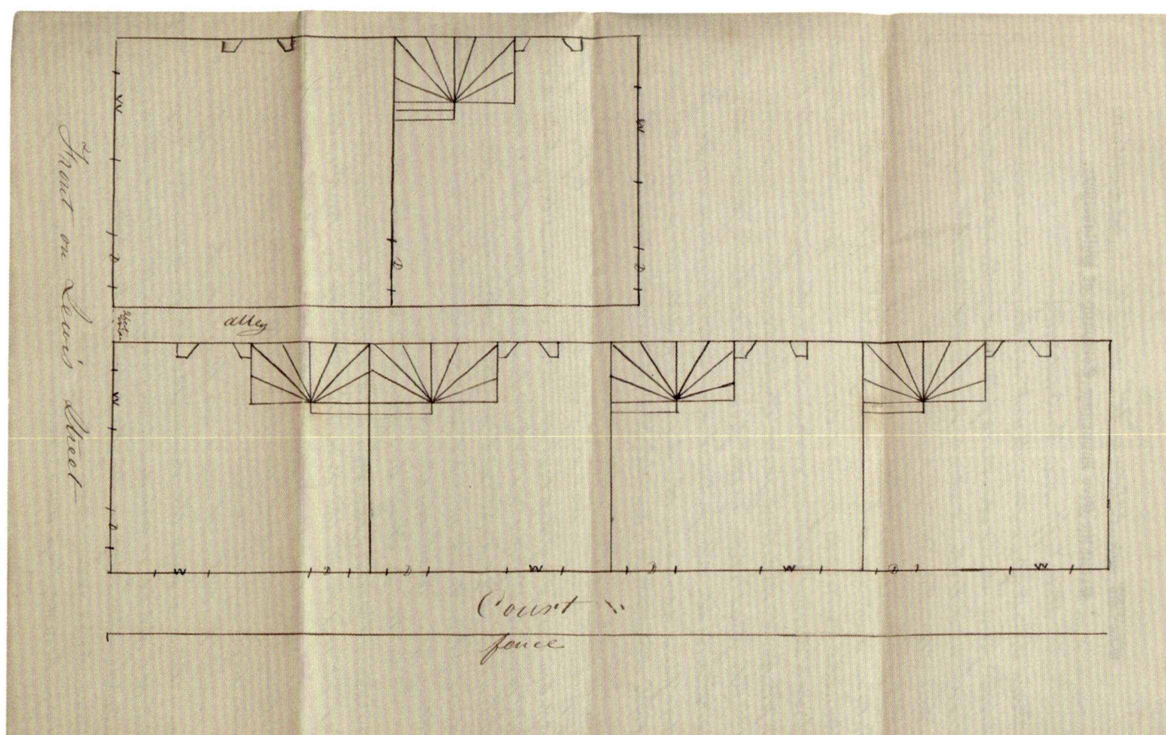


Fire has not typically been a friend to history, nor to cities. Open flames were everywhere in the eighteenth and nineteenth centuries for heating, evening light, cooking, and various craft activities. Their peril was multiplied in dense settings, spurring building regulations, organized fire responses, and, key here, fire insurance companies. Such companies provided owners compensation when an insured property burned, but through their standard practice of surveying structures, they also created a collateral boon for architectural and urban history by amassing an enormous collective archive that documents the form, chronology, and ownership of hundreds of thousands of structures in and near various American cities.

Fire insurance got an early start in Philadelphia in the mid-eighteenth century, and by the end of the nineteenth, several competing companies in the city had together surveyed well over 100,000 properties that they insured. These documented buildings were large and small, ranging from

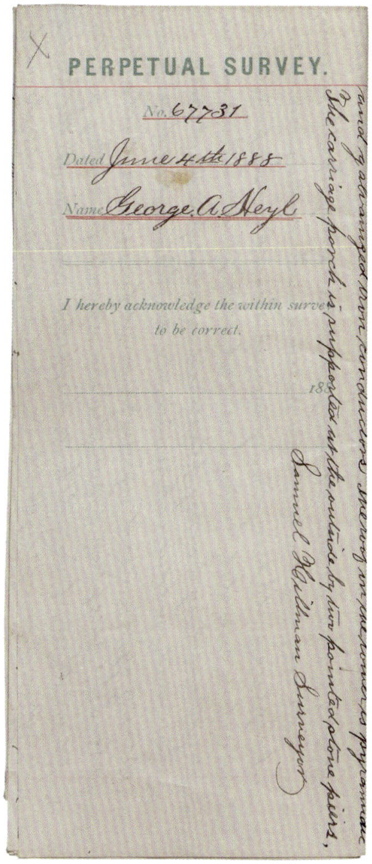


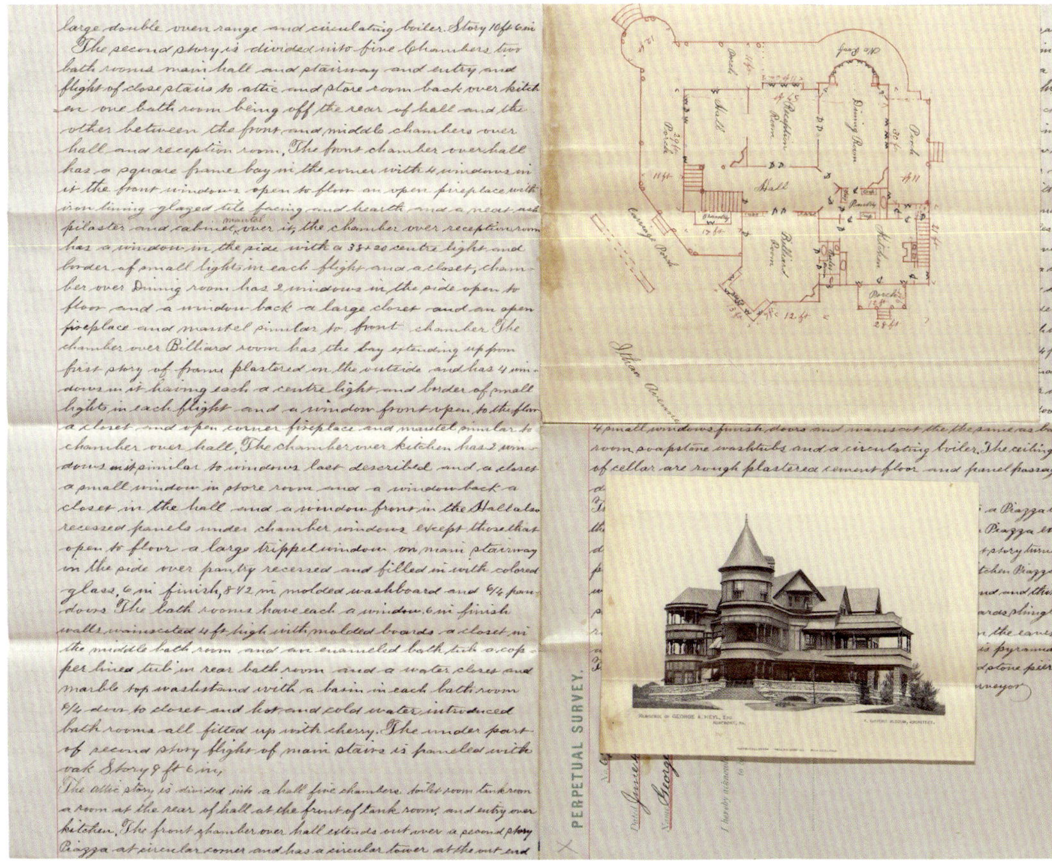


farmhouses and barns to grand country houses, city mansions, factories, stores, and stables. The leading subset, though, lay in records of Philadelphia row houses, typically with fronts that measured about thirteen to eighteen feet wide. Many rows were insured in series when they were first built, while others were surveyed individually for subsequent owners.

One of a few collections of this species at the Historical Society of Pennsylvania is the Franklin Fire Insurance Company's extensive archive of "perpetual" surveys, among the nation's richest graphically. These documents record buildings insured between the 1820s and 1890s, mostly across eastern Pennsylvania and southern New Jersey. Initially a few sentences and numbers sufficed, but in the second quarter of the nineteenth century, Franklin surveys each filled a page or two with close descriptions of spaces on all stories. The practice of including a plan of the ground story was especially common; while simplified, with single lines marking the position of walls without indicating their thickness, and with openings usually referenced by Ws and Ds, those plans nonetheless convey the use and relation of spaces, while dimensions, materials, and special features were spelled out textually.

Each survey also precisely (if often arcanely) located the property, firmly established a date by which a building was constructed, and identified the owner who insured it. For the great majority of urban houses that were built speculatively in series, these records identified the developers of houses that were meant soon to be sold to occupant-owners or to investors who might hold onto them for rental. In this way they reveal the activities of a set of elusive but essential players whose decisions were critical shapers of our cities and suburbs.

Ultimately, such surveys constitute a rich resource for historians exploring a range of questions. They serve both as tools that allow us to closely know many individual places that have long-since disappeared and, more broadly, offer visual evidence for seeing larger patterns that had characterized a now-transformed built landscape.

JEFFREY A. COHEN

## 58. **George Dubois** (1811–1888)

### *Chapel of the Lebanon Cemetery*

---

ca. 1850
Published by Frederick Kuhl (b. ca. 1812)
Hand-colored lithograph on wove paper
18 ⅜ × 25 ⅜ inches (46.6 × 64.5 cm)

Inscribed below image: *CHAPEL OF THE LEBANON CEMETERY*; below image, lower left: *Printed by F.Kuhl.*; below image, lower right: *Lith by G.Dubois.*

Historical Society of Pennsylvania Large Graphics Collection [V65]

Lebanon Cemetery was one of the most important African American institutions in nineteenth-century Philadelphia. A key node in a social network that connected religion, education, and political activism, Lebanon was itself nonsectarian and business oriented. Some sense of the esteem the establishment garnered may be gleaned through anecdotes. When reaction to John Brown's raid at Harper's Ferry prompted Underground Railroad operator William Still to seek clandestine cover for his matchless trove of incriminating documents, he chose Lebanon's chapel-cum-office. When W. E. B. DuBois (1868–1963) undertook his pioneering sociological study, *The Philadelphia Negro* (1899), he asked Lebanon's principal manager for data. More than an orderly collection of human remains, the cemetery signaled the Black community's participation in America's "rural" cemetery movement. It also helped secure that community's claims to gentility and urbanity at a time when such ambitions were regularly parodied and discounted by the city's white population.

Located some 2.5 miles south of the city on Passyunk Road, the cemetery obtained its charter from the Pennsylvania legislature on January 24, 1849. Dentist, hairdresser, and unlicensed physician Jacob C. White Sr. (1806–1872) was the institution's leading founder. A peripatetic entrepreneur, White also served as a ruling elder of the city's First African Presbyterian Church while superintending its Sunday School; although Lebanon had no official connection to the congregation, several other corporators held positions there. These men ran the cemetery as a private, for-profit company, in keeping with local precedent at Laurel Hill, Woodlands, and other well-known white cemeteries. Competition came principally from Olive Cemetery in West Philadelphia. The two institutions opened at the same time and operated (with difficulty) into the twentieth century, but Lebanon was always grander and better connected to the city's Black elite.

Whatever their respective strengths, neither cemetery could afford to alienate potential lot buyers or investors. Hints of impermanence or speculative motives could be damaging. Lebanon's managers countered such impressions by commissioning an impressive lithograph of the cemetery's building and grounds. Both were designed by (white) architect and civil engineer John E. Carver (1803–1859), who had gained notoriety for his work on the Episcopal Church of St. James the Less (1846). Standing near Laurel Hill and part of the same tourist circuit, this near-replica of a thirteenth-century English parish church made an appealing model for Lebanon's chapel, the more so, perhaps, because of shared history (Robert Ralston Sr. [1761–1836] had sponsored construction of First African Presbyterian's original house of worship. The congregation continued to remember this act when Ralston's son left funds for building St. James the Less). While gridded in plan, Lebanon's landscape bore the imprint of romanticism in its lush plantings—deciduous trees in front and evergreens within—and a Gothic gateway rendered in granite. When intramural burial bans and streetcar-era development pressures finally brought an end to the place, these gateposts were reinstalled at Eden Cemetery in Collingdale, Pennsylvania, where they can be seen to this day.

AARON V. WUNSCH

59. **Sidney & Neff**

## *Plan of Chelten Hills, Cheltenham Township, Montgomery County Penna, As Surveyed and Laid out by Sidney & Neff*

1854
Published by Friend & Aub
Hand-colored lithograph on paper mounted on linen
24 13/16 × 35 7/16 inches (63.0 × 90.0 cm)

Inscribed center right: *PLAN / OF / CHELTEN HILLS / CHELTENHAM TOWNSHIP / Montgomery County, Penn[a] / As surveyed and laid out by / SIDNEY & NEFF / PHILAD[a] / 1854 / Friend & Aub. Lith. 80, Walnut St Phil[a]*

Historical Society of Pennsylvania Map Collection

Like many American cities, Philadelphia sprouted railroad suburbs in the 1850s. Scholars tend to classify them as "planned" or "unplanned," but in fact most fall somewhere in between. More than Llewellyn Park (1853) outside Manhattan, or Glendale (1851) outside Cincinnati, Chelten Hills represents a pragmatic adaptation to existing conditions. The brainchild of developer and abolitionist Edward M. Davis (1811–1887), the project grew out of parcels he and his partners had assembled along the newly charted route of the North Pennsylvania Railroad, which had yet to run trains at the time this lithograph appeared. The property encompassed about one thousand acres on the west side of Old York Road and had been the province of Quaker farmers for the better part of two centuries. Well-connected and well-capitalized, Davis's Chelten Hills Association dedicated most of the tract to suburban villas with ample grounds. Social convention envisioned husbands commuting to law firms, clubs, and counting houses some nine miles to the south while other family members and servants sallied forth to the adjacent village of Shoemakertown for basic goods and services.

The plan presents Chelten Hills "[a]s surveyed and laid out by Sidney & Neff," a firm responsible for other swatches of railroad-related suburban development in these years. Although he had published *American Cottage and Villa Architecture* four years earlier, J. C. Sidney's (1818–1881) professional experience hewed more toward surveying and cartography, presumably prompting him to partner with James P. W. Neff around the same time. Sidney thus listed himself as "civil engineer" and Neff as "architect" in 1850s directories, though Sidney would straddle that line and others throughout his career. The precise nature and extent of the firm's work at Chelten Hills is unclear. Representing existing roads, property lines, topography, and vegetation was probably their principal charge, with greater latitude for "design" on the tract's interior. Perhaps their chief intervention was the "The Serpentine," an assertively picturesque counterpoint to the orthogonal "avenues" to the south and east. Tellingly, however, this snaking artery was already being truncated at the time the plan was published (see annotation in the right-hand corner) and would be further curtailed and "corrected" (that is, straightened) in years to come.

Over time Chelten Hills has disappeared, its south end renamed La Mott, its north side abutting Wyncote, and the whole administered as a subset of Elkins Park. One might reasonably ask, then, why Chelten Hills is worth remembering. The answer is twofold. First, there is the project's significance at the time of conception: an example of elite metropolitan development rarely studied in Philadelphia beyond the city's Main Line and Germantown Avenue corridors. Few people did more to shape that growth at mid-century than J. C. Sidney, whose efforts ranged from cemeteries, parks, and suburbs to churches, houses, and outbuildings. Credited with proposing the first cohesive scheme for Fairmount Park (1859), Sidney would return to Chelten Hills for a small church (St. Paul's Episcopal,

1860–61), a church burial ground (St. Thomas's, ca. 1861), and several residential commissions.

The way Chelten Hills evolved is also of interest. The northern and western flanks became the domains of leading Gilded Age grandees: Jay Cooke built his massive Ogontz estate there, hatmaker John B. Stetson settled nearby, and traction magnate Peter A. B. Widener eventually located his vast Lynnewood Hall in the same area. To the south, the legacy of Quaker abolitionist Lucretia Mott unfolded in land uses and place names. As Davis's in-laws, Mott and her husband kept tabs on the development from its inception and moved there in 1857. Their idyllic house, Roadside, overlooked Old York Road for decades. Behind it sprang Camp William Penn, a trailblazing Union Army training ground for Black troops, while adjacent tracts became Camptown (later La Mott), a working-class suburb remarkable for its integration of Irish and Black residents. But this radical legacy had limits. The twentieth century brought Latham Park (1912), an "enclosed and restricted" residential subdivision whose towering iron entrance gates landed feet away from where Roadside had stood.

AARON V. WUNSCH

TRANSVERSE
SECTION
THRO'
AUDITORIUM

## 60. **Gustav Runge** (1822–1900) and **Napoleon LeBrun** (1821–1901)

### *Academy of Music, Transverse Section Thro' Auditorium*

---

1855–57
Ink, graphite, and watercolor on paper
22 13/16 × 22 inches (58.0 × 55.8 cm)

Inscribed below image: *TRANSVERSE / SECTION / THRO' / AUDITORIUM*

Historical Society of Pennsylvania Large Graphics Collection [V65]
Gift of the Academy of Music, 1964

Philadelphia's Academy of Music, according to the great conductor Leopold Stokowski, is "the sleekest vehicle of musical expression ever created." Only Vienna boasted finer acoustics, said Christina Nilsson, the Victorian diva who sang in every major opera house from Moscow to Chicago. But it is hardly surprising that it could satisfy an educated European professional: its architect was himself one. Gustav Runge was the product of the leading German architectural schools, and the signs of his sophisticated training are apparent everywhere in this drawing of 1854.

The competition to design the Academy was furiously contested, and to prepare his project Runge joined forces with Napoleon LeBrun, the architect of Philadelphia's Catholic Cathedral. It was a partnership of convenience: Runge was the controlling mind, as his published treatise on the building makes clear. LeBrun and Runge won easily, besting their sixteen competitors, and this cross-section of the auditorium suggests why.

To design a complicated public building for a competition—to prepare all the necessary plans, elevations, and sections—is a calculated gamble. Typically architects will not make highly detailed drawings, knowing they can refine their designs if they win. But Runge's section has all the completeness of a fully developed working drawing. Besides the auditorium itself, with its three tiers of seats carried on slender, cast-iron columns, he addressed every aspect of construction, ventilation, and decoration. We see the mighty timber truss supporting the gambrel roof; the eight-foot-wide ventilator shaft atop the ceiling, the rising air warmed by the chandelier; and the exquisitely detailed ornament of the proscenium arch, built almost exactly as shown here. Even the gaslights above the angled seats reveal carefully placed ducts to carry away the exhaust. Runge acted as if he fully expected to break ground the next day.

And yet the auditorium's famous feature is missing. Runge was a "superb cellist," with a musician's understanding of vibration and resonance and how they affected sound. In the interval between winning the commission in February 1855 and the start of construction in July, he rethought its acoustics. The great challenge of designing a performance space is to avoid echo, but Runge attached even more importance to amplifying the resonance of the sound "at its point of origin." He accomplished this by building "enclosed hollow spaces" (*begrenzten hohlen Räume*) beneath the pliant floor of the parquet, in effect turning it into a vast vibrating soundboard. Hence the quality of living sound praised by Stokowski, Nilsson, and others.

Alas, it is no more. The Academy's acoustics were inadvertently compromised in 1960 when a concrete floor was poured into the hollow space beneath the stage to support the weight of a new movable organ.

Runge's transverse section is one of seventeen drawings from the winning competition entry in the collection of the Historical Society of Pennsylvania, which also includes the project of the Philadelphia architect Stephen Button. A gawky domed affair, it could scarcely differ more from Runge's splendidly refined essay. Unaccountably it won second prize.

MICHAEL J. LEWIS

# 61. *Inventory and Appraisement of the Estate of Capt. John Butler*

February 13, 1849
Manuscript; red and black ink on light blue wove paper
13 × 8 inches (33.0 × 20.3 cm)

Butler Family Papers [1447]
Gift of Owen J. Wister, 1947

This inventory of the "property" comprising the estate of Captain John Butler (d. 1849) listed 840 enslaved people, valued at $281,125, from the two Georgia plantations Butler co-owned with his brother Pierce Mease Butler. The account is in the large Wister and Butler Families Papers, dating from 1700 to 2004, which include diaries, correspondence, business, estate, and real estate papers, financial records, photographs, newspaper clippings, and other manuscript and printed materials that cover the lives and interests of the Butler, Wister, and related families and their connections in the United States and Great Britain. Among the principals represented in the collection is Major Pierce Butler, most famous for pushing slavery's interest at the Constitutional Convention in 1787 and acquiring (through marriage) both a sea-island cotton plantation and a rice plantation on the Altamaha River delta in Georgia. Additionally he gained more than five hundred enslaved workers that became the basis of the Butler family wealth as well as the purchase of two houses in Philadelphia that became Butler family residences thereafter. Also of note is Pierce Mease Butler, one of Major Butler's grandsons who, along with his brother Captain John Butler, inherited and then "managed" the Georgia plantations from Philadelphia as an absentee master. In March 1859 he infamously put up for sale 436 enslaved men, women, and children in the largest single auction of humans in US history, to cover debts from his mismanagement of the plantations, business speculations, gambling, and lavish lifestyle. More names from the collection include Butler's daughter Frances Kemble Butler Leigh (from his short-lived marriage to celebrated English actress Fanny Kemble), who tried to run the plantations with "free" labor after the Civil War, failed after ten years, and published in 1883 a much-read memoir defending her father and the interests of the white master class; and Leigh's nephew Owen Wister, author of *The Virginian* (1902) and resident of Philadelphia, who inherited the estate and sold the Georgia property in 1923.

The Butler papers reveal the tangled histories and interests of slaveholders and enslaved on the plantations, and then the postwar lives that former "masters" and now freed people sought to create on the sea islands, as they also speak to the many family, commercial, financial, and other ties that bound Philadelphia to slavery and the South. In the business and personal records, the Butler papers constitute one of the fullest and most sustained accountings of Black-white interactions in the Deep South during the nineteenth century. They also provide direct information on Black people's lives, such as names, immediate family and wider kin relationships, work histories and habits, foodways, and local Geechee-Gullah culture of West African linguistic, artistic, musical, and religious adaptations. Even emotionally charged documents such as the 1849 inventory and appraisement of slaves and the catalogue of the 1859 Butler auction—both of which in varying degrees describe individuals by name, family connection, "occupation," and physical characteristics (valuation of enslaved property for purposes of sale or credit usually included such factors as age, skills, strength, intelligence, and for girls and young women their child-bearing potential)—have become important in Black American's genealogical searches for family connections otherwise impossible to discover and for writing new histories of slavery from multiple perspectives. RANDALL M. MILLER

| No. | Name | Age | Value | |
|---|---|---|---|---|
| | Brought up | | $ | 191725.. |
| 548 | Die | 18 | 500.. | |
| 549 | Dorinda | 1/2 | 50.. | |
| 550 | Queen | 17 | 450.. | |
| 551 | Matty | 12 | 375.. | 1375.. |
| 552 | Tom | 38 | 550.. | |
| 553 | Harriet | 31 | 475.. | |
| 554 | Waney | 7 | 250.. | |
| 555 | Molly | 1/4 | 50.. | 1325.. |
| 556 | Jerry | 45 | 450.. | |
| 557 | Violet | 43 | 400.. | |
| 558 | Betsy | 19 | 500.. | |
| 559 | Abram | 12 | 400.. | |
| 560 | Primus | 9 | 300.. | |
| 561 | George | 7 | 250.. | |
| 562 | Mary | 3 | 150.. | |
| 563 | Ruth | 15 | 400.. | |
| 564 | Infant | | 50.. | 2900.. |
| 565 | Friday | 32 | 550.. | |
| 566 | Die | 28 | 500.. | |
| 567 | Elcey | 11 | 375.. | |
| 568 | Pheobe | 9 | 300.. | |
| 569 | Cornelia | 6 | 225.. | |
| 570 | Lavinia | 1/4 | 50.. | 2000.. |
| 571 Mason | Sancho | 53 | 500.. | |
| 572 | Nanny | 55 | 175.. | |
| 573 | Chany | 16 | 500.. | 1175.. |
| 574 Cooper | Isaac | 32 | 600.. | |
| 575 | Philis | 28 | 500.. | |
| 576 | Nanny | 9 | 300.. | |
| 577 | Rose | 4 | 175.. | |
| 578 | Priscilla | 1 | 100. | 1675.. |
| 579 Carpt. | Sunday | 56 | 400.. | |
| 580 | Rina | 53 | 225.. | |
| 581 | Justice | 20 | 600.. | 1225 |
| | Carried up | | $ | 203400.. |

| No. | Name | Age | Value | |
|---|---|---|---|---|
| | Brought up | | $ | 203400.. |
| 582 | Peter | 32 | 600.. | |
| 583 | Diana | 29 | 450.. | |
| 584 | Grace | 8 | 275.. | |
| 585 | York | 5 | 225.. | |
| 586 | Fanny | 1 | 100.. | |
| 587 | Sancho | 1/12 | 50.. | 1700.. |
| 588 | Elijah | 35 | 550.. | |
| 589 | Hagar | 31 | 450.. | |
| 590 | Jenny | 13 | 400.. | |
| 591 | Daphne | 6 | 225.. | 1625.. |
| 592 | Sinder | 73 | — | |
| 593 | Patty | 44 | 375.. | |
| 594 | Dixon | 10 | 350.. | 725.. |
| 595 Cooper | Nero | 58 | 350.. | |
| 596 | Mary | 58 | 225.. | 575.. |
| 597 Cooper | Philip | 28 | 700.. | |
| 598 | Chloe | 19 | 500.. | |
| 599 | John | 3 | 150.. | |
| 600 | William | 1/4 | 50.. | 1400.. |
| 601 Cooper | Charles | 39 | 700.. | |
| 602 | Luna | 36 | 425.. | |
| 603 | Nero | 14 | 375.. | |
| 604 | Mary | 8 | 275.. | |
| 605 | Elcey | 7 | 250.. | |
| 606 | Ephriam | 5 | 200.. | |
| 607 | Patience | 3 | 150.. | |
| 608 | George | 1/4 | 50.. | 2425.. |
| 609 | Isaac | 31 | 600.. | |
| 610 | Sue | 24 | 500.. | |
| 611 | Icy | 9 | 300.. | 1400.. |
| 612 | Worster | 36 | 500.. | |
| 613 | Mary | 30 | 300.. | 800.. |
| 614 | Ceasar | 25 | 600.. | |
| 615 | Elcey | 20 | 500 | |
| 616 | Biat | 2 | 125 | 1225.. |
| | Carried over | | $ | 215275.. |

# 62. *Freedom to the Slave*

1863–64
Published by Supervisory Committee for Recruiting Colored Regiments
Chromolithograph on paper
10 ¼ × 8 9⁄16 inches (26.0 × 21.0 cm)

p. 28 of the *John Brown Papers, 1851–1861*

Ferdinand J. Dreer Autograph Collection [0175]
Gift of Ferdinand J. Dreer, 1890

This chromolithograph was among the most popular and potent images promoting Black recruitment during the Civil War. It sometimes was sold as a stand-alone lithograph to be framed but also printed as a poster. This particular lithograph is the cover of a war song, with a note on the reverse stating that it is the "original version" of "John's Brown's Body." It is pasted in a bound-volume scrapbook entitled, "Original papers read in evidence at the trial of John Brown, for the invasion of Harper's Ferry; together with other papers relating to his life and execution," which comprises the John Brown Papers, part of the massive autograph collection that Ferdinand J. Dreer gave the Historical Society of Pennsylvania in 1890. Included in the scrapbook are letters by and about John Brown (1800–1859); coded letters planning the John Brown raid on Harper's Ferry in 1859; a copy of Brown's "A Declaration of Liberty, By the Representatives of the Slave Population of the United States of America" (1859); a broadside entitled *Address of John Brown to the Virginia Court when about to receive the sentence of death, for his heroic attempt at Harper's Ferry, to give deliverance to the captives, and to let the oppressed go free* (Boston, 1859); a codicil or part of Brown's will written December 1, 1859, specifying buying Bibles for his children; and other items. Of special significance is a letter from one of Brown's captors detailing the military action at Harper's Ferry; letters from President James Buchanan on his refusal to involve the federal government in putting down any rebellion or effort to rescue Brown; and correspondence of Virginia Governor Henry Wise regarding security during and after Brown's trial and the disposition of Brown's body to his widow.

During and after his trial and execution, Brown became the subject of intense interest. Brown's contemporaries, and later historians, were not sure if Brown was a madman or a martyr, but there was no doubt that his unflinching resolve to end slavery by any means, and to give his life to the cause of liberty, forced Americans to answer where they stood on the issue. His manly posture in facing death inspired many, including Ralph Waldo Emerson and Henry David Thoreau, who likened him to biblical prophets, even Christ, and famously asserted Brown's martyrdom would make the gallows as holy as the cross. Speeches, poems, paintings, and songs about Brown proliferated.

Collecting John Brown materials also became an obsession. People visited Harper's Ferry to see the site of the great "battle" and gather relics, especially pikes, for which there was a brisk trade. After Brown's execution, people sought planks from the scaffold, pieces of the hanging rope, coffin screws, and other objects that seemingly carried some sacred power. Getting materials from John Brown's own hand proved more difficult, for Brown refused autograph seekers. Still, Brown documents came on the market. His children, for example, sometimes turned to selling their father's letters or mementos during hard times. Reportedly, Ferdinand Greer paid Salmon Brown $1,000 for John Brown's last will written to his wife during his imprisonment. Whatever the truth of that transaction, Dreer got enough Brown-related documents to reveal important aspects of Brown's life and effect. RANDALL M. MILLER

FREEDOM TO THE SLAVE
PUBLIC
SCHOOL

## 63. **William Still** (1821–1902)

### *Journal C*

1852–57
Manuscript; ink on paper bound in half black leather and marbled paper boards
7 15⁄16 × 6 ½ inches (20.1 × 16.7 cm)

Pennsylvania Abolition Society Papers [0490]
Gift of Frances E. Still, 1931

### *William Still*

ca. 1875
Halftone on paper
5 ½ × 4 inches (14.0 × 10.2 cm)

p. 74 of *The Underground Railroad: From Slavery to Freedom*

## **Nell Irvin Painter** (1942– )

### *Arrived New Names 2*

2022
Hand-colored lino print and ink on Bristol vellum
12 × 9 ⅝ inches (30.4 × 24.4 cm)

Nell Irvin Painter Prints [4530]
Purchase, 2022
Courtesy of Nell Irvin Painter

### *William Still Triptych, 1–3*

2022
#1: one run etching and one run screenprint; #2: one run etching printed with intaglio wiping and a surface roll of transparent ink, and one run screenprint; #3: one run screenprint, one surface rolled Plexiglas flat, and one run etching
27 ⅝ × 22 ½ inches (70.1 × 57.1 cm)

Nell Irvin Painter Prints [4530]
Purchase, 2022
Published by the Brodsky Center at PAFA, Philadelphia, copyright the artist and the Brodsky Center at PAFA, Philadelphia
Photograph courtesy of the artist and the Brodsky Center at PAFA, Philadelphia, photo by Adrian Cubillas
Courtesy of Nell Irvin Painter

Page by eloquent page, William Still's journal captures the United States on the road to war over slavery. So much rushes out to grab the reader! Two realizations struck me in these pages, this daily record of self-emancipation. First, the words of rebirth, of new names as new identities, as exemplified in thirteen dates in the single year of 1854.

> Mar. 3rd 1854 Rosanna Tonnell, left Isaac Tonnell of Georgetown, Del., on Tuesday in Christmas: (New name Maria Hide) in company with another young woman, and little boy which was her son.
>
> Aug 28/54 Arrived—Wesley Kinnard, old name, Sam'l Green
>
> Sept. 2/54 Arrived. Mark Washington, new name Wm Wilson
>
> Sept 8/54 Arrived, John Henry Rickets, (new name Ed. Henry Waples)
>
> Oct. 10/54 Arrived Henry Wilson, old name Perry Wilson
>
> Nov. 2/54 Nov. Arrived—John Canon—old name London Davis
>
> Nov. 3/54 Arrived, Andrew Blow—old name Henry Levison

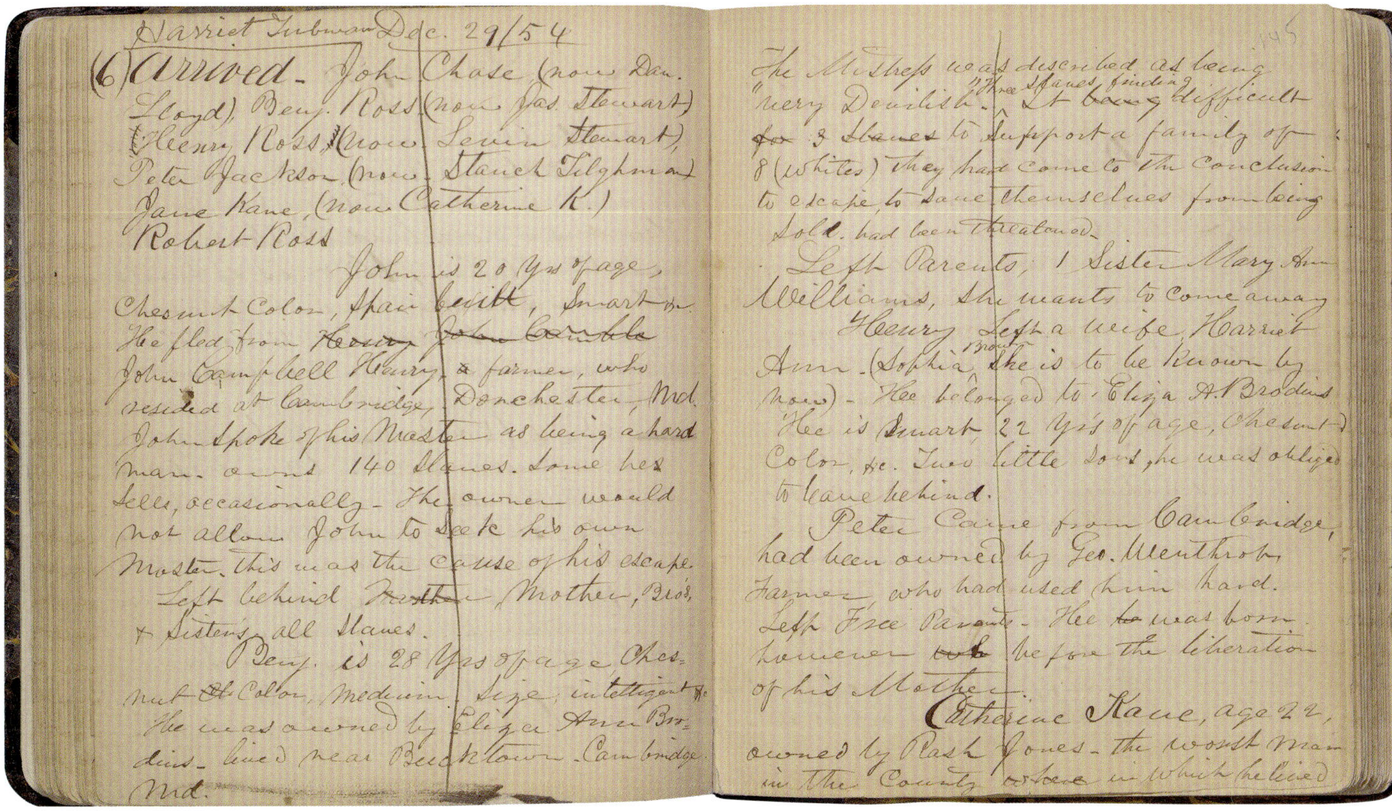

Harriet Tubman Dec. 29/54

(6) Arrived – John Chase (now Dan. Lloyd), Benj. Ross (now Jas. Stewart), Henry Ross, (now Levin Stewart), Peter Jackson (now Staunch Tilghman) Jane Kane, (now Catherine K.) Robert Ross

John is 20 Yrs of age, Chesnut Color, Spare built, Smart &c. He fled from John Campbell Henry, a farmer, who resided at Cambridge, Dorchester, Md. John Spoke of his Master as being a hard man – owns 140 slaves. Some he sells, occasionally – The owner would not allow John to seek his own Master, this was the cause of his escape. Left behind Mother, Bro's, & Sisters, all slaves.

Benj. is 28 Yrs of age, Chesnut Color, medium size, intelligent &c. He was owned by Eliza Ann Brodins – lived near Bucktown – Cambridge Md.

The Mistress was described as being "very Devilish." Three slaves finding it difficult to support a family of 8 (whites) they had come to the conclusion to escape, to save themselves from being sold, had been threatened.

Left Parents, 1 Sister Mary Ann Williams, she wants to come away

Henry Left a wife, Harriet Ann – (Sophia Brown she is to be known by now) – He belonged to Eliza A. Brodins He is Smart, 22 Yr's of age, Chesnut Color, &c. Two little sons, he was obliged to leave behind.

Peter Came from Cambridge, had been owned by Geo. Wenthrop, Farmer, who had used him hard. Left Free Parents – He was born however before the liberation of his Mother.

Catherine Kane, age 22, owned by Rash Jones – the worst man in the County in which he lived

Nov. 14/54 Arrived—Henry Allen, (new name Thos. Redden)

Nov. 15/54 Four at one arrival—Yesterday afternoon Robert Belt, (now Chas_ Williams) Nanthaniel Smith, (now John Hutchins) Ellen Cale, (now Sarah Johnson), and Mary Cale, now Jane Johnson.

Nov. 21/54 Arrived, Peter Johnson, had been known by the name of Peter Airs

Nov. 21/54 Sam'l Davis, new name Benj. Johnson

Nov 29/54 W$^{m}$ Butcher—new name W$^{m}$ T. Mitchel

Harriet Tubman Dec. 29/54 (6) Arrived—John Chase, (now Dan. Lloyd), Benj. Ross (now Jas. Stewart) ~~(Henry Ross,)~~ (now Lewis Stewart), Peter Jackson, (now Stanch Tilghman) Jane Kane, (now Catherine K.)

Here were fugitives, now remaking themselves as free people, christening themselves anew.

The second characteristic in this remarkable record is the sheer magnitude of what Still heralded as "Arrived," the flow of people taking their lives into their own hands as autonomous beings. Only some fugitives took on new names, but the rhythm of their escape was steady. I saw a repressive system leaking the people at its foundation, a fatal hemorrhage at the heart of the institution, not quite on a weekly basis in 1854 and 1855, but rapidly enough to show the slave regime's crisis. Who left? Young men, middle-aged men, young women, mothers with children, married couples, siblings. Everyone was leaving their jobs, their enslaved lives, their legal owners whether harsh, lax, cruel, careless, tightfisted, or negligent.

Still asked about their experiences of enslavement, and the people described their owners by name, vocation, and

personal habits, leaving a record for our times of exactly who (and whose descendants) prospered on stolen labor. The people were quitting a system intended for permanence that had once seemed eternal. Striking out on their own in the mid-1850s meant starting anew—most likely in Canada—beyond the reach of the American Fugitive Slave Law. Leaving home meant leaving their country.

This page dated December 29, 1854, features an unusually large group of six people who arrived together under the guidance of Harriet Tubman, who regularly coordinated with Still's Philadelphia Vigilance Committee. Here Tubman is presented as the "Moses of her people," for some of these pages' escapees were, in fact, her very own people. Her brothers Ross, for example, were embodiments of the familial dimension of freedom. NELL IRVIN PAINTER

# 64. Banneker Institute

## *Constitution*

1854
Manuscript; ink and graphite on paper
12 × 7 ½ inches (30.5 × 19.2 cm)

Leon Gardiner Collection of American Negro Historical Society Records [0008]
Gift of Leon Gardiner, 1934

In 1854, several dozen of Philadelphia's African American men established the Banneker Institute, "a young men's instruction society." According to the Institute's constitution, "the object of this association shall be, primarily, the mental improvement of its members." Named in honor of the African American mathematician who had assisted in the surveying of Washington, DC, in the 1790s and had published authoritative almanacs during those same years, the Banneker Institute set as its purpose a series of lectures, seminars, and debates on national and international topics "in various branches of knowledge." In pursuit of its goal—which it described as "the diffusion of useful knowledge"—the Banneker Institute leaders intended to create "a library, which if properly kept up, would shed a halo of literary light throughout this city, and reflect great credit on those who constitute this association."

The Banneker Institute was one of several incarnations of self-education organizations created by Black Philadelphians as early as the 1830s, aimed at developing what the Institute founders described as "discipline to the mind." Among the Institute's precursors were the Gilbert Lyceum, whose ambition was "the encouragement of polite literature," and the Rush Library and Debating Society, which is reputed to have amassed a two hundred-volume library. Like these predecessors, the Banneker Institute was short-lived: its membership—robust at its inception in the 1850s, gradually dwindled, and the Institute ceased keeping records in 1872. Perhaps the demands, distractions, and promises of the Civil War and Reconstruction diverted the Black communities' resources. However, during the sixteen years of its recorded activity, the group followed a strict discipline, with weekly meetings convening at 8:00 p.m. and closing promptly at 10:00 p.m. The Institute's meticulously kept attendance, activity, and disciplinary records reflect its commitment to high standards and thoughtful management. Admission to the organization was by invitation only; "indecorous language" (presumably swearing) was prohibited; and members were required not only to pay annual dues but also to take responsibility, by turns, for preparing to lead discussions or for arranging lectures on various scientific, literary, political, philosophical, or historical topics. And the Institute was not insular. Though self-described as a "young men's" group, some of its programs were led, attended, and economically supported by women—family or friends of members—and other nonmembers.

Thus, though its tenure was relatively short, the Banneker Institute's reach was not insignificant. Composed of members of Philadelphia's Black elite—entrepreneurs, craftsmen, clergymen, educators, and graduates of the Institute for Colored Youth (an exclusive educational institution established by Philadelphia Quakers to educate Black children)—the network surrounding the Banneker Institute encompassed the city's most influential African Americans. The Historical Society of Pennsylvania's Leon Gardiner Collection houses not only Banneker Institute records but also private papers and correspondence of many of its members and associates from as far afield as Canada, England, and Scotland.

Since the 1950s, scores of scholarly publications have mined the Gardiner Collection to investigate and highlight little-known narratives of the richness and struggles of Philadelphia's nineteenth-century African American lives. HSP has encouraged and promoted such research through fellowships, public programming for adults, and "history camps" to make these materials known to public school students.

EMMA LAPSANSKY-WERNER

# Constitution.

Title

Art. 1. Sec. 1.

The name, style and title of this association shall be The Banneker Institute of the City of Philadelphia.

Art. 1. Sec. 2. Objects

The objects of this association shall be primarily, the mental improvement of its members by means of lectures, debates and the formation of such committees in the various branches of knowledge as may be deemed most effectual ~~in~~ carrying out the designs of the Institute: secondarily, the diffusion of useful knowledge among all who may come within the pale of its influence.

Art. 2. Sec. 1. Members

The members of the Institute shall be active, contributing, ~~corresponding~~ and honorary.

Art. 2. Sec. 2. Active membership

Any male person of good moral character, and of ordinary literary attainments, may become an active member by signing the Constitution and by paying such admission fee as may be required in the By-Laws.

Art. 2. Sec. 3. Corresponding do.

Any person of good moral character can become a contributing member by indorsing the Constitution and by contributing to the funds of the Institute the sum of one dollar annually.

# MEN OF COLOR, TO ARMS! NOW OR NEVER!

This is our Golden Moment. The Government of the United States calls for every Able-Bodied Colored Man to enter the Army for the THREE YEARS' SERVICE, and join in fighting the Battles of Liberty and the Union. A new era is open to us. For generations we have suffered under the horrors of slavery, outrage and wrong; our manhood has been denied, our citizenship blotted out, our souls seared and burned, our spirits cowed and crushed, and the hopes of the future of our race involved in doubts and darkness. But now the whole aspect of our relations to the white race is changed. Now therefore is our most precious moment. Let us Rush to Arms! **Fail Now and Our Race is Doomed** on this the soil of our birth. We must now awake, arise, or be forever fallen. If we value Liberty, if we wish to be free in this land, if we love our country, if we love our families, our children, our homes, we must strike NOW while the Country calls: must rise up in the dignity of our manhood, and show by our own right arms that we are worthy to be freemen. Our enemies have made the country believe that we are craven cowards, without soul, without manhood, without the spirit of soldiers. Shall we die with this stigma resting on our graves? Shall we leave this inheritance of shame to our children? No! A thousand times No! **We WILL Rise!** The alternative is upon us; let us rather die freemen than live to be slaves. What is life without liberty? We say that we have manhood—now is the time to prove it. A nation or a people that cannot fight may be pitied, but cannot be respected. If we would be regarded *Men*, if we would forever **SILENCE THE TONGUE OF CALUMNY,** of prejudice and hate; let us rise NOW and fly to arms! We have seen what **Valor and Heroism** our brothers displayed at **PORT HUDSON and at MILLIKEN'S BEND;** though they are just from the galling, poisoning grasp of slavery, they have startled the world by the most exalted heroism. If they have proved themselves heroes, can not we prove ourselves men? **ARE FREEMEN LESS BRAVE THAN SLAVES?** More than a Million White Men have left Comfortable Homes and joined the Armies of the Union to save their Country; cannot we leave ours, and swell the hosts of the Union, to save our liberties, vindicate our manhood, and deserve well of our Country?

MEN OF COLOR! All Races of Men—the Englishman, the Irishman, the Frenchman, the German, the American, have been called to assert their claim to freedom and a manly character, by an appeal to the sword. The day that has seen an enslaved race in arms, has, in all history, seen their last trial. We can now see that **OUR LAST OPPORTUNITY HAS COME!** If we are not lower in the scale of humanity than Englishmen, Irishmen, white Americans and other races, we can show it now.

**MEN OF COLOR! BROTHERS and FATHERS! WE APPEAL TO YOU!** By all your concern for yourselves and your liberties, by all your regard for God and Humanity, by all your desire for Citizenship and Equality before the law, by all your love for the Country, to stop at no subterfuges, listen to nothing that shall deter you from rallying for the Army. Come forward, and at once Enroll your Names for the **Three Years' Service. STRIKE NOW,** and you are henceforth and forever **FREEMEN!**

E. D. Bassett,
Wm. D. Forten,
Frederick Douglass,
Wm. Whipper,
D. D. Turner,
Jas. McCrummell,
A. S. Cassey,
A. M. Green,
J. W. Page,
L. R. Seymour,
Rev. J. Underdue,
John W. Price,
Augustus Dorsey,
Rev. Stephen Smith,
N. W. Depee,
Dr. J. H. Wilson,
J. W. Cassey,
P. J. Armstrong,
J. W. Simpson,
Rev. J B. Trusty,
S. Morgan Smith,
Wm. E. Gipson,
Rev. J. Boulden,
Rev. J. Asher,
Rev. J. C. Gibbs,
Daniel George,
Robert M. Adger,
Henry M. Cropper,
Rev. J. B. Reeve,
Rev. J. A. Williams,
Rev. A. L. Stanford,
Thomas J. Bowers,
Elijah J. Davis,
John P. Burr,
Robert Jones,
O. V. Catto,
Thos. J. Dorsey,
I. D. Cliff,
Jacob C. White,
Morris Hall,
James Needham,
Rev. Elisha Weaver,
Ebenezer Black,
Rev. Wm. T. Catto,
Jas. R. Gordon,
Samuel Stewart,
David B. Bowser,
Henry Minton,
Daniel Colley,
J. C. White, Jr.,
Rev. J. P. Campbell,
Rev. W. J. Alston,
J. P. Johnson,
Franklin Turner,
Jesse E. Glasgow.

# 65. *Men of Color, To Arms! Now or Never!*

1863
Published by Frederick Douglass (1818–1895) and the Supervisory Committee for Recruiting Colored Regiments
Broadside; letterpress on paper
10 × 7 ¾ inches (25.4 × 19.7 cm)

Leon Gardiner Collection of American Negro Historical Society Records [0008]
Gift of Leon Gardiner, 1934

"Men of Color, To Arms! Now or Never!" So exhorted a broadside circulated in 1863 in response to President Abraham Lincoln's pronouncement that African Americans—after months of being barred from military service—could join the Union battle to end slavery. This call-to-arms was endorsed by more than four dozen of Philadelphia's most prominent African American teachers, ministers, craftspersons, and businessmen and widely circulated through the well-worn networks that had been distributing Black peoples' newspapers since the 1820s. It helped to recruit nearly 200,000 Black men and women to serve in the Union army. Seasoned abolitionist and newspaper publisher Frederick Douglass—though not a native Philadelphian—lent his authority to the advertisement's call for the "three years service" that these signers hoped would result in African Americans becoming "henceforth and forever FREEMEN!"

The broadside, which highlights the bravery—and the loss of many lives—of the United States Colored Troops (USCT) at Port Hudson, Mississippi (May 1863), and Milliken's Bend, Louisiana (June 1863), also helped to inspire the development of Camp William Penn, just north of Philadelphia, which was fully operational as the Union army's largest USCT training facility by July 1863. Through training grounds like Camp William Penn, Pennsylvania provided the largest number of African American Union troops of any of the Northern states.

A copy of this announcement—signed by some Black Pennsylvanians who could trace their heritage to participation in the American Revolution—is among the rich collection of African American artifacts entrusted to the Historical Society of Pennsylvania by the Negro Historical Society, founded in 1897 by the heirs and friends of many of the signers of that "Now-or-Never" call to arms. HSP's Negro Historical Society materials include correspondence of men and women who had set their life's work as protecting Black lives and furthering Black reputations, as well as advancing access to citizenship, education, and economic opportunity. The reach of the Negro Historical Society was broad, with documents dating back to the 1790s and encompassing African Americans' civic, religious, and social-justice involvements, as well as their abolitionist, journalistic, and educational endeavors. The records of the Banneker Institute—an intellectuals' study group—are also housed in the Gardiner Collection, alongside documents, such as this broadside, which were created and promoted by many of the same Black activists who had founded the Banneker Institute to support their educational aspirations. And the lyrical rhetoric of the broadside echoes the intellectual ambitions of that earlier organization's charter: "If we are not lower in the scale of humanity than Englishmen, Irishmen, white Americans and other races, we can show it now . . . by all your desired for Citizenship and Equality before the law, by all your love for the Country."

Indeed, HSP's Leon Gardiner Collection, and the Negro Historical Society records embedded therein, are a treasure-trove of inspiring chronicles awaiting exploration.

EMMA LAPSANSKY-WERNER

# 66. **John Sartain** (1808–1897), after **Christian Schussele** (ca. 1824–1879)

## *Men of Progress—American Inventors*

1862
Published by John Skirving
Mezzotint and etching on paper
26 × 38 ⅜ inches (66.2 × 97.4 cm)

Signed in graphite, lower right margin: *Artist's proof John Sartain*
Inscribed in graphite, bottom margin: *Dr. Morton Bogardis* [*sic*] / *Colt / McCormick / Saxton / Peter Cooper / Goodyear / Profr Henry Mott / Dr Nott / Emerson / Morse / Burden / Hoe / Bigelow / Jennings / Blanchard / Howe. / American Inventors*; in plate, below image: *The orig[d] Picture by C. Schussele. Phil[a] 1861. / Entered according to Act of Congress in the year 1862, by John Skirving, in the Clerk's Office of the District Court for the Eastern District of Pennsylvania. Eng[d] on steel by John Sartain, Phil[a] 1862.*; verso in graphite: *John Gossert Phila. June 1895 / Alex. McClure / John Gossert*

Historical Society of Pennsylvania Large Graphics Collection [V65]

At the Great Exhibition of 1851 in London, the range and quality of inventions displayed by American exhibitors startled their European competitors, signaling the young republic's growing involvement in the Industrial Revolution. Several years later, John Skirving, a Philadelphia-based builder and entrepreneur, persuaded iron manufacturer Jordan L. Mott (1799–1866) to commission a life-size group portrait of America's leading inventors, to be painted by Christian Schussele, a French émigré who had settled in Philadelphia in the late 1840s. At the same time, Skirving, who was a canny entrepreneur, engaged the engraver John Sartain to make a large mezzotint reproduction of the painting for publication and sale. The final painting depicts nineteen men gathered in a conference room, surrounded by drawings and models of their inventions. The twentieth inventor is Benjamin Franklin, overseeing the gathering in a portrait in the left background. Several of the men who had made their mark at the 1851 exhibition are also portrayed—including Cyrus McCormick, Samuel Colt, and Erastus Bigelow. The composition, as Skirving explained in the key that accompanied the mezzotint, formed "a *conversazione* . . . a means of presenting in a natural and picturesque manner so many likenesses together, and as free as possible from formality and stiffness." The original painting is now at the National Portrait Gallery in Washington, DC, and has been heralded as a landmark tribute to American innovation: owners of the mezzotint include circus entrepreneur John Ringling North and founder of the Goodyear Rubber Company, Frank A. Seiberling. Skirving's project was also prescient—by 1870, several of the men depicted had died, as had Skirving himself.

By partnering with Sartain, Skirving gained the talents of an accomplished and well-connected artist, publisher, and fellow entrepreneur. Sartain had emigrated from England to Philadelphia in 1830 and pioneered the art of reproductive mezzotint in the United States. In an age before photographic reproduction, numerous painters engaged him to copy their works; he also produced celebrity portraits and published the eponymous *Sartain's Union Magazine*, of which Edgar Allan Poe was a friend and contributor. Throughout his long life, Sartain was a tireless advocate for American art, even as photographic

technology rendered his mezzotint reproductions obsolete. As a director of both the Pennsylvania Academy of the Fine Arts and the Philadelphia School of Design for Women, he worked to professionalize art school curricula. He also chaired the Fine Arts Department for the 1876 Centennial Exhibition and was a founding trustee of the Pennsylvania Museum and School of Industrial Art, now the Philadelphia Museum of Art.

Thanks to a gift from Sartain's granddaughter, the Historical Society of Pennsylvania owns an extensive collection of Sartain's papers, as well as engravings by Sartain and his children, Emily, William, Samuel, and Henry. Emily followed in her father's footsteps most closely. She was an accomplished painter and printmaker as well as a pioneering advocate for women artists, serving as chair of the Women's Art Department at the 1893 Columbian Exposition and for many years as the principal of the Philadelphia School of Design for Women (now Moore College of Art).

The sitters, with (some of) their areas of innovation noted, are (from left to right): William Thomas Green Morton (1819–1868), *ether anesthesia*; James Bogardus (1800–1874) *cast-iron architecture*; Samuel Colt (1814–1862) *armaments*; Cyrus Hall McCormick (1809–1884) *mechanical reaper*; Joseph Saxton (1799–1873) *hydrometer, fountain pen, daguerrotypy*; Charles Goodyear (1800–1860) *vulcanized rubber*; Peter Cooper (1791–1883) *steam locomotive*; Jordan Lawrence Mott (1799–1866) *iron works*; Joseph Henry (1797–1878) *electromagnets, founding secretary of the Smithsonian Institution*; Eliphalet Nott (1773–1866) *coal-burning stove*; John Ericsson (1803–1889) *naval architecture*; Frederick Ellsworth Sickels (1819–1895) *steam engine valves*; Samuel Finley Breese Morse (1791–1872) *telegraphy*; Henry Burden (1791–1871) *iron works*; Richard March Hoe (1812–1886) *rotary printing press*; Erastus Brigham Bigelow (1814–1879) *textile manufacturing, power looms*; Isaiah Jennings (1792–1862) *steam engines, "instantaneous matches," artificial light*; Thomas Blanchard (1788–1864) *assembly-line manufacturing, armaments*; and Elias Howe (1819–1867) *sewing machine*.

ELIZABETH MILROY

## 67. **William McIlvaine Jr.** (1813–1867)

### *Camp of Harding's Landing, James River Va.*

July 1, 1862
Watercolor on paper
6 ³⁄₄ × 9 ³⁄₄ inches (17.2 × 25.0 cm)

Inscribed in graphite, lower left: *Camp of July 1st, 1862 / Harding's Landing, James River Va.*

Historical Society of Pennsylvania Bound Graphics Collection [V66]

Less well known than the abundant print illustrations and photographs of the Civil War, but also revealing of soldiers' views of the war they knew firsthand, are the pencil or pen drawings and sketches, painted scenes and portraits, and watercolors by soldier "artists," both amateur and professional, who provided often intimate images of soldiers' lives, especially in camp. The eighty watercolors and pencil drawings by William McIlvaine Jr. of the Fifth New York Infantry, gathered in a volume titled "Camp Views of War of Rebellion" in the collections of the Historical Society of Pennsylvania, constitute one of the finest examples of such soldier artists' work and exemplify many of the features in subject and style that characterized the genre.

McIlvaine, who was born in Philadelphia and studied at the University of Pennsylvania, was already an accomplished artist, working principally in watercolors, when he enlisted in the New York Fifth Regiment of Volunteers, a Zouave unit, in 1861. He had traveled to Europe to observe the techniques, media, and subject matter of the great masters, but in his own work, he chose to represent American subjects. In 1849 he went to the California gold fields, where he painted many watercolor scenes of mining and miners' lives, but after half a year returned to Philadelphia, traveling from California through Mexico and Panama. McIlvaine collected some of his drawings and watercolors of the places he visited along the way into a book about his journey, *Sketches of Scenery and Personal Adventure in California and Mexico* (1850). From 1851 to 1855, he remained in Philadelphia and exhibited his work at the Pennsylvania Academy of the Fine Arts and elsewhere. He then moved to New York, where he painted many scenes of transportation and town life in the region and placed his work in several galleries. When the war came, McIlvaine enlisted as a private, but his exact motive for joining is not known.

During the war McIlvaine saw action with the Army of Potomac from 1861 to 1863, when he left the army. The army fought in some of the bloodiest engagements of the war, but McIlvaine's visual record of the war largely focused on the prosaic aspects of soldiering in camp and on the march. McIlvaine's commanding officer had excused Private McIlvaine from his regular duties in order to paint a record of camp life. McIlvaine did so by portraying soldiers on picket duty, at the Army Post Office tent, in the officers' quarters, and at rest. He also drew images of forts and other structures. Such depictions humanized the soldiers and offered a counterpoint to other accounts, usually in diaries and letters, but also in photography, that the "real war" in its barbarity and human cost was hardening the men, perhaps irreparably. Whether McIlvaine consciously chose to color over or mitigate war's horrors as a palliative, we do not know. But his "Camp Views of War of Rebellion" reminds us that there was no single view or account of the war that stood for all. RANDALL M. MILLER

# 68. *Emancipation Proclamation*

1864
Published by Leland-Boker
Broadside; letterpress on paper
18 1/4 × 11 1/2 inches (46.4 × 29.5 cm)

Signed in ink: *Abraham Lincoln / William Seward / John Nicolay*

Historical Society of Pennsylvania Treasures Collection

This copy of the Emancipation Proclamation of January 1, 1863, is one of forty-eight "authorized" copies printed in Philadelphia by Leland-Boker and signed by Abraham Lincoln, expressly for sale at $10 a piece at Philadelphia's Great Central Sanitary Fair in June 1864. It was part of a long line of printings of the Proclamation. The US government printing office made a small run of copies on January 1, 1863, and on January 3, the State Department produced an edition for distribution to the diplomatic corps and also printed 15,000 copies of the official 1863 Proclamation as a broadsheet for the Adjutant's Office to distribute to the army, government agencies, and newspapers. News of the Proclamation, printings, and readings of it stirred jubilation across the Union and generated demand for more copies. Reprints soon became collectibles. Interestingly, before 1864 such reprints were almost all text-only, with no image of Lincoln as emancipator or other symbolism to enhance the meaning or significance of the document. By 1864, however, as the emancipation issue took center stage in politics and defined the presidential campaign, lithographers and engravers began to produce copies of the Proclamation with images of Lincoln in various poses as emancipator and of grateful enslaved people released from shackles. The Proclamation also became the stuff of controversy as emancipation divided the Northern public, and political cartoons about the Proclamation and Lincoln's promise or his perfidy in issuing it abounded. After Lincoln's assassination—and in many Northerners' minds, his canonization as a martyr to the Union cause—printers found a ready market for pictorial representations of the Proclamation deifying Lincoln. But interest in reprints of the original Proclamation as a text-only document continued.

To capitalize on that interest, organizers of fairs to support relief for soldiers, widows, and orphans sought copies of the Proclamation for sale. In October 1863 Lincoln donated the original handwritten manuscript of the Proclamation as a fundraising promotion at the United States Sanitary Commission Northwestern Soldiers' Fair in Chicago. The original was soon acquired by the Chicago Historical Society, where it was lost in the great Chicago fire of 1871. (By luck, a reproduction of the original was printed in Benjamin Lossing's *Pictorial History of the Civil War* in 1868.) Demand for a signed copy of a reprint was high, and Lincoln obliged by signing the "authorized" Leland-Boker copies offered by the Philadelphia fair. That Lincoln and Mrs. Lincoln also attended the Sanitary Fair on June 16 added to the document's appeal. There the president thanked the organizers of the fair and its visitors for all their "voluntary contributions, given freely, zealously, and earnestly, on top of all the disturbances of business, the taxation, and burdens [of] the war." The signed copies available for sale sold out.

Today, only about half of the surviving copies of this printed and signed edition remain. Most of them are in museums, libraries, or archives.

RANDALL M. MILLER

BY THE PRESIDENT OF THE UNITED STATES OF AMERICA.

# A Proclamation.

**Whereas**, on the twenty-second day of September, in the year of our Lord one thousand eight hundred and sixty-two, a proclamation was issued by the President of the United States, containing, among other things, the following, to wit:

"That on the first day of January, in the year of our Lord one thousand eight hundred and sixty-three, all persons held as slaves within any State or designated part of a State, the people whereof shall then be in rebellion against the United States, shall be then, thenceforward, and forever, free; and the Executive government of the United States, including the military and naval authority thereof, will recognize and maintain the freedom of such persons, and will do no act or acts to repress such persons, or any of them, in any efforts they may make for their actual freedom.

"That the Executive will, on the first day of January aforesaid, by proclamation, designate the States and parts of States, if any, in which the people thereof, respectively, shall then be in rebellion against the United States; and the fact that any State, or the people thereof, shall on that day be in good faith represented in the Congress of the United States, by members chosen thereto at elections wherein a majority of the qualified voters of such State shall have participated, shall, in the absence of strong countervailing testimony, be deemed conclusive evidence that such State, and the people thereof, are not then in rebellion against the United States."

**Now, therefore**, I, ABRAHAM LINCOLN, President of the United States, by virtue of the power in me vested as commander-in-chief of the army and navy of the United States, in time of actual armed rebellion against the authority and government of the United States, and as a fit and necessary war measure for suppressing said rebellion, do, on this first day of January, in the year of our Lord one thousand eight hundred and sixty-three, and in accordance with my purpose so to do, publicly proclaimed for the full period of one hundred days from the day first above mentioned, order and designate as the States and parts of States wherein the people thereof, respectively, are this day in rebellion against the United States, the following, to wit: Arkansas, Texas, Louisiana, (except the Parishes of St. Bernard, Plaquemines, Jefferson, St. John, St. Charles, St. James, Ascension, Assumption, Terre Bonne, Lafourche, St. Mary, St. Martin, and Orleans, including the City of New Orleans,) Mississippi, Alabama, Florida, Georgia, South Carolina, North Carolina, and Virginia, (except the forty-eight counties designated as West Virginia, and also the counties of Berkeley, Accomac, Northampton, Elizabeth City, York, Princess Ann, and Norfolk, including the cities of Norfolk and Portsmouth,) and which excepted parts are for the present left precisely as if this proclamation were not issued.

And by virtue of the power and for the purpose aforesaid, I do order and declare that all persons held as slaves within said designated States and parts of States are and henceforward shall be free; and that the Executive government of the United States, including the military and naval authorities thereof, will recognize and maintain the freedom of said persons.

And I hereby enjoin upon the people so declared to be free to abstain from all violence, unless in necessary self-defence; and I recommend to them that, in all cases when allowed, they labor faithfully for reasonable wages.

And I further declare and make known that such persons, of suitable condition, will be received into the armed service of the United States, to garrison forts, positions, stations, and other places, and to man vessels of all sorts in said service.

And upon this act, sincerely believed to be an act of justice warranted by the Constitution upon military necessity, I invoke the considerate judgment of mankind and the gracious favor of Almighty God.

In witness whereof I have hereunto set my hand and caused the seal of the United States to be affixed.

[L. S.] Done at the City of Washington this first day of January, in the year of our Lord one thousand eight hundred and sixty-three, and of the Independence of the United States of America the eighty-seventh.

By the President: Abraham Lincoln

William H. Seward *Secretary of State.*

A true copy, with the autograph signatures of the President and the Secretary of State.

Jno. G. Nicolay
*Priv. Sec. to the President.*

## 69. Social, Civil, and Statistical Association of the Colored People of Pennsylvania

*Frederick Douglass, will deliver the third lecture of the course before The Social, Civil and Statistical Association of the Colored People of Pennsylvania: on Thursday evening, Feb'y 16th, in Concert Hall. Subject, "Equality Before the Law."*

---

1865
Broadside; letterpress on paper
14 × 8 3/8 inches (35.8 × 21.3 cm)

Leon Gardiner Collection of American Negro Historical Society Records [0008]

This handbill advertised abolitionist and civil rights activist Frederick Douglass's lecture, "Equality Before the Law," for February 16, 1865, as one of a five-part series promoted as "an interesting course of lectures to suit the times." The event was sponsored by the Social, Civil, and Statistical Association of the Colored People of Pennsylvania (SCSACP), which William Still and other Black leaders in Philadelphia had formed in 1860 to "labor earnestly for the right to suffrage . . . and to gather statistics with regard to the condition and wants of the colored people in general." Over time the association lobbied for emancipation and civil rights, pushed for the recruitment of Blacks into the Union army, and used statistical and other information to show the ways Blacks contributed to improvement in society and to inform and mobilize Black participation in public affairs. The SCSACP also organized benefits for soldiers and widows and ran lecture series on public issues.

Douglass's promised speech for the association fit his particular interests in early 1865 as he thought about the moral and practical concerns affecting freedom. With Congress's passage of the Thirteenth Amendment in January 1865, Douglass and other Black leaders stepped up calls for civil rights and voting power while also emphasizing the need for Blacks to help themselves by building their own institutions, especially schools, to secure freedom. From January to May 1865, Douglass was on the lecture circuit, traveling from Massachusetts to Maryland, giving speeches on the need for Black suffrage as essential to freedom. As in his lecture, "Equality Before the Law," Douglass also weighed in on civil rights issues such as the denial of equal access to public transportation, which was of immediate concern to the SCSACP in Philadelphia trying to end Jim Crow practices on the streetcars there. For Douglass, as for other civil rights advocates, equal rights required not only equality before the law but also being treated with respect.

Douglass did not need any other attractions but himself to draw a large following, but the SCSACP wanted to provide entertainment as well as education to ensure it would fill up Concert Hall and gain donations to aid Black soldiers and their families. Included on the program was Elizabeth Taylor Greenfield, who, after being manumitted from slavery, studied music in Philadelphia and became an international star singing Italian operas and sentimental American tunes. Greenfield's participation in the program

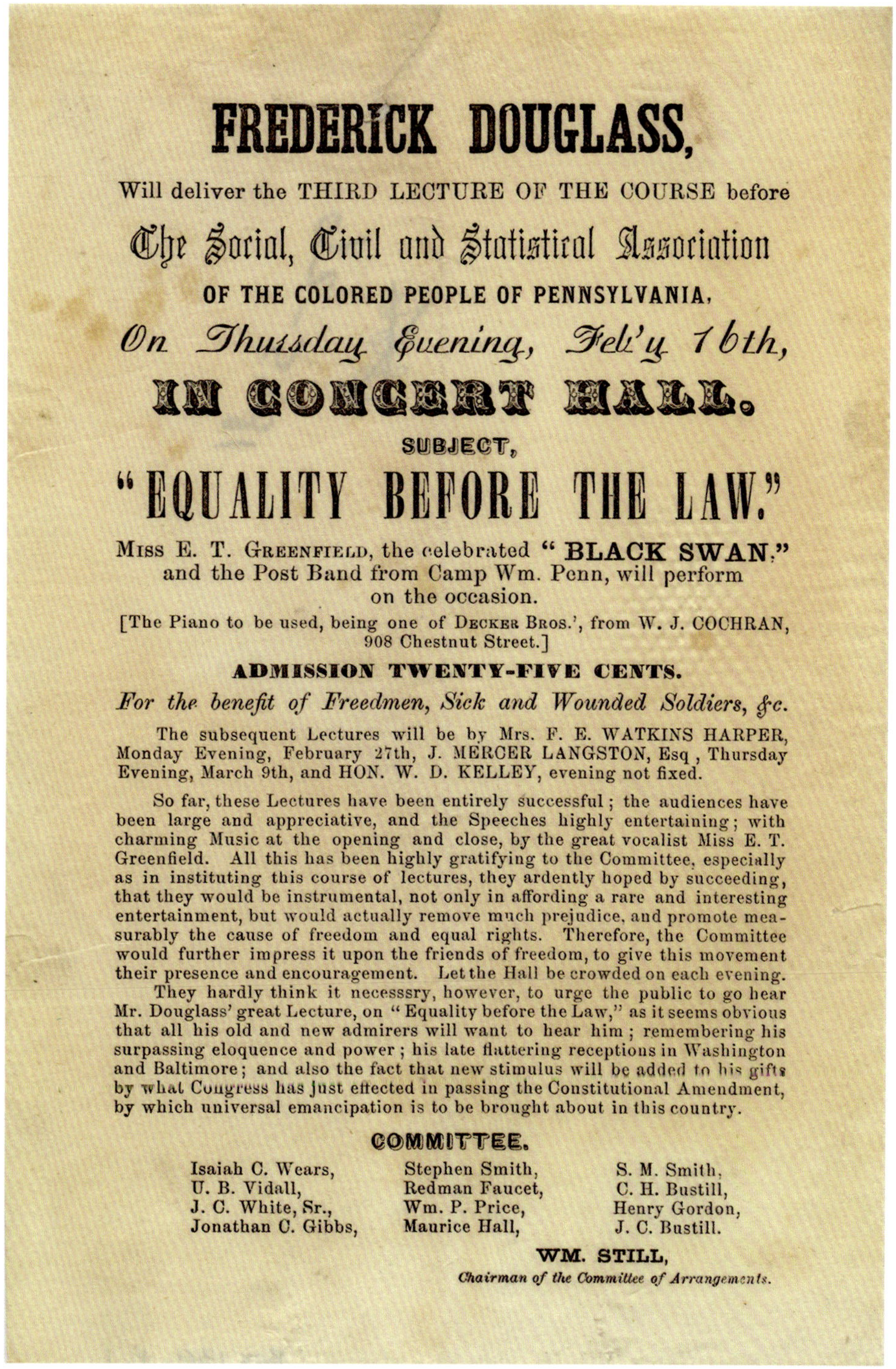

FREDERICK DOUGLASS,

Will deliver the THIRD LECTURE OF THE COURSE before

The Social, Civil and Statistical Association

OF THE COLORED PEOPLE OF PENNSYLVANIA,

*On Thursday Evening, Feb'y 16th,*

IN CONCERT HALL.

SUBJECT,

"EQUALITY BEFORE THE LAW."

Miss E. T. Greenfield, the celebrated "BLACK SWAN," and the Post Band from Camp Wm. Penn, will perform on the occasion.

[The Piano to be used, being one of Decker Bros.', from W. J. COCHRAN, 908 Chestnut Street.]

**ADMISSION TWENTY-FIVE CENTS.**

*For the benefit of Freedmen, Sick and Wounded Soldiers, &c.*

The subsequent Lectures will be by Mrs. F. E. WATKINS HARPER, Monday Evening, February 27th, J. MERCER LANGSTON, Esq , Thursday Evening, March 9th, and HON. W. D. KELLEY, evening not fixed.

So far, these Lectures have been entirely successful ; the audiences have been large and appreciative, and the Speeches highly entertaining; with charming Music at the opening and close, by the great vocalist Miss E. T. Greenfield. All this has been highly gratifying to the Committee, especially as in instituting this course of lectures, they ardently hoped by succeeding, that they would be instrumental, not only in affording a rare and interesting entertainment, but would actually remove much prejudice, and promote measurably the cause of freedom and equal rights. Therefore, the Committee would further impress it upon the friends of freedom, to give this movement their presence and encouragement. Let the Hall be crowded on each evening.

They hardly think it necesssry, however, to urge the public to go hear Mr. Douglass' great Lecture, on "Equality before the Law," as it seems obvious that all his old and new admirers will want to hear him ; remembering his surpassing eloquence and power ; his late flattering receptions in Washington and Baltimore; and also the fact that new stimulus will be added to his gifts by what Congress has just effected in passing the Constitutional Amendment, by which universal emancipation is to be brought about in this country.

COMMITTEE.

| | | |
|---|---|---|
| Isaiah C. Wears, | Stephen Smith, | S. M. Smith, |
| U. B. Vidall, | Redman Faucet, | C. H. Bustill, |
| J. C. White, Sr., | Wm. P. Price, | Henry Gordon, |
| Jonathan C. Gibbs, | Maurice Hall, | J. C. Bustill. |

**WM. STILL,**

*Chairman of the Committee of Arrangements.*

promised a thrilling evening of music while also attesting to Black genius and accomplishment that might come with freedom. Also performing that evening was the Post Army Band from the United States Colored Troops at Camp William Penn, reminding those gathered that Black men were still serving the Union's cause. Then, as now, organizers of political rallies and events understood that music was more than mere entertainment.

This handbill is in the American Negro Historical Society Records, 1790–1905, at the Historical Society of Pennsylvania. This rich and varied collection of African American documents is especially useful in recording the establishment and practices of African American institutions and their roles in community building and civil rights activism.

RANDALL M. MILLER

# 70. **James Fuller Queen** (ca. 1820–1886)

## *Buildings of the Great Central Fair*

1864
Published by P. S. Duval & Son
Chromolithograph on paper
24 1/8 × 34 5/8 inches (61.3 × 88.0 cm) (sheet)

Inscribed below image: *BUILDINGS OF THE GREAT CENTRAL FAIR, / IN AID OF THE U.S. SANITARY COMMISSION / LOGAN SQUARE, PHILADELPHIA, JUNE 1864*; below image, lower left: *Drawn from Nature & on Stone by James Queen*; below image, lower center: *H.E. Wrigley Architect*; below image, lower right: *Printed & Lithogr^d at P.S. Duval & Son. Philad*

Historical Society of Pennsylvania Large Graphics Collection [V65]

Between 1863 and 1865, more than two dozen "sanitary fairs" were organized in northern cities to raise money for medical services provided to the Union forces by the United States Sanitary Commission. James Queen's bird's-eye view depicts the largest of these that opened in June of 1864 on Logan Square in a 200,000-square-foot temporary complex of linked exhibition pavilions clustered around a central hall dubbed "Union Avenue." To the south a wooden-roofed round structure housed a restaurant; to the north was the canvas-canopied Floral Department. In the adjacent Art Gallery, visitors toured the largest art exhibition ever organized in the United States.

The first sanitary fair had been organized in the fall of 1863 by a group of Chicago women who appealed for donations from private citizens as well as from the mercantile, industrial, and agricultural sectors. The success of the Great Northwestern Sanitary Fair inspired other events, and Philadelphians were planning a similar fair by early 1864. Leading citizens eagerly volunteered to join parallel organizing committees of women and men charged with assembling displays of machinery, handmade and manufactured products, and *objets d'art*. Visitors paid admission to shop, attend dramatic performances and musical concerts, and tour special exhibits. Specific trades and industries sponsored the majority of sales booths. Young upper-middle-class women—often the daughters of the fair organizers—worked diligently to persuade visitors to part with their money for the cause.

In addition to the Art Gallery, the Floral Department, and the Arms and Trophies Department, other pavilions housed a playground, bank, post office, and police station. In the "Pennsylvania Kitchen," where antique cupboards were filled with pewter and crockery, visitors could "ruminate upon how their grandfathers lived" while watching "a venerable grandmother plying her spinning-wheel." The "William Penn Parlor" featured "relics" lent by the Historical Society of Pennsylvania, the City of Philadelphia, and private collectors, including the original charter of the city and the wampum belt allegedly presented to Penn by the Lenni Lenape. Queen's lithographic view was one of many souvenirs available for sale.

Consumer goods were arrayed to celebrate the power and progress of the Northern wartime economy. In fact, the commercial aspects of the fair created some confusion among visitors. "The amount of 'shopping' already done at the Fair is very great, and money is flowing at a rate that caused us no small degree of surprise," reported one newspaper. "Many people entered with the idea that the Fair was nothing more than a series of stores." But patriotic consumerism was an effective tactic. During the fair's fifteen-day run, average daily attendance surpassed 25,000, and organizers raised more than $1,000,000. When the fair ended, the pavilions were demolished: the lumber, bricks, and tin roofing were purchased by the Pennsylvania Railroad for a new depot in West Philadelphia.

The men and women who produced the Great Central Sanitary Fair gained invaluable experience in the logistics and financial management of large-scale public displays. That experience would serve them well a decade later when many of the same individuals participated in organizing the Centennial Exhibition, the first true world's fair organized in the United States, which Philadelphia hosted in 1876.

ELIZABETH MILROY

Further related information in the Historical Society of Pennsylvania archives can be found in the Horace Furness Papers, Sartain Family Papers, and John Welsh Papers.

# 71. *The True Issue or "Thats Whats the Matter"*

1864
Published by Currier and Ives
Lithograph on paper
13 7/16 × 17 11/16 inches (34.2 × 45.0 cm)

Inscribed below and within image: *Lincoln / "No Peace without Abolition!"; Mac./ "The Union must be preserved at all hazards!"; Jeff / "No peace without Separation!"*; below image, lower center: *Entered according to act of Congress in the year 1864 by Currier & Ives, in the Clerk's Office of the District Court of the United States, for the Southern Dist. of N.Y. /* THE TRUE ISSUE OR "THATS WHATS THE MATTER"*/ Published by Currier & Ives, 152 Nassau St. N.Y.*

Historical Society of Pennsylvania Cartoons and Caricatures Collection [3133]

During the Civil War, lithography was the principal medium providing visual depictions of war, politics, the home front, and virtually every aspect of American life. Unlike photographs and paintings, which were displayed in books or at exhibits, lithographs were mass-produced and intended for illustrated magazines and other news publications but mostly sold as single sheets to the general public in shops or by individual vendors or distributed by political parties. Readily produced, lithographs often provided immediate images of events, such as battles, which added to their popularity and made them common reference points in people's descriptions and even remembrances of the war. In politics they provided shorthand depictions of people and issues that gave them a currency and impact no other medium matched.

Printed by the prominent and market-dominant New York City lithography firm Currier and Ives, *The True Issue or "Thats Whats the Matter"* is a pro-Democratic 1864 campaign lithograph that depicts a determined Democratic presidential candidate General George B. McClellan (1826–1885) as the primary force keeping the Union from being rent apart by not allowing either Republican emancipation or Confederate separation to win the day. Political cartoons were already staples of American public life by the Civil War, and Americans had long learned how to read them for content and purpose. By 1864 caricatures of Abraham Lincoln and Jefferson Davis were common tropes in political cartoons, making it easy to focus on an issue with little need to explain the character or interest of the principals. The war generated immense interest in political matters

that the lithographers met with hundreds of thousands of prints. Political parties flooded the Union with lithographic and other images in 1864, along with all manner of campaign paraphernalia—such as hats, scarfs, buttons, badges, collars, and even cigar wrappers—printed with slogans or candidates' images to excite participation and loyalty from their supporters. Quickly produced to stay current with changing circumstances and events, and responsive to both political parties' constant demand for new materials, the lithographic political cartoons often suffered from sloppy production, as is evident in this example with its misspelling of Pennsylvania and Minnesota on the map and lack of apostrophes in its title.

The ubiquity and ephemerality of wartime lithographs, especially political cartoons, and their less aesthetic appeal than color chromolithographs and the visual potency of photography made these black-and-white prints seem of little value to collectors of Civil War material and visual culture. Many collections have some lithographs from the Civil War era, but outside of the Library of Congress, few have many and varied examples. This makes the rich and revealing Historical Society of Pennsylvania's Cartoons and Caricatures Collection especially worthwhile as a resource, which not only has multiple images of the same issue but also covers a long period of collecting. That fact makes it possible to observe the continuity and changes in tropes, subject matter, and production of political cartoons, especially over time.

RANDALL M. MILLER

## 72. **David J. Kennedy** (1816–1898)

## *Pop Corn Pavilion*

1876
Watercolor on paper
9 3/16 × 13 inches (23.4 × 33.0 cm)

Signed in graphite, lower right: *D. J. Kennedy. 1876.*
Inscribed in ink, below image: *Pop corn Pavilion. / opposite to the Tunisian Café and Bazaar, situate on Fountain Avenue north of the Pennsylvania State / Building and on the corner of the avenue south side, and south of the arch under it. Sept. 1876.*

David J. Kennedy Watercolors [V61]
Purchase, 1901

Born in Scotland, David J. Kennedy settled in Philadelphia in 1838 and worked for the Reading Railroad before poor eyesight forced him to retire in 1861. However, his true vocation was art, and undeterred by limited vision, he devoted more than fifty years to documenting Philadelphia's fast-changing urban landscape in meticulously detailed drawings and watercolors. The Historical Society of Pennsylvania owns more than 1300 of these views, most mounted on paper with extensive captions that Kennedy added with invaluable information about the sites and structures. Kennedy's interests were encyclopedic, from celebrated works of architectural design such as the State House and the Customs House to new park landscapes along the Schuylkill River, to more utilitarian structures and sites, including stores, theaters, jails, coal yards, and shipyards.

In 1869, Kennedy was hired as a draftsman by the Fairmount Park Commission, and it was likely in this capacity that he produced a series of views of the pavilions erected for the Centennial Exhibition of 1876. Commemorating the signing of the Declaration of Independence, the Centennial was the first true world's fair hosted by an American city and the first world's fair at which major exhibits were dispersed among many separate pavilions, two of which (the Art Gallery and Horticultural Conservatory) were permanent structures. In total, 180 buildings of iron, glass, and stone were erected within the 465-acre site in West Fairmount Park. Many of the fifty foreign countries participating constructed their own buildings, as did several American manufacturers and most of the participating states. They ranged in size from the Main Exhibition building—the largest structure in the world at this date, it housed 13,720 exhibitors over 20 acres—to the diminutive Singer Sewing Machine building.

Kennedy documented the Centennial's major pavilions, but he also recorded minor temporary structures that would otherwise have been lost to memory, including this view of one of two buildings devoted to the sale of popcorn (both designed by architect H. J. Schwarzmann, 1846–1891). The popcorn concession was one of many products and services contracted by the exhibition's cash-strapped organizers in advance of the fair. In 1871, when Congress approved plans to organize the fair, it had created the Centennial Commission, composed of representatives from each state, to erect exhibition buildings and oversee the reception and installation of exhibits. But the commission had no authority to raise money, and because both the federal government and the state of Pennsylvania resisted fully funding the event, in 1872, the Centennial Board of Finance was established to seek funds from private sources by selling stock and "concessions for privileges." By late 1875, newspapers across the country had seized on reports that the Board of Finance was paying inflated sums to concessions bidders, including the "popcorn capitalist"—one

J. A. Baker of Dayton, Ohio—who reportedly paid as much as $8000, "for the sole privilege of impairing the digestion of the world at the great fair." The controversy faded with the Centennial's success: between May and November 1876, an estimated ten million visitors would tour the temporary exhibition city. And already by September, the *Philadelphia Inquirer* reported that Baker was reaping "a harvest of pecuniary benefits." ELIZABETH MILROY

Further related information in the Historical Society of Pennsylvania archives can be found in the Centennial Exhibition Records, Herbert Welsh Papers, John Welsh Papers, and Sartain Family Papers.

FRASER, FURNESS, & HEWITT, ARCHTS PHILADA

SYNAGOGUE
FOR THE
CONGREGATION RODEF SHOLAM,
S.E. CORNER BROAD & MOUNT VERNON STRTS PHILA

## 73. **Benjamin Linfoot** (1840–1912)

# *Synagogue for the Congregation Rodef Sholam* [*sic*]

1869
Chromolithograph on paper
25 9⁄16 × 17 inches (64.9 × 43.3 cm)

Inscribed below image: *SYNAGOGUE / FOR THE / CONGREGATION RODEF SHOLAM* [*sic*], */ S.E. CORNER BROAD & MOUNT VERNON STR[ts] PHIL[a]*; below image, lower center: *FRASER, FURNESS & HEWITT ARCH[ts] PHILAd[a]*; within image, lower left: *Ben Linfoot. Lith. Phila[da] 1869.*

Historical Society of Pennsylvania Large Graphics Collection [V65]

Rodeph Shalom is architectural fantasy at its most rapturous; one could almost believe that the entire nineteenth century drew upon an opium pipe and fell into a dream. Baffled reporters struggled to describe it, variously calling its style "Saracenic," "Alhambraic," or "Moorish Gothic." Its architecture was revolutionary in Philadelphia, but so too was the chromolithograph that celebrated it, a happy instance where message and medium accorded so perfectly that they seemed the expression of a single thought.

The building was the fruit of a dynamic collaboration between Rabbi Marcus Jastrow and his architects, Frank Furness and George W. Hewitt, then junior partners in the firm of Fraser, Furness & Hewitt. Jastrow arrived in Philadelphia in 1866, having witnessed the construction of Berlin's dazzling New Synagogue on the Oranienburger Strasse, and wanted something similar for his new congregation. There was no sense that it was incongruous to use forms that were of Islamic origin in a Jewish house of worship; on the contrary, Furness and Hewitt, "remembering that those for whom it is erected are of Eastern origin, have happily chosen the Eastern style, thereby constructing a place of worship which, in architectural characteristics, harmonizes with the faith of those who are to worship within it."

The most startling aspect of Rodeph Shalom (it did not regularize the spelling of its name until late in the nineteenth century) was its color. The walls were warm brown Trenton sandstone from New Jersey, relieved by bright red Seneca sandstone trim from Maryland and "light Ohio Stone" from Cleveland. Meanwhile, the glistening columns at the entrance came from Scotland, "Red Aberdeen Granite, highly polished," while the dome above the corner tower was blue and gold. Such intense architectural color was a novelty in Philadelphia, and to celebrate it, the proud congregation turned to that recent innovation, the chromolithograph.

A lithograph, literally "drawing on stone," is made by drawing with a grease-based crayon on a smooth limestone plate, which was chemically treated so that the ink would adhere only to the drawing. In a chromolithograph, each color was applied by a different plate, the paper passing through the printing press repeatedly until every color was added. The process was costly and required great technical skill to ensure that the plate was precisely aligned. (In fact, the dark brown here is ever so slightly to the right of the perspective drawing.) It was made by Benjamin Linfoot, an accomplished English-born printmaker who specialized in architectural illustration (and would eventually turn to architectural practice).

Rodeph Shalom is one of the first buildings to show Furness's distinctive personal language of architecture. Among the holdings of the Historical Society of Pennsylvania are photographs and drawings of buildings from across his career, including four complete sets of plans for depots of the Baltimore & Ohio Railroad. MICHAEL J. LEWIS

## 74. Coxe Mining Company

### *Unidentified Workers*

ca. 1890
Gelatin silver print
7 7/8 × 10 inches (20.0 × 25.5 cm)

Coxe Family Mining Papers [3005]
Gift of the Trustees for the Heirs and Devisees of Tench Coxe, 1967

## Underwood & Underwood

### *Drifton Breaker*

1917
Gelatin silver print
10 × 8 inches (25.5 × 20.2 cm)

Inscribed recto in ink: *Drifton Braker* [*sic*] */ shop Garage / Jerry Futzinger [?] House / The old Branding House / Shop office*; verso in graphite: coal */ anthracite on way to brakers* [*sic*] */ Pa. Mine*

Coxe Family Mining Papers [3005]
Gift of the Trustees for the Heirs and Devisees of Tench Coxe, 1967

In 2001, scholars gained access to the largest collection of papers ever donated to the Historical Society of Pennsylvania, the business records of the Coxe Mining Company. The records span the years 1774 to 1968 and are contained in 1036 boxes, occupying 496 linear feet of shelf space. The Coxe Family Mining Papers are a prime example of the active mission of HSP to collect, house, and preserve manuscript documents revealing the American past and to facilitate research through careful cataloguing and effective search tools—even when on the scale of the Coxe collection.

The Coxe family operated mines in the eastern central coal fields of the Pennsylvania anthracite region (through Luzerne County) as a powerful independent coal company. Ninety-five percent of the supply of anthracite coal in the United States formed eons ago below the surface of a 500-square mile triangular area in northeastern Pennsylvania. Anthracite is a remarkable fossil fuel. Almost pure carbon (without inflammable impurities), it is a dense, hard coal that is difficult to light but once lit, it burns slowly, efficiently, cleanly, and with intense heat: in other words, a perfect fuel to power industrialization, a source of heat to generate steam and drive engines, to melt ores into metals, and to warm the homes of growing urban populations.

Excavating anthracite presented great challenges, but an even greater consequential obstacle involved transporting anthracite coal in bulk to urban and industrial centers. The Pennsylvania anthracite region did not have the advantage of navigable riverways. Building an infrastructure first of canals and then railroads required massive financing. Major investment firms, notably the banking house of J. P. Morgan, began to underwrite the formation of railroad companies, with the raised capital not only funding the construction of railroads but also the buying of land and mining of coal. Out of this process emerged a set of companies, such as the Philadelphia and Reading Railroad, that dominated the production and transport of anthracite coal, controlling output and prices. Independent companies were at their mercy with the shipping rates charged by the monopoly anthracite railroads. Few independents survived, and most were bought out. The Coxe Company mines reigned independently for forty years in the late nineteenth and early twentieth centuries—with nearly 4,000 employees, coal shipments in excess of 1.5 million tons annually, and land assets valued at $10 million at the time—a story better able to be understood now through the opening of the firm's records at HSP.

The genesis of the Coxe Mining Company dates to the 1790s and the purchase of 80,000 acres of land in the Pennsylvania anthracite region by Tench Coxe. Coxe, the foremost advocate of manufacturing development at the founding of the United States (and advisor to Alexander Hamilton), presciently recognized the role that anthracite coal would play. However, mining operations would await the initiative and professional engineering training of his grandson, Eckley Coxe, who formed a company in 1865 and oversaw its great expansion and success as a family business through his managerial acumen and technical innovations. His heirs would sell the mining facilities to the major Lehigh Valley Railroad Company in 1905 (taking a strong shareholder stake), but the family would also maintain property holdings, lease land for mining, and sustain earnings for the Coxe estate until a final liquidation of assets in 1965.

With its vast personal, administrative, property, engineering, operational, financial, employee, and legal and regulatory files—the latter thick for the twentieth century—the Coxe Family Mining Company Collection at HSP is a treasure trove for business and labor historians as well as students of the history of technology and government-business relations. Their full tapping lies ahead. WALTER LICHT

## 75. W. J. Morgan & Co.

*Mr. & Mrs. McKee Rankin.*
*In their New Play, "49."*

---

ca. 1882
Chromolithograph on paper
25 ½ × 32 15⁄16 inches (64.7 × 83.7 cm)

Inscribed above image: *MR. & MRS. MCKEE RANKIN.*; below image: *In their New Play, "49."*; within image, upper left: *"WESTWARD THE COURSE OF EMPIRE TAKES ITS WAY" / ARCH ST. THEATRE / JAN. 2--ONE WEEK. / MATINEES ON MONDAY, WEDNESDAY & SATURDAY*; within image, lower right: *W.J. MORGAN & CO. LITH. CLEVELAND.O.*

Historical Society of Pennsylvania Theater Posters Collection
[V06]
Gift of Stan V. Henkels, 1917

A theatre poster is more than a supersized advertisement: It is a snapshot that expands our understanding of the time and place of its creation. The Historical Society of Pennsylvania holds more than 1,300 of these visual time capsules in its Theater Posters Collection, and this illustration for *49* offers particularly rich insight into its era. Men on horseback, covered wagons, and a bare-skinned native are shorthand for an American mythos—the taming of the West. Tales of this period have inspired genres of novels, music, TV series, movies, and plays. Much of American fascination with westward expansion was driven by a single tenet—Manifest Destiny—which celebrated the inevitable conquest of the frontier by white settlers, spreading the United States from the Atlantic to the Pacific. McKee Rankin and his wife Kitty appear in *49*, a drama set against the backdrop of the California Gold Rush. The western state's population stood at 14,000 in January 1848, when the first gold was discovered there, and by the end of 1849, a flood of California Dreamers had raised that number to almost 100,000. About forty years later, so many Americans had moved west that the nation's frontier was declared closed.

The imprint of Manifest Destiny is strengthened by the words on the poster, "Westward the Course of Empire Takes Its Way," which represented the title of a mural commissioned in 1861 and produced by Emanuel Leutze for the US Capitol. Leutze apparently drew the phrase from an eighteenth-century poem by Bishop George Berkeley. The play, which was based on the recollections of Rankin's uncle who participated in the Gold Rush, became a hit in Philadelphia. Rankin received credit for contributing to its writing as well as starring in the production. While Rankin had a busy career, he could not claim great success. David Beasley, who wrote *McKee Rankin and the Heyday of the American Theater*, chose to end his account with a quotation from critic Amy Leslie: "There is no man so picturesque today, no man so capable, no man so brilliant and probably no man of such startling genius who will leave so little to commend him to posterity. Somehow he always stacked the cards against himself and overplayed the game." The Rankins' daughter, Doris Rankin, enjoyed some success in movies of the 1920s and 1930s, and she became part of the Barrymore acting dynasty after marrying Lionel Barrymore and producing two children before their marriage ended in divorce eighteen years after it had begun.

ALICE L. GEORGE

The Historical Society of Pennsylvania holds a wealth of collections related to theater history, including the Historical Society of Pennsylvania Playbill Collection, the Kenneth Trotter Collection of Theater Programs, Memoirs 1880–1946 by Richard Herndon, Archives of Mr. H. German Wilson, Francis Bosworth Papers, Deutsches Theatre Subscription Book, Frank Savaro Papers, Thomas Labrum Scrapbooks, Leona Hyneman Lowengrund Scrapbook and Photographs, Andrew Salama Papers, Specimens of Theatrical Cuts by George William Childs, Frank McGlinn Collection, and Wheatley Dramatic Association Papers.

# 76. **DeWitt Clinton Baxter** (1829–1881)

## *Elevation of 800 block of Chestnut Street, North Side*

---

ca. 1880
Ink and gouache on paper mounted on linen
8 11/16 × 34 7/8 inches (22.0 × 88.5 cm) (unfolded);
10 5/8 × 22 11/16 inches (27.0 × 57.7 cm) (volume, closed)

pl. 10 of *Streets of Philadelphia*
Inscribed verso in graphite: *N S Chestnut 8–9*

DeWitt C. Baxter Drawings [3256]
Gift of Ferdinand J. Dreer, 1885

In the middle decades of the nineteenth century, the old center of Philadelphia was quickly becoming a new place. Key through streets, including the eastern parts of Chestnut, Market, and Walnut, were undergoing a dramatic visible transformation that was allied to a functional one: businesses claimed prominent sites on blocks that had formerly accommodated a mix of homes and small shops. Ambitious merchants adapted both to fully commercial uses, with enlarged display windows, prominent signs, and dropped stoops. Then, from the late 1840s through the end of the century, an irresistible tide of new, larger buildings built specifically for business, mainly for retail and services, completely recast these downtown blocks.

This new streetscape was visually competitive, with higher-end businesses seeking architectural distinction through differentiated materials, styles, height, and degrees of elaboration. Here architects found an extraordinary opportunity to flex their design muscles. These changes created a new, densely commercial quarter serving what had become a novel city of strangers more than neighbors,

drawing visitors and residents alike who came to consume, enjoy, or do business.

In the district's new urban faces, a wood engraver, DeWitt Clinton Baxter, saw opportunity. In 1856 he and a partner, printer Harmanus Neff, promoted the idea of drawing whole blockfronts on large sheets, capturing "the Architectural characteristic of each Building as its stands, side-by-side with its neighbor . . . with the signs, numbers, and other distinguishing marks affixed" for firms subscribing as advertisers. Below the image would be an array of typeset business-card replicas identifying those subscribers. Baxter had a clear model in *Rae's Philadelphia Pictorial Directory and Panoramic Advertiser,* conceived in 1851 by another graphic entrepreneur, Julio H. Rae, who had continuously transcribed the blockfronts along Chestnut Street between Second and Tenth streets, publishing them in book form. But Baxter's project took on an expanded geography and format, issuing his views on large single sheets.

*Baxter's Panorama and Business Directory of Philadelphia* began in earnest in 1857 and was an apparent early success. By 1861 the enterprise produced about twenty views tinted in two colors showing nonsequential blockfronts chosen opportunistically to favor those rich with potential advertisers. But the series paused at the start of the Civil War, as Baxter took a prominent role in leading a regiment called Baxter's Fire Zouaves. After a long hiatus, though, he returned to the project in 1879, this time reproducing carefully inked line drawings through photolithography, without tints, and pasting on images of streetside pedestrians and signage to fill out the scene. This second series reached about three dozen additional sheets before Baxter's death in 1881.

The Historical Society of Pennsylvania's collection of Baxter's preparatory pasteups—including some blocks he apparently never published—was the gift of collector Ferdinand J. Dreer (1812–1902) in 1885. They offer an unrivaled visual record of the city's best-known commercial corridors, preeminent in memory and recorded imagery, but since the late nineteenth century, a district that has been almost completely transformed yet again. JEFFREY A. COHEN

# 77. *Construction of the Philadelphia Rapid Transit System Rail Line*

ca. 1905
Gelatin silver print
5 ¼ × 7 ⅜ inches (13.3 × 18.7 cm)

Philadelphia Rapid Transit Company Photoprints [V40]
Gift of William Twining, 1924

Philadelphia was a city on the rise in the early twentieth century. Its population surged from 1.3 million in 1900 to 1.8 million in 1920. People poured in to work for thousands of employers, making hats and rugs, locomotives and ships. As the city grew increasingly cramped and congested, boosters believed Philadelphia could rival New York City and London, but only if it developed adequate transportation. The days of horse-drawn trolleys and omnibuses clattering over cobbles to meet the city's needs were well past. Instead, to move goods and people around a growing metropolis, Philadelphia needed trolleys, subways, steel rails, and electricity.

This photo, part of a collection donated by William Twining, who served as Philadelphia's transit commissioner when the city built much of its transportation system, including its elevated lines, highlights many themes that came together in early twentieth-century Philadelphia's transportation industry.

Brick and stone had helped make the city modern in the nineteenth century, replacing miles of dirt roads. They gave horses' hooves the purchase they needed to pull carriages, but they also provided a jouncy ride. This became more problematic as carriages and omnibuses became heavier, and horses strained under the load. The Philadelphia Rapid Transit Company (PRT), which ran the city's transportation system from 1902 until the Philadelphia Transportation Company (PTC) took over in 1940, built on nineteenth-century efforts to lay track across the city. Trolleys' steel wheels on steel rails provided a much smoother ride, moved far more people at a faster pace than horses, and expanded electricity usage across the city. For two generations, Philadelphians saw trolleys as modern transit until they were replaced by automobiles.

Laying tracks across the city required an army of workers, and this photo highlights how Black Philadelphians provided much of the manual labor. Facing discrimination in area industries, African Americans found the PRT a stable employer, albeit one that segregated them into lower-level, physically demanding work. They dug out old cobblestones and bricks, laid ties, and swung rails into place. They often paid a heavy toll with smashed fingers, bruised limbs, and lacerations. Yet without them, Philadelphia could never have moved forward.

A more subtle theme in the photo is the use of public space by a private company. While boosters celebrated building a modern transit system, critics questioned how a private company could lay the track it owned and controlled down the middle of a public street. Why did profits generated by a public good flow to a private company rather than go back to the city to invest in an even better transit system? For decades PRT and its successor PTC distributed profits to stockholders until the money ran out and the Southeastern Pennsylvania Transportation Authority (SEPTA) took over. The fact that PRT built a system on public streets that everyone needed and turned the profits over to a few shareholders rankled Philadelphians for generations.

JAMES WOLFINGER

GETMAN & CO.
Semper Cigar Factory
Nearly everybody reads The Bulletin
Semper Cigar Factory
P.R.T.Co
70

# Fall and Winter Catalogue

1905-6

No. 59

John Wanamaker

PHILADELPHIA
NEW YORK
PARIS

# 78. John Wanamaker Department Store

## *Fall and Winter Catalogue, 1905–1906*

1905
Printed periodical; halftone on paper
9 5/8 × 6 3/4 inches (24.5 × 17.1 cm)

John Wanamaker Collection [2188]
Gift of Woodward and Lothrop, Inc., 1988; gift of the Wanamaker Institute of Industries, 1995

The stunning fur coat, the fashionably long hair, the audaciously billowing hat, and the lovely face open a window into another time when department stores became merchants of dreams. Shoppers flooded inside, often to look more than to buy. They wanted to breathe in the elegance of a shopping experience seemingly without limits. On display were stylish clothes, useful housewares, dazzling jewelry, and even pianos—and everything was all in one place. Particularly for the middle class, these stores became a destination: not just a place to buy but somewhere they could dine, socialize, and explore. From corsets to cutlery, furniture to feathers, silks to sporting goods, the newly emerging department stores acted as a magnet to Americans, and Wanamaker's drew crowds to Center City Philadelphia. Besides goods on sale, the store offered museumlike exhibits, ranging from films of Paris fashion shows to a depiction of the Constitution's signing.

This catalogue is a part of the John Wanamaker Collection, which traces the life of the merchant who helped to shape the twentieth-century city. Born in Philadelphia in 1838, Wanamaker introduced the city's first clothing store in 1861 and opened its first department store in 1877 at Thirteenth and Market. The Grand Depot was a repurposed train terminal. Over the years, Wanamaker developed a chain of stores in the Philadelphia area. He also planted a stake on Broadway in the heart of Manhattan and opened another store in Yonkers. Active in political, religious, and community life, Wanamaker left behind papers that offer tantalizing glimpses of Philadelphia's social history.

While casting light on Wanamaker's cutting-edge career in the retail trade of the nineteenth and twentieth centuries, the collection also traces the great entrepreneur's work as postmaster general of the United States under Republican president Benjamin Harrison from 1889 to 1893. Wanamaker decided to rebuild the store at the beginning of the twentieth century. Construction was done in stages so that Wanamaker's would never be closed, and in 1911, it opened its doors to enthusiastic shoppers. Customers were enticed by its Grand Court on the first floor, where a 2,500-pound bronze eagle dominated the open space, and a huge organ with more than 18,000 pipes and 140 stops entertained shoppers as they ogled potential deals. After his father's death in 1922, Wanamaker's son, Rodman, took over management of the company until he died in 1928, ending family leadership of the company. Wanamaker's remained the nation's largest privately held retailer until 1978, when the Wanamaker family sold it to Carter Hawley Hale. It is currently a Macy's store, but the organ and the eagle still reside there.

ALICE L. GEORGE

The Historical Society of Pennsylvania also holds materials about other department stores in Pennsylvania, including Bonwit Teller & Company, Strawbridge & Clothier, Snellenburg's, Boyd's, Lit Brothers, Kaufmann's, and Gimbel Brothers.

# 79. W. T. Littig & Co.

## *Philadelphia of To-Day*

1908
Halftone on paper
23 × 37 ½ inches (58.4 × 95.4 cm)

Inscribed above image: *THE PHILADELPHIA OF TO-DAY / THE WORLD'S GREATEST WORKSHOP / America's largest Home City with more home owners than any other City in the world*; below image: *PHILADELPHIA SHOWING IMPROVED WATER FRONT / POPULATION IN 1908, 1,550,000 / 225th ANNIVERSARY OF THE FOUNDING OF PHILADELPHIA*; within image, lower left: *W.T. Littig & Co. N.Y.*

Historical Society of Pennsylvania Print Collection [V89]

When the 1854 Consolidation Act united the city and county of Philadelphia, the two-square-mile city delineated in the Penn-Holme plan expanded to encompass 130-square miles. A half century later, Philadelphia was the nation's third largest city by population, a landscape of densely packed wharves and shipyards, commercial and industrial areas often alongside residential neighborhoods, interspersed with parks and, in the outer districts, still-rural farmland, all arrayed (roughly) along a grid of streets that echoed Penn's founding vision.

Aerial or "bird's-eye" panoramic views were a popular form of civic boosterism during the nineteenth century. This example was published for Founder's Week, which marked Philadelphia's 225th anniversary in early October 1908. The previous year newly elected mayor Andrew Reyburn had appointed a commission that included Historical Society of Pennsylvania librarian John Jordan to ascertain whether the founding of Philadelphia dated to 1683 rather than 1701, as was stated on the city seal. The commissioners found documents that affirmed Reyburn's belief, and the mayor took the opportunity to mark this correction with a citywide celebration. (It should be noted, however, that the 1701 date is legally more correct because this is the year of the first city charter signed by Penn.) Workers and schoolchildren were given a week's holiday to enjoy concerts, parades, and pageants. Each night hundreds of electric lights illuminated the tower of City Hall. Festivities even included an automobile race in West Fairmount Park. Historic sites opened for public tours, and various organizations published pamphlets and reports tracing aspects of the city's history. The Founder's Day executive committee issued this view to advertise the city's many

"firsts"—historical and contemporary—in captions framing the image. These achievements included the Declaration of Independence, the Constitution, and the Bill of Rights. Philadelphia was the nation's "greatest" workshop: with only one-sixth of the country's population, it produced one-twentieth of all manufactures in more than sixteen thousand manufacturing plants. And it boasted more homeowners than any other city in the world. Eighty-five percent of houses were lived in by one family, and twenty percent of these dwellings were less than ten years old, attesting to the city's recent explosive growth. In addition to the Delaware waterfront improvements, major landmarks and civic improvements visible in the view include Memorial Hall, the Fairmount Reservoir, and East and West Fairmount Park, as well as City Hall (completed in 1903) and the eastern section of the new parkway, construction of which had started in 1907.

The view may be based in part on photographs taken from an airship. The Philadelphia *Inquirer* hired famed aeronaut Lincoln Beechey to pilot an airship over the city several times during Founder's Week, but there is no record that he made photographs during these ascents. It is not unlikely that the unknown artist used a more traditional technique by assembling the panorama from careful sketches made on the ground combined with information gleaned from maps and earlier site views to "imagine" the elevated view. Copies of the large print were probably given away to Founder's Week sponsors and organizers; a reduced version of the view appeared in the executive committee's final report.

ELIZABETH MILROY

# 80. **Violet Oakley** (1874–1961)

## *Penn's Arrival on the "Welcome" 1682*

1908
Charcoal and watercolor on illustration board
14 7/16 × 39 1/4 inches (36.7 × 99.7 cm)

Signed in graphite, lower right: *V. Oakley*
Inscribed in ink, upper right: *Penn's arrival / on the "Welcome" / 1682*

Violet Oakley Sketchbooks [3336]

Philadelphians have a long history of being caretakers of their revered past. The city's commemoration of its 225th anniversary in 1908 was the most extensive effort of its time for historical focus and the use of municipal resources to create a dramatic public celebration. Known as Founder's Week, this effort was led by the respected local historian Ellis Paxson Oberholtzer (1868–1936). He in turn engaged the Philadelphia artist Violet Oakley for the key positions of art director and designer of the floats for the History Parade held on October 9, 1908. At the time Oakley's talents were already recognized for her historical murals in Pennsylvania's State Capitol in Harrisburg. She began this elaborate program of wall paintings in 1902 and was the first woman to receive such a large and important public commission.

The scope and size of the Philadelphia celebration cannot be overestimated for its time. Founder's Week was considered a national event and brought thousands of people into the city. Each day of the week from October 4 to 10 was planned in detail, with the opening ceremonies on Sunday, titled Religion Day. The next five days included many public and private events, but the afternoons were given over to parades. In addition to a dramatic Naval River Parade, there were four street parades: the Civil and Military Parade, the Municipal Parade, the Industrial Parade, and the History Parade. Each included historical presentations with participants in appropriate period dress. Spectators were impressed with the number of floats, horses, uniforms, and costumed men, women, and children. Special trains were added to the schedule for the number of visitors coming into the city during the week, and tickets were sold for bleacher seats on the routes. National newspapers and magazines covered the week's parades and events.

The timeline for Founder's Week was certainly limited for such a large and complex project. According to Oberholtzer's notes, Oakley received the commission on May 26, 1908. She must have begun work immediately on the parades, particularly the designs for the floats representing

The Historical Society of Pennsylvania received a large collection from the Violet Oakley Foundation that contains books, engraving plates, original watercolors, sketchbooks, professional and personal papers, photographs, posters, broadsides, Philadelphia Contemporary Club Papers, and Philadelphia Plastic Club Papers. In addition, there are Oakley's limited-edition publications, *The Holy Experiment* (1922), *The Founding of the State of Liberty* (ca. 1922), and *The Law Triumphant* (1932).

rtant events in Philadelphia's past. At the Histori-
ociety of Pennsylvania, there are twenty-four of her rcolors for the history parade floats.

ne designs were submitted to Oberholtzer for his oval and were returned to Oakley with detailed com-s. As part of the printed materials to accompany Found-Veek, there was a History Parade Booklet with a cover n by Oakley. It included sixty-eight entries on the floats ndividual groups with a description of their importance. lthough a few of Oakley's floats represented sym-classical ideals or places, such as "The City Beauti-or Philadelphia, most told stories of specific historical occurrences. In addition, there are imaginative watercolors for floats showing famous social celebrations, productive activities at home, and the city's involvement in world-wide trade. At the beginning of the history parade, an elaborate float depicted the arrival of William Penn on the Delaware River in 1682. Oakley had previously painted a mural of Penn on his ship, the *Welcome*, for the Pennsylvania State Capitol in 1902–1906. She expanded this composition to include the entire vessel complete with sails, passengers, and Penn leaning on the bow, looking out for land. Sometimes Oakley had to make changes to her designs, and for this float Penn no longer faced forward but sat with his back to the bow. The float remained an impressive sight and was pulled by six draped, white horses.

Due to the tremendous success of the History Parade with the public, Oakley's reputation became even better known. In the following decades, she continued to work as a muralist, painter, and stained glass artist, with her fame reaching its apex in the 1920s and 1930s. Her watercolor designs for the 1908 parade floats played a significant role in how Philadelphia achieved its 225th anniversary, which celebrated the city's historical accomplishments while presenting a true spectacle of the time.

MARTHA HUTSON-SAXTON

## 81. J. B. Lippincott Company

### *Sectional View of Lippincott Company's Publishing House*

April 1887
Wood engraving
5 ¾ × 9 ½ inches (14.6 × 24.3 cm)

From *Lippincott's Monthly Magazine*, vol. 39
Inscribed below image: *SECTIONAL VIEW OF J. B. LIPPINCOTT COMPANY'S PUBLISHING HOUSE, / 715 and 717 Market St., and 714, 716, 718, and 720 Filbert St., Philadelphia.*; center right: *J.P. LIPPINCOTT CO. ENG.*

### *J. B. Lippincott Company Retail Book Department*

1893
Published by J. B. Lippincott Company
Wood engraving
3 ⅛ × 4 ½ inches (8.0 × 11.6 cm)

p. 13 of *Classified catalogue of publications and importations*

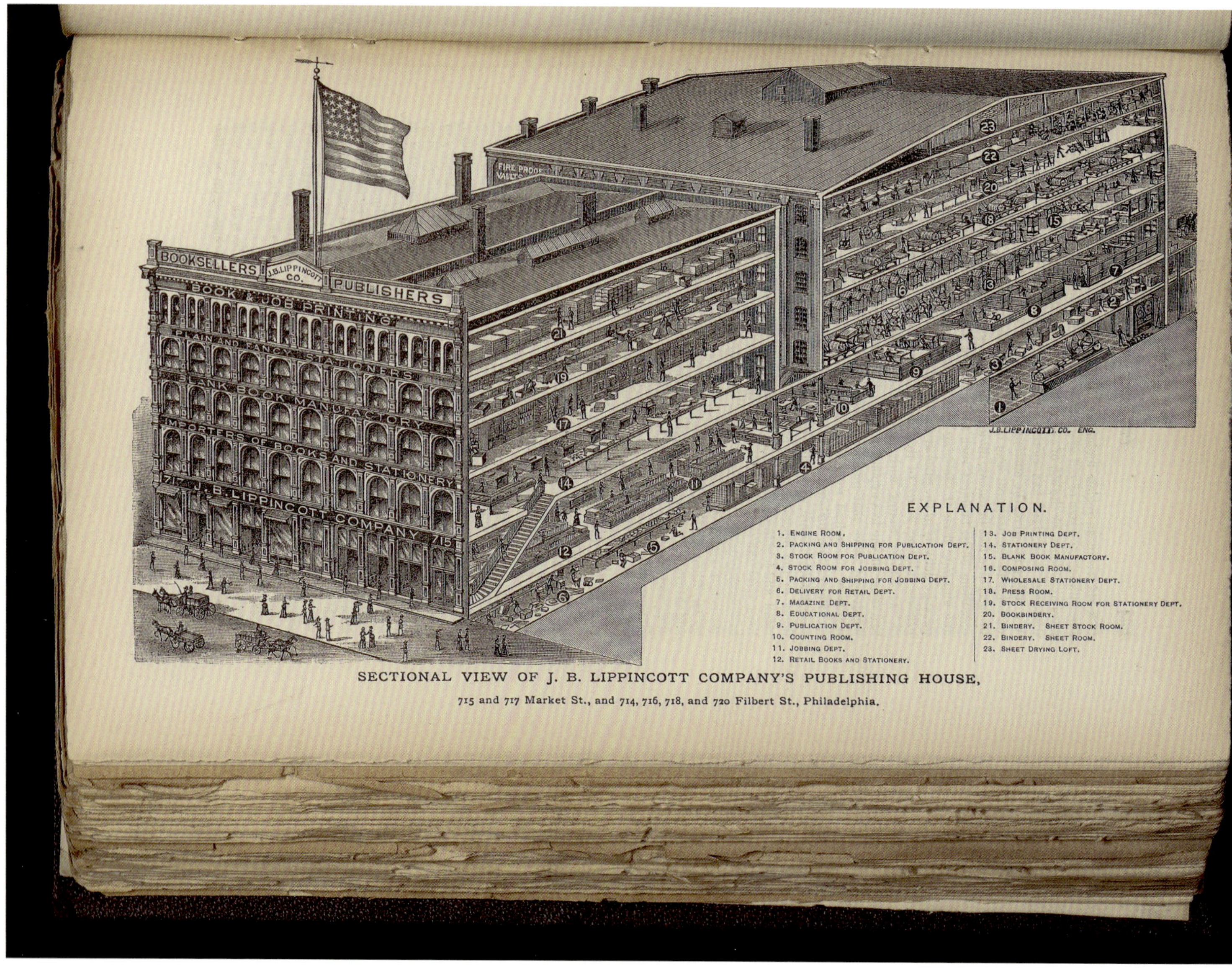

"We have here, perhaps, the largest distributing house in the world." This is how Henry Charles Carey described Lippincott, Grambo & Co. in his survey of the history and progress of the American book trade at the April 1854 festival honoring the retirement of Abraham Hart, his brother's partner at the publishing firm of Carey & Hart. And Carey certainly would have known. At age eight he had attended with his father, the pioneering publisher Mathew Carey, one of the foundational events that established that trade–the celebratory dinner at the first American book fair held in New York in June 1802; he would go on to become an important and innovative publisher in his own right. To bolster his claim, Carey explained that in many weeks the Lippincott firm sent out books and other merchandise for "an average of more than ten tons a day."

J. B. Lippincott Co., known today principally as a publisher of medical books and journals, was involved in all aspects of the book trade in the nineteenth century. A major publisher and importer of a wide range of books and periodicals, the firm was also a manufacturer and retailer of books and stationery and a job printer of custom orders for others. Above all, J. B. Lippincott Co. was the country's largest jobber, wholesaling its own publications and those of others across the nation. The broad range of its activities is clear from this sectional view of the establishment from 1887. The front building, facing the 700 block of Market Street, was dedicated to publishing, retailing, and storage of stock, while the building in the rear, stretching back to Filbert Street, housed a complete manufactory, with separate floors given over to composition, printing, and binding. As the illustration shows, Philadelphians wanting to purchase something to read could enter from Market Street into an elegant retail space where any book they might wish would have been available–stationery and fancy goods were available upstairs on the second floor.

The Lippincott establishment was gutted by fire over several days in late November 1899, and for many years scholars believed that none of the early records of the firm survived. But in 2002, Lippincott Wilkins and Wulwer donated 144 boxes of early archival material to the Historical Society of Pennsylvania. These boxes contained, among other material, 576 bound manuscript volumes, over 500 of which are letter books containing copies of outgoing letters documenting all aspects of the firm's activities. A preliminary finding aid, prepared in 2007, has recently been revised, and collection material has now been treated for mold and rehoused. To date, scholars have been particularly interested in the editorial correspondence of *Lippincott's Monthly Magazine*, launched in 1868, and the letters to and from the firm's London agency, established in 1875. But the collection remains largely unexplored and underutilized, far more so than any other major American publisher's archive surviving from the industrial era.

MICHAEL WINSHIP

## 82. **Horace Trumbauer** (1869–1938), attributed to **Julian F. Abele** (1881–1950)

## *The Free Public Library of Philadelphia*

1911–12
Ink and wash on laminated paper, mounted on card
36 × 64 inches (91.5 × 162.5 cm)

Inscribed below image: · *THE · FREE · PUBLIC · LIBRARY · OF · PHILADELPHIA · / ·MAIN BUILDING · FRONT ELEVATION* ·; below image, lower left: · *HORACE TRUMBAUER. ARCHITECT* ·; below image, lower right: *SCALE: ONE INCH EQUALS EIGHT feet* ·

Horace Trumbauer Architectural Drawings [V36]
Gift of W. Edward Franks, 1968

This vibrant ink-and-wash drawing of the Free Library was probably created in the last months of 1911 at the end of a flurry of activity. That spring the library had been assigned a prominent site on the new Benjamin Franklin Parkway, the city appropriated money to acquire the land and clear it of houses, and Horace Trumbauer was appointed its architect.

Trumbauer was the favorite designer of the intermarried Widener and Elkins families, for whom he had created gigantic suburban houses in the 1890s. They were generous supporters of the Free Library and successfully lobbied its trustees and the mayor to secure Trumbauer's appointment. He set to work immediately and presented sketch plans in June 1911.

Evidence suggests that Trumbauer assigned the further development of the project to the chief designer in his office, the hugely talented Julian F. Abele, the first African American to receive an architectural degree from the University of Pennsylvania. On October 5 it was Abele who presented a preliminary design—probably including this elevation—to the library building committee. On April 2, 1912, he would again represent the Trumbauer office before the city's new Art Jury, forebear of today's Art Commission, whose file for the meeting includes a photograph of this drawing. Although the norms of the day prevented public recognition of a Black architect (or any junior member of a firm), Abele's role was fully visible to those involved in the project.

The library had been given one of the two sites for public buildings on the north side of Logan Square, then in the process of being transected (and transformed) by the new parkway. It was presumed from the start that the library design would establish the model for the second building (ultimately the Municipal Courts); in other words, the two buildings would be twins. Thus it is unsurprising that Abele, who had a strong affection for French neoclassical architecture, took inspiration from the most famous architectural twins in the world, the pair of grandiose palaces on the Place de la Concorde in Paris (1755–63). But while Abele's initial design was influenced by those structures, he lengthened it by two bays and replaced its free-standing colonnade with a row of attached columns. The effect was somewhat drier—and arguably more modern.

In subsequent revisions, the building had to be shortened by forty feet to fit on the site and further reduced to save money. The proportions of the shorter design were nearer those of its French sisters, which it came to resemble ever more closely, with freestanding columns and a ground floor brought close to street level.

The project was bedeviled by setbacks. Only a dozen days after the Art Jury approved the preliminary design, the Titanic sank, taking its patrons George and Harry Elkins Widener to their deaths. There were also protracted squabbles over financing and contractor selection, and the design revisions required two further reviews by the Art Jury. Even so, the Free Library was the first public building on the parkway to open on June 2, 1927.

DAVID B. BROWNLEE

· THE · FREE · PUBLIC · LIBRARY · OF · PHILADELPHIA ·
· MAIN BUILDING · FRONT ELEVATION ·
· HORACE TRUMBAUER, ARCHITECT ·
SCALE: ONE INCH EQUALS EIGHT FEET ·

# 83. Fred Spear

## *Enlist*

---

1915
Published by Tudor Press
Color rotogravure on paper
43 3/4 × 26 7/8 inches (103.5 × 68.3 cm)

Inscribed within image, lower center: *ENLIST*; within image, lower right: *FRED SPEAR*; below image, lower left: *ISSUED BY THE CITY OF BOSTON PUBLIC SAFETY COMMITTEE*; below image, lower right: *THE TUDOR PRESS - BOSTON*

Historical Society of Pennsylvania War Posters Collection [V95]

A wraith-like woman, her eyes closed, her hair swept upward, sinks to the bottom of the sea. A wet gown, bare at the shoulder, reveals her firm, athletic body. Her naked foot touches moss-covered rocks. With a sleeping infant enclosed in her arms, she embodies maternal bliss. Bubbles rise from her lips. The water is dark but translucent. A fish floats by in the depths, an impassive onlooker.

What a strange, almost surreal scene this is, at once terrifying and tranquil, summoning the viewer's primordial fear of death by drowning only to merge it with an equally primordial desire to return to the maternal warmth of the womb. It pulls together two of the most powerful pairings in art and literature: Mother and Child, and Death and the Maiden. To modern eyes, this image might seem hokey and kitschy. But to thousands, if not millions, of Americans who saw it plastered on walls across the land in the summer of 1915, it must have been disturbing, even shocking. Unfortunately, the historical record does not indicate how many copies of the poster were made, where it was displayed, and what casual viewers thought or said about it. Most of the several thousand war-related images produced in the United States during this period share a similar fate.

Still, in June 1915 few viewers would have missed the poster's reference to the recent sinking of RMS *Lusitania* by a German submarine. At 2:00 p.m. on May 7, the Germans fired a torpedo at the unguarded ocean liner on its return from New York to Liverpool. The vessel went down in eighteen minutes before lifeboats could be deployed. Twelve hundred victims perished, among them 128 Americans. Most of the bodies were never recovered; only two hundred corpses washed up on the Irish coast. According to a widely circulated news report, two of these belonged to a mother and child: "On the Cunard wharf lies a mother with a three-month-old child clasped tightly in her arms. Her face wears a half smile. Her baby's head rests against her breast. No one has tried to separate them."

The poster is eloquent in its brevity. A single word, floating in space beneath the descending forms of the mother and child, conveys its message in pastel pink letters: ENLIST. Outlined with soft white contours, these letters epitomize Victorian notions of feminine frailty. By reducing the text of the poster to one well-chosen, well-rendered word, the artist, Fred Spear, displays an economy of form that must have been a model for legions of future commercial and political advertisers, whose goal was to scrub ads clean of verbiage and visual clutter to speed up communication and heighten impact. Here, a single, stand-alone word has been "enlisted" to drive home the poster's message.

And the message was simple: enlist in the armed forces to help prevent further atrocities of this magnitude. The poster addressed male and female viewers alike: Men, join the army, navy, or marines. Women, make sure your men join the army, navy, or marines. In the late spring and summer of 1915, the United States was neutral, almost two years away from going to war in Europe, but "Preparedness" advocates insisted on the importance of building up America's peacetime military to be ready for what they were sure would be a coming conflict. *Enlist* preyed on the age-old trope of imperiled femininity to stir visceral emotions in contemporary viewers. At a time when Americans were more likely to be troubled by rapidly changing sex roles in their own society than they were by the conflagration on a distant continent, posters such as *Enlist* managed to collapse two areas of concern into one. DAVID M. LUBIN

ENLIST
FRED SPEAR
ISSUED BY THE CITY OF BOSTON PUBLIC SAFETY COMMITTEE

## 84. Bethlehem Steel

### *Blast Furnaces*

ca. 1900
Published by Dando Printing and Pub. Co.
Halftone on paper
3 11/16 × 5 inches (9.4 × 12.8 cm)

p. 19 of *Bethlehem Steel Company, South Bethlehem, Pa., U.S.A.*

## Herbert Pullinger (1878–1961)

### *Bethlehem Steel*

1917
Lithograph on paper
26 5/16 × 19 inches (66.8 × 48.2 cm)

Signed and dated lower left: *Herbert Pullinger-17*
Inscribed lower left: *Blast Furnace Bethlehem Steel Co.*

Historical Society of Pennsylvania Large Graphics Collection [V65]

Visitors flock to Bethlehem, Pennsylvania, at Christmastime to delight in the holiday decorations that sparkle throughout the city's entire downtown. (This orchestrated display dates to the 1930s when city officials and business leaders mobilized during the Great Depression to attract tourist shopping dollars to boost the local economy.) Visitors now also flock to Bethlehem to gamble at the Wind Creek Resort Casino. The casino occupies a portion of a 1,600-acre tract of land once dominated by the massive facilities of the Bethlehem Steel Corporation. An overhead bridge that conveyed ores serves as part of the frontage of the casino, and a few former shops of the steelworks have been repurposed, but casino patrons sitting at slot machines and gambling tables today would have little inkling that the second largest steel-producing company in the United States operated at the site just three decades before. The name of the casino itself reflects the abrupt erasure of an important history.

German Moravians founded Bethlehem in 1741 as a North American outpost to evangelize other European settlers and Native Americans. Church-owned artisanal workshops were established. Abetted by abundances of nearby natural resources and waterway links to east coast urban centers, industrial development ensued in the mid-nineteenth century. Iron and steel production began in the city with the formation of the Bethlehem Iron Company in 1865. That precursor of the steel corporation faced stiff competition from Pittsburgh producers, and in the 1880s, company executives lobbied successfully to secure contracts from the US government to manufacture steel armor plate and ordnance for modern steam-powered naval vessels. The initiative represented the first instance of what eventually would be labeled the "military-industrial complex," and steel production in Bethlehem from that point on would be sustained by military orders. The Bethlehem Iron Company would be reorganized in the 1890s and then purchased by financial interests connected to Charles Schwab in 1901 and incorporated as the Bethlehem Steel Corporation in 1904. By World War I, Schwab had built the company into the country's second-largest steel producer (and third-largest corporation) with 34,000 workers. The company expanded with the creation of shipbuilding capacities in Baltimore and Quincy, Massachusetts, and through the acquisition of a large steelworks in Buffalo. During World War I and II, Bethlehem Steel was a major supplier of armaments and battleships. Employment would grow to 160,000 workers. Faced with foreign competition, the company began to retrench in the 1980s, and steel production came to a halt in Bethlehem in 1995.

The business records of the Bethlehem Steel Corporation have never been formally archived. Relevant manuscript materials can be found in several research libraries,

notably at the Historical Society of Pennsylvania, but here as part of different collections. For example, the company began recruiting Mexican workers in 1923. The details can only be found in *La Prensa*, a Spanish-language paper published in the US; HSP holds copies of the newspaper as part of the Balch Institute of Ethnic Studies Collection. Photographs of the steelworks and a lithograph by the Philadelphia illustrator and printmaker Herbert Pullinger that convey the mammoth facilities can be found in various HSP holdings; testimonies of company officials to government agencies during wartime, especially concerning labor disputes, are held in other collections (the disparate materials can be located through HSP search engines). HSP also helped to keep the history of the Bethlehem Steel Corporation from fading with the publication of a set of essays on the company in a November 2006 special issue of *Pennsylvania Legacies,* a general-audience journal of the Society.

WALTER LICHT

VOTES
FOR
WOMEN

# 85. *Justice Bell Tour*

June 25, 1915
Gelatin silver print
6 7/8 × 4 15/16 inches (17.4 × 12.6 cm)

League of Women Voters Records [2095]
Gift of the League of Women Voters of Pennsylvania, 1980 and 1990

In the summer and fall of 1915, woman suffragists descended on New Jersey, New York, Massachusetts, and Pennsylvania, where male voters in each state were about to decide whether to extend the franchise to women. Tours in Pennsylvania often featured the Justice Bell, a replica of the Liberty Bell intended to remind voters of the connection between women's struggle for the vote and the nation's struggle for independence. At the Historical Society of Pennsylvania, a series of photographs of the Justice Bell tour is included in the papers of the League of Women Voters (LWV) of Pennsylvania, the state affiliate of the former National American Woman Suffrage Association (NAWSA). This collection provides robust coverage of the LWV's work and scattered coverage of the Pennsylvania Woman Suffrage Association, for which other primary sources are scarce.

Suffragists often invoked the history of the American Revolution. In 1848, attendees at the Seneca Falls Convention modeled their Declaration of Sentiments deliberately on the Declaration of Independence, substituting the phrase "all men and women are created equal" for the original wording. In 1893, suffragist Lucy Stone (1818–1893) asked that a replica of the Liberty Bell, cast for the World's Columbian Exposition in Chicago, not ring until women had attained equality. Similarly, the 1915 Justice Bell was muted to reflect women's silenced voices. Chester County resident Katharine Wentworth Ruschenberger, who led the publicity campaign for the Woman Suffrage Party of Chester County and commissioned the 1915 Justice Bell, may have been directly inspired by Stone. Replica Liberty Bells also featured in suffrage parades and demonstrations before 1915.

Leading up to the referendum, suffragists brought the bell to every county in the state, where it often accompanied elaborate rallies. For example, in Philadelphia, one hundred women bearing torches and wearing the white and yellow of the suffrage movement drew the bell on a float, marching around City Hall and down Broad Street. A parade of between five and seven thousand followed. In rural areas, women drove the bell along country roads, stopping frequently to speak with farmers.

Despite these efforts, all of the 1915 referenda failed. In Pennsylvania, liquor interests actively opposed the measure, and Philadelphia machine politicians may have worked behind the scenes to sway constituents' votes with premarked sample ballots. These devastating losses, however, helped to convince NAWSA president Carrie Chapman Catt (1859–1947) of the importance of pursuing a constitutional amendment. Veterans of the Pennsylvania tour continued to use the bell in this phase of the campaign. Finally, four years after the failed referendum, Pennsylvania ratified the Nineteenth Amendment in June of 1919. The Justice Bell appeared in a procession in Harrisburg to mark the occasion. A year later, upon the ratification of the Nineteenth Amendment, it rang for the first time.

CHRISTINA LAROCCO

Further information can be found at the Historical Society of Pennsylvania in the Jane Campbell Papers [3203], Caroline Katzenstein Papers [Am .8996], and Dora Kelly Lewis Correspondence [2137].

## 86. **Broadbent & Phillips**

### *Dora Kelly Lewis*

ca. 1880
Albumen print mounted on card
6 ½ × 4 5⁄16 inches (16.5 × 11.0 cm)

Inscribed lower left of card: *Broadbent & Phillips*; lower right of card: *1206 CHESTNUT ST. PHILAD'A.*

Dora Kelly Lewis Correspondence [2137]
Gift of Dora Kelly Lewis's descendants, 1986

### *Dora Kelly Lewis Letter to Louise Lewis*

November 14, 1917
Manuscript; graphite on paper
8 15⁄16 × 5 ½ inches (22.7 × 13.9 cm)

Dora Kelly Lewis Correspondence [2137]
Gift of Dora Kelly Lewis's descendants, 1986

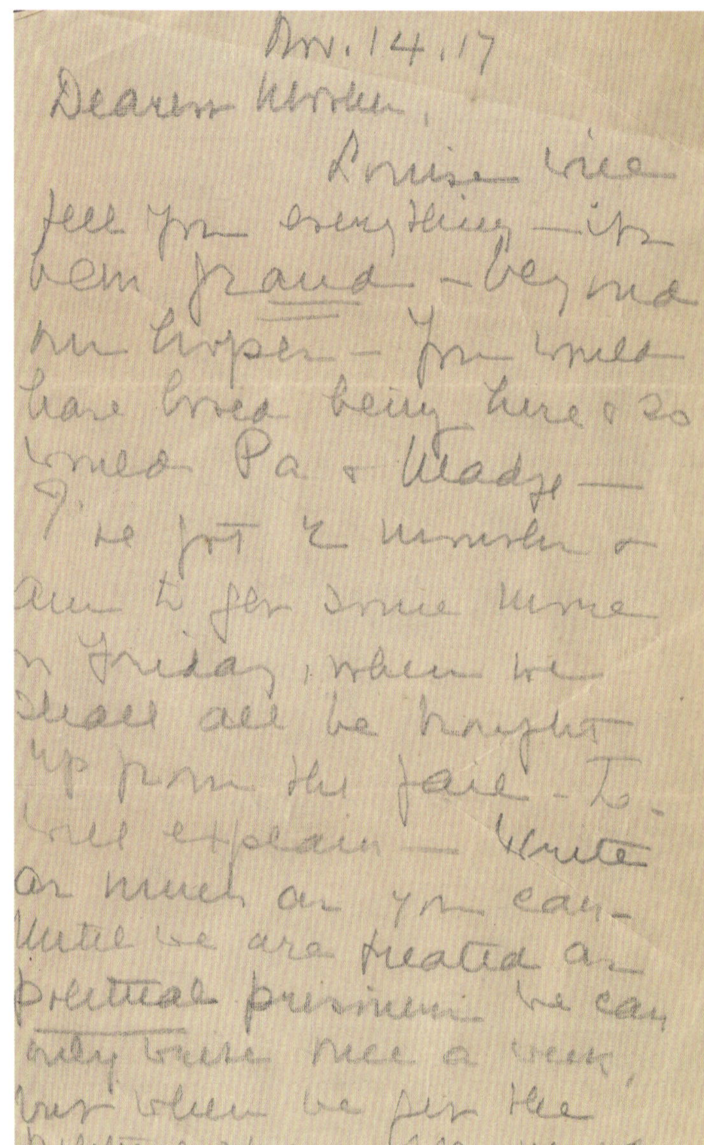

Nov. 14. 17
Dearest Mother,
Louise will tell you everything — it's been grand — beyond our hopes — you would have loved being here & so would Pa & Gladys — I've [illegible] to [illegible] & [illegible] to get some time on Friday, when we shall all be brought up from the jail — to tell explain — Write as much as you can. Until we are treated as political prisoners we can only write once a week, but when we get the political status, [illegible]

In January of 1917, members of the National Woman's Party (NWP) began picketing the White House to demand voting rights for women. Philadelphia resident Dora Kelly Lewis, whose career also included support for prison reform and workers' rights, numbered among them. Born in Chester County, Pennsylvania, to a well-off family, Lewis was a founder of both the Equal Franchise Society, a suffrage group, and (with her sister Esther) the Lighthouse, a settlement house for Kensington mill workers.

Lewis and NWP founder Alice Paul (1885–1977) worked together on local arrangements for the 1912 National American Woman Suffrage Association's (NAWSA) convention in Philadelphia. The two bonded immediately, and Lewis followed Paul to the NWP. In addition to her work on the executive committee in fundraising, Lewis served as one of Paul's closest advisors. The Historical Society of Pennsylvania holds a small but important collection of Lewis's correspondence, particularly revealing the brutality the picketers faced while imprisoned in 1917.

The decision to picket came from both Paul's experience in the British suffrage movement and the tradition of Quaker witness. Each day these "Silent Sentinels" raised banners demanding that President Woodrow Wilson support a national suffrage amendment. However, after the US entered World War I in April 1917, politicians and law enforcement officials deemed protest unpatriotic, and Wilson did not appreciate the picketers' willingness to point out his hypocrisy: the US had entered the war to make the world "safe for democracy."

Soon officials began to arrest and sentence demonstrators to prison terms of up to six months. Lewis was one of the first—and, at fifty-five, one of the oldest—women to be arrested. At the rat- and bedbug-infested Occoquan Workhouse in Virginia, Lewis led the group in demanding political-prisoner status. Prison officials retaliated with violence later known as the "Night of Terror." When guards threw Lewis into her room, she hit her head and lost consciousness. Some feared she was dead. In response to this treatment, Lewis, Paul, and other picketers went on a hunger strike. Prison officials then subjected them to a brutal force-feeding regimen. Smuggled notes eventually revealed the rampant torture and abuse that the prisoners endured.

In the fall of 1917, Lewis spoke in twelve midwestern states on behalf of the picketers, sharing her grueling experiences. In 1919, she became head of the NWP's ratification committee, lobbying politicians from Pennsylvania to California to support the newly passed Nineteenth Amendment. Her activism is less well documented after this point, though she championed the Equal Rights Amendment from its introduction in 1923. The Dora Kelly Lewis Correspondence demonstrates how suffragists revitalized the movement through a renewed focus on a federal amendment and mass public demonstrations. It also provides insight into the organization and philosophy of the NWP and highlights the dismal treatment suffragists received in prison.

CHRISTINA LAROCCO

Further information can be found at the Historical Society of Pennsylvania in the Caroline Katzenstein Papers [Am .8996], League of Women Voters of Pennsylvania Records [2095], and the Lighthouse Records [1970].

# 87. **William Shewell Ellis** (1876–1931)

## *Mary Elizabeth Hallock Greenewalt with Color Organ*

1922
Gelatin silver print
10 × 7 ⅞ inches (25.5 × 20.0 cm)

Inscribed lower left: *Wm. Shewell · Ellis*; verso: *Photo of Mrs. Mary Hallock Greenewalt (the head arrangement is fancy + only used for this photo) seated at her second development of light-color play console instrument. The color filters are of the true primary colors (see correspondence with the Eastman-Kodak Co.) and with the scale of at least visible microments* [*sic*] *made through the rheostat (see patent 1357773) makes for the first time a definite measure definite recordability for color shade and color tint. The Arabic name, it will be seen is carried on the side of the instrument.*

Mary Elizabeth Hallock Greenewalt Papers [0867]
Gift of Mary Elizabeth Hallock Greenewalt, 1936–1949

A concert pianist by training, Mary Elizabeth Hallock Greenewalt sits in this photograph not before the ebonies and ivories of the musical keyboard but rather before the rheostats and rotary actuators of the *Sarabet*. A light control console of her own design, the *Sarabet* produced slowly morphing, colorful illuminations for concerts she gave in the 1920s; as Beethoven and Debussy were heard, Greenewalt's lighting designs for each piece were seen, cast over the performance space.

Philadelphia-based Greenewalt had begun experimenting with the idea of using expressive lighting during her piano performances as early as 1905, but the first public outing of this multimedia concept came in 1911 in the Egyptian Hall of Philadelphia's Wanamaker's department store. Greenewalt had devised a relatively crude method to realize her vision in this concert: dyed transparent materials were drawn in front of a source of light by an assistant as Greenewalt played the piano. By 1918, however, her pursuit for greater control over light as a medium had led to the design of her first version of the *Sarabet*, which she named after her Syrian mother, Sara Tabet. A self-taught electrical engineer, Greenewalt made elements of her earliest instrument by hand, but she turned to companies—such as the General Electric Works, the Westinghouse Company, and the Commercial Engineering Company of Pittsburgh—to produce her later designs, such as the version pictured here, which was used for concerts in New York in 1922. As she designed and redesigned the *Sarabet*, Greenewalt obtained a total of eleven patents, covering color filters, switches, and rheostats, as well as the instrument as a whole and a system for notating light.

Greenewalt was not the first person to suggest that displays of abstract color could accompany music. An eighteenth-century French Jesuit monk, Louis Bertrand Castel, proposed a keyboard instrument that would produce a color and a sound for each key pressed. While the practicalities of making this instrument proved overly taxing for Castel, an American inventor, Bainbridge Bishop, displayed a "color organ" in New York in the 1880s—a musical organ with an attachment that lit up colored lights in coordination

with the keys played. A similar instrument, invented by the artist Alexander Wallace Rimington, translated musical pitches into colors for concerts in England in 1895.

Greenewalt's instrument differed from these earlier precedents in an obvious way: there was no musical keyboard. She strongly objected to the idea of having each musical pitch accompanied by its own color; she preferred longer-lasting colors gradually shifting in intensity, over which her rheostats—regulators of electric current—gave her subtle control. She even suggested that the *Sarabet*'s expressive power could allow it to create light art independent of music.

Greenewalt's use of immersive electric lighting foreshadows the art installations of James Turrell and Dan Flavin. Her visualizations of classical music predate similar work in film by Oskar Fischinger, Mary Ellen Bute, and, in the case of *Fantasia*, Walt Disney. The coordination of lights with music found later popularity too in the liquid-light, laser-light, and disco-lighting phenomena. While the *Sarabet* might have fallen into obscurity and no instrument survives, Greenewalt's vision nonetheless prefigured a number of later twentieth-century trends.

RALPH RICHARD WHYTE

## 88. **Albert E. Dutrieuille Catering**

### *Dutrieuille Baptist Catering Firm Chefs*

Undated
Gelatin silver print
7 ⅞ × 9 ⅞ inches (20.0 × 25.0 cm)

Dutrieuille-Baptiste Family Photographs [PG036]
The Balch Institute, gift of Peter Shelton

### *Dinner Menu for the Class of 1934 at St. Veronica's Rectory*

1938
Print on card
5 ½ × 3 ¼ inches (14.0 × 8.2 cm)

Stamped verso, upper right: *ALBERT E. DUTRIEUILLE / 4001 Spring Garden St. / Philadelphia, PA*; verso in blue ink, center: *Rev. Francis V Carr / 6200 Rising Sun Dr. / Phila. Pa.*

Albert E. Dutrieuille Catering Records [MSS052]
The Balch Institute, gift of Bernice Dutrieuille Shelton, 1973

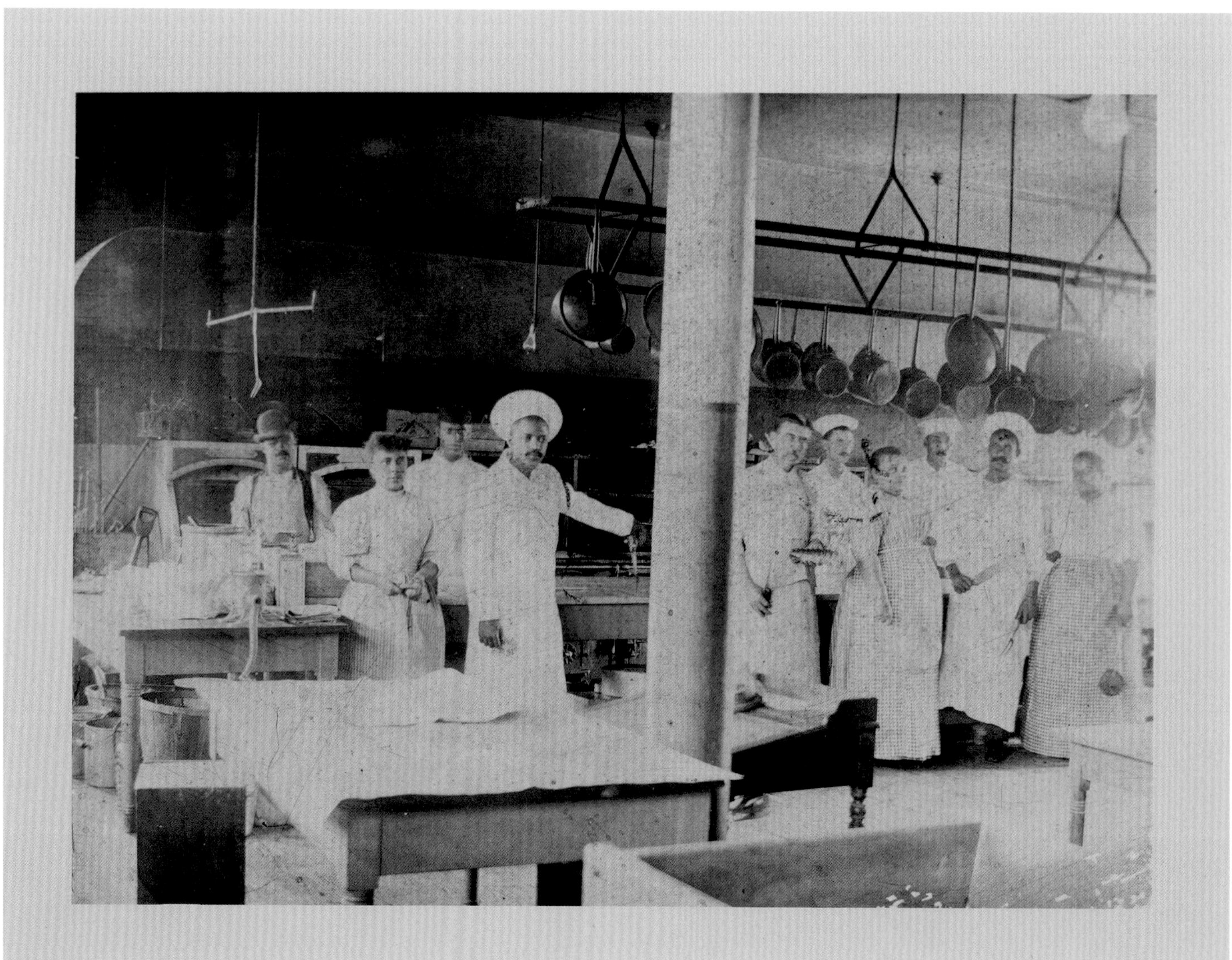

No wedding, graduation celebration, alumni gathering, or club meeting would be complete without food. Whether a casual celebration around an array of finger foods or a formal multi-course meal, Philadelphians at the end of the nineteenth century turned to caterer Peter Albert Dutrieuille (1838–1919) to elevate their events into memorable occasions.

When Dutrieuille opened the doors of his café and catering business at 108 South Eighteenth Street in 1873, he joined a long tradition of Black Philadelphia entrepreneurs who had carved a path for themselves in the food industry. From the colonial era through the nineteenth century, public waiters contracted their services to provide and serve refreshments, and public cooks commandeered kitchens to supply sumptuous meals. Robert Bogle, James Prosser, Peter and Mary Frances Augustin, and Thomas J. Dorsey are just a few early African American caterers who developed successful businesses and enjoyed a wide following. These caterers not only helped Philadelphia build its reputation as a city renowned for its cuisine but also strengthened Black communities through their volunteerism, philanthropy, and networks.

Dutrieuille nurtured his connection to Philadelphia's French and Saint Dominguan communities as well as to the wider Catholic community. He married Amelia Baptiste (also spelled Baptist), of French West Indian descent, and apprenticed with his in-laws. Their son, Albert E. Dutrieuille (1877–1974), who carried on the business after his father retired and eventually moved it to Spring Garden Street, also worshiped in the city's Catholic churches and maintained an active ecclesiastic network. Many Catholic churches, organizations, and groups, such as St. Veronica's Class of 1934, engaged the Dutrieuilles when they needed a caterer.

The St. Veronica's Class of 1934 dinner followed the format of a traditional menu. The meal progressed from fruit to soup, through entrees, vegetables, salad, and ended with dessert and nuts. In addition to this standard fare, the Dutrieuilles served terrapin. Terrapin, a freshwater relative of the turtle found in Mid-Atlantic marshes, was a specialty of Philadelphia's African American caterers and extremely popular from the nineteenth through the early twentieth centuries. This and other menus in the Dutrieuille collection illustrate African American caterers' broad range of culinary knowledge and skill.

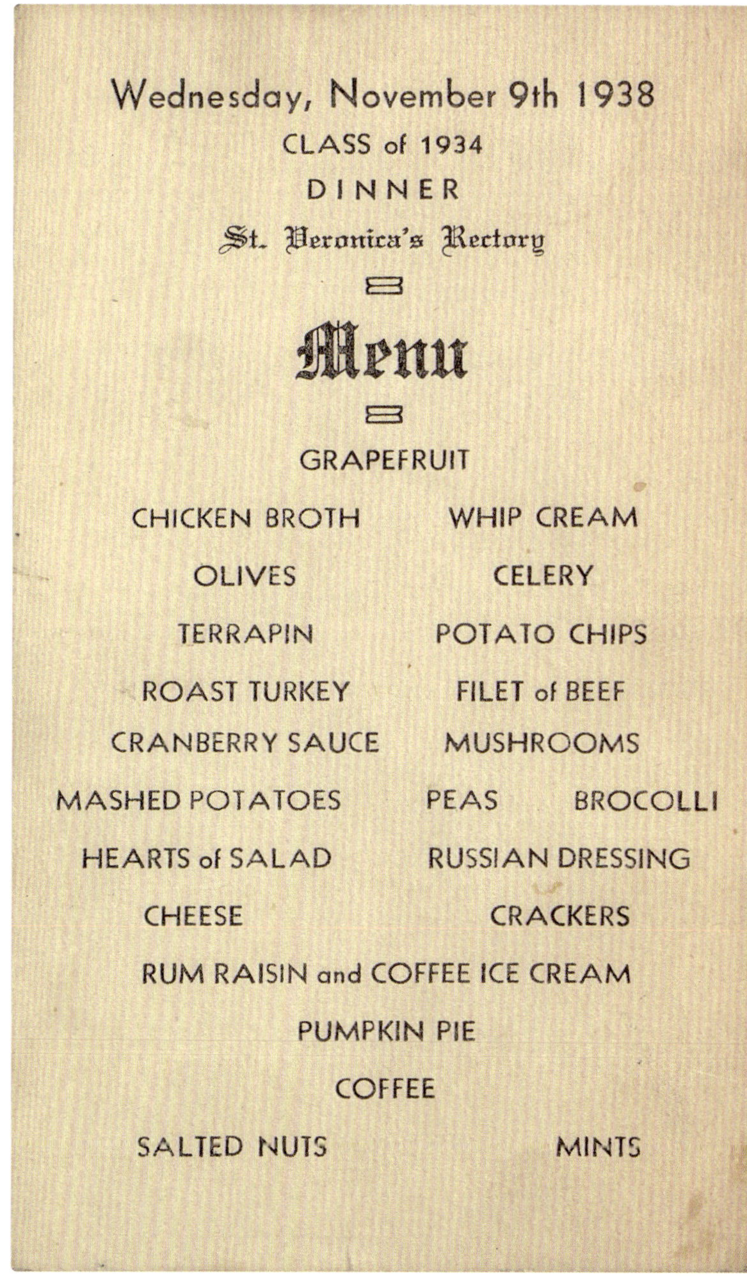
Wednesday, November 9th 1938
CLASS of 1934
DINNER
St. Veronica's Rectory

Menu

GRAPEFRUIT
CHICKEN BROTH WHIP CREAM
OLIVES CELERY
TERRAPIN POTATO CHIPS
ROAST TURKEY FILET of BEEF
CRANBERRY SAUCE MUSHROOMS
MASHED POTATOES PEAS BROCOLLI
HEARTS of SALAD RUSSIAN DRESSING
CHEESE CRACKERS
RUM RAISIN and COFFEE ICE CREAM
PUMPKIN PIE
COFFEE
SALTED NUTS MINTS

The photograph of the chefs and cooks who worked with the Dutrieuilles and Baptistes shows them in the kitchen surrounded by the apparatus of their craft. The various tables, ovens, pots, and pans are more than tools. Each represents their command of cooking materials, techniques, and methods that when combined with detailed knowledge of foodstuffs created meals that delighted patrons. This photograph of the Dutrieuille-Baptiste chefs and cooks is also an acknowledgment of the often-unheralded people who made catering businesses successful. Their work and those of people like them enabled Albert E. Dutrieuille to helm the thriving business and continue the legacy of the African American caterers into the 1960s. DANYA M. PILGRIM

# 89. **Dox Thrash** (1893–1965)

## *Charlotte*

ca. 1933–41
Carborundum mezzotint on paper
11 5/8 × 8 1/4 inches (29.5 × 21.0 cm)

Signed in graphite, lower right: *D. Thrash / WPA Art Program*
Inscribed in graphite, lower left: *Charlotte*

Works Projects Administration Posters Collection [V99]
Allocated to the Historical Society of Pennsylvania by the Work Projects Administration, War Services Project, March 3, 1943

Dox Thrash often honored women. He is known for the Opheliagraph, or the carborundum mezzotint process that he renamed after his mother, Ophelia. This example, *Charlotte,* is a portrait of an African American woman. The composition is tightly focused on the face. Only part of her carefully coiffed hair is discernible, and her neck dissolves into the velvety darkness of the paper's surface. Although many of Thrash's portraits of working-class men and entertainers are known, few are aware of his repertoire of bold Black women. Thrash, like most African American artists in the twentieth century, was compelled to provide realistic and affirming imagery to counter the negative representations of Black Americans that dominated popular culture. For his images of women, these portraits confronted the pervasive Eurocentric beauty ideals. Thrash's close, detailed lines celebrated his models' broad noses, full lips, and large piercing dark eyes. He also named most of these portraits—*Anna, Jenny, Mary Lou, Miss X.* A carborundum of *Mary Lou* at the Philadelphia Museum of Art looks like a younger version of *Charlotte.* Her features, the distinctive peaked hairline, and middle-parted bob characterize a handful of Thrash's female portraits; even the same hoop earrings recur.

Given that these images were made within the same few years, Thrash is clearly using one specific woman to serve as his muse. One could always speculate that she is his wife, Edna McAllister, or just a lifelong model and friend. Whether real, fictional, or both, naming these women, who all boldly stare out at us, was of great importance to Thrash and his audience. These women needed to rise above such denigrating, anonymous stereotypes as the mammy or the prostitute. To do so, they had to reflect a tangible personhood, an individualism rooted in an actual lived experience. Thrash often turned to women as subjects. His female portraits range from mothers with their children or going to the market to those doing their hair and a rich group of nudes. The virtual absence of the Black nude in American art before the 1970s makes Thrash's work very pertinent in American art history. Artists such as Archibald Motley Jr., Eldzier Cortor, and Thrash brought dignity and grace to the Black bodies they dared to insert into such a significant Modernist tradition. It is worth noting that these three artists all attended the School of the Art Institute of Chicago, where Motley had introduced Black models into life drawing classes soon after Thrash started taking classes there.

KYMBERLY PINDER

Charlotte
THRASH
WPA Art Program

# 90. The Philadelphia Record

## *Father Divine*

1939
Gelatin silver print
7 7/8 × 10 inches (20.0 × 25.5 cm)

*Philadelphia Record* Photograph Morgue [V07]
Gift of the Philadelphia Evening Bulletin, 1951

During the dreary and desperate days of the Great Depression, tens of thousands of people in the United States and around the globe turned to an African American preacher, Father Divine, in their quest for relief. Divine fed many hungry New Yorkers in the 1930s at his base in Harlem, and he moved his crusade to the Philadelphia area in the early 1950s.

Most striking among Father Divine's teachings was the idea that he was God on Earth. "Just as Jesus Christ came to the earth in the form of a little baby, so I, God, have arrived in the form of a Black man," he proclaimed. Born in Rockville, Maryland, as George Baker, he apparently received little or no formal education before beginning his career as an itinerant preacher.

As a spellbinding minister in the 1920s and 1930s, Divine created his own form of religious practice built around public confession and residential gatherings of his congregation. Divine established about 150 communes worldwide and called each one "heaven." People of all races lived together because Father Divine saw race as irrelevant; however, residents were segregated by gender and told to practice celibacy. This idea generated charges of encouraging "race suicide" from African American leader Marcus Garvey (1887–1940) because most of Father Divine's supporters were African American women, some of whom deserted husbands and children to enjoy the preacher's version of heaven.

Divine's Peace Mission Movement had a political component as well. The group promoted desegregation, anti-lynching legislation, confiscation of firearms, restrictions on labor unions, continuing education, and self-sufficiency. His followers often joined public protests related to these causes. For example, in the late 1940s, the movement gathered over 250,000 signatures for an anti-lynching petition presented to Congress. During his career, Father Divine faced civil and criminal trials as a result of financial disputes and disorderly gatherings. In one case, someone was stabbed during a melee that erupted during a service.

By 1940, he had amassed an estimated $15 million, equivalent to more than $290 million in the 2020s. He enjoyed sharing feasts with his disciples in the hungry years of the 1930s, and these events often were compared to Jesus Christ's biblical miracle of the loaves and the fishes. Divine saw food as tangible evidence of God's word. He died September 10, 1965, and after his death, his widow, Edna Rose Ritchings, claimed leadership of the dwindling movement until her death in 2017.

The Historical Society of Pennsylvania holds many of Father Divine's own words as well as books and articles written about him. Many images of the sect leader can be found in the vast *Philadelphia Record* Photograph Morgue, one of HSP's collections. In a highly competitive environment, the *Philadelphia Record* had to shut its doors in 1947. Founded in the late nineteenth century, its circulation peaked in the 1930s at more than 315,000.

ALICE L. GEORGE

# 91. **Sumiko Kobayashi** (1923– )

## *Internment Camp*

August 18, 1942
Graphite on paper
11 15⁄16 × 17 11⁄16 inches (30.4 × 45.0 cm)

Signed and dated in graphite, lower right: *Sumiko Kobayashi / 8/18/1942*

Sumiko Kobayashi Papers (additions) [MSS073A]
Gift of Sumiko Kobayashi, 1991–1992, 2003

At an age when many young American women were attending college, Sumiko Kobayashi found herself imprisoned in her own country because of the color of her skin, the shape of her eyes, and the land of her ancestry. In 1942, as US and Japanese forces battled in the Pacific, she became one of more than 120,000 Japanese Americans taken from their homes and confined to what the US government called internment camps, which some now label as concentration camps. Because fewer than 12,000 Caucasian German Americans were placed in these detention facilities, the World War II camps have become a symbol of racism against Asian Americans.

Franklin D. Roosevelt's administration adopted this policy in response to public fears that those of Japanese descent might be spies for their ancestral land. As a result, the government seized both Japanese Americans and Japanese permanent resident aliens in California, Washington, Oregon, and parts of Arizona.

A second-generation Japanese American, Kobayashi and her family were first taken to the Tanforan Assembly Center in San Bruno, California, and later to the Topaz Relocation Center in Utah. During her time in both places, she drew sketches of her surroundings, including this one, which shows the barracks at the Topaz camp.

Born in 1923 at Yamato, a Japanese agricultural camp near Palm Beach, Florida, Kobayashi spent part of her childhood in Geneva, Illinois, before the family settled in San Leandro, California, where she graduated from high school in 1941. A year later, authorities sent her family away from their home and into the camp system.

While at Topaz, she received assistance from the National Japanese American Student Relocation Council, which helped young detainees achieve admission to college, win scholarships, and find jobs to cover their expenses. In 1943, she applied to colleges and was able to leave the camp

to attend Brothers College, Drew University, in Madison, New Jersey.

Her family was released from Topaz in May 1944. They first moved to Connecticut and later settled near Philadelphia. Sumiko joined them in 1947. She held several jobs in the city, including work at the Franklin Institute Research Labs Computer Center. Ironically, the US Army Corps of Engineers employed her in Japan from 1952 to 1954. She later worked for Provident National Bank and finally joined FMC Corporation, an agricultural sciences company, where she remained until her retirement in 1985. She was redress chair of Pennsylvania's Japanese American League chapter, where she participated in the fight to win compensation for those who had been imprisoned. This effort came to fruition in 1988 when legislation offered an apology and $20,000 to each internee. ALICE L. GEORGE

Sumiko's sketches can be seen in the Historical Society of Pennsylvania's digital collection at https://digitallibrary.hsp.org/index.php/Detail/objects/11664. Related collections include the Sumiko Kobayashi Papers and those of her father, Susumu Kobayashi. Other detention camp prisoners whose papers can be found at the Historical Society of Pennsylvania include Shigezo and Sonoko Iwata and Saburo and Michiyo Inouye.

UNITED
we are strong
UNITED we will win
OWI Poster No. 64. Additional copies may be obtained upon request from the Division of Public Inquiries, Office of War Information, Washington, D. C.

## 92. **Henry Koerner** (1915–1991)

### *United We Are Strong, United We Will Win*

---

1943
Published by United States Government Printing Office
Halftone on paper
40 × 28 ½ inches (101.6 × 72.4 cm)

Inscribed within image, along barrel with Norwegian flag: *KOERNER*; below image, lower left: *OWI Poster No. 64. Additional copies may be obtained upon request from the Division of Public Inquiries, Office of War Information, Washington, D.C.*; below image, lower right: ☆ *U.S. GOVERNMENT PRINTING OFFICE: 1943—O—527286*

Historical Society of Pennsylvania War Posters Collection [V95]

In the two world wars, the US government hammered home its message with posters that encouraged sacrifice, unity, and bravery. In this example, taken from the Historical Society of Pennsylvania's War Posters Collection, the message is clear: The likelihood of victory in this global conflict depends not on a single nation but on an alliance that can topple the Axis powers of Germany, Japan, and Italy.

This 1943 poster produced by the Office of War Information shows flag-draped artillery guns representing Norway, the United Kingdom, the United States, China, the Soviet Union, and Australia—the nations traditionally labeled as "the Allies." By this point in the war, the tide had begun to shift in the Allies' favor, particularly after the 1942 Soviet success in driving back the Germans from Moscow and the Allies' May 1943 victory over the Germans in North Africa. Still two years from its conclusion, the war continued to claim lives on many fronts, including an Allied invasion of France, carpet bombing of cities in Europe and Japan, the Battle of the Bulge, and US use of atomic bombs in Hiroshima and Nagasaki. The Allies achieved victory in Europe on May 8, 1945, and in the Pacific on August 15, 1945. War posters reflect the nation's efforts to proliferate important messages in an age before television and the Internet provided Americans with opportunities for multiplexing information twenty-four hours a day.

HSP's War Posters Collection holds over five hundred original posters from World War I and II. Included among World War I examples are images promoting the Liberty Loan, the American Red Cross, and the US Food Administration. The World War II group represents a wide array of government bodies, including the War Production Board, the US Shipping Board, the Emergency Fleet Corporation, the US Coast Guard, the US Coast Guard Women's Reserve, the YWCA, the Women's Land Army, and all branches of the military. These posters cover rationing, enlistment, war bonds, vigilance, and conservation of resources. Some feature the work of renowned artists, including Norman Rockwell, Albert Dorne, James Montgomery Flagg, E. McKnight Kauffer, David Stone Martin, Ben Shahn, and Frederick Siebel. HSP's staff compiled this collection from donations and purchases.

ALICE L. GEORGE

---

Similar works can be found in the Balch Institute Ethnic Posters Collection, the Historical Society of Pennsylvania Poster and Broadside Collection, and the Work Projects Administration Posters Collection.

# 93. *The Balch Institute Ethnic Newspapers*

*Εθνικός Κήρυξ (Ethnikos Kyrix)*
January 30, 1923
17 5/16 × 10 5/8 inches (44.0 × 29.5 cm)

The Balch Institute Newspapers

*Korean Independence*
December 21, 1949
18 11/16 × 12 3/4 inches (47.5 × 32.5 cm)

The Balch Institute Newspapers

ΕΘΝΙΚΟΣ ΚΗΡΥΞ

ΣΥΝΤΑΓΜΑΤΑΡΧΗΣ ΠΛΑΣΤΗΡΑΣ ΕΦΘΑΣΕΝ ΕΙΣ ΤΗΝ ΛΩΖΑΝΝΗΝ

ΣΥΡΡΑΞΙΣ ΜΕΤΑΞΥ ΓΕΡΜΑΝΩΝ ΚΑΙ ΓΑΛΛΩΝ

ΔΙΑ ΤΟ ΨΩΜΙ ΤΩΝ ΟΡΦΑΝΩΝ

Σήμερον $416.15

ΜΗΝΙΑΙΟΥ ΕΙΚΟΝΟΓΡΑΦΗΜΕΝΟΥ ΕΘΝΙΚΟΥ ΚΗΡΥΚΟΣ

Korean Independence

Premier Kim Il Sung of Korea Urges:

Koreans, Unite For Peace!

'The Current Of History Can Be Determined Only By The People's Strength'

In the 1980s and 1990s, thousands of Philadelphia public school students each year visited the Balch Institute of Ethnics Studies as part of class trips. Crowds of other residents and tourists joined them in viewing well-curated and compelling exhibits on immigration, diaspora communities, and the role of race and ethnicity in US history. A devoted team of docents provided classroom presentations and tours of displays in permanent and special exhibition spaces. Scholars also entered the Balch Institute, a six-story building on Seventh Street just below Market; they headed to the library to utilize a growing collection of manuscript records illuminating the experiences of more than eighty immigrant groups.

The Estate of Emily Swift Balch, matriarch of a prominent Philadelphia family, provided the financial base for the founding of the Balch Institute of Ethnic Studies. She had created a trust fund for her two sons, but they predeceased her. After her death, the Balch Estate remained in limbo until trustees petitioned the Orphans' Court of Philadelphia to apply the funds to create a center of learning (as requested by remaining members of the Balch family). The presiding judge stipulated that the center be dedicated to the history of immigration. Thus, the Balch Institute opened its doors in May of 1976.

A premier archival collection was assembled from scratch, and popular special exhibits were mounted—the last set focused on the history of Philadelphia's Chinatown and new communities of immigrants from Latin America, the Middle East, and Africa. Unfortunately by the late 1990s, the Balch Institute faced severe fiscal constraints and inadequate facilities to preserve its manuscript holdings. The latter became a top priority, and negotiations proceeded to merge the Balch archive with the collections of the Historical Society of Pennsylvania. The Balch Institute of Ethnic Studies closed its doors in 2002.

*El Mundo*
March 4, 1952
23 × 17 5/8 inches (58.6 × 44.8 cm)

The Balch Institute Newspapers

EL MUNDO

Constitución Triunfa Con 375,740 Votos
Hay 82,917 en Contra; 3,282 Protestados

Celebran Hoy Vista Sobre Ruiz Nazario

Congresistas Elogian el Proceso Electoral

Elección Fué Muy Rápida Y Ordenada

Creen Paquete Recibido Ayer Tiene Bomba

Drew Pearson Niega Muñoz Sea Dictador

*India Abroad*
November 2, 1984
16 5/8 × 11 1/2 inches (42.2 × 29.3 cm)

The Balch Institute Newspapers

2 Security Guards Open Fire Striking Premier 16 Times

Incident Takes Place at New Delhi Home; End Comes After 2-Hour Emergency Surgery On Bullet Wounds to Her Chest and Abdomen

India Abroad

INDIRA SHOT DEAD

Census Reports Indians In U.S. are Prosperous

Karnataka Chief Undergoes Biopsy for Throat in Boston

A Statistical Portrait of Asian Indians in the U.S.

MONTESSORI

FOODS OF INDIA

SINHA TRAVELS LTD.

HSP now holds one of the nation's most valuable research collections on immigration and the immigrant experience. The Balch Collections include the archives of other institutions, for example, the American Friends Service Committee (which contains 20,000 refugee case files), the Philadelphia Jewish Archive Center, and the Scotch-Irish Foundation Library. The collection is rich in the records of ethnic fraternal orders (such as the Russian Orthodox Mutual Aid Society), churches (such as the Estonian Evangelical Lutheran Church), and veteran's groups. Additionally, there are papers of leading figures in immigrant communities, including politicians, businessmen, educators, artists, and labor activists. Volumes of relevant pamphlets, broadsides, magazines, books, photographs, scrapbooks, sheet music, and radio program tapes are available for research.

Prominent in the Balch Collections are ethnic newspapers, 130 in all, printed in 30 languages, and published in 25 states (the holdings are particularly strong for the Pennsylvania anthracite region). The scope is notable: an African American newspaper from Charlestown, West Virginia, 1944–57; a Japanese American paper published in Denison, Arkansas, during the World War II period of Japanese American internment; and *La Prenza*, printed in Antonio, Texas, 1913–28, which uniquely reported on cross-border migration of Mexicans in the opening decades of the twentieth century. The newspapers are replete with personal announcements and stories and coverage of local church, recreational, and cultural events, but also with evidence of ongoing political mobilizations, labor organizing, and strong ties to homelands that is completely absent in the mainstream press. The Balch newspaper holdings at HSP take diaspora communities out of the shadows.

WALTER LICHT

## 94. Holy Redeemer Chinese Catholic Church

### *Basketball Game at Holy Redeemer*

1948
Gelatin silver print
$4\frac{15}{16} \times 7$ inches ($12.5 \times 17.9$ cm)

Holy Redeemer Chinese Catholic Church Photograph Collection
[PG120]
The Balch Institute, Gift of Holy Redeemer Chinese Catholic Church

When many people think about Chinese American culture, basketball may not be the first thing that comes to mind. But basketball is an integral part of Chinese American community life. Since 1981 teams from Chinatowns around the country vie yearly in a national championship, and regional tournaments existed as early as the 1930s. In Philadelphia's Chinatown, basketball has always been played in the basement gymnasium of the Holy Redeemer Chinese Catholic Church and School.

The first Chinese Catholic Church in the western hemisphere, Holy Redeemer opened at Tenth and Vine Streets in 1941 and quickly became an important institution in the Chinatown community, not only for worship but also because it provided the only school, playground, and gym in the neighborhood. Such spaces were critical for families raising children in a historically marginalized community adjacent to "Skid Row."

The youth club at Holy Redeemer was named for Bishop Paul Yu Pin, vicar of Nanking, China, whose visit in 1939 inspired the church's opening. The Yu Pin Club shaped the lives of generations of young Chinese Americans who grew up in Chinatown from the 1940s through the 1970s, hosting an annual Chinese New Year dance, various sports teams, and an annual field day. Many activities fostered relationships with Chinese clubs in other eastern cities, particularly New York and Washington, DC. The Yu Pin basketball team played all comers: groups in the city Catholic league and from other Chinatowns along the northeast coast, even a team composed entirely of local waiters.

Like other ethnic enclaves around the country, Philadelphia's Chinatown was threatened by urban renewal in the 1960s when plans for creating a crosstown expressway included the destruction of Holy Redeemer. Residents, many of them women and young people, organized a "Save Chinatown" movement that successfully protected the beloved church and went on to redevelop the area to serve the community's unique needs. Holy Redeemer was (and is) an important symbol of Chinatown "beyond the restaurants," the living neighborhood of families, schools, churches, playgrounds, and family associations that residents fought to defend.

The Holy Redeemer papers provide a window into the activities, values, and priorities of an ethnic community in the mid-twentieth century and are typical of the kinds of materials found in the Balch Institute for Ethnic Studies Collection. Merged with the Historical Society of Pennsylvania in 2002, the Balch Collection documents the immigrant experience of more than eighty ethnic groups in the United States, including African, African American, Chinese, German, Greek, Irish, Italian, Japanese, Polish, Puerto Rican, Slovak, and Ukrainian. Balch collections encompass materials related to ethnic mutual aid, political history, women's history, and labor history and include newspapers, pamphlets, and other printed materials. Many of these resources were created by ethnic groups themselves and document the activities and contributions to American life through the communities' own perspectives. KATHRYN E. WILSON

Further related information in the Historical Society of Pennsylvania archives can be found in the Jung Family Photographs, 1910–1960, Reverend Tam Tong Hoh Papers, Philadelphia Chinatown Development Corporation Papers, Mary E. Scott Chinese Sunday School, First Baptist Church, Philadelphia, Photographs, 1900–1944, *Yellow Seeds* Newspaper, 1972–1977, Rose Lanu Quong Papers, 1897–1972, and the Tsiwen Law Papers, 1984–1991.

# 95. *Albert M. Greenfield*

1955
Gelatin silver print
8 1/8 × 10 inches (20.7 × 25.4 cm)

Albert M. Greenfield Collection [1959]
Gift of Albert M. Greenfield Foundation, 1968

Albert M. Greenfield's remarkable career was much celebrated during his lifetime, not least by Greenfield himself. It was the story of a feisty and combative Russian immigrant who rose from Philadelphia office boy to ruler of an immense East Coast business empire, encompassing real estate, department stores, banks, hotels, newspapers, even the Loft Candy Corporation. It was also the story of a Jewish outsider who challenged Philadelphia's entrenched Protestant plutocrats and ultimately supplanted them as the favored confidant of mayors, governors, senators, and US presidents. While some Philadelphians perceived Greenfield as a cunning octopus, monopolizing and choking everything within the grasp of his many tentacles, Greenfield saw himself as a happy warrior, exuberantly harnessing the creative forces of a free society to shatter the antiquated structures of a repressive past.

For such a man, who reinvented himself half a dozen times, two factors were critical: high visibility and control over his narrative. As a driven young real estate broker at the turn of the twentieth century, Greenfield plastered his name across Philadelphia homes and office buildings. From the Ben Franklin Hotel (the world's largest when it opened in 1925) to the renewal of Society Hill (which he spearheaded in the mid-1950s), Greenfield changed not only Philadelphia's physical face but also its tentative soul. He violated social taboos with gleeful abandon—challenging Philadelphia's Republican political machine, forming alliances between Jews and Catholics, hiring the first Black drivers for the city's bus lines, and promoting women to executive positions. In the process, he helped transform Philadelphia from an exclusive oligarchy based largely on bloodlines into an inclusive meritocracy.

In his avuncular later years, Greenfield bequeathed his personal and business papers—more than a thousand boxes containing about 18,000 folders dating back to 1918—to the Historical Society of Pennsylvania. Greenfield intended to weed out any adverse items beforehand but never got around to it. Consequently, today any visitor to HSP can find such nuggets as letters to Greenfield from people claiming to have known him at Philadelphia's elite Central High School (which Greenfield falsely claimed to have attended), as well as personal notes from Greenfield attesting to his impatience with whiners and complainers ("I'm sorry Sophie isn't feeling well, but in a large family, there's always someone who isn't feeling well.")

In my definitive Greenfield biography (*The Outsider,* Temple University Press, 2013), I contended that Greenfield's legacy lies not in his peripatetic business deals, his civic activities, his political maneuvers, or his philanthropy, but in his cheerful refusal to accept such age-old obstacles to human progress as pessimism, timidity, prejudice, fear of immigrants, and resistance to change.

Future scholars who comb through those 1,000-plus boxes at HSP may reach different conclusions. Greenfield's papers have already inspired four other books on diverse subjects (including a biography of Greenfield's partner, the motion picture pioneer William Fox). Thanks to Greenfield's willingness to leave his papers to posterity, the task of understanding this extraordinary individual may have just begun.

DAN ROTTENBERG

NEWBURGER & CO.
THE JOB
SAM MILLER PHOTOGRAPHER

# 96. *Richardson Dilworth Speaking in Front of the Bellevue Hotel*

November 5, 1951
Gelatin silver print
7 15/16 × 9 13/16 inches (20.2 × 25.0 cm)

Inscribed verso in ink: *Day before election in front of Bellevue, 1951*

Richardson Dilworth Papers [3112]
Donated by Deborah D. Bishop, Louis G. Hill, Aubrey Lees, and the Estate of Richardson Dilworth

This 1951 photo captures key elements of one notably consequential year in Philadelphia's modern political history. Standing on the campaign car are Joseph Clark (right) and Richardson Dilworth (left), Democratic candidates for mayor and district attorney, respectively. The city's Democratic newspaper, the *Public Record*, had closed in 1947, making these campaign speeches critical. Yet the film camera in the photo suggests a further change: televisions, a novelty in the previous election cycle, were in 12 million American homes by 1951. The Clark-Dilworth campaign made effective use of the new medium. The photo also shows an almost entirely male audience, but closer to the car and facing the audience are a few of the many women who worked for the campaign (Dilworth's wife Ann is the woman farthest to the left) and who were crucial to its success.

Both candidates won their elections, making Clark the first Democratic mayor since 1881. Democrats also won every other citywide office and fourteen out of seventeen city council seats—a dramatic reversal for Philadelphia, which Republicans had dominated since the Civil War. Democrats' success in 1951 was the culmination of a local reform movement and a national party realignment, beginning with Franklin Roosevelt's election as president in 1932, even as Pennsylvania and Philadelphia remained Republican stalwarts. Philadelphia's dominant Republican party operated through a vast system of patronage and kickbacks, electoral fraud, and the genuine allegiance of voters—it was, after all, a manufacturing city that strongly favored Republican backing of a protectionist tariff. Yet Republicans' support was eroding. Municipal unionization, New Deal welfare programs and patronage that bypassed city officials, and a municipal budget ravaged by the Depression that required layoffs all decimated the Republican patronage machine.

After World War II, Philadelphia Democrats joined forces with a new generation of white-collar political activists, including Clark, Dilworth, Walter Phillips, and Edmund Bacon. Much of this activism was channeled through existing reform groups such as the Committee of Seventy, the Economy League of Pennsylvania, and the Philadelphia Bureau of Municipal Research (PBMR). But there also were new organizations, such as the City Policy Committee; the uniquely influential Greater Philadelphia Movement (GPM), a council of business leaders; and the Philadelphia chapter of Americans for Democratic Action, where white collar reformers joined with Democratic party regulars, labor unions, and intellectuals. There were also increasingly influential civil rights groups, such as the Philadelphia Fellowship Commission, that allied with the reformers, reflecting the growing discontent of the city's swelling Black population.

The GPM, PBMR, and Economy League used a blue-ribbon committee organized by Mayor Bernard Samuel to investigate and report on gross inefficiencies and criminal corruption in city government, leading to dismissals, arrests, indictments, suicides, further investigations, and a wave of negative publicity that provided a window of opportunity for reformers. Thus in 1949 Dilworth was elected city treasurer, Clark was elected controller, and Democrats won several other offices, thereby setting the stage for the 1951 party realignment and establishing the Democratic city we know today. RICHARDSON DILWORTH

# 97. *Charlotte Ives Montgomery at Ardrossan*

ca. 1930
Gelatin silver print
6 ⅞ × 9 inches (17.5 × 23.0 cm)

Montgomery, Scott, and Wheeler Families Papers [4470]
Gift of the Montgomery, Scott, and Wheeler families, 2021

In the years leading up to World War I, a young Philadelphia investment banker, Robert L. Montgomery (1879–1949), and his wife, Charlotte H. B. Tyler Montgomery (1881–1970), heir to a Philadelphia business and banking fortune, began piecing together a country estate in the farmland rolling west from the city. Wealthy Philadelphians, grown rich on the profits from steel and department stores and locomotives, were buying land along the Pennsylvania Railroad's Main Line and building mansions replete with crenelated walls, banquet halls, and porte cocheres. In the decades that followed, the Montgomerys' nearly eight-hundred-acre expanse in Villanova, called Ardrossan, came to exemplify the insular, leisured world of the WASP establishment—a world of horses and hounds, charity balls, society weddings, summer "cottages" in Maine, and, in the Montgomerys' case, a dairy herd of three hundred Ayrshire cows. Horace Trumbauer (1868–1938), whose architectural firm would go on to design the Philadelphia Museum of Art and Widener Library at Harvard, made for the Montgomerys a fifty-room, English Renaissance Revival–style house, around which would eventually orbit three generations of descendants, ensconced in fieldstone farmhouses, along with the families of their Irish immigrant retainers. The eldest of the Montgomerys' children, Helen Hope, married an heir to a Pennsylvania Railroad fortune, Edgar Scott. In 1929, Scott would found, with his father-in-law, Montgomery, Scott & Company, a forerunner of the stock brokerage Janney Montgomery Scott. Playwright Philip Barry would dedicate his 1939 play, *The Philadelphia Story*, to Helen Hope and Edgar, having borrowed from Ardrossan much of the play's setting and from Helen Hope some of the inspiration for the character of Tracy Lord, whom Katharine Hepburn would immortalize on Broadway and in the film that followed. Ardrossan—the history and cultural significance of which can be traced in this collection of family papers, letters, photographs, diaries, scrapbooks, invoices, and other documents donated to the Historical Society of Pennsylvania—remained intact until Helen Hope's death in 1995 at age ninety-one. It had outlasted nearly every other Main Line estate of its day.

In this photograph, Charlotte Ives Montgomery (1912–1981), the youngest of the Montgomery children and an accomplished horsewoman, appears on the lawn of "the big house" in fox-hunting attire, with Trumbauer's stone-trimmed gables and Palladian dormers in the background. Many decades later, Robert Montgomery Scott (1929–2005), a Montgomery grandson and newly retired president and chief executive officer of the Philadelphia Museum of Art, spent years meticulously restoring the exterior and much of the interior of the house. Draperies were reproduced, furniture reupholstered, needlepoint seat covers refurbished, light fixtures rewired, silk damask wall coverings rewoven, and walnut paneling returned to mint condition. The project, paid for largely out of his own pocket, was an act of love for a house he did not own. After the restoration's completion, Scott died at age seventy-six.

JANNY SCOTT

# 98. *Portrait of John Fryer*

ca. 2000
Inkjet print
4 7/8 × 5 inches (12.4 × 12.5 cm)

John Fryer Papers [3465]
Gift of Kathy Fryer Helmbock, 2003

## **John Fryer** (1937–2003)

## *Speech to the American Psychiatric Association*

May 2, 1972
Manuscript; ink on yellow paper
11 1/8 × 8 1/2 inches (28.2 × 21.6 cm)

John Fryer Papers [3465]
Gift of Kathy Fryer Helmbock, 2003

With eight words ("I am a homosexual. I am a psychiatrist.") Dr. John Fryer, a Philadelphia psychiatrist, began a process that would tumble American laws, impact the collecting scope and programming of the Historical Society of Pennsylvania, and change the lives of millions of gay men and lesbians around the world.

Fryer was on the faculty of Temple University's school of medicine when he addressed the American Psychiatric Association in 1972. However, since the APA's own *Diagnostic and Statistical Manual of Mental Disorders* (DSM) listed homosexuality as a mental illness (and there were scarce legal protections for gay men and lesbians), Fryer made his speech wearing a mask and bulky clothes to alter his appearance and using a special microphone to distort his voice. He declared himself to be both gay and an APA member. Based in part on his testimony, the APA removed homosexuality from the DSM the following year. However, it took more than a year for discriminatory laws to follow suit. If gays and lesbians were not, literally, crazy, why was it legal to discriminate against them? Finally in 2003, with *Lawrence v. Texas*, the Supreme Court decriminalized homosexuality. In 2010 Congress repealed the gay military ban. In 2015, the Supreme Court struck down all state bans on same-sex marriage with *Obergefell v. Hodges*. The Supreme Court, with *Bostock v. Clayton County*, ruled in 2020 that the Civil Rights Act of 1964 also covered homosexuality and gender identity. Homosexuality was no longer a crime, the military and marriage bans were overturned, and employment rights were upheld—all because gay men and lesbians were no longer considered mentally ill.

At the Historical Society of Pennsylvania, the 1990s began to see changes that reflected the larger gay rights movement. HSP has always held archival items of gay men and lesbians: Walt Whitman, Alice Paul, and Ludwig II, among others. But they were never identified or promoted bibliographically as such. Then HSP began to catalogue its uncatalogued serials. They found early issues of *Drum*, a gay pride magazine first published in Philadelphia in 1964, and started to document local gay community activity by collecting newsletters and miscellaneous archival material. But nothing prepared them for the seventy-six linear feet of John Fryer's papers in 2004. This was something truly momentous.

In the late 2000s, HSP began to participate in the Artist Embedded project funded by the Pew Center for Arts & Heritage. Writer and director Ain Gordon spent two years at HSP combing Fryer's 217-box archive as the basis for his original play *217 Boxes of Dr. Anonymous*. It debuted in Philadelphia in 2016, then performed in New York in 2018 and Los Angeles in 2019.

For HSP staff, personally, the changes of 2003, 2010, 2015, and 2020 were most notable in that staff (both active and former) were able to finally marry their long-term partners legally. It really all comes down to dignity and respect. It's just a shame it took forty-seven years to get there.

LEE ARNOLD

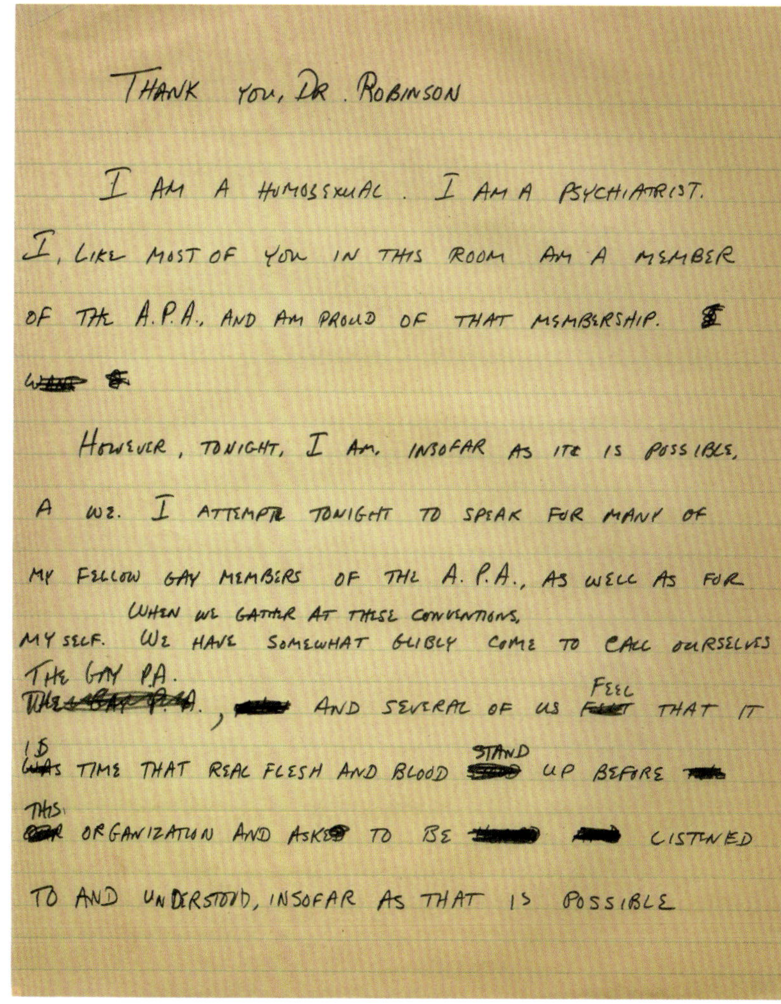
THANK YOU, DR. ROBINSON

I AM A HOMOSEXUAL. I AM A PSYCHIATRIST.
I, LIKE MOST OF YOU IN THIS ROOM AM A MEMBER OF THE A.P.A. AND AM PROUD OF THAT MEMBERSHIP.

HOWEVER, TONIGHT, I AM, INSOFAR AS IT IS POSSIBLE, A WE. I ATTEMPT TONIGHT TO SPEAK FOR MANY OF MY FELLOW GAY MEMBERS OF THE A.P.A., AS WELL AS FOR MYSELF. WHEN WE GATHER AT THESE CONVENTIONS, WE HAVE SOMEWHAT GLIBLY COME TO CALL OURSELVES THE GAY PA., AND SEVERAL OF US FEEL THAT IT IS TIME THAT REAL FLESH AND BLOOD STAND UP BEFORE THIS ORGANIZATION AND ASK TO BE LISTENED TO AND UNDERSTOOD, INSOFAR AS THAT IS POSSIBLE

Other notable gay and lesbian materials at the Historical Society of Pennsylvania include: *Center City Magazine,* Philadelphia: Center City Magazine, 1980; *Drum,* Philadelphia: Janus Society, 1964; *The Gay Alternative,* Philadelphia: Gay Activists Alliance, 1972; Lou Meehan, *Barbara Gittings at "Crossroads"* (photograph), Philadelphia: Historical Society of Pennsylvania, 1994 [Society Portrait Collection]; *New Gay Life,* Philadelphia: Spruce Street Press, 1977; and Donald Vining, *Donald Vining* (typescript) *Diary* [Am .137452].

## 99. **Tony Auth** (1942–2014)

### *Gave Proof Through the Night that our Flag Was Still There*

---

1972
Ink and gesso on paper
11 × 14 15⁄16 inches (27.9 × 38.0 cm)

Signed upper left: *Philadelphia Inquirer / Auth*

Historical Society of Pennsylvania Medium Graphics Collection [V64]

As US bombs lit up the night sky in Vietnam during 1972, the *Philadelphia Inquirer*'s editorial cartoonist Tony Auth was reminded of another war in which a fragile, new nation struggled to defend its independence. In 1814, Francis Scott Key anxiously watched British forces attack Baltimore's Fort McHenry during the War of 1812. The early nineteenth-century scene prompted Key to write the lyrics of the United States' national anthem, "The Star-Spangled Banner" **(no. 54)**. Auth's cartoon draws a connection between Key's observations and the situation that many Vietnamese citizens experienced.

During 1972, the United States pummeled North Vietnam and Viet Cong bases in South Vietnam as President Richard Nixon tried to force the North Vietnamese to negotiate a peace settlement. By this time, Nixon had reduced the number of US servicemen in Vietnam by more than fifty percent since taking office in 1969. Nevertheless, he stood firm on the need to maintain aerial bombing, which was intended to generate fear as much as devastation. The attacks sparked protest marches across the United States. The year 1972 ended with a post-Christmas flourish that included the war's largest B-52 strike, with 120 bombers hammering North Vietnam.

The Historical Society of Pennsylvania's collection of cartoons and caricatures covers a period beginning in the mid-eighteenth century and continues through the 1970s. The first known American political cartoon appeared in 1754 when Benjamin Franklin published the famous image of a segmented snake with the words "Join or Die." At the time, Franklin was attempting to draw the colonies together to fight the French and Indian War. The cartoon found new life over a decade later as the possibility of a revolution began to crystallize because of growing discontent with British rule among the thirteen colonies. Technological advances enabled newspapers and periodicals to expand their use of cartoons in the nineteenth century. As geographical divisions deepened around the time of the Civil War and Reconstruction, the images became more caustic. The majority of cartoons in HSP's collection date from that period. Ranging from small to oversized, they are predominantly in English, although a few are in French. This collection assembled by HSP staff members also includes uncatalogued materials gathered by the Balch Institute for Ethnic Studies.

Auth's cartoons have been collected and published in two books. He started his career as a biological illustrator in 1965 while producing editorial cartoons for an alternative newspaper. *The Inquirer* hired him in 1971, and his work served as a centerpiece on the paper's editorial pages for over forty years, winning him a Pulitzer Prize in 1976. He left the newspaper in March 2012 to provide work for an online editorial website. Auth died in 2014. ALICE L. GEORGE

The J. Hampton Moore Papers contain a large collection of political cartoons, and other cartoons are part of the Historical Society of Pennsylvania's graphics collection

# 100. *Angela Davis Urges – Declare Your Independence: Vote for Hall and Tyner*

1976
Published by Communist Party of the United States of America
Offset lithograph on paper
22 ¼ × 15 ½ inches (56.5 × 39.4 cm)

Inscribed within image: *Angela Davis urges- / Declare your Independence / Vote for Hall and Tyner*; below Declaration of Independence: *Hoffman '76*; lower center: *Issued by: Hall-Tyner Election Campaign Committee, 156 Fifth Ave., Suite 1100, NYC 10010 / '76 Campaign Souvenir - $1.00*

Thelma McDaniel Collection [3063]
Purchase, 2003

The message is strong: "Declare Your Independence," and the face of African American activist Angela Davis (born 1944) adds power to that battle cry, which endorsed the Communist Party's 1976 presidential election ticket. This poster, along with many other traces of mid-twentieth-century American activist campaigns, resides in the Thelma McDaniel Collection at the History Society of Pennsylvania. From 1935 to 1989, McDaniel collected pamphlets, flyers, newspapers, and posters that reflected left-leaning causes, including Black power, African solidarity, and communism.

Pressure for equal rights grew in the 1930s, especially in the wake of the unjust 1931 imprisonment of nine African American youths charged with rape in Scottsboro, Alabama. The teens were accused of attacking two white women on a freight train. Following their initial convictions, the Communist Party joined the case, fighting for the defendants' rights. Later, civil rights leaders also supported them. The Scottsboro 9 faced more than a decade of court battles before all were freed. Despite repeated convictions by Alabama juries, each ultimately was cleared. The great sense of injustice within the Black community helped to kindle expanded activism that reached its peak in the mid-1950s through the early 1970s.

This poster highlights a fiery activist who stepped into the spotlight in the late 1960s. After spending her youth in segregated Birmingham, Alabama, Angela Davis attended Brandeis University. As a graduate student at the University of California at San Diego, she joined several radical organizations, including the Black Panthers and the Che-Lumumba Club, an all-Black section within the Communist Party. She became a professor at UCLA, but because of her political activities, she clashed with the university administration and was fired. She regained her job in court but left UCLA in 1970.

That same year she became a supporter of three African American inmates, known as the Soledad Brothers, who were accused of killing a white prison guard. During inmate George Lester Johnson's trial, his brother, Jonathan, took the courtroom hostage in hopes of freeing his accused brother and others. A superior court judge and two inmates died in the shootout that followed. Because Johnson used weapons apparently registered to Davis, she was suspected of complicity and went into hiding. She became one of the FBI's Most Wanted before being captured two months later. She faced several charges, including murder, and spent eighteen months in prison before her acquittal in June 1972.

In the poster she is endorsing the ticket of Gus Hall and Jarvis Turner, who attracted about 60,000 votes. In 1980 and 1984, Davis herself was the Communist Party's vice-presidential candidate, with Hall still holding the ticket's top spot. Neither campaign equaled the 1976 contest's vote total.

Though little is known about the poster's donor, Thelma McDaniel, her collection offers a window into a time of volatility and public advocacy. ALICE L. GEORGE

---

In the Historical Society of Pennsylvania archives, the Justine J. Rector Papers also follow the fight for African American rights, beginning in the late 1960s. Rector, who was active in both journalism and politics, founded the African American Male Resource Center.

# Selected Bibliography


Baltzell, E. Digby. *Philadelphia Gentlemen: The Making of a National Upper Class*. Philadelphia: University of Pennsylvania Press, 1958.

Bartram, William. *Travels through North and South Carolina, Georgia, East and West Florida, the Cherokee Country, the Extensive Territories of the Muscogulges or Creek Confederacy, and the Country of the Chactaws. Containing an Account of the Soil and Natural Productions of Those Regions; Together with Observations on the Manners of the Indians*. Philadelphia: James & Johnson, 1791.

Bell, Richard. *We Shall Be No More: Suicide and Self-Government in the Newly United States*. Cambridge, MA: Harvard University Press, 2012.

Bellion, Wendy. *Citizen Spectator: Art, Illusion, and Visual Perception in Early National America*. Chapel Hill: Published by the Omohundro Institute of Early American History and Culture by the University of North Carolina Press, 2011.

Beveridge, Albert J. *Abraham Lincoln, 1809–1858*. 2 vols. Boston: Houghton-Mifflin, 1928.

Blackett, R. J. M. *The Captive's Quest for Freedom: Fugitive Slaves, the 1850 Fugitive Slave Law, and the Politics of Slavery*. New York: Cambridge University Press, 2018.

Blakney, Sharece, et al. *Stories We Know: Recording the Black History of Bartram's Garden and Southwest Philadelphia*. Edited by Aislinn Pentecost-Farren. Philadelphia: The John Bartram Association and Mural Arts Philadelphia, 2017.

Bourque, Monique, and R. Joseph Anderson. *A Guide to Manuscript and Microfilm Collections of the Research Library of the Balch Institute for Ethnic Studies*. Philadelphia: Balch Institute for Ethnic Studies, 1992.

Boyd, Julian P. "The Declaration of Independence: The Mystery of the Lost Original." *Pennsylvania Magazine of History and Biography* 100, no. 4 (Oct. 1976): 438–67.

Branson, Susan. *"Those Fiery Frenchified Dames": Women, Politics, and Culture in Early National Philadelphia*. Philadelphia: University of Pennsylvania Press, 2008.

Braund, Kathryn H., ed. *"The Attention of a Traveller": Essays on William Bartram's Travels and Legacy*. Tuscaloosa: University of Alabama Press. 2022.

Brigham, David R. *Public Culture in the Early Republic: Peale's Museum and Its Audience*. Washington, DC: Smithsonian Institution Press, 1995.

Brinton, Daniel G. *A Lenape-English Dictionary*. Philadelphia: Historical Society of Pennsylvania, 1889.

Brown, John K. *The Baldwin Locomotive Works, 1881–1915: A Study in American Industrial Practice*. Studies in Industry and Society, series edited by Philip B. Scranton. Baltimore: Johns Hopkins University Press, 1995.

Brownlee, David B. *Building the City Beautiful: The Benjamin Franklin Parkway and the Philadelphia Museum of Art*. 2nd ed. Philadelphia: Philadelphia Museum of Art, 2017.

Cohen, Steve. "Unfairly Maligned: The Glory Years and Beyond for Philadelphia's Academy of Music." *Totaltheater.com* (Aug. 2003). https://totaltheater.com/?q=node/467.

Covello, Leonard. *The Heart is the Teacher*. New York: McGraw-Hill, 1958.

Davis, Emilie Frances. *Emilie Davis's Civil War: The Diaries of a Free Black Woman in Philadelphia, 1863–1865*. Edited by Judith Giesberg. University Park: Pennsylvania State University Press, 2014.

Davis, Susan G. *Parades and Power: Street Theatre in Nineteenth-Century Philadelphia*. Berkeley: University of California Press, 1986.

Doerflinger, Thomas M. *A Vigorous Spirit of Enterprise: Merchants and Economic Development in Revolutionary*

*Philadelphia*. Chapel Hill: University of North Carolina Press, 1986. Published for the Omohundro Institute of Early American History and Culture, Williamsburg, VA.

Drinker, Elizabeth Sandwith. *The Diary of Elizabeth Drinker.* Edited by Elaine Forman Crane. Boston: Northeastern University Press, 1991.

Dunbar, Erica Armstrong. *A Fragile Freedom: African American Women and Emancipation in the Antebellum City*. New Haven, CT: Yale University Press, 2008.

Ebert-Schifferer, Sybille. *Deceptions and Illusions: Five Centuries of Trompe l'Oeil Painting.* Washington, DC: National Gallery of Art, 2002.

Erben, Patrick M. *A Harmony of the Spirits: Translation and the Language of Community in Early Pennsylvania*. Chapel Hill: University of North Carolina Press, 2012. Published for the Omohundro Institute of Early American History and Culture, Williamsburg, VA.

Fahs, Alice. *The Imagined Civil War: Popular Literature of the North & South, 1861–1865*. Chapel Hill: University of North Carolina Press, 2001.

Faulkner, Carol. *Lucretia Mott's Heresy: Abolition and Women's Rights in Nineteenth-Century America*. Philadelphia: University of Pennsylvania Press, 2011.

Foner, Eric. *Free Soil, Free Labor, Free Men: The Ideology of the Republican Party*. New York: Oxford University Press, 1995.

———. *Gateway to Freedom: The Hidden History of the Underground Railroad*. New York: W. W. Norton & Co., 2015.

Freehling, William W. *The Road to Disunion*. Vol. 2, *Secessionists Triumphant, 1854–1861*. New York: Oxford University Press, 2007.

Fry, Joel, ed. *Bartram's Garden Catalogue of North American Plants, 1783*, Special Issue, *Journal of Garden History* 16, no. 1 (1996).

Garvan, Beatrice B. "An East Prospect of the City of Philadelphia." In *Philadelphia: Three Centuries of American Art.* Edited by Darrel Sewell. Philadelphia: Philadelphia Museum of Art, 1976.

Gonzalez, Aston. "The Art of Racial Politics: The Work of Robert Douglass Jr., 1833–46." *The Pennsylvania Magazine of History and Biography* 138, no. 1 (Jan. 2014): 5–37.

Gough, Deborah Mathias. *Christ Church, Philadelphia: The Nation's Church in a Changing City*. Philadelphia: University of Pennsylvania Press, 1995.

Heath, Andrew. *In Union There Is Strength: Philadelphia in the Age of Consolidation*. Philadelphia: University of Pennsylvania Press, 2019.

Heinrich, Thomas R. *Ships for the Seven Seas: Philadelphia Shipbuilding in the Age of Industrial Capitalism*. Baltimore: Johns Hopkins University Press, 1997.

Hill, Draper, ed. *The Satirical Etchings of James Gillray.* New York: Dover Publications, 1976.

Johanek, Michael C., and John L. Puckett. *Leonard Covello and the Making of Benjamin Franklin High School: Education as if Citizenship Mattered*. Philadelphia: Temple University Press, 2007.

Kammen, Michael. *A Machine that Would Go of Itself: The Constitution in American History*. New York: St. Martin's Press, 1994.

Lanmon, Lorraine. "American Caricature in the English Tradition: The Personal and Political Satires of William Charles." *Winterthur Portfolio* 11 (1976): 1–52.

———. "William Charles and His War of 1812 Caricatures." In *Philadelphia Printmaking: American Prints Before 1860*, edited by Robert F. Looney, 93–98. West Chester, PA: Tinicum Press, 1976.

Lapsansky-Werner, Emma J. *The Black Presence in Pennsylvania: "Making it Home."* University Park: Pennsylvania Historical Association, 2001.

Laurie, Bruce. *Working People of Philadelphia, 1800–1850*. Philadelphia: Temple University Press, 1980.

Lawson, Melinda. *Patriot Fires: Forging a New American Nationalism in the Civil War North*. Lawrence: University of Kansas Press, 2002.

Lewis, Michael J. *Philadelphia Builds.* Philadelphia: Paul Dry, 2021.

Library Company of Philadelphia and Historical Society of Pennsylvania. *Afro-Americana, 1553–1906*. 2nd ed. New Castle, DE: Oak Knoll Press, 2008.

Licht, Walter. *Getting Work: Philadelphia 1840–1950*. Cambridge, MA: Harvard University Press, 1992.

———. *Working for the Railroad: The Organization of Work in the Nineteenth Century*. Princeton, NJ: Princeton University Press, 1983.

Lyons, Claire A. *Sex Among the Rabble: An Intimate History of Gender & Power in the Age of Revolution, Philadelphia*. Chapel Hill: University of North Carolina Press, 2006.

Manion, Jen. *Liberty's Prisoners: Carceral Culture in Early America*. Philadelphia: University of Pennsylvania Press, 2015.

McCabe, James D. *The Illustrated History of the Centennial Exhibition*. Philadelphia: The National Publishing Company, 1876.

McKee, Guian A. *The Problem of Jobs, Race, and Deindustrialization in Philadelphia*. Chicago: University of Chicago Press, 2008.

Meyers, Amy, ed. *Knowing Nature: Art and Science in Philadelphia, 1740–1840*. With Lisa Ford. New Haven, CT: Yale University Press, 2011.

Milroy, Elizabeth. *The Grid & the River: Philadelphia's Green Places, 1682–1876*. University Park: Pennsylvania State University Press, 2016.

Mires, Charlene. *Independence Hall in American Memory*. Philadelphia: University of Pennsylvania Press, 2002.

Nash, Gary B. *First City: Philadelphia and the Forging of Historical Memory*. Philadelphia: University of Pennsylvania Press, 2002.

———. *Forging Freedom: The Formation of Philadelphia's Black Community, 1720–1840*. Cambridge, MA: Harvard University Press, 1988.

Newman, Richard S. *Freedom's Prophet: Bishop Richard Allen, the AME Church, and the Black Founding Fathers*. New York: New York University Press, 2008.

———. *The Transformation of American Abolitionism: Fighting Slavery in the Early Republic*. Chapel Hill and London: The University of North Carolina Press, 2002.

Parker, Peter J. "Plan of Philadelphia." In *Philadelphia: Three Centuries of American Art*, edited by Darrel Sewell. Philadelphia: Philadelphia Museum of Art, 1976.

Paskoff, Paul F. *Industrial Evolution: Organization, Structure, and Growth of the Pennsylvania Iron Industry, 1750–1860*.

Studies in Industry and Society, edited by Glenn Porter. Baltimore and London: Johns Hopkins University Press, 1983.
Pencak, William A., and Daniel K. Richter, eds. *Friends and Enemies in Penn's Woods: Indians, Colonists, and the Racial Construction of Pennsylvania*. University Park: Pennsylvania State University Press, 2004.
Powell, Richard J. *Cutting a Figure: Fashioning Black Portraiture*. Chicago: University of Chicago Press, 2019.
Rawls, Walton. *Wake Up America: World War I and the American Poster.* New York: Abbeville, 1988.
Rilling, Donna. *Making Houses, Crafting Capitalism: Builders in Philadelphia, 1790–1850*. Philadelphia: University of Pennsylvania Press, 2001.
Roberts, Cokie. *Founding Mothers: The Women Who Raised Our Nation*. New York: William Morrow, 2004.
Rudolph, William Keyse, and Carol Eaton Soltis. *Thomas Sully: Painted Performance*. Milwaukee: Milwaukee Art Museum, 2013. Distributed by Yale University Press.
Salvatore, Nick. *We All Got History: The Memory Books of Amos Webber*. New York: Times Books, 1996.
Scharf, J. Thomas, and Thompson Westcott. *History of Philadelphia, 1609–1884*. 3 vols. Philadelphia: L. H. Everts, 1884.
Scranton, Philip. *Figured Tapestry: Production, Markets, and Power in Philadelphia Textiles, 1885–1941*. New York: Cambridge University Press, 1989.
———. *Proprietary Capitalism: The Textile Manufacture at Philadelphia, 1800–1885*. Philadelphia: Temple University Press, 1983.
Scranton, Philip, and Walter Licht. *Work Sights: Industrial Philadelphia, 1890–1950*. Philadelphia: Temple University Press, 1986.
Sewell, Darrell, et al. *Philadelphia: Three Centuries of American Art.* Philadelphia: Philadelphia Museum of Art, 1976.
Shepherd, William R. *History of Proprietary Government in Pennsylvania*. New York: Columbia University Press, 1896.
Sinha, Manisha. *The Slave's Cause: A History of Abolition*. New Haven, CT: Yale University Press, 2016.
Smith, Billy G., ed. *Down and Out in Early America*. University Park: Pennsylvania State University Press, 2004.
———. *The "Lower Sort": Philadelphia's Laboring People, 1750–1800*. Ithaca, NY: Cornell University Press, 1990.
Snyder, Martin P. "The Contracted Scull and Heap East Prospect, 1756." In *City of Independence: Views of Philadelphia Before 1800.* New York: Praeger, 1975.
Soderland, Jean. *William Penn and the Founding of Pennsylvania: A Documentary History*. Philadelphia: University of Pennsylvania Press/Historical Society of Pennsylvania, 1983.
Spady, James G. "The Afro-American Historical Society: The Nucleus of Black Bibliophiles, (1897–1923)." *Negro History Bulletin* 37, no. 4 (June/July 1974): 254–57.
Stampp, Kenneth M. *America in 1857: A Nation on the Brink.* New York: Oxford University Press, 1990.
Stieverman, Jan, and Oliver Scheiding. *A Peculiar Mixture: German-Language Cultures and Identities in Eighteenth-Century North America*. University Park: Pennsylvania State University Press, 2013.
Tatum, George B. *Penn's Great Town: 250 Years of Philadelphia Architecture Illustrated in Prints and Drawings*. Philadelphia: University of Pennsylvania Press, 1961.
Varon, Elizabeth R. *Disunion: The Coming of the American Civil War, 1789–1859*. Chapel Hill: University of North Carolina Press, 2008.
Verplanck, Anne. "The Silhouette and Quaker Identity in Early National Philadelphia." *Winterthur Portfolio* 43, no. 1 (Spring 2009): 41–78.
Vitiello, Domenic. *The Sellers Family and the Industrial Metropolis*. Ithaca, NY: Cornell University Press, 2013.
Von Erffa, Helmut, and Allen Staley. *The Paintings of Benjamin West*. New Haven, CT: Yale University Press, 1986.
Wadwhani, R. Daniel. "The Philadelphia Saving Fund Society and the Culture of Thrift in 19th-Century Pennsylvania." *Legacies* 12, no. 2 (Nov. 2012): 6–11.
Wallace, Anthony. *Rockdale: The Growth of an American Village in the Early Industrial Revolution*. New York: Knopf, 1977.
Wainwright, Nicholas B. *Philadelphia in the Romantic Age of Lithography*. Philadelphia: Historical Society of Pennsylvania, 1958.
Walters, Kerry. "'All Equally Dear to God': William Bartram's Antislavery Manuscript." In *William Bartram: The Search for Nature's Design*, edited by Thomas Hallock and Nancy E. Hoffman, 372–80. Athens: University of Georgia Press, 2010.
Warner, Sam Bass. *The Private City: Philadelphia in Three Periods of its Growth*. Philadelphia: University of Pennsylvania Press, 1968.
Watson, John Fanning. *Annals of Philadelphia and Pennsylvania, in the olden time; being a collection of memoirs, anecdotes, and incidents of the city and its inhabitants, and of the earliest settlements of the inland part of Pennsylvania, from the days of the founders.* 2nd ed. Philadelphia: John Penington and Uriah Hunt, 1844.
Weatherwax, Sarah. "Peter S. Duval, Philadelphia's Leading Lithographer." In *Philadelphia on Stone: Commercial Lithography in Philadelphia, 1828–1878*, edited by Erika Piola, 97–117. University Park: Pennsylvania State University Press, 2012.
Weslager, C. A. *The Delaware Indians: A History*. New Brunswick, NJ: Rutgers University Press, 1972.
Wilentz, Sean. *The Rise of American Democracy: Jefferson to Lincoln*. New York: W. W. Norton & Company, 2005.
Winch, Julie, *A Gentleman of Color: The Life of James Forten.* New York: Oxford University Press, 2002.
Wulf, Karin. *Not All Wives: Women of Colonial Philadelphia.* Ithaca, NY: Cornell University Press, 2000.

# List of Contributors

Lee Arnold
*Librarian Emeritus*
Historical Society of Pennsylvania

David Barnes
*Associate Professor of History and Sociology of Science*
University of Pennsylvania

Katy Bodenhorn Barnes
*Director of Genealogical Programs and Services*
Historical Society of Pennsylvania

Georgia B. Barnhill
*Curator Emerita*
American Antiquarian Society

Wendy Bellion
*Associate Dean for the Humanities and Sewell C. Biggs Chair in American Art History*
University of Delaware

Rebecca Brannon
*Associate Professor of History*
James Madison University

David R. Brigham
*Librarian and CEO*
Historical Society of Pennsylvania

Kathleen M. Brown
*David Boies Professor of History and Core Faculty, Gender, Sexuality, and Women's Studies, and the Center for Feminist, Queer, and Transgender Research*
University of Pennsylvania

David B. Brownlee
*Frances Shapiro-Weitzenhoffer Professor Emeritus*
University of Pennsylvania

Jane E. Calvert
*Director and Chief Editor, The John Dickinson Writings Project and Associate Professor of History*
University of Kentucky

Mark Clague
*Professor of Musicology*
University of Michigan

Jeffrey A. Cohen
*Term Professor, Growth & Structure of Cities Department*
Bryn Mawr College

Marie A. Conn
*Professor Emerita of Religious Studies*
Chestnut Hill College

Charles T. Cullen
*President and Librarian Emeritus*
Newberry Library

Susan G. Davis
*Professor Emerita Communication and Information Sciences*
University of Illinois, Urbana-Champaign

Richardson Dilworth
*Professor of Politics*
Drexel University

Megan J. Elias
*Director of the Gastronomy Program*
Boston University

Patrick M. Erben
*Professor of English*
University of West Georgia

Joel T. Fry
*Curator*
Bartram's Garden

Alice L. George
*Independent Historian*

James N. Green
*Librarian Emeritus*
The Library Company of Philadelphia

Emma Hart
*Professor of History and Richard S. Dunn Director, the McNeil Center for Early American Studies*
University of Pennsylvania

Sandra M. Hewlett, CG®
*Genealogy Professional*

Martha Hutson-Saxton
*Art Historian*

Emma Lapsansky-Werner
*Professor of History and Emerita, and Curator of Special Collections, Emerita*
Haverford College

Christina Larocco
*Editor of Pennsylvania Magazine of History and Biography and Scholarly Programs Manager*
Historical Society of Pennsylvania

Michael J. Lewis
*Faison-Pierson-Stoddard Professor of Art*
Williams College

Walter Licht
*Walter H. Annenberg Emeritus Professor of History*
University of Pennsylvania

David M. Lubin
*Charlotte C. Weber Professor of Art*
Wake Forest University

Anna O. Marley
*Chief of Curatorial Affairs and Kenneth R. Woodcock Curator of Historical American Art*
Pennsylvania Academy of the Fine Arts

Holly A. Mayer
*Professor Emerita of History*
Duquesne University

Amy Meyers
*Retired Director*
Yale Center for British Art

Randall M. Miller
*Professor Emeritus of History*
Saint Joseph's University

Elizabeth Milroy
*Professor Emerita of Art & Art History Westphal College of Media Arts & Design*
Drexel University

Kristen Nassif
*Andrew W. Mellon Postdoctoral Curatorial Fellow*
The Walters Art Museum

Therese O'Malley
*Retired Associate Dean*
*Center for Advanced Study in the Visual Arts*
National Gallery of Art

Nell Irvin Painter
*Edwards Professor of American History, Emerita, and visual artist*
Princeton University

Robert McCracken Peck
*Senior Fellow and Curator of Art and Artifacts*
Academy of Natural Sciences of Drexel University

Danya M. Pilgrim
Assistant Professor of History
Temple University

Kymberly Pinder
*Stavros Niarchos Foundation Dean*
Yale School of Art

John H. Pollack
*Curator of Research Services*
*Kislak Center for Special Collections, Rare Books and Manuscripts*
University of Pennsylvania

Daniel K. Richter
*Roy F. and Jeannette P. Nichols Professor of American History Emeritus*
University of Pennsylvania

Jessica Choppin Roney
*Associate Professor of History*
Temple University

Dan Rottenberg
*Journalist, Editor, and Author*

Janny Scott
*Journalist and Author*

Matthew Skic
*Curator of Exhibitions*
Museum of the American Revolution

Patrick Spero
*Executive Director*
George Washington Presidential Library

Laurel Thatcher Ulrich
*300th Anniversary University Professor, emerita*
Harvard University

John C. Van Horne
*Director Emeritus*
The Library Company of Philadelphia

Anne A. Verplanck
*Associate Professor, Emerita*
Penn State Harrisburg

David Waldstreicher
*Distinguished Professor of History*
The Graduate Center, City University of New York

Sarah J. Weatherwax
*Senior Curator of Graphic Arts*
The Library Company of Philadelphia

Ralph Richard Whyte
*Adjunct Assistant Professor*
Columbia University

Kathryn E. Wilson
*Associate Professor*
Georgia State University

Michael Winship
*Iris Howard Professor of English II Emeritus*
University of Texas at Austin

James Wolfinger
*Dean of the School of Education and Professor in the Department of Curriculum and Instruction and in the Department of History*
St. John's University

Karin Wulf
*Beatrice and Julio Mario Santo Domingo Director and Librarian John Carter Brown Library and Professor of History*
Brown University

Aaron V. Wunsch
*Associate Professor*
*Graduate Program in Historic Preservation and Department of Landscape Architecture*
*Stuart Weitzman School of Design*
University of Pennsylvania

Library of Congress Cataloging-in-Publication Data

Names: Brigham, David R., editor.
Title: Two hundred years : the Historical Society of Pennsylvania, 1824–2024 / edited by David R. Brigham
Other titles: Historical Society of Pennsylvania, 1824–2024
Description: Philadelphia : Historical Society of Pennsylvania, [2023] | Includes bibliographical references.
Identifiers: LCCN 2023006601 | ISBN 9798218133306 (hardcover)
Subjects: LCSH: Historical Society of Pennsylvania—History. | Pennsylvania—History—Sources. | History—Societies, etc.
Classification: LCC F146 .T86 2023 | DDC 974.8/006—dc23/eng/20230215
LC record available at https://lccn.loc.gov/2023006601

Published by the Historical Society of Pennsylvania
1300 Locust Street
Philadelphia, PA 19107
www.hsp.org

Distributed by the University of Pennsylvania Press
www.pennpress.org

Produced by Marquand Books, Seattle
www.marquandbooks.com

Edited by Melissa Duffes
Designed by Ryan Polich
Typesetting and layout by Tina Henderson
Proofread by Laura Lesswing
Color management by I/O Color, Seattle
Printed and bound in China by C&C Offset Printing Co.

Cover image: Thomas Birch, *Penn's Treaty Tree*, 1800–1801 (no. 38)
pp. 2–3: William McIlvaine Jr., *Camp of Harding's Landing, James River Va.*, July 1, 1862 (no. 67)
p. 4: Albert Newsam, *P. S. Duval Lithography Trade Card*, 1843 (no. 53)
p. 10: David J. Kennedy, after Thomas Sully, *Grand Civic Arch*, ca. 1867 (no. 46)
pp. 36–37: William H. Horstmann & Sons, *Ribbon Sample Book*, 1850–72 (no. 56)
Back cover: *Students Engaging with Original Documents in the Reading Room at the Historical Society of Pennsylvania*, July 2018

Photo credits:
All images by the Historical Society of Pennsylvania, except items indicated.

Jaime Alvarez: pp. 50, 100 [foldout], 102–3, 149, 150, 213
Photograph courtesy of the artist and the Brodsky Center at PAFA, Philadelphia, photo by Adrian Cubillas: pp. 174–75
The Philadelphia Inquirer. © [1972] Philadelphia Inquirer, LLC. All rights reserved. Used under license: p. 246
Ryan Brandenberg Photography: back cover